Canine Colorado

Where to Go and What to Do with Your Dog

Cindy Hirschfeld

FULCRUM PUBLISHING
GOLDEN, COLORADO

To Clover:
May you always bark softly
and carry a big stick.

Book design by Alyssa Pumphrey

Library of Congress Cataloging-in-Publication Data
Hirschfeld, Cindy.
    Canine Colorado : where to go and what to do with your dog / Cindy Hirschfeld.
        p. cm.
    Includes bibliographical references and index.
    ISBN 1-55591-375-X (paperback)
    1. Travel with dogs—Colorado—Guidebooks. 2. Colorado—Guidebooks. I. Title.
SF427.4574.C6H56   1998
917.88'0433—dc21   98-4562
                                                              CIP

Printed in the United States of America
0 9 8 7 6 5 4 3 2 1

Fulcrum Publishing
350 Indiana Street, Suite 350
Golden, Colorado 80401-5093
(800) 992-2908 • (303) 277-1623
website: www.fulcrum-books.com • e-mail: fulcrum@fulcrum-books.com

Contents

Acknowledgments

This book was made a reality with the support and encouragement of many people. A special thank-you for research assistance goes to Jamie Kim. Thanks also to Michelle Asakawa for her conscientious copyediting and to the staff at Fulcrum Publishing. The scores of hotel owners, Forest Service rangers, National Park representatives, Bureau of Land Management staffers, state parks personnel, animal control officers, and others with whom I spoke during the course of my research provided essential information.

Dr. Steve Peterson at Alameda East Veterinary Hospital deserves special credit for repairing Clover's two torn ACLs that occurred right in the middle of our research efforts. Thanks to Rick Kahl and Lindsey Diforio at SKIING magazine for allowing me to take the time I needed from my job there to finish this book. And I'm extremely grateful to the following friends, who accompanied Clover and me on outings, provided valuable tips on dog-friendly places, hosted us as houseguests during our travels, helped with research, or supplied photos: Kathy Caponera; Carolyn and Patterson Carstens; Peggy and Bailey Chamblin; Jennifer and Dakota Cook; Teri Craig; Amy Ditsler; Terry DuBeau; Arlan Flax; Stacy Gardner; Tim and Bismarck Hancock; Lowell Hart; Tamra and Camper Hoppes; Diane Kane and John Eakin; Carol Kauder; Beth Litz; Jim Margolis; Sean and Frostbite McCullough; Judy Nishimoto; Connie and Bess Oehring; Karen Pauly; Pam and Bart Simich; Erik and Sunny Skarvan; Helmut and Jasmine Tingstad; Claire Walter; Anne, Don, Cara, and DeChelly Webster; Mary and Tundra Winquest; and Sarah and Burley Woodberry.

Of course, thanks go to my family, most especially my mother. And finally, thanks to my cat, Blue, for putting up with all this dog stuff and for accepting the fact that there will be no "Feline Colorado."

Introduction

A survey by the American Animal Hospital Association (AAHA) shows that 66 percent of dog owners in the United States bring along their pets when they travel. This proves something that you and I have known for a long time: Dogs are part of the family—if not your primary family—and vacations can be a lot more fun when shared with a furry, four-legged companion. Traveling with Rover in tow, however, requires a bit of prep work because, believe it or not, not everyone loves our dogs as much as we do! To this end, my faithful research assistant, Clover (herself a native Coloradan), and I have scoured the state searching out dog-friendly activities and accommodations. We hope the results of our research will help you and your dog discover that Colorado is a great place for canines!

In this introduction, you'll find some of the headings that are used throughout the book, with explanations of what each section contains, the criteria for selection, and other tips that will help you and your dog make informed travel decisions.

The information in this book is accurate as of March 1998. Please keep in mind that policies, prices, or regulations are always subject to change. Just because you read it here doesn't mean a detail is set in stone. It's best to call ahead, especially for lodging, to confirm that Rover is indeed still welcome. Traveling with a dog can be like traveling with kids: The keys to success are to be flexible and have some alternate plans to fall back on, if necessary.

The maps in this book are for general reference purposes only. You'll need to consult a topographic map for specifics on the trails described herein.

Don't let your dog do the driving! (photo by Cindy Hirschfeld)

BEFORE ↑

↓ AFTER

V

THE MUCH-MALIGNED DOG

Allow me to mount my soapbox for a minute in defense of dogs. During the course of researching this book, I encountered many people who visibly flinched at the mere mention of the word "dog." People like these don't want dogs to be able to hike on trails, stay at hotels, or participate in a whole range of day-to-day activities with their owners. As a result of such attitudes, dogs have acquired a strange status: not quite human, not quite animal. They're not allowed in most public places because they're, well, dogs, yet many people believe dogs should be restricted in the natural world as well. One woman at a Forest Service office, who will remain unidentified, patiently explained to me that dogs must be kept leashed in designated Wilderness areas so that they won't harass wildlife. As she spoke, my eyes were drawn to a hunting guide prominently displayed on the counter. I mentioned that it seemed ironic that hunting is allowed in these areas yet dogs are required to be restrained; the woman responded with a blank look. "Well," she finally said, "all those animals would just starve to death otherwise." Oh.

I firmly believe that dogs—and humans, too—are a part of nature, not apart from it. We should all do our best to reasonably minimize our impact. Yet dogs have the same right to be outside, to run in the grass, to follow a scent, to play in the snow as any other animal. Those who would scowl at a dog are missing out on one of life's greatest opportunities to share and to bond with another living creature.

Okay, it's time to dismount and get on with the nitty-gritty.

TAIL-RATED TRAILS

Clover and I have "sacrificed" many hours to hike most of the trails described in this book and determine their dog suitability. We considered several factors that seem to make a trail particularly enjoyable for dogs: whether or not they can be off leash, if water is readily available for a drink or for swimming, and if other dogs (and their owners) frequent the trail. For your sake I've also taken the scenic component into account.

Trails are rated on a scale of one to four tail wags, with four signifying the hikes that were our favorites. Also included are trails or areas where dogs are *not* allowed—indicated by a drooping tail symbol—so you'll know ahead of time to leave the dog at home. Naturally there are many more dog-suitable trails than I've been able to describe in this book. When making the final selection, I deferred to my faithful companion. (Of course, because golden retrievers are always happy, I really couldn't go wrong no matter what I chose!) Consider our recommendations either a jumping-off point or a foolproof list if you have limited time to spend in an area.

Four tail wags

Drooping tail

Land-Use Policies

Following are general guidelines for the different types of land you may encounter on your excursions. For more specifics, refer to the descriptions of the individual trails and parks in each chapter.

National Parks and Monuments

First, the bad news: In general, dogs are not allowed on any of the trails in Colorado's national parks and monuments. And you cannot leave your dog unattended anywhere, be it at a campsite, at a trailhead, or in your car. The good news is that they're not banned entirely. As long as you keep your dog on a leash no longer than six feet, you can bring him (or her) to the campgrounds and picnic areas. And you can take a walk with your leashed dog on closed roads (i.e., during the winter, when they're not plowed), though your dog must not venture more than 100 feet from the roadside or parking area. So if you're planning to center your trip on hiking or backpacking in a national park or monument, Rover will need to stay home.

As with most rules, however, a few exceptions exist. Leashed dogs are allowed to hike at the Great Sand Dunes National Monument near Alamosa (which doesn't have defined trails), and they're permitted on a few short trails in the Black Canyon of the Gunnison National Monument. You can also bring your dog to visit Bent's Old Fort in eastern Colorado and Hovenweep National Monument, which straddles the Colorado/Utah border. And, finally, dogs are allowed on the trails at Curecanti National Recreation Area, which is managed by the National Park Service, outside Gunnison.

An entry fee is required at all national parks and monuments.

National Forest and National Forest Wilderness Areas

Here's a "secret": Dogs are not *required* to be leashed on National Forest land unless it is a designated Wilderness area (though the Forest Service often *advises* that they be on a leash). I call this a secret because, unfortunately, many of the Forest Service employees with whom I spoke are not familiar with their own agency's policy. If you ask about dogs on trails at a ranger district office, chances are the person behind the desk will insist that dogs have to be leashed everywhere. In actuality, leash laws apply only in the following situations: (1) You are in what's considered a "developed recreation site," such as a campground or picnic area; or (2) the Forest Service supervisor in a particular district has issued an "order" specifying that dogs be leashed on a particular trail (some of the more heavily used trails have leash regulations and should be signed as such at the trailhead).

Dogs *are* required to be leashed, however, within most designated Wilderness

---

TRAVEL TIPS

Make sure your dog's vaccinations are up-to-date when planning your trip. Bring along copies of his rabies certificate and proof of other vaccinations in case you need to day-board him while traveling.

When traveling by car, avoid feeding your dog for at least three hours before you leave to help prevent carsickness.

Flying your dog requires careful advance planning. If your dog is small enough to fit in an airline-approved carrier that can be stashed under the seat in front of you, he can travel under your supervision. Otherwise he'll have to ride in an airline-approved cage, labeled "Live Animal," in the baggage compartment. You'll need to feed and water Fido within four hours of the flight's departure. Provide a fresh water dish in his cage; you might want to freeze the water first so it won't spill during transport but will melt in time for a midflight drink. Ten days or less before the date of your flight, bring Rover to his vet to undergo an exam and get a current health certificate and proof of rabies vaccination, which you'll often need to present at the airport. Tranquilizing your dog before travel is controversial. Many animal experts now advise against it—dogs who have a bad reaction to sedatives or who receive too large a dose can die. If you have a particularly hyperactive dog, talk to your vet about alternatives to sedating him. Your airline of choice may have additional requirements, which you should inquire about when making your reservation.

Consider having a tag made up with a friend or neighbor's phone number that you can attach to your dog's collar when traveling. If you and your dog become separated while on the road, the person who (hopefully) finds him will be able to actually get in touch with someone rather than just reaching your answering machine. PetsMart stores also offer a nifty new option for ID'ing your pet: in-store machines that produce customized tags in just a few minutes. If you'll be in one location for most of your stay, stop by PetsMart and make up a tag with your temporary phone number on it.

areas. You and your dog will know you're entering a Wilderness area from signs either at the trailhead or on the trail if a Wilderness boundary lies along your route. (Note that mountain bikes are not allowed in Wilderness areas.) Wilderness boundaries are also clearly indicated on topographic maps. And a handful of Wilderness areas in Colorado actually don't have a leash requirement (another little-known fact). Refer to individual chapters for more information.

State Parks

In general, you must keep your dog on a leash no longer than six feet in all state parks. The exceptions are the handful of state parks that have off-leash dog areas: Cherry Creek, Chatfield, and Lathrop. And some parks don't allow any dogs whatsoever: Roxborough, Harvey Gap, and Mueller (dogs can stay at Mueller's campgrounds). Keep in mind that dogs are not permitted in any swim or water-ski beach areas in any of the state parks.

An entry fee is required at all state parks. If you're a frequent visitor, you'll save a bundle by getting a season pass, which is good at all the parks.

Bureau of Land Management (BLM) Land

The BLM has the most liberal policies regarding dogs of any land overseer in Colorado. Dogs are not required to be leashed anywhere on BLM land, even in Wilderness Study Areas. Of course, much BLM land is undeveloped, meaning there aren't nearly as many trails as on National Forest land. The flipside is, because these areas can be remote, you're less likely to encounter other people who may be bothered by your dog.

Hunting Season

When fall comes, so comes hunting season in Colorado. And that means that from about mid-September to the beginning of November you should take extra care when hiking with your dog in National Forest (including Wilderness) areas. This is definitely not the time to let your dog run around wearing those fake antlers you bought him last Christmas. One of my friends went to her local WalMart and bought a bright orange hunting vest—for her dog to wear. You can take a precaution as simple as tying bright orange tape to your dog's collar. The point is to avoid having your dog wind up like Tripod, a dog we met near Aspen who had been shot in the leg by a hunter's errant bullet. For information about specific hunting seasons, contact the Colorado Division of Wildlife office in Denver at 303-297-1192.

Trail Etiquette
The Leash

I'm lucky in that Clover is well behaved on trails: She doesn't stray, she doesn't chase deer or elk, she waits for me to catch up if she gets too far ahead, and she goes off the trail to poop. Nevertheless, I always carry her leash, just in case. If your dog can be an unruly hiker, keep him leashed on heavily used trails; your outing will be more pleasant without the glares of other hikers. And if your dog is a wildlife chaser, definitely keep his leash at the ready. *According to Colorado state law, dogs can be shot for harassing livestock or wildlife.* Some people claim that you can never control a dog in time to keep him from taking off after a deer. I disagree, simply because I've seen otherwise. If you pay attention to your dog and your surroundings, you can nab him and put him on his leash before he dashes. But you know your dog the best. If you feel you can't control him or don't want to stay on the alert during a hike, keep him leashed.

Ask Before He Sniffs

You and your dog will win many friends if you train him not to approach other people or dogs uninvited. When your off-leash dog encounters an on-leash dog, communication is especially important. That dog may be leashed for reasons other than simple owner control: He may be sick, skittish around other dogs, or even downright unfriendly.

The Clean-up Routine

Those plastic bags that your newspaper comes in serve double duty as handy pooper scoopers. Many forward-thinking towns also provide dispensers of plastic pet-pickup baggies at popular parks and trailheads.

If you're on a trail in a National Forest or other more remote location, I think it's perfectly acceptable to train your dog to poop off trail; or you can fling the poop off the trail into the woods with a stick. After all, no one's cleaning up after all those other animals that use the outdoors as their restroom!

CYCLING FOR CANINES

As an added activity bonus, Clover and I have scoped out places where your dog and your mountain bike can travel in tandem. For the fit dog, nothing beats a run beside one's pedaling owner for exercise efficiency. But—and this is an important but—you must approach biking with your dog differently than a solo ride. This should be a shared activity; if you're a hardcore rider, for example, don't expect your dog to keep up while you try to ride faster than your friends—the results could be fatal! And cycling with your dog is not the time to engage in screaming descents; in fact, you should stop often, allowing your dog plenty of time to catch up with you and to rest. The bottom line is that your dog, not you, should dictate the pace of the ride. If your primary purpose in riding is to get an intense cardiovascular workout, leave Fido at home.

Your dog should be in good condition before you ask him to keep up with you when you're biking. (Though if you're on a very technical trail, he may well outrun you!) You are the best judge of your dog's physical fitness; if he gets regular exercise and is generally healthy, he's probably able to accompany you on a short bike ride. The fact that you're reading this book is a good sign that you keep your dog fairly active. Just remember that your dog can't tell you that he's too tired to keep running. Make sure that he will have access to water and bring extra for rides in dry areas. And save those 30-mile cycles for a time when your dog is at home resting.

The rides listed range from easy to moderately technical in terms of terrain and are generally under 10 round-trip miles in length (keep the distance under 10 miles for the few rides described that have slightly higher mileage). I've only included areas where dogs can safely be off leash. Unfortunately, this leaves out a lot of good biking terrain. If you've figured out how to ride on singletrack or otherwise technical trails with your dog on a leash, more power to you! None of the rides involves traveling on paved roads, even for a short segment. Traffic and dogs just don't mix. And, as a final caveat, I've steered away from some of the more heavily trafficked biking trails, popular as they may be, because I know you'd hate to have your pooch mowed down by one too many kamikaze cyclists.

POWDERHOUNDS

Most dogs I know *love* the snow, so what better way to enjoy the winter together than to take your dog along skiing or snowshoeing? Most chapters include a few suggestions on where you can do this. As with cycling, however, you'll need to modify your activity level to suit your dog. Plowing through snow when you have four legs and are only a foot or so off the ground takes a lot of effort and can even result in injury. Trails or roads that have been packed down by other skiers or snowshoers are the most canine friendly. If Rover is lagging behind or is otherwise obviously tired, shorten your outing so he'll still be able to accompany you on the next one. It's also a good idea to invest in some booties to protect your dog's paws from painful snow and ice buildup; dogs with webbed feet are especially prone to this. See the "Gearhound" appendix for more information.

As this book is by no means intended to be a backcountry ski guide, I've only included trails that have minimal avalanche danger and are fairly straightforward. In addition, you'll see that several Nordic ski areas have some trails set aside for dogs and their owners, ideal for the type of short ski outings that will keep your dog healthy and happy.

CREATURE COMFORTS

Before I began researching accommodations that accept dogs, I envisioned quaint bed and breakfasts (B&Bs) that would welcome canine guests with open arms, presenting them with freshly baked dog biscuits and perhaps even a resident play companion. Clover and I would spend the day frolicking in a beautiful mountainside setting and then return to a charmingly furnished room. Well, I quickly discovered that such was not the case. Many hotels, motels, and, alas, B&Bs in Colorado want nothing to do with four-legged visitors. (Some proprietors, however, admitted regret at not being able to put out the canine welcome mat; said one innkeeper, "If it makes you feel any better, we don't accept children, either!") Diligent research, however, turned up many places that do accept pets, with a broad range of prices and lodging styles from rustic to ultraluxurious. You may be pleasantly surprised at how many accommodations *will* welcome you and your dog.

I've included any and every place I could track down that accepts pets. (By the way, tourism brochures, while helpful, were by no means always accurate or comprehensive.) This means not every accommodation listed is a place you, let alone your dog, would choose to spend the night. But sometimes the need to find somewhere to stay (especially one that's within your budget) outranks preference. A few places will accept pets on a case-by-case basis, depending on who else is staying there, the dog's temperament, and so on, but didn't want to be listed in this book. If you have your heart set on a particular hotel, it doesn't hurt to ask if they'll take your dog, too.

Here's a brief rundown of what you can expect to find in the lodging listings:

Price symbols: Because rates are often in flux, I've devised a simple scale to guide your expectations rather than give specific prices. Rates are based on two people per night unless otherwise indicated:

$ = up to $50
$$ = $50–$100
$$$ = $100–$150
$$$$ = $150 and up

You'll notice that many lodgings straddle price categories.

Name, address, phone number: Many of the toll-free phone numbers listed for chain hotels and motels go to a national reservations center. Though you can find out rates and room availability through these centers, contact the individual lodging directly to notify the management that you'll be bringing your dog and to confirm the pet policy.

Brief description: For places other than chain accommodations or standard motels, I've provided a summary of the lodging set-up and amenities. If an owner or manager seemed particularly friendly toward dogs, I mentioned it.

Dog policy: A frequent response to the question "Do you allow dogs?" was "Yes, if they're well behaved and housebroken."

cathy®   by Cathy Guisewite

Because it should almost go without saying that you should not impose your dog on any hotel, motel, or other accommodation if he doesn't match that description, I didn't mention it repeatedly in every lodging write-up. But I'll say it here: *Please, for the sake of the rest of our dogs, leave your dog at home until you've trained him to be a courteous guest.* I have heard earfulls of stories from disillusioned lodging owners who used to allow pets but stopped doing so because they had too many bad experiences.

When inquiring about dog policy, I asked if a fee or deposit is required; about any guidelines that dictate the size, type, or number of dogs in a room; and whether a dog can be left unattended in the room. As you'll note, the answers varied among lodging providers. I've noted which places request a fee or deposit, and how much; if a listing doesn't include either, you can assume your pet is gratis, though it's always a good idea to double-check. Some places will put up you and your dog in a smoking room only—good news if your dog is a smoker (though personally I don't think that dog breath is anywhere near as foul-smelling as stale smoke!). Some managers I spoke with were adamant that guests not leave their dogs unattended in the rooms, while others didn't have a problem with it as long as the housekeeping staff is notified—presumably so that a housekeeper won't be licked to death while trying to change your sheets! If a listing has no specific information on dog policy, it means that no fee or deposit is charged, you and your dog can stay in any room, and you cannot leave your dog unattended inside.

Some experts advise against leaving a dog unattended in a hotel room. If your lodging choice allows this, I feel it's a useful option to have as long as you're confident that your dog can stay on his best behavior. Though I don't recommend leaving Fido for more than a couple of hours, it's a far better alternative than leaving him in a car in warm weather if you're headed into "absolutely no dogs" territory (e.g., a

restaurant). Of the lodging operators who permit this, many rationalized that a dog's owner is the one who will best know if the dog can be left alone. All emphasized that dogs on their own must be quiet and non-destructive. Some places will allow you to leave Rover unattended as long as he's in a travel kennel—an item you might consider bringing along just for that purpose. If you're staying at a place where your dog cannot be left unattended, please don't jeopardize the pet policy for the rest of us by ignoring the rules.

Following each chapter's listing of accommodations is a selection of nearby campgrounds, in case your dog decides he'd rather "ruff" it for the night.

Worth a Paws

This is a catch-all category. I've included out-of-the-ordinary dog activities, ranging from benefit events in which you can participate with your four-legged friend to Frisbee competitions and self-service dog washes. Not only are these diversions fun for the pooch (well, except for the dog washes, maybe), they allow you to mingle with other dog owners who may be just as nuts about their canines as you are about yours.

Doggie Daycare

Despite your best intentions, you may want to do or attend something while traveling that your dog just can't join in on (e.g., a day at a national park, a hike up a challenging "fourteener," or that fancy-dress family reunion party). Although I don't think road-tripping with your canine friend should entail stashing him in a kennel on a regular basis (after all, you could have just left the dog at home), it's handy to know there are places that will welcome your dog for a day or even for just a few hours. Most "daycare providers" require reservations a few days in advance as well as proof that your dog is up-to-date with his vaccinations, including rabies, distemper, and bordatella (kennel cough). Moreover, if your dog is not a Colorado resident, he's technically supposed to have a health certificate from his hometown veterinarian in order to cross state lines. While only a few of the kennels included here actually require this, it wouldn't hurt to procure a certificate before leaving home if you think you might need to board Rover.

PET PROVISIONS

You've run out of Iams halfway through your trip, and your dog only turns up his nose at supermarket dog food. I've included selected lists of where to restock. Note that for ethical reasons, I've tried to avoid listing pet stores that market puppies and kittens along with supplies. If you're far from the nearest pet emporium, remember that most vets carry specialty dog foods and other supplies. Look under "Canine ER" for locations of the nearest veterinarians in each region.

CANINE ER

One of the worst potential travel scenarios for your dog would be to get sick or injured while on the road, far from the friendly scalpel of the hometown vet. The veterinarians and clinics listed throughout the book offer either 24-hour or on-call emergency service. I used a few methods to narrow down the listing of veterinarians within each area. If a region has veterinary clinics that are open 24 hours a day—generally cities such as Boulder, Denver, Colorado Springs, and Fort Collins—I've listed only these clinics, since they'll be able to serve all your dog's needs at any time. In areas that have no 24-hour clinics but still offer a wide range of veterinary services, I honed the list to include just those veterinary hospitals that are certified by the American Animal Hospital Association; you'll see "AAHA certified" in parentheses after the hospital's name. The AAHA has stringent standards that a hospital must meet in order to be certified, including complete diagnostic and pharmacy facilities, sanitary conditions, proper anesthetic procedures, modern surgical facilities, nursing care, dental service, medical records for each patient, and emergency service.

Though my method of selection undoubtedly omits many caring and qualified veterinarians, relying on the AAHA certification allowed me to point your pet in the right direction without actually evaluating each vet. And, finally, in areas that have neither 24-hour clinics nor AAHA-certified hospitals, I've listed all the veterinarians that provide on-call emergency service. Hopefully you and your dog will never need to use any of this information.

RESOURCES

Here you'll find addresses and phone numbers of tourist information centers, chambers of commerce, and land-use agencies that can provide additional information for your travels.

WHY YOU WON'T FIND PLACES TO EAT WITH YOUR DOG IN THIS BOOK

It's often nicer to have your best friend at your feet during mealtime than stashed in a room or a car (assuming, of course, that Rover is not up for membership in "Beggers Anonymous"). Unfortunately, Colorado law prohibits dogs from being in any area where food is served, even if it's an outdoor patio. Of course, this doesn't mean that you won't see dogs and their owners enjoying a bite to eat together at outside dining venues. But I didn't want to get any of these accommodating restaurants in trouble by letting the dog out of the bag, so to speak. Your best bet is to scope out places that offer dining al fresco and then ask if Rover can join you.

CLOVER'S PACKING LIST

portable food/ water bowl	brush
	fluffy toy
leash	***Optional:***
dog food/biscuits	dog bed or blanket
doggie backpack	medication
booties (in winter)	travel kennel or
towel	crate

FIRST AID FOR FIDO

Can my dog be affected by the altitude?
Dogs who already have some sort of heart or respiratory illness at sea level may have trouble at higher altitude. But, in general, healthy, active dogs should have no problems. Chances are good that if you're doing okay at a higher altitude, your dog definitely is.

Will my dog get giardia from drinking out of streams?
Just like humans, dogs can get giardia, a single-cell parasite that often causes cramps and diarrhea, from drinking untreated water. Many dogs who have been exposed to it, however, never show any symptoms. Or your dog might get the runs for just a few days. Bottom line: When you're out hiking with your dog, it's going to be difficult to prevent him from slurping out of streams. And he'll probably be fine. Of course, if your dog has persistent diarrhea or other gastrointestinal problems, bring him to a vet to be treated with antibiotics.

Can my dog get dehydrated?
Yes! Remember that your dog is probably working harder than you during most physical activities. Dogs seem to cover about twice the mileage of their owners, running back and forth on the trail. And they have those fur coats to deal with. Sticky gums are a sign of dehydration. Make sure that your dog always has an ample water supply, whether you're carrying it (along with something he can drink out of) or from streams or ponds in the area you'll be hiking, running, or biking through.

What should I do if my dog gets heatstroke?
Difficulty breathing or rapid breathing, vomiting, high body temperature, or out-and-out collapse are all signs of heatstroke. Submerge your dog briefly in cool (not ice) water. Keep him wet and cool—wrap him in a wet towel if you have one—and encourage but don't force him to drink water. Follow up immediately with a visit to the vet.

What should I do if my dog gets hypothermia?
Low body temperature, a decreased breathing rate, and shivering are all signs of excessive chilling or hypothermia. Move your dog to a sheltered area or, ideally, inside, and wrap him up in a sleeping bag or multiple blankets. *Gently* rub him to help rewarming. Never put an electric heating pad against your dog—it can easily burn him.

What should I do if my dog is bitten by a snake?
Restrain and calm him so that the venom won't spread further. Apply a flat tourniquet if he's been bitten on the leg. Encourage the wound to bleed and wash the bite area with soap and water. Apply a cold compress, if possible. Take Fido to the vet ASAP.

For more information on helping your dog if he's injured, refer to *First Aid for Dogs: What to Do When Emergencies Happen,* by Bruce Fogle, D.V.M., or *Emergency First Aid for Your Dog,* by Tamara S. Shearer, D.V.M.

CENTRAL COLORADO

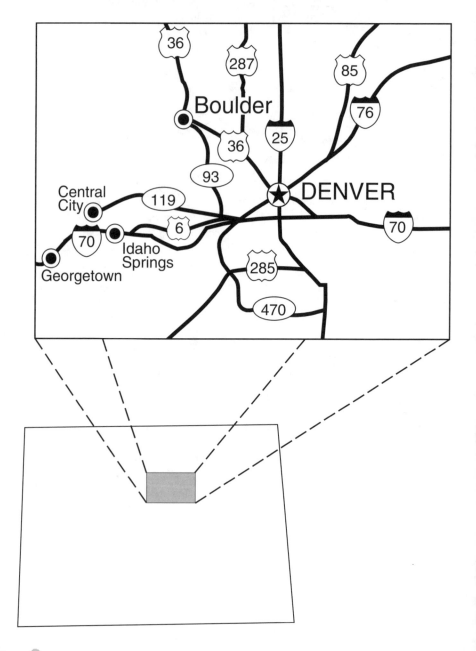

1
Denver and Vicinity

THE BIG SCOOP

For a city, Denver's not a bad place in which to be a dog. Lots of hotels and motels welcome four-legged travelers, and there's plenty to do out of doors. The mile-long 16th St. pedestrian mall in the heart of Denver's downtown is the perfect place for the urban dog to catch up on his people watching. Chic dogs will want to stroll with their owners through Cherry Creek, the city's toniest shopping district. Or they might want to visit trendy LoDo, which includes Coors Field; though not allowed inside the baseball stadium, dogs can gaze longingly at the exterior and imagine all the balls that could be chased down inside.

Within the City and County of Denver, as well as in surrounding towns in the Denver metro area, dogs must be leashed when not on private property. Resident dogs must be vaccinated annually against rabies once they're six months and older, and dogs are required to wear a city license tag within thirty days of moving to the city.

Both Jefferson and Adams Counties (west of Denver and northeast of Denver, respectively) have leash laws as well. Dogs may be walked under voice command, however, in the unincorporated parts of Arapahoe and Douglas Counties (east of Denver and south of Denver, respectively).

TAIL-RATED TRAILS

As might be expected in a city that is home to an active population, it's not difficult to find a great selection of easily accessible hiking trails near Denver. You and your dog will have to travel to the outskirts of the city and beyond to reach many of the trails that will allow you to enjoy a "less developed" hiking experience. Denver and its surrounding communities, however, have an extensive network of paved bike paths and trails, often known as greenways, that your dog will enjoy exploring. Some extend for several miles, others for just a few blocks. An excellent resource that maps out many of these trails is "Your Guide to Colorado Trails: Denver Metro Area," a free brochure put out by Colorado State Parks and the Colorado Lottery (once you've read the brochure, you'll understand the connection). Look for it at visitor centers and Forest Service offices.

You'll find some of the best hiking opportunities in the Jefferson County Open Space parks, many of which are described in this section. Not all of these parks, however, are necessarily suitable for dog hikes, due to heavy mountain-bike use. If you don't want to worry about Fido and his leash having a too-close encounter with spokes (or don't want to put up with the exasperated looks of riders who think you didn't get out of their way quickly enough), bring your dog somewhere other than White Ranch (north of Golden), Apex (on Golden's western side), and Matthews Winters (next to Red Rocks) parks. Mount Falcon Park is also popular with mountain bikers, though most seem to start out on the front side, so I've described access via the "back way" here. Of course, when the trails are snowy or especially muddy, you and your dog will encounter relative solitude in these latter parks—just make sure to bring a large towel for after-hiking paw and leg cleanup.

For more information on specific trails west of Denver, refer to *Foothills to Mount Evans: West-of-Denver Trail Guide* (sixth edition), by Linda McComb Rathbun and Linda Wells Ringrose. For information on other trails in the Denver area, look at the *12 Short Hikes* series, by Tracy Salcedo (three volumes cover the Denver foothills). The Pike National Forest southwest of Denver, including the Lost Creek Wilderness Area, has an extensive trail system. The South Platte Ranger District (see "Resources") provides informative, detailed written descriptions of a wide range of hikes in this area.

Denver

There are 210 city-maintained parks throughout Denver. Three of the most popular are described here, but there are plenty more for your dog to explore. For a "Parks and Recreation Facility Map" that details all of them, contact the Denver Parks office at 303-964-2500.

 Washington Park. Denver dogs in the know come to "Wash Park" to participate in one of the city's best canine social scenes. Bordered by Virginia Ave., Franklin St., Louisiana Ave., and Downing St., the 154-acre park is also one of Denver's largest, with two small lakes, colorful flower gardens (one a duplicate of George Washington's gardens at Mount Vernon), an indoor recreation center, playground, lawn bowling court, soccer field, and lighted tennis courts. You and your dog have several strolling options: a 2.6-mile crushed-gravel trail goes around the park's outer edges, while a paved inner trail makes two loops within the park, each about a mile in length. *Dogs must be leashed.*

 Cheesman Park. Close to Capitol Hill, 82-acre Cheesman Park is between 13th and 8th Aves., Humboldt and Race Sts. The park is a pleasant oasis, with gardens, a pavilion, and a view west to the mountains. Make sure your dog takes time to sniff the flowers here, as he's not permitted in the adjoining Denver Botanic Gardens. Two main walkways wind around the park: a gravel-surfaced one that's 1.6 miles long, and a paved one at 1.4 miles. *Dogs must be leashed.*

 City Park. Denver's largest park at 314 acres, City Park is also the site of the Denver Museum of Natural History, the Denver Zoo, and a public golf course. Dogs will have to content themselves with a saunter around the park's two lakes and its gardens. A 1.6-mile paved trail encircles City Park Lake, while a 3-mile natural surface trail tours the park's perimeter. You'll also find playing fields, a band shell, playgrounds, picnicking spots, and lighted tennis courts on park grounds. The park is located north of 17th Ave. between York St. and Colorado Blvd. *Dogs must be leashed.*

North of Denver

 Golden Gate Canyon State Park. Located 16 miles northwest of Golden, this 14,000-acre mountainous park offers almost 35 miles of trails, all with animal names, that you and your dog can enjoy together. The main access from the eastern side, which will bring you by the park's visitor center, is via Golden Gate Canyon Rd., a signed turnoff from Highway 93 just north of Golden. The drive to the park is 13 miles from the turnoff. *Dogs must be leashed.*

One particularly nice hike follows the **Horseshoe Trail,** a 3.6-mile round-trip route from the Frazer Meadow trailhead to Frazer Meadow and back. To reach the trailhead, turn right at the T-intersection just after the visitor center, pass the Ralston Roost trailhead on the left, then pull into the next trailhead parking area on the left. You'll ascend a moderate uphill alongside a creek for most of the hike, then will reach a large meadow flanked by stands of aspen. Head right for a few minutes on the intersecting Mule Deer Trail to view the old homestead in the meadow. Other park trails that follow streams for a good portion of their length include the 2.5-mile **Raccoon Trail**, which makes a loop from the Reverend's Ridge Campground in the park's northwestern corner; the **Mountain Lion Trail**, which forms a 6.7-mile loop that begins and ends at the Nott Creek trailhead in the northeastern corner of the park; the 2.4-mile round-trip **Buffalo Trail**, which goes from the Rifleman Phillips Group Campground in the northern part of the park to Forgotten Valley; and the 2.5-mile **Beaver Trail**, which follows a loop beginning and ending at the visitor center and includes a short detour to Slough Pond.

Camper and Tamra Hoppes enjoy a break in the Pike National Forest southwest of Denver. (photo courtesy of Tamra Hoppes)

abled exercisers. Note that dogs are not allowed on the nature trail that loops around Kestral Pond in the northwest part of the park—the area is designated as a wildlife sanctuary.

Crown Hill Park. From Lakewood, take Kipling Ave. north to W. 26th Ave. and make a right. Two parking areas for the park are on the lefthand side of the block. *Dogs must be leashed.*

This 177-acre Jefferson County Open Space park is a perfect spot for an after-work stroll with Rover. The most obvious route to take is the 1.2-mile **Lake Loop Trail**, a paved path that encircles Crown Hill Lake and its resident ducks; just keep your dog on a short leash so that he doesn't have any entangling encounters with a bicyclist or in-line skater. The **Outer Loop Trail** takes you around the park's perimeter, but you won't be near the water. A number of unnamed horse trails, on which dogs are allowed, too, wind through the park. There's also a 1-mile fitness course near the lake that includes access for dis-

Van Bibber Park. Located in Arvada, the park has two main access areas with parking lots: off Indiana St. and off Ward Rd., both just south of W. 58th Ave. *Dogs must be leashed.*

From either side of the park, you'll start out on the paved **Van Bibber Creek Trail**, which is 1.5 miles from end to end. You'll soon reach a small network of natural-surface trails that meander through the 130-acre Jefferson County Open Space park. Van Bibber Creek, which runs through the park's northern section, is often dry midsummer but has water at other times of the year. As you and your dog walk (or jog—this is a good venue for a run), you'll glimpse the somewhat odd combination of farmland and suburban palaces that's becoming common to the metro area. If you're starting out at the eastern side of the park, you'll reach the middle before leaving behind the rush of traffic on busy

Ward Rd. No dogs are allowed on the Jimmy Go Trail, which leads to an observation deck in the wetlands section of the park; if your dog wants to walk a large loop, you and he will need to briefly exit, then reenter the park.

West of Denver

 Maxwell Falls Trail. 3.5 miles round-trip. From the stoplight on Highway 74 in downtown Evergreen, head south on Highway 73 for about a mile. Make a right on Brook Forest Rd. Drive for 3.6 miles to the lower trailhead parking in a small fenced area on the left side of the road. *Dogs can be off leash.*

One of the closest National Forest trails to Denver, the Maxwell Falls Trail has recently been rerouted (including a new trailhead) because of some private property issues along the old trail. This hike features plenty of access to water, lots of trees to sniff, and a brief scenic vista. Begin by heading up the path marked by the brown carsonite post in the southwest corner of the parking area. You'll make a moderate ascent through a forest of fir, pine, and aspen, contouring southwest across a hillside and following the route of an unnamed creek. The trail eventually fords the creek and switchbacks up to a clearing on a small saddle (this is where you'll get the view). Cross an old dirt road and follow the trail down the other side of the saddle. From here the trail stays fairly level as it goes into the Maxwell Creek drainage. After

Sean McCullough and Clover on the Maxwell Falls Trail. (photo by Cindy Hirschfeld)

crossing the creek, head left (upstream); you've now joined up with the original portion of the Maxwell Falls Trail. The falls themselves are about a quarter mile ahead.

After viewing the falls, you can either return the way you came or, if your dog is up for a longer hike, follow a loop that adds about 1.25 miles to the total distance. To access the loop, backtrack from the falls a few hundred yards to an intersection. Follow the intersecting trail as it switchbacks uphill and then runs above the creek. In about a third of a mile, this trail ends at the upper trailhead for Maxwell Falls, at an unmarked parking pullout off of Brook Forest Rd. Before reaching trail's end, however, ford the creek and head left on a wide dirt path that doubles back along the creek. This path, which is actually the old dirt road that you crossed earlier in the hike, starts to head away from the creek. After about a mile, you'll come out on the same saddle that you traversed earlier. Look for the intersection with the Maxwell Falls Trail (unmarked) and go right to return to the lower trailhead parking area.

 Elk Meadow Park. From Denver, take I-70 west to Exit 252, then head toward Evergreen on Highway 74 east. At 5.3 miles from the first traffic light after crossing over I-70, turn right (west) on Stagecoach Blvd. Drive 1.25 miles to the parking area on the right. *Dogs must be leashed, except in the dog training area.*

This Jefferson County Open Space park, on 1,280 acres, has 11.5 miles of trails, including a 4.7-mile (one-way) ascent of 9,600-foot Bergen Peak, which will give you a panoramic view of the Continental Divide. Your dog might be most interested, however, in sniffing out the off-leash area. To access it, cross Stagecoach Blvd. from the parking area and go through the gate. A quarter-mile trail leads off to the right, with signs for the dog training area (you're supposed to keep your dog leashed on this trail). The training area itself is a large field, bordered by aspen along one side. Though a couple of footpaths lead into the field it's not really a hiking area. But it's a fine place to let your dog go through his paces, retrieve a stick or ball, or play with another four-legged friend. And if he needs to pause for a drink, there's a running spigot alongside the access trail for easy refreshment.

 Pine Valley Ranch Park. Head south on U.S. Highway 285, going through Morrison, Aspen Park, and Conifer. In Pine Junction, make a left at the traffic light onto Pine Valley Rd. Head southeast on Pine Valley Rd. for about 6 miles, until you come to a hairpin turn in the road. Go right on Crystal Lake Rd. and follow the signs to Pine Valley Ranch. *Dogs must be leashed.*

Pine Valley Ranch Park, on 820 acres, has a beautiful, wide-open feel. And though somewhat removed from the madding crowd, it's still a Jefferson County Open Space property. In the middle lies small, scenic Pine Lake, and the North Fork of the South Platte River runs across the park. As a bonus, the park's southern boundary abuts Pike National Forest, where your dog can hike leash free. To hike along the rushing waters of the South Platte, take the 2-mile **Narrow Gauge Trail** in either direction from the parking area; the trail follows the route used by the Colorado and Southern Railroad in the early part of the century. A very short trail loops around Pine Lake. To head into the National Forest, follow the **Buck Gulch Trail** for 1 mile to the park boundary; the trail then continues for another 2.2 miles as a Forest Service trail. It's possible to do a long loop (5.3 miles) by combining the **Buck Gulch, Skipper,** and **Strawberry Jack Trails;** note that these are also popular mountain-biking trails.

 Lair o' the Bear Park. From Morrison, take Highway 74 west toward Evergreen. After going

through Idledale (don't blink), look for the signed park entrance on the left. *Dogs must be leashed.*

Tucked into the side of Bear Creek Canyon, this 319-acre Jefferson County Open Space park offers a healthy-sized stream with easy access for dog dips as well as 4 miles of trails. And because the park is relatively small, you're not likely to encounter the mountain bikers who frequent many of the other Jeffco Open Space areas. The **Creekside Trail** parallels Bear Creek for nearly 1.5 miles; head toward the creek from the parking area and pick up the trail going in either direction. If you go left (east), you'll eventually cross the Ouzel Bridge—keep an eye out for these small gray birds plunging into the water—and meet up with the **Bruin Bluff Trail.** Keep heading east to connect with Little Park in about a quarter mile, primarily a picnic spot. Another portion of the Bruin Bluff Trail forms a 1.3-mile loop through the forest above the creek's south side.

 Lookout Mountain and Beaver Brook Trails. Up to 16.5 miles round-trip. This hike starts across from the Lookout Mountain Nature Center, which you can reach in one of two ways: From Highway 6, coming from Golden or Lakewood, turn west on 19th St., which becomes Lookout Mountain Rd., and follow the switchbacks up, past Buffalo Bill's grave, to Boettcher Mansion and the nature center. From I-70 west from Denver, take Exit 256, make a right at the stop sign, and follow the brown signs along Paradise and Charros Rds. to Lookout Mountain Rd., where you'll turn right to head up to the nature center. Either way, look for the parking pullout on the other side of the road from the nature center main entrance. *Dogs must be leashed.*

The Lookout Mountain Trail drops down a hillside in the cool shade of lodgepole pine for a mile before intersecting with the Beaver Brook Trail. Take a left at the trail intersection; the right ends at a busy trailhead on Lookout Mountain Rd. known as Windy Saddle. As you hike, you and your dog can take in a bird's-eye view of Clear Creek Canyon below and the Front Range's northern foothills—as well as of the gamblers speeding toward Black Hawk and Central City on curvy Highway 6. Shortly after joining up with the Beaver Brook Trail (there's no brook along this part), you'll encounter two short talus fields, which may test your pooch's rock-hopping skills. The next section of trail includes a few places where you'll have to scramble up and over some rocks; the trail then mellows out again as it continues to wind along the south side of the canyon. If you and your dog are particularly ambitious, or if you've arranged a car shuttle, you can hike for a total of about 8.25 miles from the Lookout Mountain trailhead to the Beaver Brook Trail's western terminus in Genesee Mountain Park (Exit 253 off I-70).

 Meyer Ranch Park. Head south on U.S. Highway 285 from Denver. Before you reach the town of Aspen Park, you'll see a turnoff for South Turkey Creek Rd. and a sign for the park on the left. From South Turkey Creek Rd., the parking area is almost immediately on the right. *Dogs must be leashed.*

This 397-acre Jefferson County Open Space park has about 4 miles of trails that wind through the forested hillside to the south. This is a particularly nice place to hike in September when the aspen change color. The trails are wide and well graded, with benches conveniently placed along them if you or your dog need to stop for a breather. In the early 1940s, a small ski area was located on the southern end of the property, now overgrown with aspen. The **Old Ski Run Trail** takes you to this spot, though you probably won't be able to recognize the formerly skiable terrain. There's no water along any of the trails, just a small creek near the parking lot.

 Mount Falcon Park. Head south on U.S. Highway 285, which can be accessed from C-470 just past Morrison, to the Parmalee Gulch Rd. exit. Drive north on this road for 2.5 miles; you'll see a sign for the park indicating a right turn. From here, follow the signs through a residential area to the parking lot. *Dogs must be leashed.*

This park, another Jefferson County Open Space property, features 11.2 miles of trails spread over 1,415 acres. It's located on land formerly owned by John Brisben Walker, a wealthy gent who lived here at the turn of the century until his house burned down in 1918 (you can visit the remains). The directions I've given take you and your dog to the west parking lot, which receives a little less mountain-bike use than the east parking lot, off Highway 8 outside of Morrison. However, if you are in the eastern part of the park, your dog might want to sniff out the 3.4-mile out-and-back **Turkey Trot Trail**, which is for hikers only. From the western side, a nice 3-mile loop involves taking the **Castle Trail**, passing by the castlelike Walker Home Ruins, to the aptly named **2-Dog Trail**, which ends at a lookout with a view of Denver and Lakewood, Red Rocks Amphitheater, and the plains to the east. Return via the **Meadow Trail**, which hooks up with the Castle Trail not too far from the parking area. There's no water along this route.

 Clear Creek and Tucker Gulch Trails. Located in the town of Golden, the trails can be accessed from Vanover Park, one block east of Washington St. (the main downtown thoroughfare) at Ford and 10th Sts. Parking is available. *Dogs must be leashed.*

Though admittedly not the most scenic hike, this is nonetheless a fine option if your dog wants to stretch his legs while you're visiting the former territorial capital of Colorado. To reach the 0.9-mile-long Clear Creek Trail, cross the larger bridge from the parking area and then pick up the red dirt trail across the street. When you come to Washington St. one block later, you'll need to pick up the trail on the north side of the creek. Your walk will take you along Clear Creek to Lions Park and the Golden Community Center. The trail continues for about a quarter mile past the park before crossing under Highway 6 and turning into a gravel road; it becomes decidedly less scenic from this point on. The paved Tucker Gulch Trail begins at the east end of the parking lot at Vanover Park and runs for 1.1 miles along a stream through a peaceful suburban landscape before ending at Ford Rd. across from Normandy Park.

 O'Fallon Park. Part of Denver's Mountain Parks system, O'Fallon is located just east of Kittredge off Highway 74. If you're coming from Denver, look for a large, three-sided chimney/fireplace structure after passing Corwina Park—this is your cue that the entrance to O'Fallon is coming up on the left. Follow the road from the entrance as it goes left, until it ends in a parking area. *Dogs must be leashed.*

Though there are some picnic sites near the park entrance, O'Fallon, like most other Denver Mountain Parks, doesn't have a developed trail system. Yet there are certainly hiking opportunities within the park, and because they're not mapped out, you and your dog may be less likely to encounter the hiking masses here. From the parking area, cross the bridge over Bear Creek and walk up a dirt service road (closed to regular vehicle traffic). The road ascends amid stands of caramel-scented ponderosa pine. As there's no particular destination for this hike, let your dog determine the length of your outing.

 Dog Training Area at the Jefferson County Government Center. From Den-ver, take Highway 6 west to Golden. Make a right on Jefferson County Parkway, which is just past the Taj Mahal–like government building. Turn left on Illinois. Drive to the parking lot on the right, near the end of the road. *Dogs can be off leash.*

The dog training area is a small field at the north end of the parking lot (look for the sign). There's not much to recommend the site except that dogs can be off leash (Clover seemed to like it well enough). If you really need to find a place where your dog can run, and you're on the west side of Denver, check it out.

South of Denver

 Chatfield State Park. You can easily access the park, which is southwest of Denver, via C-470 east or Wadsworth Blvd. south. If you're coming from C-470, take the Wadsworth Blvd. exit and drive south for 1 mile to the park entrance on the left. *Dogs must be leashed, except in the dog training area.*

Like Cherry Creek State Park, Chatfield is best known for its reservoir and the water recreation it provides, but dogs will be much more interested in the off-leash area set aside for them. Located in the northeast corner of the park, the dog training and exercise area, as it's officially known, encompasses 160 acres. There's even a pond, where several dogs were practicing their stick-in-the-water retrieval skills when we visited. To reach the site, turn left (north) at the T-intersection after going through the park entrance station. Follow the road up and around the top of the dam to the Stevens Grove picnic area, where parking is available. From there, a trail leads around the pond. You and your dog can also head east on the trail (away from the pond), but Fido will have to leash up when crossing the marked dog area boundary; you'll connect with the paved **Centennial Trail,** which runs along C-470. The dog training area also extends on the other side of the road from Stevens Grove as well as from the next picnic area, Cottonwood Grove; your dog can either follow some small social trails here or explore among the trees—just keep an eye out for the boundary markers. For the best meet-and-greet opportunities, however, the pond's the place.

The park has some paved trails that run along the west and south sides of the reservoir. And the **Highline Canal Trail** is just outside the park's south and east boundaries.

 Cherry Creek State Park. The park, located in Aurora, has two main entrance gates: The east entrance station is off of Parker Rd., 1.5 miles south of I-225; the west entrance station is reached via Yosemite St., south of I-225, and Union Ave. Currently, if you walk (or bike) into the park from one of the numerous trail accesses (pick up a park map for locations), you don't need to pay an entrance fee. The park is conducting a feasibility study to determine whether this policy will be retained. *Dogs must be leashed, except in the dog training area.*

Though known primarily for its reservoir, Cherry Creek State Park rates high among the canine set because of the off-leash dog area at the southern end of the park. To reach this area, which covers about 60 acres, drive south on the main park road from the east entrance station and park in the lower parking lot for the 12 Mile House group picnic site. You'll need to keep your dog leashed for about the first 500 yards, until you pass the dog area boundary sign. You can also access the off-leash area by heading west on Orchard Ave., off Parker Rd., for about a half block to a small parking area (there's a self-service fee station). The dog area consists mainly of open grassland traversed by a wide gravel trail; water-loving hounds will seek out the small creek. There's plenty of room for your dog to get a good workout, play with a friend, or chase down a ball.

If he tires of the scenery, put him back on his leash and bring him to explore the rest of the park, which has about 12 miles of trails. The paved **Cherry Creek Trail** runs through the park from north to south; north of the dam, outside the park boundary, a portion connects to the **Highline Canal Trail**. A network of trails lies west of the Shop Creek trailhead, which is off the main park road south of the east entrance station—note that these trails can get very muddy in late winter and spring. Another trail goes along the southern end of the reservoir, from the marina area east to the Shop Creek area. The park is still in the process of mapping out and improving the signage on its trails, so you and your dog should expect to do some exploring rather than following a set route. Dogs are not allowed at the reservoir's swim beach.

 Castlewood Canyon State Park. This day-use park is in Franktown, south of Denver and east of Castle Rock. From Denver, take either Highway 83 (S. Parker Rd.) south or I-25 south to Castle Rock, then Highway 86 east 6 miles to the intersection with Highway 83. The main park entrance (and visitor center) is 5 miles south of this intersection, on the right. There's also a west entrance, reached via Castlewood Canyon Rd. off Highway 86 from Castle Rock. *Dogs must be leashed.*

Castlewood Canyon seems something of an anomaly, a small canyon set near the edge of the eastern plains. The park provides a nice alternative to a mountain hike; you and your dog will be surrounded by farmland yet can still view the peaks of the Front Range in the distance, including Pikes Peak. A pleasant short hike (about 2 miles) combines the **Lake Gulch** and **Inner Canyon Trails.** From the parking area, the Lake Gulch Trail (there is no lake) begins as a paved path before changing to gravel surface. You'll hike among ponderosa pine and juniper before descending to Cherry Creek and its riparian habitat. After crossing the creek, go right to pick up the Inner Canyon Trail. You may want to make a short detour to the left, however, to view the ruins of the dam, which collapsed in 1933. The **Inner Canyon Trail** follows the course of the creek before crossing it and switchbacking up to the parking area. If your dog is interested in a much longer hike, you can add on a loop of the **Creek Bottom** and **Rim Rock Trails** (about 3.6 miles), which cover the park's western section. Castlewood Canyon is also popular with rock climbers, so your dog shouldn't be alarmed if he spots a gear-laden human spider.

 Roxborough State Park. Dogs are not permitted in this day-use state park southwest of Denver.

 Waterton Canyon. You'll have to leave your dog at home if you want to hike or bike the 6.2-mile trail that winds through this scenic canyon along the South Platte River. The northern terminus of the Colorado Trail, which traverses the state for 469 miles, is at the end of the canyon. You will need to bypass the first part of the trail and pick it up at County Rd. 96 (S. Platte River Rd.) if you're planning a cross-state hike with Rover.

CYCLING FOR CANINES

One of the nearest places to Denver for singletrack mountain biking with Rover in tow is the **Buffalo Creek** area, about 45 miles southwest of the city. All trails are in the Pike National Forest. To access the area, take U.S. Highway 285 south, then either Highway 126 south from Pine Junction or County Rd. 68 southeast from Bailey. Both routes lead to Forest Rd. 550 and the trailheads. Ten short trails can be ridden in a variety of combinations. The **Miller Gulch** and **Homestead Trails** form a 6.1-mile loop on easy to moderate terrain. For a shorter loop (about 4.7 miles), ride Miller Gulch to Homestead but take **Charlie's Cut Off,** which goes off to the left about 0.4 mile up the Homestead Trail. Reach these trails

from the Miller Gulch trailhead off Forest Rd. 553. Farther up the road is the Buck Gulch trailhead, from which you can ride the **Buck Gulch, Strawberry Jack,** and **Skipper Trails,** a 5.3-mile loop of moderate to difficult terrain. (Note that you won't be able to ride with your dog in adjoining Pine Valley Ranch Park, as dogs must be leashed.) Both the Miller Gulch and Buck Gulch Trails have water nearby. The **Colorado Trail** also runs through the Buffalo Creek area and can be accessed from the trailhead at the intersection of Highway 126 and Forest Rd. 550.

Other recommended biking options are the **Maxwell Falls Trail,** especially if you do the loop option (see "Tail-Rated Trails"), and trails in **Clear Creek County** (see chapter 3).

POWDERHOUNDS

See chapters 2 (Boulder and Vicinity) and 3 (Central City, et al.) for some of the nearest canine-suitable skiing and snowshoeing trails.

CREATURE COMFORTS

Unless otherwise stated, dogs should not be left unattended in the room or cabin.

Arvada

$$$ On Golden Pond Bed and Breakfast, 7831 Eldridge St., 303-424-2296. The B&B has one room where dogs may stay, and it comes complete with a fireplace and private patio. There's a $10 one-time fee for a small dog, and $20 for a large dog. The house is situated on ten acres of land with a private pond. You must keep your dog leashed on the property.

Aurora

$ Ranger Motel, 11220 E. Colfax, 303-364-3386. Dogs are permitted with a $50 deposit, of which $40 is refunded if there's no damage. You can leave your dog unattended in the room at your own discretion.

$–$$ Blue Spruce Motel, 12500 E. Colfax, 303-343-3303. Dogs are allowed in most rooms with a $200 deposit. If Fido doesn't do any damage to the room, you'll get back 80 percent of the deposit; the motel keeps $40 for a carpet-cleaning fee. You can leave your dog unattended in the room if he's in a travel kennel.

$$ La Quinta, 1011 S. Abilene, 303-337-0206 (800-531-5900)

$$–$$$ Holiday Inn Denver Southeast, 3200 S. Parker Rd., 303-695-1700 (800-962-7672). There's a $50 one-time fee for a dog, and he can be left unattended in the room. The hotel is near Cherry Creek State Park, which boasts an off-leash dog area (see "Tail-Rated Trails").

$$$–$$$$ Holtze Executive Village Southeast, 15196 E. Louisiana Dr., 303-743-5100 (800-422-2092). The hotel offers standard guest rooms as well as one- and two-bedroom apartment-style suites with fully outfitted kitchens. There's a $200 deposit to stay with your dog as well as a $5 fee per dog, per night. You can leave your dog unattended inside as long as you let the front desk know so that arrangements can be made for housekeeping.

Castle Rock
$ Castle Rock Motel, 125 S. Wilcox, 303-688-9728. Dogs are welcome in some of the motel's rooms for stays of one or two nights.

$ Super 8 Motel, 1020 Park St., 303-688-0880 (800-800-8000). Dogs are permitted in smoking rooms only.

$$ Comfort Inn, 200 Wolfensberger Rd., 303-660-2222 (800-228-5150). Dogs are allowed in smoking rooms only, for $7.50 extra per night. You can leave your dog unattended in the room as long as you let the motel management know. The motel requests that you not walk Fido through the lobby when the continental breakfast is being served; he'll have to use the back entrance.

Denver—Downtown
$ Motel 6–Central, 3050 W. 49th Ave., 303-455-8888. Dogs under 50 pounds make the guest grade here.

$$ Denver Downtown Super 8 Hotel, 2601 Zuni St., 303-433-6677. Dogs under 30 pounds are welcome at this Super 8, and they can be left unattended in the room.

$$ Ramada Inn–Downtown West, 1975 Bryant, 303-433-8331. With a $50 deposit your dog can stay here and enjoy the view of Mile High Stadium out the window. He can be left unattended in the room.

$$ Ramada Limited, 1150 E. Colfax Ave., 303-831-7700 (800-542-8603). With a $10 deposit you can bring your dog here and even leave him unattended in the room.

$$–$$$ The Holiday Chalet, A Victorian Hotel, 1820 E. Colfax Ave., 303-321-9975 (800-626-4497). "We're puppy-dog friendly," says the owner of this small, homey hotel in a restored 1896 former private residence, "but they have to be well mannered." For $5 extra per night, your dog can stay with you in one of the ten rooms, each with Victorian-style furnishings and fully equipped kitchen. Cheesman Park is only two blocks away.

$$–$$$ Marriott–City Center, 1701 California St., 303-297-1300

$$–$$$ Residence Inn by Marriott, 2777 Zuni St., 303-458-5318 (800-331-3131). The Residence Inn offers studio or penthouse suites, both with fully equipped kitchens. There's a $10 fee per night per dog, for up to fifteen nights, and you can leave your dog unattended in the suite.

$$–$$$$ Warwick Hotel–Denver, 1776 Grant St., 303-861-2000 (800-525-2888). All you'll be asked to do when you bring your pooch to this plush, European-style hotel is sign a pet contract. You can leave your dog unattended in the room.

$$$ The Burnsley Hotel, 1000 Grant St., 303-830-1000 (800-231-3915). This apartment-style suite hotel accepts dogs under 20 pounds, with a $25 deposit. All suites include one bedroom and full kitchen.

$$$–$$$$ The Westin Hotel Tabor Center Denver, 1672 Lawrence St., 303-572-9100 (800-228-3000). The hotel accepts dogs 20 pounds and under, with some exceptions to the size limit occasionally made. You can leave your dog unattended in the room while you peruse the shops downstairs in the Tabor Center.

$$$$ Adam's Mark Hotel, 1550 Court Pl., 303-893-3333 (800-444-2326). Dogs under 40 pounds can stay at this posh hotel near the 16th St. pedestrian mall. A $100 deposit per pet is required.

$$$$ Executive Tower Hotel, 1405 Curtis St., 303-571-0300 (800-525-6651). You'll need to give a credit-card imprint as a deposit, and you can leave your dog unattended in the room. The hotel features an athletic club on premises.

Denver—East
$ Motel 6 Denver East, 12020 E. 39th Ave., 303-371-1980. One small dog (e.g., poodle size) is allowed per room.

$–$$ Travelodge, 6090 Smith Rd., 303-388-4051. Dogs are allowed with a $25 cash deposit. They can be left unattended in the room.

$$ Best Western Executive Hotel, 4411 Peoria St., 303-373-5730 (800-848-4060). There's a $10 fee per night for executive dogs, and you can leave your dog unattended in the room (but not to do his business!).

$$ Drury Inn Denver, 4400 Peoria St., 303-373-1983 (800-325-8300)

$$ Holiday Inn Central, 4040 Quebec, 303-321-6666. Dogs are permitted in first-floor smoking rooms only.

$$ La Quinta Inn–Denver Airport, 3975 Peoria Way (15 miles from DIA), 303-371-5640 (800-687-6667). You can leave your dog unattended as long as you let the front desk staff know.

$$ Quality Inn and Suites, 4590 Quebec St., 303-320-0260 (800-677-0260). Dogs

are allowed in standard smoking rooms only—not in any of the suites—with a $25 deposit.

$$ Rodeway Inn, 12033 E. 38th Ave., 303-371-0740 (800-228-5160). Dogs are allowed in the motel's older rooms for a $10 fee per night.

$$–$$$ Amerisuites, 16250 E. 40th Ave. (8 miles from DIA), 303-371-0700 (800-833-1516). Dogs 25 pounds and under are allowed in designated pet rooms for a $10 one-time fee. Rooms come equipped with microwave and refrigerator. You can leave your dog unattended inside if you're confident he won't make a peep.

$$–$$$ Doubletree Denver Hotel, 3203 Quebec St., 303-321-3333 (800-222-TREE). Located across from the former Stapleton Airport, the hotel permits dogs with a $50 deposit or a credit-card imprint.

$$–$$$ Holiday Inn Denver International Airport, 15500 40th Ave. (10 miles from DIA), 303-371-9494 (800-511-2118). The hotel allows dogs for a $10 fee per night.

$$–$$$ Ramada Inn Airport, 3737 Quebec St., 303-388-6161 (800-999-8338). The "Airport" in the hotel's name actually refers to the old Stapleton Airport, which is across the street. Dogs are allowed in designated pet rooms (both smoking and non-) with a $25 cash deposit or a credit-card imprint. You can leave your dog unattended in the room.

$$$ Embassy Suites Denver International Airport, 4444 N. Havana St., 303-375-0400 (800-345-0087). Located about 15 miles from DIA, Embassy Suites offers two-room units with refrigerator, microwave, and coffee maker. There's a $50 deposit for a dog, and you can leave yours unattended in the room.

Denver—North
$ Valli Hi Motor Hotel, 7320 Pecos Ave., 303-429-3551. There's a $3 fee per night.

$ Western Motor Inn, 4757 Vasquez Blvd., 303-296-6000. Dogs are welcome for $5 extra per night.

$–$$ Super 8, 5888 N. Broadway, 303-296-3100 (800-800-8000). Dogs under 20 pounds are permitted, and they can be left unattended in the room, though the housekeepers probably won't come in during that time.

$$ La Quinta Inn Central, 3500 Park Ave. W. (Fox St.), 303-458-1222 (800-531-5900). You can leave Fido in the room unattended as long as you let management know.

$$ Regency Hotel, 3900 Elati St., 303-458-0808 (800-525-8748)

Denver—South
$ Cameron Motel, 4500 E. Evans, 303-757-2100. Lap-sized dogs are allowed in five of the smoking rooms for $5 extra per night.

$–$$ Mark I Guest Suites, 1190 Birch, 303-331-7000. The suites, located in four separate buildings, range in style, but all are basically one- or two-bedroom apartments with fully equipped kitchens. For a $100 one-time fee ($50 for each additional dog), your dog can stay with you in one of ten smoking suites, and you can leave him unattended inside. The Cherry Creek shopping district is nearby.

$$ Best Western Landmark Hotel, 455 S. Colorado Blvd., 303-388-5561 (800-528-1234). There's a $25 deposit, and you can leave your dog in the room unattended (perhaps while you dash to the upscale Cherry Creek Mall, nearby). The Cherry Creek bike path runs right behind the hotel, convenient for walks with Rover.

$$ La Quinta Inn Denver South, 1975 S. Colorado Blvd., 303-758-8886 (800-531-5900). You can leave your dog unattended in the room.

$$–$$$ Denver Marriott Southeast, 6363 E. Hampden Ave., 303-758-7000 (800-228-9290). Dogs are permitted in ground-floor rooms only, most of which are smoking.

$$–$$$ Marriott Denver Tech Center, 4900 S. Syracuse St., 303-779-1100 (800-228-9290). Dogs 20 pounds and under are permitted. You can leave your dog unattended in the room as long as he's in a travel kennel.

$$–$$$$ Loews Giorgio Hotel, 4150 E. Mississippi Ave., 303-782-9300 (800-345-9172). This posh hotel allows dogs in twenty of its smoking rooms on the second floor. You can leave Fido unattended inside—then take him for a stroll on the Cherry Creek bike path, two blocks away.

Denver—West
$–$$ Days Inn Central, 620 Federal Blvd., 303-571-1715. There's a $25 deposit for a dog.

Englewood
$$ Days Inn Denver South, 5150 S. Quebec, 303-721-1144 (800-329-7466). The hotel has about fifteen designated pet rooms (both smoking and non-) in which dogs can stay with a $50 deposit.

$$ Hampton Inn Southeast Denver, 9231 E. Arapahoe, 303-792-9999 (800-423-9323). You can leave your dog unattended in the room.

$$ Super 8, 5150 S. Quebec, 303-771-8000 (800-800-8000). Dogs are allowed in most of the motel's rooms with a $50 deposit. You can leave your dog unattended inside.

$$–$$$$ Embassy Suites–Denver South, 10250 E. Costilla (near I-25 and Arapahoe Rd.), 303-792-0433 (800-654-4810). Dogs 25 pounds and under are welcome in second-floor rooms for a $10 nightly fee. (Note that the Embassy Suites–Denver Southeast, on Hampden Ave., does *not* take pets.)

$$–$$$$ Holtze Executive Village, 6380 S. Boston St., 303-290-1100 (800-422-2092). The hotel offers standard guest rooms as well as one- and two-bedroom apartment-style suites with fully outfitted kitchens. There's a $200 deposit to stay with your dog as well as a $5 fee per night. You can leave your dog unattended inside as long as you let the front desk know so that arrangements can be made for housekeeping.

$$–$$$$ Residence Inn by Marriott Denver South, 6565 S. Yosemite, 303-740-7177 (800-331-3131). You and your dog can stay in either studio or penthouse suites, both with fully equipped kitchens. There's a $10 fee per night, per pet, with a maximum charge of $180 per pet (so if you're on a long-term stay, dogs are free after the eighteenth night). You can leave Rover unattended inside.

$$$–$$$$ Summerfield Suites Hotel, 9280 E. Costilla Ave., 303-706-1945 (800-833-4353). You'll find one- and two-bedroom suites here with lots of amenities as well as fully equipped kitchens. There's a $100 one-time fee for a dog if you're staying seven nights or less, $150 if your stay is more than seven nights. In addition, dogs are charged $10 extra per night. The hotel generally puts dogs in smoking units, but some nonsmoking rooms are available, so be sure to ask. And you can leave your dog unattended inside, but housekeeping won't enter during that time.

Golden

$ Golden Motel, 510 24th St., 303-279-5581. There's a $5 fee per night, per dog.

$$ Days Inn Denver West–Golden, 15059 W. Colfax Ave., 303-277-0200 (800-329-7466). It's smoking rooms only for dogs, with a $4 fee per night. You can leave your dog unattended in the room, but the housekeeping staff won't pay a visit during that time.

$$ La Quinta, 3301 Youngfield Service Rd., 303-279-5565 (800-531-5900). You can leave your dog unattended in the room.

$$–$$$ Holiday Inn, 14707 W. Colfax Ave., 303-279-7611 (800-HOLIDAY).

Dogs are permitted in outside-facing, ground-level rooms only with a $50 deposit. You can leave your dog unattended inside the room.

$$–$$$ Marriott West, 1717 Denver West, 303-279-9100. For $10 extra per night, dogs can stay in first-floor rooms at the hotel. And you can leave your dog unattended inside.

$$–$$$ A Touch of Heaven/Talmar Bed and Breakfast, 16720 W. 63rd Pl., 303-279-4133. This B&B offers several elaborately decorated rooms, including the Royal Suite, which features a sunken bathroom with waterfall, Jacuzzi, and sauna as well as a sitting room with marble fireplace and a white baby-grand piano. Small dogs are welcome on a case-by-case basis, and an outside run is available for times when you may need to leave your pooch behind. There's a $5 fee per night. Horseback riding lessons are also available, as the B&B is home to several Arabian stallions—as well as Willie the schnauzer, billed as the official greeter.

Greenwood Village

$–$$ Motel 6, 9201 E. Arapahoe Rd., 303-790-8220 (800-466-8356). The motel accepts small dogs (e.g., lap size or slightly larger).

$$$ Woodfield Suites, 9009 E. Arapahoe Rd., 303-799-4555 (800-338-0008). The suites range from studios to one bedrooms, some with kitchens that include a stove but no oven, some with minirefrigerator and microwave only. Cooking utensils are supplied on request. Dogs are allowed in twenty of the suites, all of them smoking units.

Highlands Ranch

$$–$$$ Residence Inn by Marriott–Highlands Ranch, 93 W. Centennial Blvd. 303-683-5500 (800-331-3131). The apartment-style suites range from studios to one and two bedrooms. All have fully equipped kitchens, and the two-bedroom units have gas fireplaces, too. There's a $100 one-time fee for a dog, and he can be left unattended inside. You'll want to let the front desk know if your dog's alone so they can alert housekeeping.

Lakewood

$ Motel 6, 480 Wadsworth Blvd., 303-232-4924 (800-466-8356). Dogs up to 30 pounds get the nod here.

$$ Best Western Denver West, 11595 W. 6th Ave., 303-238-7751 (800-841-0462). With a $25 deposit, you and your dog can stay in ten rooms (half are nonsmoking). Fido can stay inside unattended, but your room won't be cleaned as long as he's there alone. There's a courtyard at the hotel where you can walk him.

$$ Comfort Inn and Suites–Southwest Denver, 3440 S. Vance St., 303-989-5500 (800-228-5150). Dogs are allowed in smoking rooms and suites with a $50 deposit. You can leave Fido unattended inside. (Note that the Comfort Suites on W. 6th Ave. does *not* accept pets.)

$$ Ramada Inn Denver West, 7150 W. Colfax Ave., 303-238-1251 (800-321-7187). There's a limit of one dog per room, and a $50 cash deposit or credit-card imprint is required. You can leave your dog unattended in the room.

Northglenn

$$ Days Inn Northglenn, 36 E. 120th Ave., 303-457-0688 (800-874-4513). There's a $6 fee per night for a dog. You can leave your dog unattended in the room as long as he's in a travel kennel and you put up the "do not disturb" sign to alert housekeeping.

$$ Holiday Inn Northglenn, 10 E. 120th Ave., 303-452-4100. Your dog will be charged $10 extra per night; you can leave him unattended inside if he promises to remain on his best behavior.

$$ La Quinta Inn Denver North, 345 W. 120th Ave., 303-252-9800 (800-531-5900).

$$ Ramada Inn Limited Denver North, 110 W. 104th Ave., 303-451-1234. Dogs are allowed in three smoking rooms only with a $25 deposit. You can leave your dog unattended in the room.

Thornton

$ Motel 6, 6 W. 83rd Pl., 303-429-1550 (800-466-8356). Though the motel prefers small dogs, you probably won't be turned away if your pooch weighs in on the larger side.

Westminster

$ Turnpike Motel, 7151 Federal Blvd., 303-429-2569

$–$$ Super 8, 12055 Melody Dr., 303-451-7200. The motel permits dogs with a $25 deposit or a credit-card imprint.

$$ Country Inn, 10179 Church Ranch Way, 303-438-5800. Dogs 18 pounds and under are allowed in smoking rooms with a $50 deposit.

$$ La Quinta Inn Westminster, 8701 Turnpike Dr., 303-425-9099 (800-531-5900). You can leave your dog unattended in the room if you let the front desk staff know.

Wheat Ridge

$ Motel 6, 9920 W. 49th Ave., 303-424-0658 (800-424-0658). Dogs 20 pounds and under are permitted, and you can leave your dog unattended in the room.

$ Motel 6, 10300 S. I-70 Frontage Rd., 303-467-3172 (800-466-8356). This Motel 6 doesn't impose a size limit on dogs.

$$ Holiday Inn Express, 4700 Kipling, 303-423-4000 (800-HOLIDAY). Dogs are welcome with a $25 deposit, and you can leave yours unattended in the room.

$$ Quality Inn–Denver West, 12100 W. 44th Ave. (Exit 266 off I-70), 303-467-2400 (800-449-0003). The motel has only two rooms (one smoking, one nonsmoking) where dogs 25 pounds and under can stay. A $50 deposit is required. You can leave your dog unattended inside, but housekeeping won't enter during that time.

Mountain Communities Southwest of Denver

Bailey

$$ Glen Isle Resort, 573 Old Stage Coach Rd., 303-838-5461. This longtime family-owned resort is situated on the South Platte River. The lodge building, which dates from 1900, is on the National Register of Historic Places. Dogs are permitted only in the resort's nineteen cabins, almost all with fireplaces and some with kitchens, for $2 extra per night. The resort is in full operation from June through Labor Day. During the winter, only nine of the cabins remain open.

$$ Mooredale Ranch Resort, U.S. Highway 285 (2.5 miles south of Bailey), 303-838-2775. The resort offers lodge rooms and suites as well as two four-bedroom cabins that sleep up to ten guests. Dogs are welcome for $10 extra per night, per dog, and they can stay unattended inside. You'll need to keep your dog leashed while on the property, which borders the South Platte River. Open year-round.

Evergreen

$$ Bauer's Spruce Island Chalets, 5937 S. Brook Forest Rd., 303-674-4757. Located on nineteen acres, these eight cabins range from studios to four bedrooms. The studios come with microwave and refrigerator; the multiroom units have full kitchens, and some have fireplaces. There's a $10 fee per night for dogs, and you can leave Rover unattended inside as long as he's in a travel kennel.

$$ Evergreen Lodge, 5331 Highway 73, 303-674-6927. Only friendly dogs are welcome at the lodge, which has a resident golden retriever. (No mean dogs or biters, says the owner.) The ten units, which are housed in four buildings, include studios as well as one- and two-bedroom suites, most with full kitchens. There's a $10 fee per night. A stream runs along the front of the property, and acres of Jefferson County Open Space are out the back door.

$$$ Abundant Way Chalet Lodge, 4980 Highway 73, 303-674-7467. The lodge allows dogs in one of its units, a fully equipped two-bedroom cabin. You might be able to leave your dog unattended inside if you can convince the owners that he's exceptionally well behaved. And you'll be able to exercise Fido, on his leash, on the surrounding acre of mountain property.

Pine

$$ The Piney Inn, 16935 Highway 126, 303-838-2616. This B&B accepts very well-behaved dogs on a case-by-case basis. The three individually decorated rooms all have private baths, and one room overlooks the South Platte River, allowing you to be lulled to sleep by the water's rush. There's also a caboose on the property that the owners plan to convert into a guest room.

$$–$$$ Anchorage Farm, 12889 Parker Ave., 303-838-5430. Located about half a mile off U.S. Highway 285, this horse ranch on fifteen acres also offers three B&B rooms with private baths. The lodging rates include a one-hour trail ride, and you can leave your dog unattended inside while you're out trotting in the fields. In addition to horses, there are other dogs who call the ranch home and with whom your dog might want to socialize.

Campgrounds

Bear Creek Lake Park, Lakewood. Off Morrison Rd., 0.25 mile east of C-470 (52 sites).

Chatfield State Park. 1 mile from the intersection of C-470 and Wadsworth Blvd. southwest of Denver (153 sites).

Cherry Creek State Park. 1.5 miles south of I-225, off Parker Rd. in Aurora (102 sites).

WORTH A PAWS

Furry Scurry. The first weekend in May, dogs from all over the metro area and their owners convene in Denver's Washington Park to participate in this walk/run, which raises money for the Denver Dumb Friends League. The 2-mile course circles one of the park's lakes. After the "race," dogs can check out the booths purveying pet products and information, enjoy a variety of treat samples, or enter competitions such as best trick or closest owner/dog look-alike. Owners can fuel up on bagels and other snacks and model their Furry Scurry T-shirts. It's the canine social event of the year! You can register in advance or on race day; in addition to the registration fee, funds are raised through pledge donations collected by participants. For more information, contact the Dumb Friends League at 303-696-4941.

Colorado Petfitters, 2075 S. University, Denver, 303-282-0020. The Denver area has long had a multitude of mountaineering stores to supply the gear needs of outdoor recreationists. Now dogs have a specialty gear store to call their own. Colorado Petfitters carries everything for the outdoor dog. Before heading to the mountains, bring Fido here to choose from a fine assortment of packs, booties, bowls, leashes, and treats. The store also sells pet-related books, premium dog food, and maps. Your dog is welcome to accompany you inside; store policy is, "if he pees on it, he buys it."

Cosmo's Dog Biscuit Bakery, 1224 E. 6th Ave., Denver, 303-777-6500 (888-88-COSMO). Does your dog have a hankering for a barbecued mail carrier? Or perhaps he'd like to bite the hand that feeds? Does he deserve a good dog star? He'll find all these and more in the form of natural, nutritious treats at this dog-dedicated bakery. There are even oat-flour-based biscuits for dogs who are allergic to wheat! The one thing you won't find here are cat-shaped dog treats, perhaps because namesake Cosmo is himself of the feline variety. Clover readily chowed down on the free samples available at the counter but had a hard time deciding on just one favorite. Is your dog's birthday coming up? Cosmo's sells personalized mutt cakes, a whole-wheat oatmeal carrot cake with cream cheese and carob frosting. You can also order an assortment of biscuits, which are sold by the half pound and pound, by phone or on-line (www.dogbakery.com/cosmos).

Ashley Whippet Canine Frisbee Invitational. One of a series of canine Frisbee events held annually in Colorado, this competition takes place the first Saturday in August, usually at Littleton's Progress Park (at the corner of Belleview and Hickory). Frisbee-loving Fidos compete in two categories: the minidistance, in which they receive points for catching distance and style in sixty-second rounds; and the free flight, in which they demonstrate their best freestyle tricks. Bring your dog to

The Furry Scurry is the canine social event of the year in Denver. (photo by Sean McCullough)

participate or just to watch; there's no entry fee, and no previous competitive experience is required. The Front Range Flyers Canine Disc Club organizes the event. For more information, contact club president Rick Brydum at 303-843-9540.

Ooh la Poochez, 2625 East 2nd Ave., Denver, 303-355-4444. This pet emporium, billed as a boutique and spa, is much more than the run-of-the-mill pet store, which makes it worthy of a paws. In addition to grooming services and a selection of premium dog food, your dog can browse among items such as high-end feed bowls, mailman- and veterinarian-shaped chew toys, and a backpack in which small (lazy) dogs can be toted around by their owners; get clean in the do-it-yourself pet wash (that means you do the washing, not Fido); or indulge in a therapeutic canine massage. According to Ooh la Poochez's brochure, the owners were inspired by a visit to Paris, where dogs have universal access to public places and "are treated with the respect and dignity they deserve." Woof! Open 9 A.M.–5 P.M., Monday to Saturday (9 A.M.–7 P.M. on Wednesday).

Red Rocks Park and Ampitheater. Red Rocks is a spectacular outdoor concert venue nestled among a natural amphitheater of—as the name implies—striking red sandstone. Though your dog is unable to come howl and cheer with the crowd during the annual summer concert series, he can pay a visit with you during nonevent times. You can even bring him onstage to play air guitar and imagine an appreciative audience of thousands before him—as long as he stays on a leash. Some hiking trails run through the park, including a 1.5-mile loop trail at the Trading Post gift shop. To reach Red Rocks, take I-70 west from Denver to the Morrison exit (259); head south on Highway 26 for about a mile to the park entrance on the right.

Buffalo Bill's Grave. Okay, so it's not quite Graceland, but your dog may be interested in sniffing out a bit of the Wild West with a visit to the final resting place of William F. Cody, a.k.a. Buffalo Bill. Rover won't be able to enter the Memorial Museum or gift shop, but he can walk with you (on leash) to the gravesite as well as enjoy the view from Lookout Mountain. From Highway 6, coming from Golden or Lakewood, turn west on 19th St. and follow the switchbacks up to the signed turnoff for the grave. From I-70 west coming from Denver, take Exit 256, make a right at the stop sign, and follow along Paradise and Charros Rds. to Lookout Mountain Rd. Go right at the T-intersection and follow Lookout Mountain Rd. to the signed turnoff for the grave. The museum is open 9 A.M.–5 P.M., every day, from May 1–October 31; 9 A.M.–4 P.M., Tuesday through Sunday, from November 1 to April 30. Call 303-526-0747 for additional information.

The Museum of Outdoor Arts. Does your dog complain that he never gets to go to museums? Bring him to The Museum of Outdoor Arts, a "museum without walls," located in Englewood's Greenwood Plaza, just west of I-25 on Orchard Rd. The fifty-five pieces of artwork—90 percent of which is outdoor sculpture—are spread out among seven locations in this office-park complex. Stop in at the museum offices, at the corner of Orchard Rd. and Greenwood Plaza Blvd., to pick up a map. Guided tours can also be arranged for $3 per person ($1 for 17 and under). Call 303-741-3609.

Bathing Beauty. Fido's been tromping through the mud all afternoon, and you don't want him to leave paw prints all over your hotel room. Lucky for you (he may have a different opinion), the Denver area has several self-service dog washes. **Mutt Puddles,** with two locations, offers rental of a small washing bay for $8 per hour, a large one for $10 per hour. Prices include shampoo and cream rinse as well as use of a towel, blow dryer, and groom ing tools: **8700 Wadsworth Blvd. in Arvada** (303-403-9901) and **120th St. and Colorado Blvd. in Thornton** (303-255-7611). Also in Thornton is **Pawz 'n' Clawz Dog and Cat Grooming, at 88th and York** (303-286-7297). Washing-bay rental is $15 ($5 per additional dog) and includes shampoo, towels, and use of brushes and a blow dryer. **Denver Dog-o-Mat, at 1842 S. Parker Rd. in Denver** (303-695-1213), charges $7–$10, depending on the size of dog, and includes shampoo and the use of towels, brushes, and

Peggy Chamblin brings Bailey to sample the treats at Cosmo's Dog Biscuit Bakery in Denver. (photo by Cindy Hirschfeld)

a dryer. **Laund-Ur-Mutt, 7175 E. Arapahoe Rd., Suite 18, in Englewood** (303-850-7266), provides washing-bay rental and use of a dryer and brushes for $8 for the first half hour, $6 per additional half hour, and $2 per additional dog. Towel rental is available for 75 cents, and you can buy shampoo, including one-wash-size bottles, at the store. Or bring your own towel and shampoo. And **Chow Down Self-Service Doggie Wash, 28608 Buffalo Park Rd. in Evergreen** (303-674-8711), provides washing-bay rental, shampoo, and the use of towels, shampoo, grooming tools, and blow dryer—as well as treats—for $12 per dog.

DOGGIE DAYCARE

Because there are so many boarding kennels in the Denver area, veterinarians that also offer boarding haven't been listed here. But if you're having difficulty finding a place for your loyal companion to spend the day, you might try the vet option.

Arvada

Action Kennel, 12975 W. 80th Ave., 303-423-2243. $4/day. Open 8 A.M.–5 P.M., Monday to Thursday and Saturday; 8 A.M.–6 P.M., Friday; 9–9:30 A.M. and 7–7:30 P.M., Sunday.

Alpine Pet Center, 9530 W. 80th Ave., 303-421-3758. $9–$10/day, depending on the size of dog. Open 7:30 A.M.–7 P.M., Monday to Friday; 7:30 A.M.–5 P.M., Saturday.

Aurora

Academy Acres Kennels, 16501 E. Arapahoe Rd., 303-690-1188. $8–$12/day, depending on the size of dog. Open 7 A.M.–6 P.M., Monday to Friday; 7 A.M.–noon, Saturday.

B&B for Dog LLC–Large Breeds, 10 S. Potomac, 303-361-0061. $12/day. Monday to Friday, dropoff is between 6:30 A.M. and 6 P.M., and pickup is any time until 10 P.M.; Saturday and Sunday, dropoff is between 7 A.M. and 6 P.M., and pickup is until 10 P.M.

Broadview Kennels, 2155 S. Havana, Aurora, 303-755-0471. $7–$8/day, depending on the size of dog. Open 7 A.M.–6 P.M., Monday to Friday; 7 A.M.–noon, Saturday.

Dogtown Boarding Kennels, 2250 N. Chambers, 303-364-3713. $7–$10/day, depending on the size of dog. Open 8 A.M.–6 P.M., Monday to Saturday.

Pets Control, 16255 E. 4th Ave., 303-364-8586. $10/day. Open 7 A.M.–6 P.M., Monday to Friday; day boarders can come on Saturday if they're dropped off before 9 A.M. and picked up after 5:30 P.M.

Tenaker Pet Care Center, 895 Laredo St., 303-366-2376. $9–$11/day, depending on the size of dog. Veterinarians are on staff, and there's even a recreational swimming pool on the premises. Open 7:30 A.M.–5 P.M., Monday to Friday; 7:30 A.M.–2 P.M., Saturday.

Broomfield

Colorado Dog Academy, 12180 N. Sheridan Blvd., 303-465-1703. $5/day. Open 8 A.M.–5:30 P.M., Monday to Saturday.

Castle Rock

Beau Monde Kennels, 660 E. Happy Canyon Rd., 303-688-9578. $10/day. The kennel features a one-acre fenced-in exercise and play area for its guests. Open 7:30 A.M.–6 P.M., Monday, Tuesday, Thursday, Friday; 7:30 A.M.–noon, Wednesday and Saturday.

Commerce City

Irondale Kennels, 6950 E. 88th Ave., 303-286-7944. $8–$12/day, depending on the size of dog. Open 8 A.M.–6 P.M., Monday to Friday; 9 A.M.–noon, Saturday.

Denver

Allbrick Boarding Kennels, 8700 Zuni, 303-429-2433. $7.50–$8.50/day, depending on the size of dog. Open 7 A.M.–6 P.M., Monday to Friday; 7 A.M.–5 P.M., Saturday.

B&B for Dog LLC–Small Breeds, 1842 S. Parker Rd., 303-745-8538. $12/day for dogs 35 pounds and under (larger dogs go to the B&B for Dog in Aurora). Monday to Friday, dropoff is between 6:30 A.M. and 6 P.M., and pickup is any time until 10 P.M.; Saturday and Sunday, dropoff is between 7 A.M. and 6 P.M., pickup until 10 P.M.

Englewood

Doggy Day Camp, 15350 E. Hinsdale Dr., 303-680-4001. $12/day. Open 7 A.M.–6:30 P.M., Monday to Friday; daycare is not available on weekends.

Sandylake Boarding Kennels, 200 W. Lehow Ave., 303-730-1715. $10/day. Open 8 A.M.–5 P.M., Monday to Friday; 8 A.M.–noon, Saturday.

Golden

Sage Valley Pet Center, 16400 W. 54th St., 303-279-6969. $11–$14/day, depending on the size of dog. Open 8 A.M.–6 P.M., Monday to Friday; 8 A.M.–noon and later by appointment only, Saturday.

Waggin' Tails, 17731 W. Colfax, 303-215-0413. $13/day on weekdays; $10/day on weekends. Half-day boarding is also available for $8 (five hours or less). Open 7 A.M.–6:30 P.M., Monday to Friday; 7–10 A.M. for dropoff and 4–7 P.M. for pickup, Saturday and Sunday.

Highlands Ranch

Tenaker Pet Care Center, 5790 E. County Line, 303-694-5738. $10–$14/day, depending on the size of dog. Veterinarians are on staff. Open 7:30 A.M.–6:30 P.M., Monday to Friday; 7:30 A.M.–1 P.M., Saturday; 5–6 P.M. for pickups only, Sunday.

Lakewood

Mantayo Kennels and Dog School, 1220 S. Wadsworth Blvd., 303-985-4011. $8–$11/day, depending on the size of dog. Open 8 A.M.–5 P.M., Monday to Friday; 8 A.M.–noon, Saturday.

Pinehurst Animal Center, 6500 W. Hampden Ave., 303-985-1845. $5/day. Open 8 A.M.–noon and 1:30–5:30 P.M., Monday to Friday; 8 A.M.–noon, Saturday.

Littleton

High Country Kennels, 8290 W. Coal Mine Ave., 303-979-3353. $5/day. Open 7 A.M.–5:30 P.M., Monday to Friday.

Pampered Pets, 13906 Kuehster, 303-697-6824. $18/day. This is a home-based boarding service run by a certified vet technician. Dogs have four fenced-in acres on which to romp and no cages or kennels. Arrangements made by appointment only. Note that though the address is officially Littleton, the house is located in the mountains, close to Conifer.

Pet Ranch Kennel, 12725 W. Belleview Ave., 303-973-0542. $6/day. Open 7 A.M.–5:45 P.M., Monday to Friday; 8 A.M.–noon, Saturday.

Parker

Cherry Creek Kennels, 9665 S. Parker Rd., 303-840-2035. $10/day. Open 8 A.M.–6 P.M., Monday to Friday; 9 A.M.–3 P.M., Saturday.

Club Pet, 10719 Parker Rd., 303-841-3227. $10/day. Open 9 A.M.–6 P.M., Monday to Saturday. Earlier dropoff times are available by appointment.

Wheat Ridge

American School of Dog Training, 4219 Xenon St., 303-940-9188. $7/day. Open 8 A.M.–7 P.M., Monday to Thursday; 8 A.M.–6 P.M., Friday; 8 A.M.–5 P.M., Saturday and Sunday.

Pet Village, 11440 W. 44th Ave., 303-422-2055 (888-FOR-PETS). $9/day. The kennel is part of a national chain. Open 8 A.M.–6 P.M., Monday to Friday; 8 A.M.–5 P.M., Saturday; 3–6 P.M. for pickups only, Sunday.

PET PROVISIONS

Arvada

Dakotah Feed and Supply, Inc., 5870 Olde Wadsworth Blvd., 303-431-5285

Great America's Pet Castle, 5366 Sheridan Blvd., 303-433-6375

Pet World, 5735 Independence, 303-422-9545

Aurora

Petco, 16960 E. Quincy Ave., 303-699-5061, and 13750 E. Mississippi, 303-695-1223

PetsMart, I-225 (Abilene) and Mississippi Ave., 303-695-4532

Brighton

Brighton Feed and Farm Supply, 370 N. Main, 303-659-0721

Broomfield

Clarkston Feed and Supply, 11177 Dillon Rd., 303-469-1951

Willow Run Feed and Supply, 5700 W. 120th Ave., 303-466-5971

Castle Rock

Castle Rock Feed and Western Wear, 420 Third, 303-688-3016

Rampart Feed and Pet, Inc., 1233 N. Park, 303-688-7360

Commerce City

Qual-Pet Feed Store, 6450 Highway 2, 303-286-8931

Denver

Colorado Petfitters, 2075 S. University, 303-282-0020

Curve Feed and Supply, 6750 W. Mississippi Ave., 303-934-1249

PetsMart, Pecos Ave. (off Highway 36), 303-428-4231

Pooch! 2817 E. 3rd Ave., 303-333-4677

Sherlock's 6th Ave. Pet Supply, 810 E. 6th Ave., 303-733-6410

Englewood

Petco, 9505 E. County Line Rd., 303-708-0616

South Side Feed and Supplies, 4332 S. Broadway, 303-761-1075

Evergreen

Chow Down, 28608 Buffalo Park Rd., 303-674-8711

Glendale

PetsMart, Colorado Blvd. and Alameda Ave., 303-394-4406

Golden

Animal Feed and Supply, 865 Lupine, 303-279-1043

Greenwood Village

Pet Outfitters, 5942 S. Holly, 303-290-0430

Highlands Ranch

Pets USA, 6435 Business Center Dr., 303-683-4650

Lakewood

PetsMart, West First Ave. and Wadsworth Blvd., 303-232-0858

Pets-n-Stuff, 7777 W. Jewell, 303-989-5380

Littleton

PetsMart, northwest corner of C-470 and I-25 (Park Meadows location), 303-799-3575

PetsMart, South University Blvd. and County Line Rd., 303-220-0215

PetsMart, Wadsworth Blvd. and Quincy Ave., 303-971-0019

Northglenn
Petco, 450 E. 120th Ave., 303-255-4528

Parker
AmeriPet, 10530 S. Parker Rd., 303-840-6640

Parker Feed and Garden Supplies, 11703 N. Highway 83, 303-841-3955

Westminster
Petco, 6735 W. 88th Ave., 303-432-9230

Pets Express, 9100 W. 100th Ave., 303-421-1225

PetsMart, 92nd Ave. and Sheridan Blvd. (Westlake Shopping Center), 303-426-4999

Wheat Ridge
PetsMart, 32nd Ave. and Youngfield St., 303-424-0123

Walkers Quality Cage and Feed Supply, 9075 W. 44th, 303-424-0305

Wardle Feed and Pet Supply, W. 42nd Ave. and Wadsworth, 303-424-6455

CANINE ER
Denver
Alameda East Veterinary Hospital (AAHA certified), 9870 E. Alameda Ave. (2 blocks west of Havana), 303-366-2639. Open 24 hours.

Englewood
Animal Hospital Center (AAHA certified),

250 W. Lehow Ave., 303-794-2200. Open 24 hours.

Greenwood Village
Tendercare Veterinary Medical Center (AAHA certified), 5930 S. Holly St., 303-689-9500. Open 24 hours.

Lakewood
Animal Emergency Service (AAHA certified), 9797 W. Colfax Ave., 303-232-6227. Open 6 P.M.–8 A.M. the following morning, Monday to Friday; from noon Saturday until 8 A.M. the following Monday; 24 hours on holidays.

Thornton
Northside Emergency Pet Clinic, 123rd and Washington, 303-252-7722. Open 6 P.M.–8 A.M. the following morning, Monday to Friday; from noon Saturday until 8 A.M. the following Monday; 24 hours on holidays.

Wheat Ridge
Wheat Ridge Animal Hospital (AAHA certified), 3695 Kipling, 303-424-3325. Open 24 hours.

RESOURCES
Denver Metro Convention and Visitors Bureau, 1668 Larimer, Denver, 303-892-1112 (800-645-3446); www.denver.org.

South Platte Ranger District, Pike and San Isabel National Forests, 19316 Goddard Ranch Ct. (past the N. Turkey Creek Rd. turnoff from U.S. Highway 285 South), Morrison, 303-275-5610.

A visit to Denver wouldn't be complete without a treat. Surprise Fido with one of these:

- A Barker's Dozen, 13 Milkbones dipped in white chocolate. The bones come in two sizes and can also be purchased individually. Rocky Mountain Chocolate Factory, 1512 Larimer St. in downtown Denver.
- Ice-cream sandwiches for dogs—two biscuits with vanilla ice cream in between. Bonnie Brae Ice Cream, 799 S. University Blvd., Denver.
- A "sundae"—a scoop of vanilla ice cream topped with two biscuits. Soda Rock Fountain, 2217 E. Mississippi Ave. (near Washington Park), Denver.

2
Boulder
and Vicinity

THE BIG SCOOP

The communities of Boulder County, including Boulder, Louisville, Lafayette, Longmont, and the mountain town of Nederland, provide lots of great outdoor opportunities for dogs, even though development in the area increases at a rate faster than a wagging tail.

Boulder is in general a dog-friendly town, though environmental and shared-use concerns have recently made dogs on trails the subject of occasionally heated debate. A local group known as FIDOS (Friends Interested in Dogs and Open Space) has become an advocate of canine rights, working to keep the majority of trails accessible to dogs. Given the occasionally lukewarm reception that some Boulder residents may give you and your dog, therefore, be sure to help your own Fido brush up on etiquette before hitting the trails.

Dogs are not allowed on Boulder's downtown, pedestrian-only Pearl Street Mall, which limits their sightseeing and shopping options somewhat. A leash law is enforced within the city limits of all towns in Boulder County, though not in unincorporated Boulder County. And though there's no direct ordinance against public tethering, the City of Boulder leash law can be interpreted as prohibiting it. So you're better off leaving your dog in the car with the windows wide open when running that quick errand than tying him up outside the store.

TAIL-RATED TRAILS

Boulder dogs are extremely lucky. Current regulations allow dogs to be off leash on most City of Boulder Open Space and Mountain Parks trails (but not on Boulder *County* Open Space), though they must always be within their owner's sight and under voice control. (Voice control means a dog must come immediately when called, no matter what distractions of other dogs, wildlife, or people may tempt him to do otherwise.) Rangers will test your dog's obedience level on occasion (a pocketful of treats can be helpful in such situations—for your dog, not the ranger!). Plastic "pet pickup" baggies are considerately provided at many trailheads to encourage you to clean up after your dog's pit stops—use them!

The trail map put out by the Colorado Mountain Club (Boulder Group) includes many hiking options in addition to the ones suggested here. Look for it at the Chatauqua Park ranger's cottage as well as at local mountaineering stores. *Boulder Hiking Trails,* by Ruth and Glenn Cushman, is another good resource.

Boulder

Marshall Mesa. 2.1 miles round-trip. Take Highway 93 (S. Broadway) south out of Boulder to the intersection with Highway 170 (Eldorado Springs Dr.) and the turnoff for Eldorado Springs. Turn left; the trailhead is 0.9 mile ahead on the right. *Dogs can be off leash.*

Though less than a mile from a major thoroughfare, the trails on Marshall Mesa convey the flavor of Boulder County's less-developed past, allowing you and your dog to experience some solitude among the ponderosa pines. In fact, cows sometimes roam on the mesa; if your pooch is prone to chase them, it's wise to keep him leashed. This is Clover's favorite evening hike, as the views west to the foothills (and Longs Peak) provide good sunset watching.

Begin on the **Community Ditch Trail,** which heads left shortly after the trailhead. After a short climb this wide gravel service road parallels an irrigation ditch, usually filled during the spring and summer, where your dog can have lots of fun frolicking in the water. After 1.3 miles the trail meets up with the **Marshall Mesa Trail** to the right, on which wet dogs get a little under a mile to dry off before arriving back at the trailhead (and the car). As an added bonus for the literate canine, signs along the loop describe the history and geology of the mesa.

 Mount Sanitas. Either 3.1 or 2.2 miles round-trip. Drive on Mapleton Ave. west from Broadway in downtown Boulder; after the Mapleton Center for Rehabilitation on the corner of 4th St., you'll see several parking turnouts on the right that provide access to the trailhead. Recommended starting point is the picnic shelter right before the small bridge. *Dogs can be off leash.*

The Sanitas trails are "doggie central" in Boulder. Your dog will love you for bringing him here if he's the social type, as there are always plenty of opportunities to do the "doggie handshake" (i.e., butt sniffing). And you'll enjoy the panoramic vistas of Boulder and the eastern plains offered at a couple of vantage points as well as the sense of being miles away from population density when you're really just a few minutes from downtown.

Clover's favorite route—best for the aerobically fit dog and owner—involves

Steve Schlachter and Jazz savor the view from Mount Sanitas. (photo by Suisaidh Schlacter)

climbing on the **Mount Sanitas Trail,** which branches off to the left after the bridge. You'll reach the summit after 1.2 miles of steady climbing (a gain of 1,280 feet). Descend 0.8 mile by the steep **East Ridge Trail** (shoes with good tread or hiking boots come in handy) and walk along the ridge past the trophy homes until you reach the top of the **Sanitas Valley Trail.** This wide gravel path descends gradually for 1.1 miles back to your launching point. (If you're into practicing your rock-climbing moves, there are some good bouldering sites along the hike up Sanitas—just look for the signs and chalk marks.)

A less strenuous alternative would be to forgo the vertical and hike along the Valley Trail, which affords views of rolling green hills capped by the famous Flatirons. Or your dog may prefer to hike up the Valley Trail and return on the 1-mile **Dakota Ridge Trail,** which begins to the right of the Valley Trail's "summit" and eventually rejoins this trail about three-quarters of the way down.

A small brook by the picnic shelter provides a cooling rest for your dog after hiking and socializing. A "swimming hole" about halfway up the Sanitas Valley Trail on the left is usually full of water in the summer, and a trickling rivulet on the trail's right provides the opportunity for some slurps. As there are no water sources on the **Mount Sanitas Trail,** you may want to bring extra water to share with your dog.

Chautauqua Park. Drive west on Baseline Rd.; the park entrance is on the left after 9th St. *Dogs can be off leash except in the large lawn area that fronts the Chautauqua Auditorium and restaurant.*

This is perhaps Boulder's best-known spot for hiking and playing, with a stunning location at the base of the town's signature Flatirons. It's wise to avoid this area midday on warm, sunny weekends (summer or winter), when everyone and their dog seem to come here (pardon the play on words). Several trails originate from here, including the popular **Mesa Trail,** which runs almost 7 miles south to Eldorado Springs. For great views of Boulder, hike to Saddle Rock or Royal Arch (both are slightly more than 2 miles round-trip and involve some climbing).

Doudy Draw (from the Flatirons Vista trailhead). About 5 miles round-trip. Take Highway 93 (S. Broadway) south from Boulder. About 2 miles south of the stoplight at the Eldorado Springs turnoff, you'll see a fenced-in parking area on the right. The trailhead is here. *Dogs can be off leash.*

This is a popular trail with horses as well as hikers. If your dog has an aversion to equine creatures, note the number of horse trailers in the parking lot before setting out. Begin by hiking west on a service road, taking in, as the trailhead name implies, a beautiful vista of the Flatirons, the vertical rock slabs that front the foothills. After the second livestock gate, the trail narrows, winding along a ridge through fragrant ponderosa pine. It then follows a couple of switchbacks down to a small gully, where you'll come to a dog rest stop

(i.e., stream). After crossing, follow the trail sign to the right (note that dogs are prohibited on the other side of the interior fence you'll pass). A good turnaround point for your hike is a bridge you'll come to just before the Community Ditch Trail, which allows your dog another respite near water. Hiking further would bring you to a final paved portion of the trail that ends at a trailhead on Eldorado Springs Dr. (Highway 170), a total of 3.4 miles from the Flatirons Vista trailhead.

Boulder Creek Path. Runs 9 miles from the mouth of Boulder Canyon to east of 55th St. *Dogs must be leashed.*

If possible, avoid bringing your dog on the downtown section of this often crowded paved path—in the wink of an eye he could easily become tangled up with the multitude of bicyclists, in-line skaters, runners, and amblers who use this popular route. The stretch of path that runs east of Foothills Highway and initially parallels Pearl St., however, offers more breathing space, especially on weekdays. See if your clever canine spots the "paw prints" embedded in the concrete just east of the office park on Pearl—they lead to a small, refreshing pool where dogs can partake of the waters while you relax on a nearby bench.

Despite the many places in and around Boulder where you can hike with your dog, certain areas lie at the other end of the spectrum—that is, dogs are banned. Fido is not welcome on the following trails on City of Boulder and Boulder County Open Space as well as on Mountain Parks land:

- a portion of the **Lindsey property,** via County Rd. 67 off Eldorado Springs Dr. You must keep your dog on the road and trail in this hiking area—when the trail forks, dogs are permitted on the right branch; there's a no-dog policy on the left branch;

- the 1.5-mile section of the **South Boulder Creek Trail** that runs south of South Boulder Rd. (also known as the Van Vlete property);

- the White Rocks section of the **East Boulder Trail,** bounded to the south by Valmont Rd. and to the north by a trail through the Gunbarrel Farm open space area;

- the **Hogback Trail,** which branches off the Foothills Trail north of Wonderland Lake;

- various city open space properties that have no established trails—check fence lines for "no dogs" postings;

- the relatively new **Hall Ranch** area north of Boulder, off Highway 36—a dog moratorium has been extended through the end of 1998 and will be reevaluated by the county commissioners in January 1999;

- the **McClintock Trail,** a self-guided nature walk between the Enchanted Mesa and Mesa Trails in Chautauqua Park.

 South shore of Boulder Reservoir. During the summer, dogs are prohibited from this area.

Eldorado Springs

 Eldorado Canyon State Park. From Highway 93 just south of Boulder, turn right on Highway 170 at the Eldorado Springs turnoff. The park is about 3 miles ahead. *Dogs must be leashed.*

When your dog has had his fill of watching climbers attempt the numerous technical routes for which "Eldo" is renowned, he'll probably be interested in doing a bit of hiking. At 2.8 miles round-trip, the **Rattlesnake Gulch Trail** begins off

the one road through the park. It climbs gradually but steadily to a flat overlook, former site of the Crags Hotel, which burned in 1912. The only remains of this once-luxurious retreat are a couple of fireplaces, sections of the foundation, and scattered pieces of charred dinnerware—as well as a spectacular view of the canyon and the plains beyond on one side and the rugged Indian Peaks on the other. Though the trail continues to an upper loop near the railroad tracks (you might spot an Amtrak train traveling high above during your hike), the overlook makes a good turnaround point. The **Eldorado Canyon Trail** takes off from the end of the park road, climbing, at times steeply, through ponderosa pine and intersecting after a couple of miles with the **Walker Ranch Loop Trail,** a popular mountain-biking area on Boulder County Open Space. Taking a left at the intersection puts you on the Crescent **Meadows Trail,** which leads to another parcel of state park land (known as Crescent Meadows). The trail eventually ends at the Gross Dam Rd.; the round-trip distance from the trailhead is 11 miles.

Louisville

 Rock Creek Farm. 5 miles of trails. Take Dillon Rd. east from McCaslin Blvd. Look for a trailhead and parking area on the right, shortly after the intersection with 104th St. An alternate entrance on 104th St. brings you directly to Stearns Lake: From Dillon Rd., go south on 104th St. The trailhead is 0.7 mile ahead on the left. *Dogs must be leashed.*

Don't confuse this Boulder County Open Space area with the monolithic Rock Creek subdivision visible from Highway 36. In fact, with the wide openness of this area, you and your dog might think you're in Nebraska, except for the stunning view of Longs Peak to the west. This would be a great place for a sunset walk. The most scenic hiking section begins from the Dillon Rd. trailhead, where a wide, flat trail leads through fields, then goes almost all the way around Stearns Lake (keep an eye out for the wildlife area closure signs). From Stearns Lake, you can also continue hiking south from the dam; after going through a horse pasture, stay to the right, where a dirt service road will eventually bring you out on an unpaved section of 104th St. that's closed to traffic.

Nederland

 Lost Lake. 4 miles round-trip. From Nederland, take Highway 72 east. Make a right on County Rd. 130 (toward Eldora Mountain Ski Resort). Stay on this road, going past the ski area turnoff and through the small hamlet of Eldora, after which the road turns to dirt. At the signed fork, stay left, to Hessie. In the spring, when the road past this point becomes streamlike, you may want to park near the fork. But if your vehicle has good clearance, the most available parking is at Hessie townsite, less than a quarter of a mile farther along. The trailhead is just up the road from here, at the North Fork of Boulder Creek. *Dogs can be off leash on this particular trail because it doesn't enter the Indian Peaks Wilderness.* If you continue hiking on one of the other trails accessed from here, be ready to leash your dog as soon as you cross the Wilderness boundary.

This area is extremely popular on weekends year-round; midweek would be the best time to explore it. The first part of this trail follows an old mining road up a gradual ascent. Midsummer, you'll be greeted by a colorful profusion of wildflowers on the slopes alongside the trail. After about half a mile, cross a bridge over the South Fork of Boulder Creek and hike up parallel to it. A sign for

Burley poses at a vista west of Boulder. (photo by Sarah Woodberry)

Lost Lake soon indicates a turnoff to the left. From there, it's a short way to the lake itself, where your dog can frolic in the water while you pick out the mining ruins on the hillside across the lake.

Cycling for Canines

Of the handful of trails near Boulder where you can bike, only a few allow free-running dogs: the **Community Ditch** and **Greenbelt Plateau Trails** on Marshall Mesa (see "Tail-Rated Trails"); the part of the Community Ditch Trail that also runs for 1.8 miles on the west side of Highway 93 (access this portion either by parking alongside Highway 93 or from the Doudy Draw trailhead off Eldorado Springs Dr. in order to avoid a dangerous crossing of the road with bike and dog in tow); the **Boulder Valley Ranch** and **Foothills Trails** off Highway 36 just north of Boulder (dogs are required to be leashed around Wonderland Lake, however); and the Teller Farm section of the **East Boulder Trail,** which runs by two lakes between Valmont Dr. and Arapahoe Ave. east of Boulder. Note that the popular Walker Ranch and Betasso Preserve loop trails both have a leash law.

You'll have more biking options outside of Nederland. The "Mountain Bike Map of Boulder County," published by Latitude 40° and available at area bike and mountaineering shops, is a good resource. Try the **Sourdough Trail,** a great moderate ride that runs about 7 miles (one way) from Rainbow Lakes Rd. to Brainard Lake Dr.; access it by driving 7 miles north of Nederland on Highway 72 and turning left at the University of Colorado Mountain Research sign. The **Switzerland Trail** fol-

lows a former narrow-gauge railroad track and has great views. There are several access points; one is reached via Sugarloaf Mountain Rd. out of Boulder Canyon, and another is about 3.5 miles past the town of Gold Hill, via Mapleton Ave./Sunshine Canyon Rd. out of Boulder. The trail runs about 4 miles down to Fourmile Creek from both of these starts. The **Bunce School Rd.** (now a jeep road) goes for about 6 miles from just past Peaceful Valley Campground, off Highway 72 north, to Highway 7; you'll have to do an out-and-back to avoid riding on the highway. Water is available near or along all of these trails.

POWDERHOUNDS

You and your dog will need to venture into the mountains around Nederland to find reliable snow for skiing or snowshoeing. Note, however, that certain trails are completely closed to dogs from December 1 through April 30: the Little Raven, Waldrop, and CMC Trails at the popular Brainard Lake area; the Jenny Creek and Guinn Mountain Trails by the Eldora Nordic Center; and the Buchanan Pass Trail in the northern Indian Peaks Wilderness.

Some good routes to consider include the **Sourdough Trail** (see "Cycling for Canines"); the **Coney Flats Trail,** a jeep road that begins at Beaver Reservoir, off Highway 72 north of Ward; and **Jenny Lind Gulch,** about 4 miles in on the Rollins Pass Rd. outside Rollinsville. For more detailed descriptions of these routes as well as other options, refer to *Skiing Colorado's Backcountry,* by Brian Litz and Kurt Lankford (Fulcrum).

CREATURE COMFORTS

Unless otherwise stated, dogs should not be left unattended in the room or cabin.

Boulder

$ Foot of the Mountain Motel, 200 Arapahoe Ave., 303-442-5688. The small, simply furnished, wood-paneled rooms are contained in rustic-looking cabins. There's a $5 fee per night for a dog. A big plus is the motel's location across the street from Boulder Creek and Eben G. Fine Park; though dogs must be leashed, the park and adjacent Creek Path provide great sniffing opportunities. You may leave your dog unattended in the room as long as you notify housekeeping.

$–$$ Boulder Mountain Lodge, 91 Four Mile Canyon Rd., 303-444-0882 (800-458-0882). This motel complex, located streamside several miles from town, has a casual, summer-camp feel. In fact, campsites are available in addition to rooms. There's a $50 deposit for a dog, $15 if you're camping. Dogs can be left in rooms, if necessary, but housekeeping will not come in.

The outskirts of Boulder have some canine-friendly biking trails. (photo by Arlan Flax)

Keep your dog leashed when outside.

$$ Best Western Boulder Inn, 770 28th St., 303-449-3800. Dogs are allowed in smoking rooms only, and a $100 deposit is required. Don't confuse this motel with the other Best Western in Boulder, the Golden Buff, which doesn't allow pets.

$$ Days Inn, 5397 S. Boulder Rd. (at Foothills Parkway), 303-499-4422. Dogs under twenty pounds are allowed in smoking rooms only.

$$ Holiday Inn, 800 28th St., 303-443-3322 (800-465-4329). Dogs are allowed in outside-facing rooms only but can be left unattended if housekeeping is notified. A $25 deposit is required. (Note that the Holiday Inn Express, in north Boulder, does not accept pets.)

$$ Lazy L Motel, 1000 28th St., 303-442-7525. Not for the discriminating dog.

$$ Super 8 Motel, 970 28th St., 303-443-7800. Dogs are allowed in smoking rooms only. A $100 deposit is required if you pay for your room with cash; no deposit is required with a credit-card payment.

$$–$$$ The Broker Inn, 30th St. and Baseline, 303-444-3330. Dogs can only stay in smoking rooms.

$$$ Homewood Suites, 4950 Baseline Rd. (behind the Meadows Shopping Center), 303-499-9922 (800-225-5466). An apartment-style hotel. There's a $50 one-time fee for dogs, which can be left unattended when housekeeping is notified.

$$$ Residence Inn by Marriott, 3030 Center Green Drive, 303-449-5545. There's a $50 one-time fee for dogs who stay up to ten nights; it's $5 per night thereafter. You can leave your dog unattended in the room.

Longmont

$ Bar-L Motel, 1524 S. Main, 303-776-7856. There's a $5 fee per night, and you can leave your dog unattended in the room.

$ Budget Host, 3815 Highway 119, 303-776-8700. The motel has designated pet rooms (both smoking and nonsmoking available) and charges $5 extra per night. You can leave your dog unattended in the room.

$ First Interstate Inn, 3940 Highway 119, 303-772-6000 (800-462-4667). Dogs are charged a $5 one-time fee.

$$ Del Camino Super 8, 10805 Turner Ave. (intersection of Highways 25 and 119), 303-772-0888 (800-800-8000). Dogs can be left unattended in the rooms.

$$ Ellen's Bed and Breakfast, 700 Kimbark St., 303-776-1676. Your dog may well appreciate this alternative to Longmont's chain motels. Set in a 1910 Victorian house, Ellen's offers two rooms, one with a queen-size bed and private bath, the other with bunk beds and a shared bath. Two schnauzers serve as host dogs. You are able to leave your dog unattended inside the room.

$$ Twin Peaks Super 8, 2446 N. Main, 303-772-8106 (800-800-8000). Dogs can stay in upstairs rooms only, and a $25 deposit is required if you're paying in cash. You can leave your dog unattended in the room.

$$–$$$ Raintree Plaza, 1900 Ken Pratt Blvd., 303-776-2000. Dogs are allowed in the main hotel but not in the suites, which are in a separate building. You must sign a release form and leave a credit-card imprint, or $50 if you're paying in cash, as a security deposit. Dogs can be left unattended in the rooms.

Louisville

$$ Comfort Inn, 1196 Dyer Road, 303-604-0181. Dogs are allowed in smoking rooms only, but they can be left unattended.

$$ La Quinta Inn, 902 Dillon Rd., 303-664-0100 (800-531-5900). Dogs under 40 pounds are permitted, and you can leave yours unattended in the room as long as he stays in a travel kennel.

Nederland

$ American Youth Hostel, 8 W. Boulder, 303-258-7788. If you're young, not picky, and are on a low budget, go for it. Otherwise, by-pass this bare-bones set-up. Dogs can be left unattended in the rooms. (By the way, you don't have to be a member of a hostel association to stay here.)

$$ Arapaho Ranch, 1250 Eldora Rd., 970-258-3405. This guest ranch near the Indian

Peaks Wilderness offers ten rustic cabins, all fully equipped, that range in size from two to four bedrooms. Before the middle of June and after Labor Day, the cabins are available for nightly rentals, with a $5 fee per night for a dog. Otherwise, stays at the ranch are on a weekly basis, with a $25 one-time fee for your dog. Families will find a variety of recreational opportunities close at hand (though horseback riding is no longer offered), and dogs will appreciate Middle Boulder Creek, which runs through the property. You can leave your dog unattended in the cabin for a couple of hours at a time. Open mid-May to October 1.

$$ Nederhaus Motel, 686 Highway 119, 303-258-3585. Suites with kitchens are available in addition to standard motel rooms.

$$–$$$ Above-Boulder Wildlife Safari Lodge, 3.5 miles outside of Nederland (you'll get more specific directions when you make a reservation), **303-258-7777.** The lodge offers three B&B rooms, each with its own, but separate, bath and decorated in a full safari theme. Small, "well-behaved" dogs and older dogs can stay with you in the rooms. The lodge also maintains outside kennels for large dogs.

Campgrounds

National Forest campgrounds: **Kelly-Dahl Campground,** 3 miles south of Nederland off Highway 119 (46 sites); **Rainbow Lakes Campground,** off Highway 72, 7 miles north of Nederland (16 sites); **Pawnee Campground,** at Brainard Lake Recreation Area, 14 miles north of Nederland off Highway 72 (55 sites).

Private campgrounds: **Boulder Mountain Lodge** (see "Creature Comforts").

WORTH A PAWS

A Cause for Paws. Your dog (and his leash) can accompany you on this 4-mile walk-a-thon along the Boulder Creek Path with lots of other dogs and their owners. Ideally you would register in advance, at the Humane Society of Boulder Valley, 2323 55th St., and collect pledges from fellow dog-lovers. However, if you're just in town for the weekend (the walk takes place mid-September), you can register on the morning of the event. Call the Humane Society at 303-442-4030 for more details.

Dog Walk. This 3-mile pledge walk is held on the first or second weekend of May, to coincide with Be Kind to Animals week. The course follows the bike path along Rogers Grove in Longmont, and proceeds benefit the Longmont Humane Society. You'll need to collect a minimum of $20 in pledges (or you can register for $20 the morning of the event), and you'll receive a T-shirt and snacks for you and your dog. Call the Humane Society at 303-772-1232 for more info.

Laund-Ur-Mutt, Table Mesa Shopping Center (near the King Soopers), Boulder, 303-543-9592. Okay, this probably won't be as much fun for your dog as for you, but if he's starting to smell like a Deadhead-type who's been on the road too long, this self-service dog wash may be just the ticket. Washing bays rent for $8 for a half hour, which includes dog-friendly hoses, a scrubbing mitt, and use of a dryer. (Towels, at 75 cents, and shampoo are extra. Or you can bring your own.) The **Blue Hills Dog and Cat Shop in Longmont** (see "Pet Provisions") also has a self-service dog wash; they provide everything, including shampoo, towels, and blow dryer, for $9.

Boulder dogs take to the Creek Path for the annual A Cause for Paws walk. (photo by Cindy Hirschfeld)

Alfalfa's Dog Wash. If you're in the neighborhood of Alfalfa's Market in Boulder (Broadway and Arapahoe) on the August weekend when this annual dog wash is held, bring your pooch by for a scrub. Proceeds benefit the Humane Society of Boulder Valley (303-442-4030).

Dog Wash. Consider this a "spa day" for your dog. The wash usually is held during July, at the Pioneer Bank in Longmont at Hover and 16th St. In addition to washers, groomers are on hand to coif drying fur and clip too-long nails. Every dog gets a bandanna to top off the look. Proceeds benefit the Longmont Humane Society (303 772-1232).

DOGGIE DAYCARE
Boulder

Allpets Clinic, 5290 Manhattan Cr. (at Highway 36 and S. Boulder Rd.), 303-499-5335, and 805 S. Public Rd., Lafayette, 303-665-4230. $16/day. Day boarding is available at both locations. A vet will do a short health exam on your dog if he or she has not been to the clinic before. Open 24 hours.

Arapahoe Animal Hospital, 5585 Arapahoe Ave. (behind the Boulder Dinner Theatre), 303-442-7033. $9–$12/day, depending on the size of the dog. Open 8 A.M.–5:30 P.M., Monday to Friday; 8 A.M.–3 P.M., Saturday.

Broadway Animal Medical, 1405 S. Broadway (1 mile south of Table Mesa Dr.), 303-499-5505. $8/day. Your dog will get to go

> Bring Rover to brush up on his hiking manners at a session of "Trail Dog Tips," free clinics put on about once a month in spring, summer, and fall by the City of Boulder Open Space Department. Each clinic is held at a different trailhead in Boulder. Call 303-441-4142 for details and times.

out and play with the other dogs every couple of hours. Open 7:30 A.M.–7:30 P.M., Monday and Thursday; 7:30 A.M.–5:30 P.M., Tuesday, Wednesday, and Friday; 7:30 A.M.–3 P.M., Saturday.

Gunbarrel Veterinary Clinic, 55th St. and Diagonal Highway, 303-530-2500. $6–$7/day, depending on the size of dog. If you don't have your dog's vaccination records along, the clinic can phone your vet. Open 8 A.M.–5:30 P.M., Monday and Friday; 8 A.M.–7 P.M., Tuesday and Thursday; 8 A.M.–noon, Wednesday and Saturday.

Lafayette

Akasha's Doggy Daycare, 307 W. Oak, 303-666-0905. $15/day. Out-of-state dogs will need to present a health certificate in addition to the required proof of vaccination. You and your dog will be asked to participate in an interview to make sure everyone's comfortable. Once in daycare, your dog will get to be out of his kennel and playing outside as much as possible; a wide selection of toys is also available for his chewing and carrying pleasure. Open 6:30 A.M.–7 P.M., Monday to Friday; weekend boarding available by appointment only.

Longmont

Blue Hills Kennel, 14360 N. 83rd St. (off Hover Rd. heading north), 303-776-3907. $6/day. A health certificate is required for out-of-state dogs in addition to proof of all vaccinations. Open 8 A.M.–noon and 3:30–6 P.M., Monday to Friday; 8 A.M.–noon, Saturday.

Longs Peak Animal Hospital, 9727 Ute, 303-776-6666. $8/day. Open 8 A.M.–8 P.M., Monday to Thursday; 8 A.M.–6 P.M., Friday; 8 A.M.–5 P.M., Saturday; 10 A.M.–4 P.M., Sunday.

Nederland

Peak to Peak Animal Hospital, 75 E. 2nd St., 303-258-7004. $12.50/day. Open 8 A.M.–

6 P.M., Monday, Wednesday, and Friday; 7 A.M.–7 P.M., Tuesday and Thursday; 8 A.M.–noon, Saturday.

PET PROVISIONS

Boulder

Animal Crackers Pets and Supplies, 2877 28th St., 303-402-0626

Exotic Aquatics, 1750 30th St., 303-442-5363. Despite the name, there's a whole range of dog supplies and food.

McGuckin Hardware, 2525 Arapahoe Ave. (in the Village Shopping Center), 303-443-1822. You and your leashed dog are welcome to browse among the cornucopia of pet items and just about anything else you can think of.

PetsMart, 2982 Iris (in the Albertson's shopping center), 303-939-9033

RAD Table Mesa Hardware, Table Mesa Shopping Center (next to World Gym), 303-499-7211

Lafayette

Bark Avenue, 101 E. Chester St., 303-664-9663

Lafayette Feed and Grain, 816 E. Baseline Rd., 303-665-5055

Longmont

Blue Hills Dog and Cat Shop, 2255 Main St., 303-651-2955

Diagonal Feed and Pet Supply, 1240 Ken Pratt Blvd., 303-776-9397

Longmont Pet Supply and Feed, 2334 Main, 303-651-2535

Rocky Mountain Feed and Pet, 208 S. Main, 303-651-6226

Lyons

St. Vrain Feed, 505 W. Main, 303-823-6882

Nederland

Nederland Feed and Supply, 45 E. 2nd St., 303-258-7729

CANINE ER

Boulder

Allpets Clinic (AAHA certified), 5290 Manhattan Cr. (at Highway 36 and S. Boulder Rd.), 303-499-5335. The clinic is staffed 24 hours, and walk-ins are welcome, though you should refrain from bringing in your pet for a routine checkup in the wee hours.

Boulder Emergency Pet Clinic, 1658 30th St. (in the Sunrise Shopping Center), 303-440-7722. Open 5:30 P.M.–8:30 A.M., the following morning, Monday through Friday; noon on Saturday to 8 A.M. Monday morning. On holidays, the clinic remains open 24 hours.

North Boulder Companion Animal Hospital (AAHA certified), 2750 Glenwood, 303-443-9003. Open 7 A.M.–midnight daily.

RESOURCES

Boulder Chamber of Commerce, 2440 Pearl St., Boulder, 303-442-1044 (visitor.boulder.net)

Boulder Ranger District, Arapaho and Roosevelt National Forests, 2995 Baseline Rd., Rm. 100, Boulder, 303-444-6600

FIDOS (Friends Interested in Dogs and Open Space), 303-447-FIDO (the Yap Line)

Nederland Visitor Center, 1st and Bridge St., Nederland, 303-258-3936

3

Central City, Clear Creek County, and Vicinity

THE BIG SCOOP

Traveling dogs will find it all here: scenic trails, 14,000-foot mountains, welcoming lodging, and mountain air, everything within a short drive of Denver. One thing your dog won't be able to do, however, is frequent the casinos in Black Hawk and Central City; to the best of our knowledge, paw-friendly slot machines have yet to be invented.

All the towns in this area have leash laws, as do Clear Creek and Gilpin Counties, though the county leash ordinance is not enforced on Forest Service trails that allow dogs under voice control.

TAIL-RATED TRAILS

The area surrounding Mount Evans, south of Idaho Springs, has the most concentrated selection of trails in the vicinity. Because of their proximity to Denver, many of these trails receive heavy use, especially on summer weekends, something to keep in mind if you're into more solitary hiking with your dog. And most of the trails are in the Mount Evans Wilderness Area or the Mount Evans Elk Management Area—where dogs must be kept leashed—for all or part of their length. A great resource for the Mount Evans trails is *Foothills to Mount Evans: West-of-Denver Trail Guide* (sixth edition), by Linda McComb Rathbun and Linda Wells Ringrose.

If you and your dog are staying near Idaho Springs, refer to the "West of Denver" section in chapter 1's "Tail-Rated

Trails" for more nearby options. And it's only a short drive to trails near Nederland (see chapter 2) from the Central City area.

 Herman Gulch. 5 miles round-trip. Take Exit 218 off I-70 (past Silver Plume). If you're coming from the east, turn right at the stop sign at the end of the exit ramp and double back on the dirt road that leads to the trailhead parking area; from the west, cross over the highway and turn right on the dirt road to the parking area. *Dogs can be off leash.* According to the Forest Service, the posted "dogs must be on leash" sign applies to the parking lot and trailhead area. There's no regulation that dogs must be kept leashed on the trail. However, because this is a popular hike on summer weekends, you might want to keep Fido leashed if you visit during that time.

This hike has become increasingly popular, especially with dogs and their owners, as the secret's out that a beautiful route hides behind the unmarked highway exit. The well-maintained trail first leads through a section of forest before popping out into a series of meadows, studded with colorful wildflowers in July and August. You'll then reenter the woods as you ascend the gulch, following closely along a stream. There are several nice areas along this stretch where you can sit on a downed log and enjoy a snack while Rover tests out the water. In the final half mile or so of trail, you'll hike above timberline, following a few steep switchbacks before reaching Herman Lake, nestled right at the base of the Continental Divide below the rocky slopes of 13,553-foot Pettingell Peak. Before heading back down valley, take a breather on one of the boulders along the shoreline and soak in the rugged surroundings; your dog will probably want to brave the frigid water for a quick dip. If he's lucky, he may even find a snowfield or two in which to play.

 Silver Dollar Lake. 3 miles round-trip. From the Georgetown exit (228) off I-70, follow the signs to Guanella Pass at the western end of town. From the beginning of Guanella Pass Rd. (at the mileage signs), drive 8.6 miles, past the Guanella Pass Campground, to a T in the road and a sign for the Silver Dollar Lake Trail. Turn right and drive a mile to the parking area at the side of the road and the trailhead. *Dogs can be off leash.*

This short, scenic hike brings you and your dog to a lake, popular for fishing, near the base of the Continental Divide. The trail heads southwest from the parking area, winding through a stately forest of Douglas fir on a moderate ascent. Shortly after passing timberline, you'll reach the lake. To the southwest lies Square Top Mountain. After your dog enjoys splashing in the lake, you and he may want to do some exploring to the northwest to visit nearby Murray Lake, which is also above timberline, before hiking the return route.

 Golden Gate Canyon State Park. The park has several access points, a couple of which are near Central City and Black Hawk. From Black Hawk, take Highway 119 north for about 5 miles to Highway 46; the park visitor center is 11 miles east on 46. Or, continue about 3 miles past the Highway 46 turnoff, then turn right on

Gap Rd., which leads into the park. For more details, see "Tail-Rated Trails" in chapter 1.

 Hells Hole. 7 miles round-trip. From Idaho Springs, drive southwest on Highway 103 for 5.5 miles. Make a right onto West Chicago Creek Rd. (Forest Rd. 188) and drive for 3 miles. The trailhead is past the West Chicago Creek Campground at the end of the road. *Dogs can be off leash until the wilderness boundary, about a mile in.*

Despite the ominous name, this is a beautiful hike, especially during the autumn when the aspen change color, and one of the less crowded ones in the Mount Evans area. Because the very first part of the trail passes by some quasipicnic areas popular with families, you might have to keep a close eye on Fido or leash him up so he doesn't make a nuisance of himself. The trail begins in forested terrain and follows West Chicago Creek, crossing various tributaries as well. After about a mile,

A new breed of mountain goat on Grays Peak. (photo by Cindy Hirschfeld)

you'll start to climb away from the creek, gradually at first, then more steeply as the trail switchbacks up amid a high wooded canopy of pine, fir, and aspen. Gray Wolf Mountain and Sugarloaf Peak come into view to the south and east, respectively.

Eventually, you'll break out of the trees into a spectacular high-alpine, marshy meadow bounded by a rocky cirque that includes the 13,602-foot Gray Wolf. The trail ends among the scree in a basin at the bottom of the cirque—the Hells Hole.

CYCLING FOR CANINES

Most of the biking routes in this area follow four-wheel-drive roads rather than singletrack trails. One recommended option is the **Old Squaw Pass Rd.,** which parallels Highway 103 east of Mount Evans for 3.25 miles. The trail has four access points from the south side of 103: 4.5 miles east of Echo Lake, 5.8 miles east, 7.4 miles east, and 8.4 miles east.

The **Devil's Canyon jeep road** runs for 2.5 miles one way, ending on a ridge with views of the Mount Evans area. There are also some loop options in this area, on the small network of jeep roads. Drive on Highway 103 from Idaho Springs for 10 miles, then make a left just after the big curve beyond the Ponder Point Picnic Area onto Forest Rd. 246. The ride begins here. Bring extra water for Rover on Old Squaw Pass Rd. and Devil's Canyon.

The **Bard Creek road** provides several miles of riding on an old mining roadbed that follows the path of the creek; access it via Bard Creek Dr. off U.S. Highway 40 through Empire.

For more specifics on rides, pick up the "Four-Wheel Driving" information sheet from the Clear Creek Ranger District (see "Resources") and the Trails Illustrated biking map for Idaho Springs/Clear Creek County.

POWDERHOUNDS

The Clear Creek County area has several fine trails for ski touring or snowshoeing with your dog. The 4-mile round-trip **Butler Gulch Trail** is a personal favorite because it holds snow well and has fun telemarking terrain in the bowls at trail's end (rife with avalanche danger, however). It can get quite busy on weekends, so a midweek tour, if possible, would be your dog's best bet. To reach the trailhead, take the Empire exit off I-70 and follow U.S. Highway 40 west to the sharp switchback at Henderson Mine (about 8 miles past Empire). The ski begins across from a small parking area, on a road. Watch out for snowmobilers on this first part; soon the Butler Gulch Trail splits off to the left and you'll leave motorized traffic behind.

The **Old Fall River Road** to Fall River Reservoir is a 6-mile round-trip easy ski on gentle terrain. From Exit 238 off I-70, turn north on Fall River Rd. Drive 6.5 miles to a right-hand switchback. The trail, which follows a jeep road, travels westnorthwest from here.

The **Waldorf Road,** which follows a very gradual, wide ascent off the Guanella Pass Rd. outside of Georgetown, also makes a good dog ski. With the Sidney Mine as the turnaround point, it's a 7-mile round-trip. To access the trail, head up the Guanella Pass Rd. for 2.5 miles to a pair of switchbacks; at the second switchback,

Laska evokes some interest from the locals. (photo by Jim Margolis)

you'll see a small parking area on the right. The Waldorf Rd. begins near the parking area.

For more information on these and other routes, refer to *Skiing Colorado's Backcountry*, by Brian Litz and Kurt Lankford.

CREATURE COMFORTS

Unless otherwise stated, dogs should not be left unattended in the room or cabin.

Black Hawk

$$ Chase Mansion, 201 Chase Gulch, 303-582-0112. "I like pets," says the owner of this "B" (bed without the breakfast), housed in a 120-year-old Victorian. She allows dogs ("no barkers or biters") in three of the inn's six rooms, which are furnished in a "casual Victorian" style. You can leave your dog unattended in the room while you gamble away his dog-food allowance. Or the owner is happy to dog sit, if your pooch would prefer some company.

$$ Gold Dust Lodge, 5312 Highway 119, 303-582-5415. The motel allows dogs for a $10 one-time fee, and you can leave your dog unattended in the room "as long as it doesn't bark or tear up the furniture."

$$ The Shamrock Inn, 351 Gregory St., 303-582-5513. This B&B welcomes "responsible pets with responsible owners" in any of its three rooms. The house was built in 1870, and the rooms are furnished "grandma style," as the owner calls it. You can leave your dog unattended in the room.

Central City

$$ Carriage House Bed & Breakfast Guest Cottages, 355 Spring St., 303-582-3636. A "very small, well-controlled" dog is welcome to join you in one of these two cottages. Each one is studio-sized and equipped with a kitchen. You can leave your dog unattended as long he remains on his best manners. Breakfast is supplied in your cottage to enjoy at your leisure.

$$ Chateau L'Acadienne, 325 Spring, 303-582-5209 (800-834-5209). The Chateau, which bills itself as a Cajun B&B, accepts lap-size dogs (about 20 pounds or under) in any of its three rooms. The rooms are individually decorated, one with Victorian furnishings, one in a Mardi Gras theme, and one in a mountain scenery mode. You can leave your dog unattended in the room only if you have a travel kennel in which to keep him.

Georgetown

$ Swiss Inn, 1414 Argentine St., 303-569-2931. With a Swiss-chalet style and seven rooms, the inn welcomes people-friendly canines. Dogs can be left unattended in the room as long as they don't terrorize the housekeeping staff. There's a small yard around the inn where a leashed dog can stretch his legs. The inn is closed from the end of October to the end of November and from the beginning of May through mid-June. Also, the office is closed on Wednesdays, so you'd need to make prior arrangements to check in that day.

$–$$ Georgetown Motor Inn, 1100 Rose, 303-569-3201 (800-884-3201). The motel allows dogs in smoking rooms only, with a $20 deposit if you're paying with cash. You can leave your dog unattended in the room, an option to consider if you're skiing nearby Loveland, Arapahoe Basin, or Keystone.

$$–$$$ Clear Creek Bed and Breakfast, 2717 County Rd. 308, 303-567-2117 (800-757-2117). This five-room B&B, with "country Colorado casual" decor, will take dogs on a case-by-case basis. The ground rules are that a dog should be under 50 pounds and interact well with people. And there's a $25 fee per night. Guanella Pass, and its National Forest hiking trails, are about 3 miles away.

Idaho Springs

$ Blair Motel, 345 Colorado Blvd., 303-567-4661. The motel prefers mellow, small

(20–30 pounds) dogs, with a $20 cash deposit. Dogs are permitted in four rooms, one of which is nonsmoking.

$ 6 & 40 Motel, 2920 Colorado Blvd., 303-567-2691 (800-524-9999). Dogs are accepted on a case-by-case basis. The motel is situated along Clear Creek, where you can walk your dog on leash along the banks.

$ Top's Motel, 2725 Colorado Blvd., 303-567-4177. In an unusual twist, the motel takes medium and large dogs, but not small dogs, as they're more likely to be barkers. However, there are only two dog-designated rooms, both of which are smoking.

$–$$ Columbine Motel, 2501 Colorado Blvd., 303-567-0948. Dogs are allowed in one room, which is smoking, with a $25 deposit and a $10 fee per night.

$–$$ H & H Motor Lodge, 2445 Colorado Blvd., 303-567-2838 (800-445-2893). Dogs are allowed in five of the motel's rooms; if your dog barks too much and disturbs other guests, however, you will be asked to leave if you can't quiet him down. Clear Creek runs behind the lodge, and you can walk your dog here on leash.

$$–$$$ Dakota Guest House, 1608 Miner St., 303-567-0709. As there are two resident dogs at the guest house, located in historic downtown Idaho Springs, the owners will do a "dog-to-dog test" to make sure everyone gets along. If not, your dog will have to sniff elsewhere for lodging. But in the past year only two dogs have been rejected, so if yours is friendly, chances are good he'll pass muster. The guest house itself is on the National Register of Historic Places, and the building's claim to fame is that Buffalo Bill quaffed his last drink there before he died. All rooms are suites with kitchenettes, and you can leave your dog unattended inside.

Campgrounds

Golden Gate State Park. The easiest way to access the campgrounds is via Gap Rd., a right turn off Highway 119, about 8 miles north of Black Hawk. The Reverend's Ridge Campground (106 sites) and Aspen Meadow Campground (35 sites) are both in the northwest part of the park. There are also four backcountry shelters and twenty-three backcountry tent sites throughout the park.

National Forest campgrounds: **Columbine Campground,** 2.1 miles northwest of Central City on County Rd. 279 (47 sites); **Cold Springs Campground,** 4 miles north of Black Hawk on Highway 119 (38 sites); **West Chicago Creek Campground,** Forest Rd. 188, off Highway 103, south of Idaho Springs (16 sites); **Guanella Pass Campground,** about 8 miles out of Georgetown on Guanella Pass Rd. (18 sites).

WORTH A PAWS

Mount Evans Road. For the quickest way to take your dog to the top of a fourteener (that's a 14,000-foot mountain, or, in this case, 14,264 feet), drive him up the paved road to the top of Mount Evans. Take Highway 103 south of Idaho Springs to

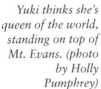

Yuki thinks she's queen of the world, standing on top of Mt. Evans. (photo by Holly Pumphrey)

Echo Lake; the road to the summit begins here. Fourteen miles later, your dog will feel like he's standing on top of the world. And he'll probably get excited at seeing the mountain goats that usually hang around roadside—viewing them from behind a car window, of course. The road is open to the summit from Memorial Day to the day after Labor Day; a fee per car is collected just beyond Echo Lake.

Argo Gold Mill. Does your dog harbor a secret desire to don a helmet, grab a pickax, and burrow into a hillside? If so, he might be interested in accompanying you on a forty-five-minute tour of this former gold mill, which dates from 1913 and supplied much of the gold for the Denver Mint. The mill is now on the National Register of Historic Places. The tour includes a van ride up to the Double Eagle Gold Mine, which you'll be able to walk 300 feet into. Look for the big red building on the hillside in Idaho Springs—it's hard to miss. Call 303-567-2421 for more information

Georgetown Loop Railroad. If your dog can comfortably fit on your lap, you can bring him along on this scenic narrow-gauge train trip between Georgetown and neighboring Silver Plume. When the railroad originally was constructed in the 1880s, it was quite a feat of engineering, relying on hairpin curves and bridges to climb the steep grade to Silver Plume. Today a round-trip train ride takes a little over an hour, and you can board at either the Silver Plume Depot or the Devils Gate Boarding Area in Georgetown (when you purchase tickets at the Old Georgetown Station, 1106 Rose St., you'll get directions for driving to the boarding area). The rail-road operates daily from Memorial Day through the first weekend of October, with a limited midweek schedule after Labor Day. Call 303-569-2403 (or 303-670-1686 in Denver) for more information and current ticket prices.

DOGGIE DAYCARE
Genesee
Lookout Mountain Pet Lodge, 24059 Highway 40, Lookout Mountain, 303-526-0436. Part of the Lookout Mountain Animal Hospital. $9–$11/day, depending on the size of your dog. Dropoffs from 8–10 A.M. and pickups from 4–6 P.M., Monday to Saturday; pickups only from 4–6 P.M. Sunday.

CANINE ER
Genesee
Lookout Mountain Animal Hospital (AAHA certified), 24059 Highway 40, 303-526-2652. Open 8 A.M.–5:30 P.M., Monday, Tuesday, Thursday, Friday; 8 A.M.–noon, Wednesday and Saturday.

RESOURCES
Clear Creek County Visitor Information, 800-882-5278

Clear Creek Ranger District, Arapaho and Roosevelt National Forests, 101 Chicago Creek Rd., Idaho Springs, 303-567-2901

Georgetown Information Center, 404 6th St., 800-472-8230

Gilpin County Chamber of Commerce, 303-582-5077 (800-331-LUCK)

Idaho Springs Visitor Information Center, 2200 Miner St., Idaho Springs, 303-567-4382

NORTHEAST
COLORADO

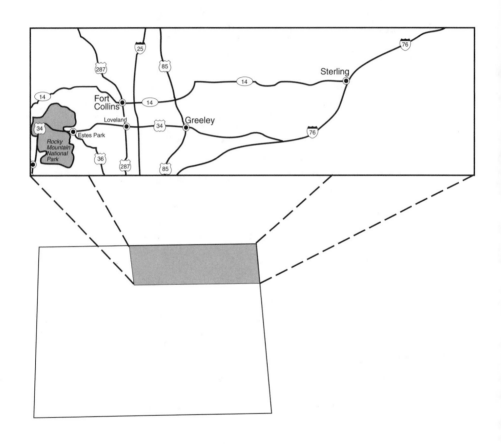

4
Fort Collins and Vicinity

THE BIG SCOOP

Close to the foothills of the northern Front Range, Fort Collins and neighboring Loveland offer a variety of opportunities for canine recreation. If you're looking for a more rustic getaway, the Poudre River Canyon (which begins about 10 miles northwest of Fort Collins) and the village of Red Feather Lakes (about 50 miles northwest of Fort Collins) have cabin resorts, most of which allow canine guests. And your dog can rest easy about his health during a visit to Fort Collins: Colorado State University is home to one of the best veterinary schools in the country, and the Veterinary Teaching Hospital operates a 24-hour critical care clinic.

You'll have to keep your dog leashed within Fort Collins and Loveland city limits; in unincorporated Larimer County areas, dogs may be under voice command. There's been talk of creating a dog park in Fort Collins where canines can socialize off leash, but the concept is still in the planning stage.

TAIL-RATED TRAILS

Dogs in Fort Collins can enjoy several open space areas, three major recreational trails within or close to town, and two parks with hiking trails just west of Horsetooth Reservoir. None of them, however, include any off-leash dog areas. To find trails where Fido can hike leash-free, head up scenic Poudre Canyon (though note that the popular Greyrock National Recreation Trail has a leash policy) or to the Red Feather Lakes area. One close-by option in the canyon—Young Gulch—is described here. The Forest Service office in Fort Collins (see "Resources") has a good range of maps and trail descriptions for other hikes.

 Young Gulch. Up to 8 miles round-trip. Head north from Fort Collins on Highway 287 to the turnoff for Highway 14 and the Poudre Canyon (about 9 miles). Turn left onto a dirt road 12.8 miles up the canyon, just past the Ansel Watrous campground on the right. Follow the dirt road to the parking area and trailhead. *Dogs can be off leash.*

This is a perfect trail for the dog who likes to get his paws muddy. Water-loving hounds will appreciate the numerous creek crossings (none on bridges), which apparently run into the forties (we lost count after about twenty). There's really no set destination for this hike, and the scenic factor remains about the same throughout, so don't feel that you must cover all 4 miles (one-way). You and your dog will have an enjoyable trip no matter how far you decide to go.

The easy-to-follow trail makes a very gradual ascent up a forested gulch, winding through sweet-smelling ponderosa and lodgepole pine, Rocky Mountain juniper, Douglas fir, and aspen. The last mile or so travels across open meadow, where the trail narrows to a small footpath. A final climb up an old road brings you to a cattle fence signed for private property, and at the end of the trail; just beyond, you'll see Stove Prairie Rd.

Horsetooth Mountain Park. From College Ave. in Fort Collins, head west on Horsetooth Rd. (south of downtown). Drive 2 miles to Taft Hill Rd.; turn left, then take a right at the next traffic light (County Rd. 38E). Follow the road around the southern end of Horsetooth Reservoir (you'll also see signs for the park). The parking area will be on the right. Note that there's a $5 entry fee. *Dogs must be leashed.*

The park offers more than 20 miles of trails, including an ascent to the distinctive Horsetooth Rock, from which you get an encompassing view of the peaks on the eastern side of Rocky Mountain National Park. (Note that, with the exception of part of the **Horsetooth Rock Trail,** the trails are multi-use, so you'll be sharing them with bikes and horses.) Most people stick to the first couple miles of trails, hiking to Horsetooth and Culver Falls, and Horsetooth Rock. So if you're looking for more solitude with your pooch, venture a little farther. You'll find water along the 2-mile-long **Spring Creek Trail** (which requires about 1.5 miles of hiking to reach) and the nearly 3-mile **Mill Creek Trail** (which begins at the end of the Spring Creek Trail). If you're really ambitious, you can even hike into neighboring Lory State Park via two of the trails. Backcountry camping is allowed in Horsetooth Mountain Park, so you can do longer hikes broken up by an overnight. Remember to keep your dog leashed at all times; rangers do patrol, and they have a no-tolerance policy, which means you're pretty much guaranteed a fine if Fido's romping freely.

 Lory State Park. From Fort Collins, take 287 North. After Laporte, go left on County Rd. 52E to Bellvue. Drive about 1 mile to County Rd. 23N; head south for about 1.5 miles to County Rd. 25G, on the right, and the park entrance. *Dogs must be leashed.*

The park offers 30 miles of well-marked trails for you and your dog to enjoy together. A few options that your dog may prefer: The 2-mile round-trip **Well Gulch Trail** heads west from the park road, up a drainage with a stream at the bottom. The trail up to **Arthur's Rock,** which provides a panoramic view of Horsetooth Reservoir and Fort Collins, is now for hikers only (there used to be a separate trail for horses and riders, but it's been flooded out); the route is 3.4 miles round-trip, and an intermittent stream alongside is a potential water source. If your dog wants to visit water's edge, bring him on the **Shoreline Trail,** a 2-mile round-trip to the reservoir and back from the park road. There are also six backcountry campsites within the park, all of them along the 3.5-mile **Timber Trail,** where you can overnight with your dog.

 Foothills Trail. Runs 5 miles from Dixon Reservoir, near the south end of Horsetooth Reservoir, to the Campeau/Reservoir Ridge Open Space Area, near the north end of the reservoir. To access the trail at Dixon Reservoir, head west from downtown Fort Collins on one of the major cross streets (e.g., Prospect) to Overland Trail (a road). Go south on Overland Trail to County Rd. 42C and turn right. Just before the hairpin turn, an unsigned gravel road leads down to a parking area next to the water and the trail. *Dogs must be leashed.*

This is a great trail for water-loving dogs, as you start out near a small reservoir and eventually gain access to large, scenic Horsetooth Reservoir. Begin hiking at the northwest corner of the parking lot. After descending a short hill, stay left at the next two forks. Cross County Rd. 42C and pick up the trail again at the white City of Fort Collins sign that lists park regulations. The trail parallels a service road through the Maxwell Open Space Area west of Colorado State University's Hughes Stadium, then switchbacks up a dry hillside of grassland, yucca plants, and sagebrush. Shortly after reaching the hilltop, cross Centennial Rd., the north-south artery for Horsetooth Reservoir, and look for the continuation of the trail at the northeast corner of the paved parking area. Stay left at the first fork. The trail goes along the bluffs above the reservoir before descending toward shoreline. Several spur trails lead down to the water, so your dog can take a dip, well deserved on a hot day. If you continue hiking, follow the trail along the shore; it eventually ascends and crosses Centennial Rd. again to reach the parking area at Campeau/Reservoir Ridge Open Space Area.

If you want a shorter hike, or if your dog wants quicker access to water, you can access portions of the Foothills Trail from several parking areas off Centennial Rd. between Dixon Dam and Soldier Canyon Dam. You can also hike south from Dixon Reservoir; a trail follows the western shoreline before heading east to end at Taft Hill Rd.

Poudre River Trail. Runs 8.35 miles from North Taft Hill Rd. west of downtown Fort Collins, to East Drake Rd., near the Prospect Ponds open space area. *Dogs must be leashed.*

This paved bike and hike path parallels the Cache La Poudre River, passing several open space areas and city parks along its route. It's a great place to take your dog for a stroll that's close to town, and it's usually less traveled than the Spring Creek Trail. As you head east from downtown, the trail passes through less developed surroundings.

Spring Creek Trail. Runs 6.6 miles from West Drake Rd. to East Prospect Rd., where it ends in the Poudre River Trail. *Dogs must be leashed.*

This paved trail follows Spring Creek and also passes through several park and open space areas. As it runs close to the Colorado State University campus, it's more of a transportation corridor than a hiking trail, but it nonetheless provides your dog with some off-street walking space.

CYCLING FOR CANINES

You'll have to head up Poudre Canyon to find the closest areas to town where you can ride with a dog. The 8-mile round-trip **Young Gulch Trail** (see "Tail-Rated Trails") has the advantage of lots of water for dogs to run through; the first mile or so will have you walking up some rocky sections, but if you stick with it you'll reach some nice rolling singletrack. The 7-mile round-trip **Hewlett Gulch Trail,** out of the town of Poudre Park, follows Gordon Creek up a moderate ascent; your dog will have a chance to sniff among the remains of early homesteads. **The Mt. Margaret Trail,** just outside Red Feather Lakes, is a scenic, rolling 8-mile round-trip to the top of Mt. Margaret and down.

POWDERHOUNDS

To find consistent snow for skiing or snowshoeing, you and your dog will need to drive to Cameron Pass at the top of Poudre Canyon, about 65 miles west of Fort Collins on Highway 14. A great short tour follows an old jeep road to **Zimmerman Lake,** a 2.2-mile round-trip from the

A canine trio—Amber, Hunter, Quinn—is ready for some ski action on Cameron Pass. (photo by Amy Ditsler)

Zimmerman Lake parking area off Highway 14, past Joe Wright Reservoir and about 2 miles below the pass. Another tour begins at the pass summit and follows the **Michigan Ditch Rd.** south into the upper part of the Michigan River drainage; a 2.6-mile round-trip brings you to some old cabins and back, though you can easily ski farther along the ditch. See *Skiing Colorado's Backcountry,* by Brian Litz and Kurt Lankford, for more details on these and other routes.

CREATURE COMFORTS

Unless otherwise stated, dogs should not be left unattended in the room or cabin.

Fort Collins

$ Lamplighter Motel, 1809 N. College, 970-484-2764

$ Motel 6 Fort Collins, 3900 E. Mulberry, 970-482-6466 (800-4-MOTEL 6). You can leave your dog unattended in the room for short periods of time.

$–$$ Days Inn, 3709 E. Mulberry, 970-221-5490 (800-DAYS-INN). The motel has some designated pet rooms, where dogs can stay for a $5 fee per night. You can leave your dog unattended in the room.

$–$$ El Palomino, 1220 N. College, 970-482-4555. There are six pet rooms, and the charge is $5.50 per night, per dog.

$–$$ Fort Collins Plaza Inn, 3709 E. Mulberry, 970-493-7800 (800-434-5548). Dog guests are usually placed in ground-floor rooms, for quicker outdoor access, with a $5 fee per night. You can leave your dog unattended in the room, but housekeeping won't enter unless he's safely contained in a travel kennel.

$–$$ Inn at Fort Collins, 2612 S. College, 970-226-2600. The motel has large, comfortable rooms and is a few blocks from the Colorado State University Veterinary Teaching Hospital. There's a $4 fee per night for a dog; if your dog is visiting Fort Collins to receive treatment at the Vet Center, you'll get a $4 per night discount (so, in effect, no extra charge). And you can leave your dog unattended in the room.

$–$$ Mulberry Inn, 4333 E. Mulberry, 970-493-9000 (800-234-5548). Some of this motel's rooms have hot tubs in them. There's a $5 fee per night, per dog, and you can leave your dog unattended in the room; just warn him not to take a soak while you are away.

$–$$ Super 8 Motel, 409 Centro Way, 970-493-7701. The motel offers a few pet rooms. You'll be asked to put down a $20 deposit if you're paying with cash.

$$ Holiday Inn I-25, 3836 E. Mulberry, 970-484-4660 (800-HOLIDAY). Dogs are put in outside-facing rooms and can be left unattended in the room.

$$ Sleep Inn, 3808 E. Mulberry, 970-484-5515 (800-627-5337). There's a $10 one-time fee per dog.

$$–$$$ University Park Holiday Inn, 425 W. Prospect, 970-482-2626 (800-HOLIDAY). The hotel has minisuites in addition to regular rooms. You can leave your dog unattended inside.

Laporte

$ Mile Hi KOA, Highway 287 at the entrance to Poudre Canyon, 970-493-9758 (800-KOA-2648). Dogs are allowed in the camping cabins; you'll have to supply your own bedding and cooking gear. Open May 1 to October 15.

Loveland

$ Budget Host Exit 254 Inn, 2716 S. E. Frontage Rd., 970-667-5202 (800-825-4254). Small dogs (i.e., poodle size) are allowed from about October to April. No dogs, no matter what size, are permitted during the summer.

$ Rose Bud Motel, 660 E. Eisenhower Blvd., 970-669-9430. There's a $5 fee per night for Citizen Canines.

$–$$ Hiway Motel, 1027 E. Eisenhower Blvd., 970-667-5224. Dogs are allowed in most rooms, for $3 extra per night. You can leave your dog unattended in the room only if he's in a travel kennel.

$–$$ Kings Court Motel, 928 N. Lincoln Ave., 970-667-4035. Dogs can stay in smoking rooms only, with a $50 deposit and a $10 one-time fee.

$$ Best Western Coach House, 5542 Highway 34, 970-667-7810. It's smoking rooms only for dogs here. You can leave your dog unattended in the room, but the housekeepers won't come in to clean during that time.

Poudre Canyon

$ Sportsman's Lodge, 44174 Poudre Canyon Rd. (54 miles from Fort Collins), 970-881-2272. Sportdogs are permitted in the twelve rustic one-room cabins for $5 extra per night. Open year-round.

$–$$ Glen Echo Resort, 31503 Poudre Canyon Rd. (41 miles from Fort Collins), 970-881-2208 (800-348-2208). Of the fifteen cabins at this riverside family resort, some are modern, with fireplaces; some are rustic, with no running water and shared bath facilities, and one is a large apartment that sleeps up to twelve guests. All have cooking supplies, however, and there's a restaurant and general store at the resort. Currently, management does not charge an extra fee for dogs, though that policy may change. You are required to keep your dog leashed on the property. The full resort is open from mid-May to November 1; two winterized units stay open year-round.

$–$$ Indian Meadows Lodge, 29839 Poudre Canyon Rd. (40 miles from Fort Collins), 970-881-2281. The lodge offers four recently renovated riverside cabins (two with kitchens, one with fireplace) as well as seven motel units with kitchenettes. A restaurant is also at the lodge so you don't have to drive to eat out. You can leave your dog unattended inside. Open year-round.

$–$$ Mountain Greenery Resort, 32595 Poudre Canyon Rd. (40 miles from Fort Collins), 970-881-2242. The resort offers eight motel-style units (five with kitchens) as well as several mobile homes. Dogs are welcome for $5 extra per night, with a limit of one dog per unit. You can take your dog for a walk along the Poudre River on a short trail that runs through the property. The resort also has a restaurant. Open from the beginning of May through the end of November.

$$ Poudre River Resort, 33021 Poudre Canyon Rd. (45 miles from Fort Collins), 970-881-2139. There are eight one- and two-bedroom, fully equipped cabins at the resort, and dogs are allowed in five of them for a $20 one-time fee. The owners ask that you keep your dog leashed on the 7.5 acre riverside property. Open year-round.

Red Feather Lakes

$ Alpine Lodge, 157 Prairie Divide Rd., 970-881-2933. Located about half a mile from the village of Red Feather Lakes, the lodge has three fully furnished cabins and two mobile homes that you and your dog can stay in. Open year-round.

$ Hilltop Outpost, 99 Hiawatha Highway, 970-881-2206. Your dog can stay with you

Hewlett Gulch, near Fort Collins, is a dog-friendly mountain bike route. (photo by Amy Ditsler)

in one of six one-room cabins as long as you keep him leashed at all times when outside. The cabins have small kitchens, and a few have fireplaces. Open year-round.

$$ Trout Lodge, 1078 Ramona Dr., 970-881-2964. You and your dog have your choice of nine fully equipped cabins, ranging from studio to two bedrooms, in the village of Red Feather Lakes. You'll need to keep your dog leashed when outside. Open year-round.

$$–$$$ Beaver Meadows Resort, 100 Marmot Dr., 970-881-2450 (800-462-5870). Though dogs are not permitted in the lodge or condos at the resort, they can have their pick of five cabins to stay in for a $20 one-time fee. Four of the five cabins are equipped with kitchens, and some have wood-burning stoves or fireplaces and decks. You can leave your dog unattended inside. The resort borders National Forest land and maintains 22 miles of hiking trails that you can bring your dog on. During the winter, however, the trails are groomed for skiing, and dogs are not permitted on them. There's also a restaurant on the premises. Open year-round.

Wellington
$ KOA Fort Collins North, Exit 281 off I-25, 970-568-7486 (800-KOA-8142). Dogs are allowed in the camping cabins; you'll have to supply your own bedding and cooking gear. Open year-round.

Campgrounds
Boyd Lake State Park. East of Loveland off Highway 34 (148 sites).

Larimer County Parks: **Carter Lake,** on County Rd. 31, about 5 miles west of Loveland (7 campgrounds); **Horsetooth Reservoir,** east of Fort Collins via County Rd. 38E (7 campgrounds, all but one near the reservoir's south end—note that dogs are not allowed at South Bay and Little Turkey Campgrounds); **Flatiron Reservoir,** off County Rd. 18E, about 7 miles west of Loveland (1 campground); **Pin-**

ewood Reservoir, at the end of County Rd. 18E, about 10 miles from Loveland (1 campground).

National Forest campgrounds: Several campsites are right off Highway 14 in Poudre Canyon, including **Ansel Watrous Campground** (19 sites); **Stove Prairie Campground** (9 sites); **Narrows Campground** (9 sites); **Mountain Park Campground** (55 sites); and **Kelly Flats Campground** (23 sites). Campgrounds near Red Feather Lakes include the **Ballaire Lake Campground,** Red Feather Lakes Rd. to Forest Rd. 162 (26 sites); **Dowdy Lake Campground,** 1.5 miles from the village on Forest Rd. 218 (62 sites); and **West Lake Campground,** 1 mile from the village on Forest Rd. 200 (29 sites).

Worth a Paws
Doggie Olympics. Do you think you have a potential gold medalist in the Marathon Beg event, just waiting for an opportunity to demonstrate his skills? Or maybe your dog would prefer to strut his stuff in the 25-Yard Dash, the Hot Dog Retrieve, or the Biscuit Walk. Bring him down to Fort Collins's City Park in September for the Doggie Olympics, where he can compete in these and other events, such as Best Tidbit Catcher and the Pentathlon. Proceeds benefit the Larimer Animal–People Partnership (LAPP). You can register in advance on the day of the competition. Call 970-226-4146 or 970-568-3379, ext. 129, for more information.

Fire Hydrant Five. Held in early May in Edora Park in Fort Collins, the Fire Hydrant Five consists of a 5K run for humans only and a 3K fun run and 5K walk for leashed dogs and their owners. In addition to your registration fee, you and your dog can collect donations, all of which will benefit the Humane Society for Larimer County's pet adoption program. Call the Humane Society at 970-226-3647 for more information.

Ashley Whippet Canine Frisbee Invitational.
The Fort Collins area hosts two of these
annual canine Frisbee events. The first is held
mid-May at Seven Lakes Park in Loveland
(1975 Park Dr.). The second is held the third
weekend in June at City Park in Fort Collins
(1500 W. Mulberry St.). Both events feature
the same format: the minidistance, in which
dogs compete in sixty-second rounds, earning points for catching distance and style;
and the free flight, in which they're judged
on difficulty, execution, leaping agility, and
showmanship while performing freestyle
tricks. The Northern Colorado Disc Dogs
puts on the events. For more information,
contact Chris Sexton at 970-495-0141 (Fort
Collins event) or Todd Stevens at 970-207-
1575 (Loveland).

Dirty dogs should try one of these do-it-
yourself dog washes: In Loveland, stop into
**Happy Tails Self-Service Pet Wash and
Boutique, 1710 W. Eisenhower, Unit 5B,
970-669-1182.** The cost is $7, which in-
cludes shampoo, conditioner, and a towel.
Dryers are available for an extra charge:
$1 for the forced-air dryer; $3 for the ken-
nel-sized walk-in dryer (so your dog can
really feel like he's at the beauty salon).
Open Tuesday to Saturday. In Fort Collins,
try **Laund-Ur-Mutt, 1119 W. Drake (in
Cimerron Plaza), 970-223-8225.** Washing-
bay rental is $8 for the first half hour and
$2 for each additional dog in the same tub.
Additional half hours are $6 each. You'll
also have use of an apron, a scrub mitt,
one towel per dog, combs and brushes, and
the fur dryer. You'll need to either supply
your own shampoo or buy it separately
from Laund-Ur-Mutt's stock. Open Tuesday to Sunday.

DOGGIE DAYCARE
Fort Collins
Andelt's Pet Motel, 3200 E. Mulberry, 970-
484-5776. $10/day. Open 7:30 A.M.–1 P.M.
and 2–5:30 P.M., Monday to Friday; 7:30
A.M.–noon and 3:30–5:30 P.M., Saturday;
8–9 A.M. and 3:30–4:30 P.M., Sunday.

Ashcroft Boarding Kennels, 5020 S.
County Rd. 3, 970-221-5689. $9–$12,
depending on the size of dog. Open 7 A.M.–
7 P.M., Monday to Friday; 7 A.M.–noon,
Saturday; 6–7 P.M., Sunday (pickup only).

Country Squire Pet Resort, 3320 N.
Shields, 970-484-3082. $6/day. Open 8
A.M.–6 P.M., Monday to Saturday; 5-6 P.M.,
Sunday (pickup only).

Crystal Glen Kennel, 720 W. Willox Lane,
970-224-3118. $5/day for an indoor/out-
door run. There's a small extra charge if
you want to have your dog walked during
the day. Open 8 A.M.–6 P.M., Monday to
Saturday; 5–6 P.M., Sunday (pickup only).

Moore Animal Hospital Pet Camp, 2550
Stover, 970-416-9101. $5.25/day. Open 7
A.M.–6 P.M., Monday to Friday; 7 A.M.–
noon, Saturday; 9–11 A.M., Sunday (pickup
only).

The Pet Lodge (at South Mesa Veterinary
Hospital), 3801 S. Mason, 970-226-6526.
$6/day. Open 7:30 A.M.–5:30 P.M., Mon-
day to Friday; 7:30 A.M.–noon, Saturday;
5–7 P.M., Sunday (pickup only).

Rover's Ranch, 4837 Terry Lake Rd.,
970-493-5970. $8–$11/day, depending
on the size of dog. Open 8 A.M.–6 P.M.,
Monday to Saturday; by appointment
only on Sunday.

Loveland
Creature Comforts Pet Retreat, 808 S.
County Rd. 23E, 970-669-2084. $8/day.
Optional exercise sessions included a 1-
mile nature hike, for $3 extra, or a super-
vised play session, for $2 extra. Open 8
A.M.–5 P.M., Monday to Friday; 8 A.M.–
noon, Saturday; 9–10 A.M. and 4–5 P.M.,
Sunday.

Loveland Veterinary Clinic, 1403 N.
Monroe Ave., 970-667-3252. $7–$8/day,
depending on the size of dog. Open 8 A.M.–
5 P.M., Monday to Friday; 8 A.M.–noon,
Saturday.

PET PROVISIONS
Fort Collins
Cache La Poudre Feeds, 1724 N. Overland Trail, 970-482-8251

Feeders Supply South, 4229 S. Mason, 970-223-1364

Fins and Skins, 1232 W. Elizabeth, 970-416-8788

PetsMart, 4330 S. College, 970-228-9502

Poudre Feed Supply, 208 N. Howes, 970-482-2741 and 6204 S. College, 970-225-1255

Vetline, 425 John Deere Rd. (behind the Holiday Inn I-25), 970-484-1900 (800-962-4554). The store carries a complete line of animal vaccines, medications, and other medical supplies.

Loveland
Canine Corner, 1402 W. 8th, 970-663-3293

High Point Feed and Supply, 530 E. Eisenhower Blvd., 970-667-2950

Sage Valley Feed and Supply, 5623 W. Highway 34, 970-663-1261

Town and Country Pet Center, 130 S. Cleveland Ave., 970-667-9669

CANINE ER
Fort Collins
Animal Emergency Services of Northern Colorado, 2005 S. College, 970-407-1905. The clinic is open 6 P.M.–8 A.M. the next morning, Monday to Friday, and 24 hours on weekends and holidays.

Colorado State University Veterinary Teaching Hospital (AAHA certified), 300 W. Drake Rd., 970-221-4535. The clinic is staffed 24 hours a day for emergency patients.

RESOURCES
Fort Collins Convention and Visitors Bureau, 420 S. Howes St., Suite 101, Fort Collins, 970-482-5821 (800-274-FORT; www.ftcollins.com)

Redfeather and Estes/Poudre Ranger Districts, Arapaho and Roosevelt National Forests, 1311 S. College Ave., Fort Collins, 970-498-2770

5
Greeley and Northeastern Plains

THE BIG SCOOP

For the most part, the plains of eastern Colorado are travel-through country (although the tourism organizations, which market part of the area as "Colorado's Outback," don't want you to think this). But frankly, unless your dog is fascinated by pioneer history or into long car rides, he'll want to keep heading toward the mountains. You will, however, find plenty of dog-friendly lodgings, most of them lower-priced motels.

Greeley, somewhat of a gateway to the plains and home to the University of Northern Colorado, is a town of great smells—for dogs. When the wind's blowing just right, evidence of the area's agriculture industry permeates the airwaves, so to speak. That's one of the few thing dogs will find to enjoy, however, as all parks in Greeley are closed to canines. For a more scenic walk than the average curbside stroll, take your dog to the UNC campus (but be sure to keep him on leash, in compliance with the citywide regulation).

TAIL-RATED TRAILS

Though the observant dog will note that there are three state parks in the region—Bonny Lake, North Sterling Reservoir, and Jackson Lake—he might be disappointed to hear that hiking trails within them are virtually nonexistent (though North Sterling is in the process of developing a trail network). They all make great destinations,

however, to camp with your dog and hang out by the water on a hot day. Dogs are not allowed on any of the swim beaches, but there are other areas in each park with water access where Fido (on leash) can dip a paw. (For park locations, see the campgrounds section in "Creature Comforts.")

Pawnee Buttes. 4 miles round-trip. Depending on your starting-out point, head either east or west on Highway 14 to County Rd. 390 (about 13 miles east of Briggsdale or 10 miles west of Raymer). At Keota, head north on County Rd. 105 for 3 miles, then turn right on County Rd. 104 and go another 3 miles to County Rd. 111. Go left for 4.5 miles, then follow the signed road to the trailhead parking area, next to a windmill. *Dogs can be off leash.*

The buttes are two dramatic, 300-foot-tall blocks of eroded sandstone within the Pawnee National Grasslands, a shortgrass prairie preserve. They top out at 5,500 feet elevation. Your dog will enjoy this hike most during the spring or fall, when intense daytime temperatures subside a bit. And you might enjoy it most in the spring, when the abundant wildflowers bloom. Regardless of when you choose to hike, bring plenty of water along. Because the area is home to several species of birds of prey that nest here in the spring, you might want to keep your dog on a leash if he's a wanderer. The easy-to-follow, primarily flat trail goes through a couple of drainages before ending at a fenceline near the buttes. En route, your dog might sniff out yucca, prickly pear cactus, and rabbitbrush, as well as some juniper. If you decide to explore more of the grasslands, be aware that dogs are not allowed on the nature walk at the Crow Valley recreation area (at the campground).

Staying cool—Bismarck lets it fly.
(photo by Tim Hancock)

CREATURE COMFORTS

Unless otherwise stated, dogs should not be left unattended in the room or cabin.

Evans

$ Motel 6, 3015 8th Ave., 970-351-6481. The Motel 6 policy is one small pet per room (although if your medium- to large-sized dog is well behaved, chances are the motel can accommodate him).

$ Winterset Inn, 800 31st St., 970-339-2492 (800-777-5088). Dogs are allowed with a $10 deposit per pet.

$–$$ Sleep Inn, 3025 8th Ave., 970-356-2180 (800-SLEEP-INN). There's a $10 one-time pet fee.

$$–$$$$ Heritage Inn, 3301 W. Service Rd., 970-339-5900 (800-759-7829). A little bit of Las Vegas comes to Greeley in the form of fourteen "Dreamscape" suites, each elaborately decorated according to a particular theme, such as Arabian Nights, Cupid's Corner, Space Odyssey, the Jungle Retreat, and, since this is Colorado, after all, the Broncos Room. The motel has plenty of nonthemed rooms as well. Dogs are allowed in the regular rooms for a $5 fee per night, and they can be left unattended in the room. Occasionally dogs are permitted to stay in one of the suites, too, but you'll have to convince management that yours is very well behaved.

Greeley

$ Greeley Inn, 721 13th St., 970-353-3216. There's a $5 fee per night. Dogs are relegated to the smoking rooms, but they can be left unattended as long as they don't cause problems.

$$ Best Western Ramkota Inn, 701 8th St., 970-353-8444 (800-528-1234)

$$ Holiday Inn Express, 2563 West 29th St., 970-330-7495. You can leave your dog unattended in the room. (Note that the Holiday Inn in Windsor does not accept pets.)

$$ Ramada Inn, 609 8th St., 970-356-3000 (888-GREELEY). There's a $5 fee per night, per dog.

Northeastern Plains
Akron

$ 4 B's Motel, 60 Hickory Ave., 970-345-2028. This friendly motel, which used to be a railroad lodge, allows dogs for $10 extra per night and with a credit-card imprint as a deposit. There's a nearby field where you can exercise Fido on leash.

Brush

$ Budget Host Empire Motel, 1408 Edison, 970-842-2876. There's a $2 fee per night, and dogs can be left unattended in the room.

$ Kozy Kort Motel, 717 Edison, 970-842-2736. The motel usually takes only small dogs during the summer; dogs of all sizes are accepted in the fall and winter to accommodate hunters.

$$ Best Western Brush, 1208 North Colorado Ave., 970-842-5146. Small dogs (20 pounds and under) are preferred; they can stay in smoking rooms only, however.

Fort Morgan
$ **Central Motel,** 201 W. Platte, 970-867-2401. Dogs are allowed in most of the motel's rooms, for a $5 one-time fee.

$ **Country Comfort Motel and RV Park,** 16466 W. Highway 34, 970-867-0260. Small dogs can stay in the motel for no charge; larger dogs have to pay $5 per night. There's a limit of one dog per room.

$ **Madison Hotel,** 14378 Highway 34, 970-867-8208 (800-634-6868). This motel has four rooms where dogs can stay, with a $25 deposit. Small dogs are preferred, but well-behaved larger ones won't necessarily be turned away.

$ **Morgan Manor Motel,** 19987 Highway 34, 970-867-2497. The motel allows pets in most of the rooms, for nightly rentals only (it also has weekly rentals).

$ **Sands Motel,** 933 West Platte Ave., 970-867-2453. You can leave your dog unattended in the room.

$–$$ **Best Western Park Terrace,** 725 Main St., 970-867-8256 (800-528-1234). With a $25 deposit, dogs can stay in eight of the smoking rooms.

$–$$ **Econo Lodge,** 1409 Barlow Rd. (Exit 82 off I-76), 970-867-9481. Dogs are only allowed in two smoking rooms, with a $5 fee per night. But they can be left unattended in the room, and there's a small pond in back that you can bring your dog to visit off leash.

Haxtun
$ **Tip Top Motel,** Highway 6 (it's a small town; you'll see the motel), 970-774-9200

Holyoke
$ **Cedar Motel,** 525 E. Denver, 970-854-2525. Dogs are allowed in some of the rooms.

$ **Golden Plains Motel,** 1250 S. Interocean Ave., 970-854-3000 (800-643-0451). Dogs

are allowed in smoking rooms only, for a $5 one-time fee. They can be left unattended in the rooms.

Julesburg
$ **Grand Motel,** 220 Pine, 970-474-3302. Dogs can stay in smoking rooms only.

$ **Holiday Motel,** Highway 138, 970-474-3371

$–$$ **Platte Valley Inn,** I-76 and Highway 385, 970-474-3336 (800-562-5166). It's smoking rooms only for dogs here. There is a gravel and grass pet area where they can be walked on leash.

Sterling
$ **Crest Motel,** 516 S. Division Ave., 970-522-3753. The motel allows dogs in some of its rooms and might charge a nightly fee if you have a long-haired or other type of dog that might require extra cleaning of the room.

$ **First Interstate Inn,** 20930 Highway 6, 970-522-7274 (800-462-4667). Dogs are charged $5 extra per night. They can stretch in the motel's yard off leash.

$ **Super 8,** 12883 Highway 61 (Exit 125 off I-76), 970-522-0300 (800-800-8000). Dogs can stay in smoking rooms only. They can be left unattended in the room.

$$ **Best Western Sundowner,** Overland Trail St. , 970-522-6265 (800-528-1234). Dogs are allowed in eleven of the smoking rooms. There's a large yard outside the motel where dogs can exercise off leash.

$$ **Ramada Inn,** I-76 and E. Highway 6, 970-522-2625 (800-835-7275). Dogs are welcome with a $25 deposit. Though you can't leave your dog in the room unattended, there is a makeshift kennel in back of the motel where he can stay, at no extra charge.

Wray
$ **Butte Motel,** 330 E. 3rd, 970-332-4828. A dog in a travel kennel can be left unattended in the room.

$ Sandhiller Motel, 411 NW Railway, 970-332-4134 (800-554-7482). Dogs are accepted, but if another guest complains, the offending dog has to pack up his biscuits and go. Only one smoking room is open to furry travelers, with a $25 deposit.

Yuma

$ Harvest Motel, 421 W. 8th Ave., 970-848-5853 (800-273-5853). Quiet dogs are welcome, for $5 extra per night.

$ Sunrise Inn, 420 E. 8th Ave., 970-848-5465. There's a $3 one-time fee.

Central Eastern Plains
Burlington

$ Chaparral Motor Inn, 405 S. Lincoln St. (Exit 437 off I-70), 719-346-5361. Dogs are allowed in smoking rooms only. A field where they can stretch their legs is beside the motel.

$ Kit Carson Motel, 700 Rose Ave. (Exit 438 off I-70), 719-346-8513. The motel has a yard where dogs can be walked on leash.

$ Sloan's Motel, 1901 Rose Ave., 719-346-5333 (800-362-0464). Dogs 40 pounds and under are allowed in seven smoking rooms at this recently renovated motel, one dog per room.

$ Super 8, 2100 Fay St., 719-346-5627 (800-800-8000). There's a $5 fee per night, per dog. Only two nonsmoking rooms are available to dogs (in addition to the smoking rooms). Though the motel doesn't really have any size restrictions for dogs, the management notes that "if your dog needs a horse trailer, it shouldn't be here!"

$ Travel Lodge/Burlington Inn, 450 S. Lincoln St., 719-346-5555. Dogs are allowed in twenty of the smoking rooms, for a $5 fee per night. They can be left unattended in the room.

$ Western Motor Inn, 2222 Rose Ave., 719-346-5371 (800-346-5330). Dogs are allowed in smoking rooms only. They can

be left unattended inside as long as you're willing to pay for any damage.

Idalia

$ Prairie Vista Motel, 26995 Highway 36, 970-354-7237

Kit Carson

$ Stage Stop Motel, 208 W. Highways 287 & 40, 719-962-3277. There's a $10 fee per night, and dogs can be left unattended in the rooms.

$ Wagon Wheel Motel, 601 W. Highways 287 & 40, 719-962-3291. Dogs are allowed in two of the motel's smoking rooms for a $5 fee per night. They can be left unattended in the room. There's a front yard and a farmyard area where dogs can be walked off leash.

Limon

$ Bonn's Motel, 1510 Main, 719-775-2074 (888-922-6667). The motel has some designated pet rooms, and you can leave your dog unattended as long as he's in a travel kennel.

$ Econo Lodge of Limon, 985 Highway 24, 719-775-2867. It's smoking rooms only for dogs, with a $25 deposit, but you can leave your dog unattended in the room.

$ Silver Spur Motel, 514 Main, 719-775-2807. Half of the rooms are dog friendly, with a $10 fee per night. Dogs can walk off leash in a field behind the motel.

$–$$ K S Motel, 385 Main, 719-775-2072. The motel allows dogs in five of its smoking rooms. There's a small park area in the back where you can exercise your dog off leash.

$–$$ Preferred Motor Inn, 158 E. Main, 719-775-2385 (800-530-3956). Dogs are allowed in about half of the rooms here, and a third of the pet rooms are nonsmoking. There's a $2 fee per night, and you can leave your dog unattended in the room.

$–$$ Safari Motel, 637 Main, 719-775-2363 (800-330-7021). For $4 extra per night, dogs can stay in several of the motel's smoking rooms.

$–$$ Travel Inn, 250 Main St., 719-775-2821. Dogs are allowed in smoking rooms only, for $6 extra per night.

$$ Best Western Limon Inn, 925 T Ave., 719-775-0277 (800-528-1234). There are six designated pet rooms; the fee for pets is $10 per night.

$$ Super 8 Motel, 937 Highway 24, 719-775-2889 (800-800-8000). Four of the smoking rooms are available to dog guests, with a $10 fee per night. Dogs can be left unattended in the rooms.

Strasburg

$ Denver East/Strasburg KOA and Kamping Kabins, 1312 Monroe St., 970-622-9274 (800-KOA-6538). The campground's management doesn't necessarily like allowing dogs in the cabins because they've had "too many poopy dogs." However, they will consider dogs on a case-by-case basis, so if you're in the area and need to find a place to stay, you might give it a try. Open year-round.

Stratton

$–$$ Best Western Golden Prairie Inn, 700 Colorado Ave., 719-348-5311 (800-626-0043). The motel has several smoking rooms that dogs can stay in. They can be left unattended in the room if they're in a travel kennel.

Campgrounds

Pawnee National Grasslands. The campground is at the Crow Valley Recreation Area, about 25 miles east of Greeley near the intersection of Highway 14 and County Rd. 77. There are ten individual sites (seven single and three double), plus some group sites that must be reserved in advance.

State Park campgrounds: **Bonny Lake State Park,** near Idalia, off Highway 385 (200 sites); **Jackson Lake State Park,** northwest of Fort Morgan, off Highway 144 (270 sites); **North Sterling Reservoir State Park,**

northwest of Sterling off County Rd. 33 (141 sites).

WORTH A PAWS

Paws and Sneakers. This annual run/walk for dogs and their owners is held in Greeley on a Saturday during the first half of September. The 2-mile course winds through the University of Northern Colorado campus, and the event's proceeds, raised through registration fees, pledges, and community sponsors, benefit the Northern Colorado Animal League. Participation gets you a T-shirt, your pooch a goodie bag, and the both of you a great time. After the run, stick around for the ten-event Canine Carnival, in which your dog can compete for honors such as best trick or best kisser. There's also a Feline Photofest for the stay-at-home cat contingent. For more information, call the Northern Colorado Animal League at 970-356-3550.

DOGGIE DAYCARE
Fort Morgan

Platte Valley Veterinary Clinic, 20804 E. Highway 34 (Fort Morgan Industrial Park), 970-867-2520. $9.70/day. Open 8 A.M.–5:30 P.M., Monday to Friday. Pickup or dropoff available on Saturday by appointment.

PET PROVISIONS
Fort Morgan

Pets R People Too, 835 E. Platte Ave, 970-867-4860

Holyoke

Tail Waggers Pet Shop, 118 W. Denver, 970-854-4130

Sterling

Cher's Pet Shop & Dog Grooming, 415 N. Front, 970-522-2577

CANINE ER
Greeley

West Ridge Animal Hospital (AAHA certified), 6525 W. 28th St., 970-330-7283.

Open 8 A.M.–5:30 P.M., Monday to Friday; 8 A.M.–noon, Saturday.

Fort Morgan

Fort Morgan Veterinary Clinic, 1215 E. Burlington, 970-867-9477. Open 8 A.M.–5 P.M., Monday to Friday; 9 A.M.–noon, Saturday.

Platte Valley Veterinary Clinic, 20804 E. Highway 34 (Fort Morgan Industrial Park), 970-867-2520. Open 8:00 A.M.–5:30 P.M., Monday to Friday.

Limon

Limon Veterinary Clinic, 1005 Immel, 719-775-9773. Open 8 A.M.–6 P.M., Monday to Friday; 8 A.M.–4 P.M., Saturday.

RESOURCES

Colorado Gateway Information Center, 122 W. 1st, Julesburg, 970-474-3504

Colorado Welcome Center, I-70 near Colorado/Kansas border, Burlington, 719-346-5554

Greeley Convention and Visitors Bureau, 902 7th Ave., Greeley, 970-352-3567

Northeast Colorado Information Center, Exit 125B off I-76, Sterling, 970-522-7649

Northeast Colorado Travel Region, 451 14th St., Burlington, 719-346-7019 (800-777-9075)

Pawnee National Grasslands Ranger District, 660 O St., Greeley, 970-353-5004

6
Estes Park

THE BIG SCOOP

This area's primary tourist draw—Rocky Mountain National Park—becomes a lot less attractive if you're visiting with your dog: You can't bring him on any hikes within the park. To the north, east, and south of Estes Park, however, is a range of National Forest trails that you and your furry cohiker can enjoy together.

Dog guidelines to live by when in Estes: (1) remind your owner to keep you leashed within the city limits and not to leave you unattended in front of a store or restaurant; (2) leave the elk alone—they don't want to play with you; and (3) keep your paws off the park trails—otherwise your owner will have to pay a fine, which just might come out of your dog-treat allowance.

TAIL-RATED TRAILS

A couple of years ago, the Forest Service proposed a management plan that would have banned dogs completely from the eastern half of the Indian Peaks Wilderness Area, south of Rocky Mountain National Park, if compliance with the mandatory leash law was less than 90 percent five years after the plan's enactment. Though the plan was not approved, be extra diligent about keeping your dog leashed when in this area so that the ban idea is not resurrected (none of the trails described here are in the Wilderness area). Note that if you decide to hike St. Vrain Mountain outside of Allenspark, you're supposed to turn around before reaching trail's end:

Part of the trail goes through a couple-hundred-foot section of Rocky Mountain National Park, and dogs are not allowed on this part. (You could also skirt this section altogether by heading off-trail, but you didn't hear it from me.) And though the Twin Sisters Trail is in a separate location, it's on National Park property and is therefore off limits to dogs. In addition to the trails listed below, you could hike with your dog in the Pierson Park and Johnny Park areas (see "Cycling for Canines").

 Crosier Mountain. 8 miles round-trip. From the intersection of Highways 34 and 36 in Estes Park, take Highway 34 west, past the Stanley Hotel. Make a right onto Devil's Gulch Rd. After about 7 miles, you'll reach the hamlet of Glen Haven. Look for the Crosier Mountain Trail sign on the right, just before a horse rental operation. You'll need to park across the street, however, as the road leading to the trailhead is a private drive. *Dogs can be off leash.*

This is a marvelous hike that will capture both your and your dog's interest with a variety of terrain and landscape. Walk up the private road (you'll probably want to keep your dog on a leash during this part) and hook up with the actual trail on the right. Be aware that the trail gets high horse use in the summer, which means that if your dog is like most, he'll try to help himself to "snacks" along the way. The trail begins by switchbacking up, though not too steeply, through stands of ponderosa pine. At half a mile, you'll pass a signed turnoff to the H-G Ranch, the first of a couple you'll come to. Shortly after, your dog can pause for refreshment at a small stream. The trail then narrows and leads you to perhaps the most beautiful part of the hike, Piper Meadow, a vast expanse studded with wildflowers in the summer. The Mummy Range and other mountains in the park stretch out to the west. Stay left at the fork, and follow the trail as it crosses above the meadow. After passing another trail junction, you'll climb a series of switchbacks leading up the hillside above the meadow. Hike past another junction atop a small saddle. The final ascent to the peak goes through thick stands of lodgepole pine, passing yet another trail junction. The very last part before the summit gets rocky and steep. The trail ends at a spectacular vista atop the 9,250-foot peak.

 Lily Mountain. 4 miles round-trip. Take Highway 7 south from Estes Park. At 5.7 miles, look for a small parking pullout on the right as well as a small brown "Lily Mountain" sign and blue call-box sign. *Dogs can be off leash.*

A popular hike close to Estes Park, 9,786-foot Lily Mountain lies just outside the park boundary; therefore, dogs are allowed, and because it's on National Forest land, they can even explore leash-free. You'll need to bring water for the both of you, as there's none along the trail. Clover liked this hike because it remains primarily in ponderosa and lodgepole pine, which meant she found an ample supply of sticks to carry around. The first half of the trail parallels Highway 7, though as you make the moderate climb, the noise from the busy highway begins to fade. And during the ascent, you'll pass lots of vista points that look down into the Estes valley. The peaks

Frostbite is a local Estes Park trouble-maker. (photo by Cindy Hirschfeld)

of Twin Sisters rise directly to the east. Stay left at an unmarked fork; from this point, the trail switchbacks up the mountain. As you approach the top, the trail becomes harder to follow; look for the rock cairns. The final ascent involves a bit of rock scrambling, but nothing that the agile dog won't be able to handle. The reward is a panoramic view of the park's lofty peaks.

 Lion Gulch. 5 miles round-trip to Homestead Meadows. From Estes Park, head south on Highway 36 for 8 miles. Then look for the parking area and trailhead on the right. *Dogs can be off leash.*

The hike begins with a short descent down to the Little Thompson River. After crossing this, the trail follows a smaller stream on the ascent up the gulch, criss-crossing it several times via bridges and logs laid across. You'll enjoy the sweet smell of pine as you travel. Shortly before reaching the first meadow, a great spot for summer wildflowers, the trail turns into an old dirt road. Pause to read the trailside sign that will educate you and your dog about the Homestead Act of 1862, in case you've forgotten that part of your high school history class. Once at the meadows, you can hike to as many as eight homesteads or a sawmill (distances range from 0.25 mile to 2 miles one way). The homesteads, which

date from 1889 to 1923, are in various states of degeneration, but you'll still be able to appreciate their scenic settings. Fido, in the meantime, can enjoy the open terrain and, if thirsty, refresh himself at the horse trough in the first meadow.

Lake Estes Trail. Runs a little under 2 miles from the Lake Estes marina to Riverside Plaza downtown. The easiest place to pick up the trail is behind the Chamber of Commerce building, just east of the intersection of Highways 34 and 36. Or, from downtown Estes, walk south toward the river. *Dogs must be leashed.*

Great for a short, scenic stroll, this paved path follows the Big Thompson River through town and then east to Lake Estes, where your dog can do a bit of on-leash splashing in the water and, perhaps, gaze longingly at the ducks. And you'll get a nice view of the park's eastern peaks. Plans call for the path to eventually encircle the whole lake.

Rocky Mountain National Park. In case your dog missed the explanation at the beginning of the chapter, here's a recap: The park is just not a dog-friendly place. Dogs can come along to campgrounds and picnic areas in the park as long as they're on a leash six feet long or less. And they can venture up to 100 feet from roadways or parking areas. That's it—all trails have been designated canine-free. And in case you're thinking of leaving Fido in the car or tied up at a trailhead or campsite, that's a no-no, too. Your best bet is to stay at a place where you can leave your dog unattended in the room or to board him during the time you plan to be in the park.

CYCLING FOR CANINES

Several four-wheel-drive roads on National Forest land provide good spots for taking the pooch for a pedal. The **Pierson Park** area is accessible from Fish Creek Rd., near the east end of Lake Estes. The **Johnny Park** area can be reached from either Highway 36 south (at the Forest Service access sign for Big Elk Meadows) or from Big Owl or Cabin Creek Rds. off Highway 7 south. To reach Pole Hill, follow the Forest Access sign off Highway 36 north, just before the final descent into the Estes valley. The Forest Service office (see "Resources") has maps of all these areas.

POWDERHOUNDS

Finding places to ski and snowshoe with your dog in the Estes Park area generally means having to venture southwest toward Nederland (see chapter 2). The Estes valley does not hold snow for very long, making National Forest trails iffy for skiing. Rocky Mountain National Park, of course, is off-limits, and trails just south of Estes are in the Indian Peaks Wilderness, with leashes a requirement.

CREATURE COMFORTS

Unless otherwise stated, dogs should not be left unattended in the room or cabin.

Allenspark

$$ Sunshine Mountain Inn, 18078 Highway 7 (2 miles south of Allenspark), 303-747-2840. Dogs are welcome in both the fully equipped one- and two-bedroom cabins or in the main lodge, where dorm space is available (retreat groups usually use the latter). You can leave your dog unattended in the cabin. Open year-round.

$$$$ Lane Guest Ranch, 12 miles south of Estes Park off Highway 7, 303-747-2493. A vacation at this family-oriented guest ranch would be heaven on earth for everyone, including the dog. In operation since 1953, the ranch accommodates up to eighty-five guests and has a staff of about forty-five. There are twenty-five cozy one- and two-bedroom cabin and A-frame units, most with private patios or decks, and more than half with private hot tubs. You can leave your dog unattended inside or on the deck while you go horseback riding or whitewater rafting. Other ranch offerings include guided hikes and fishing trips, outings to Central City and Grand Lake, evening entertainment, and a whole slate of children's activities. And of course there's plenty of hiking and biking nearby that you can do on your own with your dog (you'll need to keep your dog leashed on the twenty-five-acre ranch property). The best deals are the week-long package plans, which include three meals a day and all activities. And your pooch is sure to salivate when you tell him that free dog meals—steak, prime rib, or chicken breast—are available! Open beginning of June to end of August.

Estes Park

$–$$ Elkhorn Lodge, 600 W. Elkhorn Ave., 970-586-4416. Though the main lodge does not allow pets, you can stay with your dog in the cottages, studio cabins, or "the woodshed," a detached building with five units inside. All of these are fully furnished but don't have kitchen facilities. There's a $10 fee per dog, per night, and you can leave your dog unattended as long as you inform the management. Open from April to the end of October.

$–$$ Four Winds Motor Lodge, 1120 Big Thompson Ave., 970-586-3313 (800-527-7509). The motel accepts dogs for a $5 fee per dog, per night. In addition to standard rooms, two- and three-room suites and units with kitchens are available. A three-bedroom house can also be rented. Open year-round.

$–$$ Hobby Horse Motor Lodge, 800 Big Thompson Ave., 970-586-3336 (800-354-

8253). Dogs are allowed in most rooms, for a $5 fee per night (three rooms with fireplaces are available). Many of the rooms are at ground level, providing easy access for dog walking, and the motel is on five acres of wooded property. You can leave your dog unattended in the room only if he's in a travel kennel. Open year-round.

$–$$ Lazy T Motor Lodge, 1340 Big Thompson Ave., 970-586-4376 (800-530-8822). There's a limit of one dog per room, and a credit-card imprint is required as a deposit. Kitchenette units are available. Open May 1 to the end of October.

$–$$ Palisade Motel, 1372 Big Thompson Canyon (about halfway between Estes Park and Loveland), **970-663-5532.** The motel's units are more like cabins; some are separate, some share a wall, all but one have fully equipped kitchens. There's a $5 fee per night, per pet, and you must keep your dog leashed at all times when outside (you'll be able to take him to explore the Big Thompson River at property's edge). Open from the beginning of May to the end of September.

$–$$ Swiftcurrent Lodge, 2512 Highway 66, 970-586-3720 (888-639-9673). The riverside lodge allows small dogs (poodle size) during the off season, which includes most of May and from mid-September to April. Six motel rooms, two with kitchens, are available year-round; the seven fully furnished cottages are closed from October 15 to April 30. There's a $10 fee per night for dogs.

$–$$ A Telemark Resort, 650 Moraine Ave., 970-586-4343 (800-669-0650). The resort offers twenty fully equipped cabins with fireplaces, from studio to two-bedroom, along the Big Thompson River. There's a $10 fee per night, per dog. Open year-round.

$$ Aspen Grove Cottages, 238 Riverside Dr., 970-586-4584. Dogs 20 pounds and under can stay in these fully outfitted cabins close to downtown. There's a $5 fee per night, and you can leave your dog unat-

Is Fido craving a cool drink in downtown Estes Park? Bring him to Riverside Plaza, where a fountain and surrounding pool (as well as the nearby Big Thompson River) can provide some relief.

tended in the room if he's in a travel kennel. Open Memorial Day to October 1.

$$ Cliffside Cottages, 2445 Highway 66, 970-586-4839. The only restriction on dogs at this small resort is that they be walked in a certain area on the property. The three fully equipped cabins vary in size, from sleeping two to six, and all have fireplaces. You can leave your dog unattended inside. Open May 1 through mid-October.

$$ Edgewater Heights Cottages, 2550 Big Thompson Canyon, 970-586-8493. For $5 a night extra, your dog can have his pick of eight fully equipped cabins (most are one bedroom), all with fireplaces. "I enjoy having pets," says David, the owner. And you can take Fido to explore the surrounding fifteen acres along the Big Thompson River leash-free. Open April 1 to November 1.

$$ Estes Park Center YMCA, 2515 Highway 66, 970-586-3341. The YMCA complex is scenically situated on 860 acres right next to the national park. Though dogs are not permitted in the lodge rooms, you'll be able to choose from more than 200 fully equipped cabins, ranging in size from two to four bedrooms and some with fireplaces, that can accommodate Fido. You can leave your dog unattended in the cabin; keep him leashed when outside it. Open year-round.

$$ Inn at Estes Park, 1701 Big Thompson Ave., 970-586-5363 (800-458-1182). The motel allows dogs 25 pounds and under in its ground-floor rooms for a $10 one-time fee.

$$ Olympus Motor Lodge, 2365 Big Thompson Ave., 970-586-8141 (800-248-8141). Teeny dogs (those under 10 pounds) are allowed in certain rooms, with a credit-card imprint as a deposit. Open year-round.

$$ Triple R Cottages, 1000 Riverside Dr., 970-586-5552. These seven fully equipped cabins (from studio to three bedroom) accommodate smaller dogs (about 30 pounds and under) for $5 extra per night, per pet. Open April to the end of December.

Bruno pauses for refreshment on a trail near Estes Park. (photo by Cindy Hirschfeld)

$$–$$$ American Wilderness Lodge, 481 W. Elkhorn Ave., 970-586-4402 (800-762-5968). "We want the people who treat their pets like their babies," says the management here. So if your dog is suitably pampered and weighs less than 40 pounds, bring him along. The lodge offers motel rooms as well as two-room suites with kitchens and fireplaces. Six pet rooms are available; one canine is allowed per room, and a $5 fee per night is charged. Open year-round.

$$–$$$ Anderson's Wonder View Cottages, 540 Laurel Lane, 970-586-4158 (800-327-0113). Located on seven acres with great views of Longs Peak, these ten fully equipped cottages range in size from one to three bedrooms, and all have fireplaces and decks. Six motel rooms are also available. There's a limit of two dogs per unit, and the fee is $10 per night. Be sure to keep your dog leashed on the property. Open year-round.

$$–$$$ Machin's Cottages in the Pines, 2450 Eagle Cliff Rd., 970-586-4276. Dogs less than twenty pounds may stay in any of the seventeen fully equipped, quaintly furnished cabins, which have from one to three bedrooms and fireplaces. Because the cottages are surrounded by national park, you won't be able to walk Fido very far from them. There's a two-night minimum stay. Open from May through the end of September.

$$–$$$ Mountain Haven Inn and Cottages, 690 Moraine Ave., 970-586-2864. Dogs are welcome in four of the six fully furnished, two-bedroom cabins at this friendly complex situated on the Big Thompson River. (The inn itself, a three-bedroom house, is off-limits to canines.) Built about six years ago, the cabins are among the newer ones that you'll find in Estes. You'll need to keep Fido on his leash when outside on the property. Open year-round.

$$–$$$ National Park Resort Cabins and Campground, 3501 Fall River Rd., 970-586-4563. The resort's location just outside the park may not be worth the premium price to your dog. Nevertheless, he is welcome to join you in one of the motel rooms (two have kitchens) or one of the four fully outfitted cabins. There's a $25 deposit as well as a $5 one-time fee, both per pet, with a limit of two pets in a unit. The motel rooms (and campsites) are available from May to October 1; the cabins are open year-round.

$$–$$$ Skyline Cottages, 1752 Highway 66, 970-586-2886. Your dog will join a long line of canine visitors with a stay at Skyline, as the owner has welcomed pets for more than two decades. The eight fully equipped cottages range in size from one-room units to two bedrooms. Most have fireplaces, and a couple have decks overlooking the Big Thompson River; one even has a separate spa room with a whirlpool bath. There's a $6 fee per night, per pet, and you are able to leave your dog in the cottage unattended. The property also features a large stand-alone riverside deck with picnic tables and other seating. Be sure to bring Fido by the office for a treat from the basket of dog biscuits; poop pickup bags and plastic gloves are also dispensed on request. Open mid-May through the end of October, with two units staying open through mid-January.

> The Shining Mountains group of the Colorado Mountain Club (CMC) includes "doggie hikes" in its annual schedule of trips and activities. For information on joining this CMC group, call 970-586-6623.

$$–$$$$ Castle Mountain Lodge, 1520 Fall River Rd., 970-586-3664 (800-852-PINE). Dogs are allowed in about ten of the cottages here, which range from one to three bedrooms, for a $10 fee per night. The cottages are fully equipped, and many have fireplaces. Your dog will enjoy the scenic location along Fall River, close to the national park. Open year-round.

$$$ Canyon River Inn, 2395 Big Thompson Canyon (4 miles east of Estes Park), 970-586-9689. The inn is actually a two-story, two-bedroom cabin available for nightly rental (it sleeps up to eight). The decor is "updated mountain style," with a fireplace, wood floors, and an open floor plan upstairs that includes a full kitchen and living area. You can leave your dog unattended inside if he's in a travel kennel or if he's extremely well trained and well mannered. Available from the beginning of May through the end of September.

$$$–$$$$ Stanley Hotel, 333 Wonderview Ave., 970-586-3371 (800-976-1377). The Stephen King–loving dog will certainly appreciate a visit to the venerable Stanley, which served as the inspiration for King's book *The Shining* and, more recently, was the site of filming for a TV miniseries of the novel. If you train your dog to bark just right, he might even be able to freak out fellow guests with a passable imitation of the famous "red rum" line from the movie version of *The Shining*. In real life, the Stanley, listed on the National Register of Historic Places, offers a range of rooms, from standard to deluxe, many furnished with antiques. A $25 pet deposit is required. Open year-round.

Campgrounds

Rocky Mountain National Park. The park has four campgrounds on the eastern side, and dogs are permitted at all of them.

National Forest campgrounds: **Camp Dick** (41 sites) and **Peaceful Valley Campgrounds** (17 sites) are off Highway 72 (via Highway 7 south past Allenspark) at Peaceful Valley; **Olive Ridge Campground,** off Highway 7, is near the Wild Basin area of the national park (56 sites).

Private campgrounds: **National Park Resort Cabins and Campground** (see "Creature Comforts").

WORTH A PAWS

Strong Dog Weight-Pull Competition. Bring your dog to drool over the Arnold Schwarzeneggers of the canine world. Sanctioned by the International Weight Pulling Association, this two-day competition, held mid-February in Estes Park, allows about fifty dogs to show off their pulling prowess. Each dog is put into a competitive class based on his own weight. The competitors then vie to see who can pull the most weight on a sled on snow one day, the most wheeled weights the next. Contact the Chamber Resort Association at 800-44-ESTES for more information.

DOGGIE DAYCARE
Estes Park

Animal Medical Center of Estes Park (AAHA certified), 1260 Manford Ave., 970-586-6898. $5/day. Open 8 A.M.–5:30 P.M., Monday to Friday; 8 A.M.–noon, Saturday. Later pickups on Saturday and boarding on Sunday can be arranged in advance.

Boarding House for Pets, 863 Dry Gulch Rd., 970-586-6606. $1/hour per run (each run can hold two dogs). Open 7:30 A.M.–5:30 P.M., Monday to Saturday, and for check-in at 11 A.M. and pickup at 4 P.M. on Sunday (other times available by advance arrangement).

PET PROVISIONS
Estes Park

Boarding House for Pets, 863 Dry Gulch Rd., 970-586-6606

Pets of Estes, Upper Stanley Village, 970-586-8442

CANINE ER
Estes Park

Animal Medical Center of Estes Park (AAHA certified), 1260 Manford Ave., 970-586-6898. Open 8 A.M.–5:30 P.M., Monday to Friday; 8 A.M.–noon, Saturday.

RESOURCES

Estes Park Chamber Resort Association, 500 Big Thompson Ave., Estes Park, 970-586-4431 (800-44-ESTES; www.rockymtn trav.com/estes/ or www.estes-park.com/lodging/)

Estes Park Forest Service Office, Arapaho and Roosevelt National Forests, 161 2nd St., Estes Park, 970-586-3440

NORTHWEST COLORADO

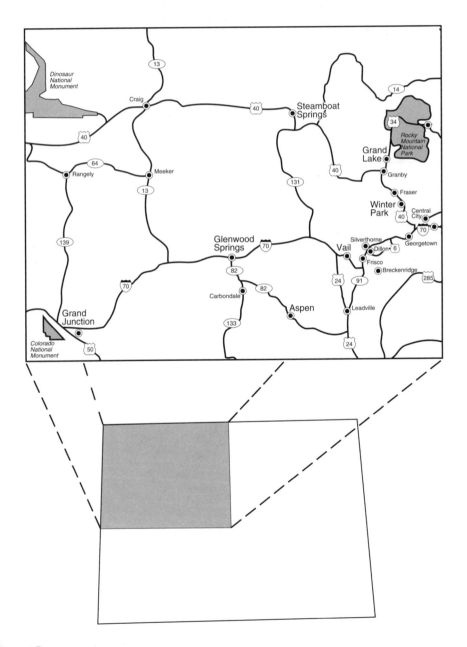

7
Winter Park, Grand Lake, and Granby

THE BIG SCOOP

The area from Winter Park to the town of Grand Lake, which runs along the western side of the Continental Divide, has fantastic views of the rugged peaks along the Divide, several lakes nestled at the base of the mountains, and abundant recreational opportunities. And Grand Lake itself is Colorado's largest natural lake. So what's in it for Rover? Not quite as much as for you, unfortunately, primarily because dogs are not allowed on any of the trails in Rocky Mountain National Park, which lies adjacent to Grand Lake. And many of the other trails enter the Indian Peaks Wilderness Area, where dogs must be leashed. But there are some great trails where your dog can hike off leash with you (including the Never Summer, Byers Peak, and Vasquez Wilderness Areas, where dogs can be under voice command) as well as suitable mountain biking terrain for the both of you. And there's even a backcountry hut you can ski to with your dog!

Within the town limits of Winter Park, Fraser, Tabernash, Granby, Grand Lake, and Hot Sulphur Springs, you'll need to keep your dog leashed. In unincorporated parts of Grand County, you can walk your dog under voice command.

TAIL-RATED TRAILS

For additional trail info, stop by the Sulfur Ranger District office in Granby (see "Resources"), which puts out a few pamphlets with short hike descriptions. Or pay a visit to **Flanagan's Black Dog Mountaineering,** on Highway 40 in downtown Winter Park, which carries a range of guidebooks and maps. (Because the store also sells ice cream, you won't be able to bring Rover inside; bring him a scoop as a reward for waiting.) If you're starting a hike at the Monarch Lake Trailhead, note that dogs are required to be on leash on trails by the lake, even though it's not within the Wilderness boundary. And you can hike with your dog at the Winter Park Ski Area as long as he stays on leash.

 Baker Gulch. 12 miles round-trip. Note that to access this trail, you will have to enter Rocky Mountain National Park and pay the requisite entrance fee. Even though the first half mile of trail is on park property, dogs are allowed because the rest is on National Forest land. Access to the trail is closed for the week before hunting season each fall, so call the park (970-627-3471) first to check on the access if you're hiking in late September or early October. Take Highway 34 to the West Entrance Station of the park. From here it's 6.2 miles to the turnoff for the trailhead. Look for the Bowen–Baker Gulch trailhead sign on the right; a large parking area is on the left. *Dogs can be off leash.*

This beautiful hike, which ascends to the top of Baker Pass, allows you to enjoy

A rest along the Baker Gulch Trail outside of Grand Lake. (photo by Cindy Hirschfeld)

the same scenery and terrain as other trails on the western side of Rocky Mountain National Park—but your dog can come too. For the first half mile, hike along a dirt service road that begins by crossing the Colorado River, and stay right at the signed fork; since you're on park property, keep your dog leashed on this section. A sign board marks the entrance into the National Forest. (During hunting season, you'll be able to drive up this road to the forest boundary.) The trail itself starts out next to a creek. After a bit you'll head away from the creek but will never be far from its hearty roar during the first few miles of the hike. Aside from an occasional switchback, the trail remains moderate and is well maintained as it winds through lodgepole pine and subalpine fir. About 2 miles from the trailhead, you'll pop out into a treeless area with a grand view of Fairview Mountain ahead, part of a spectacular alpine cirque. The trail crosses a talus slope, then reenters the trees, following the general uphill course of the creek below. You'll come to a dirt road that parallels the Grand Ditch, a water-diversion project planned in 1890 and completed in

1936 that captured snowmelt and brought it to farmers on the eastern side of the Continental Divide. Cross the ditch via the log footbridge up ahead to pick up the trail again. You'll then skirt the flanks of Mount Baker before heading north toward the pass, at 11,253 feet. The trail crisscrosses the creek a few times as it traverses open meadows. The final section is marked by cairns. Directly east of the pass lie Mounts Cumulus, Nimbus, and Stratus, all above 12,000 feet. On the return trip, you'll be treated to a view of the peaks in the park.

Alternate hikes in this area include the **Parika Lake Trail,** which branches off the **Baker Gulch Trail** at about 5 miles; from there it's 2.4 miles to the lake. The Bowen Gulch Trail begins from the same trailhead as Baker Gulch; stay left at the signed fork on the park service road. It's a 16.2-mile round-trip to the top of Blue Ridge to the south.

High Lonesome Trail. 6 miles round-trip. Take County Rd. 83 off Highway 40, at the south end of Tabernash (you'll see a sign for the Devil's Thumb Ski Area and a forest access/Meadow Creek Reservoir sign). Stay left at the next two forks—the first left will put you on County Rd. 84—following the signs to the reservoir, which is about 9 miles away. About 0.7 mile after Forest Rd. 128 comes in from the right, you'll come to an unmarked fork; stay right. Once you reach Meadow Creek Reservoir, follow the sign to Junco Lake. The parking area and trailhead are by a small Forest Service cabin. *Dogs can be off leash.*

The trail, which is also designated as part of the 3,100-mile-long Continental Divide National Scenic Trail (CDT), brings hikers to Devil's Thumb, a prominent rock feature on the Continental Divide; from here you'll be treated to expansive views of the Fraser River valley, the Indian Peaks Wilderness Area to the east, Winter Park Ski Area and surrounding peaks to the west and south, and the Never Summer Range to the north. From the trailhead, head right (south) along the High Lonesome Trail. The trail winds through a fragrant forest of lodgepole pine and spruce. In a half mile you'll come to a road; cross it, following the CDT markers. Soon you'll come to a series of beautiful, high-mountain meadows. Their open expanse allows sensational views of the high peaks that form the Continental Divide. These meadows also allow you to glean a better understanding of forest succession. They started as beaver ponds (if you look closely you can still see where the waterline was). As the streams feeding the ponds continued to transport waterborne silt and sediments, the ponds gradually filled in, becoming the lush meadows surrounding you. In time, these meadows, too, will change: The rich soil will nourish the same lodgepole pine and spruce through which you've been hiking. And, in the far-off future, some enterprising beavers might take a liking to the landscape and use the trees to dam the stream, creating suitable habitat—and beaver ponds. And so it goes.

After a little less than 3 miles of easy hiking, the trail reaches a junction with another access trail; stay left on the CDT. After the junction you'll start to climb toward the peaks to the east. Soon you'll be able to spot the Devil's Thumb, a lone spire rising from the ridgeline. The trail ultimately passes just south of the thumb (it makes a good landmark, as the trail becomes faint near the ridgeline) into the Indian Peaks Wilderness Area. Stop at the pass and savor the outstanding views in all directions before returning the way you came.

 Columbine Lake. 5.6 miles round-trip. Follow the directions to the trailhead for the High Lonesome Trail (see previous entry). *Dogs can be off leash until the Wilderness boundary, about 1.75 miles in.*

Begin hiking up an old road, which crosses a couple of streams and then as-

cends gradually through subalpine fir. At the entrance to a large meadow, you'll cross the Wilderness boundary, which means it's time to leash up. Ahead on the right, Mount Neva comes prominently into view. The road skirts the meadow on the left, eventually becoming a narrower trail. Shortly after passing the turnoff for the Caribou Trail, you'll ascend away from the meadow into the woods; you should be on the left side of a creek. The trail then skirts a couple of other meadows before the final ascent to the lake. The last part of the trail is a bit trickier to follow, so you may want to let Rover sniff out the way. You'll ascend the left side of a scree-filled drainage, hiking next to a melodic stream. The trail then crosses a plateau, which includes some marshy areas, as it angles southeast toward the lake. The lake itself is at the base of a cirque and makes for a scenic lunch spot before the return hike.

 Jim Creek Trail. About 3 miles round-trip. From Highway 40 West, 0.6 mile past the turnoff for Mary Jane Ski Area, make a right on an unmarked dirt road (it's actually Forest Rd. 128). Drive 1.6 miles, staying left at the fork, to a small parking area by a water diversion dam. The trail begins from the right side of the parking lot, through the bushes. *Dogs can be off leash.*

This hike, which stays below tree line, doesn't include any spectacular vistas of the peaks on the Continental Divide or a specific destination. But your dog will be more interested in the fresh aroma of pine and spruce and the cooling waters of Jim Creek—as well as the fact that he can enjoy them leash-free. During the summer, wildflowers dot sections adjoining the trail; this would also be a nice fall hike, as a hillside of aspen rises above the trail. About the first half mile follows an old roadbed, gradually descending to creek level. The trail then winds uphill of the creek, alternately passing through stands of fir and alpine meadows. Eventually you'll cross a series of small streams coming down the hillside and come creekside again. A small open area makes a good turnaround point; the trail continues but gets increasingly sketchy from here onward.

Rocky Mountain National Park. To reiterate (see chapter 6), the park is just not a dog-friendly place. Dogs can come along to campgrounds and picnic areas in the park as long as they're on a leash six feet long or less. And they can venture up to 100 feet from roadways or parking areas. That's it—all trails have been designated canine-free. And in case you're thinking of leaving Fido in the car or tied up at a trailhead or campsite, that's a no-no, too. Your best bet is to stay at a place where you can leave your dog unattended in the room or to board him during the time you plan to be in the park.

Shadow Mountain and East Shore Trails and part of the Knight Ridge Trail. Dogs are not allowed on the East Shore Trail, which runs along the east shore of Shadow Mountain Lake, or the Shadow Mountain Trail, which branches off it, because both are within Rocky Mountain National Park. Half of the 7-mile-long Knight Ridge Trail, starting at the Green Ridge Recreation Complex, also runs across park land, making it inaccessible to dogs. However, if you begin at the Roaring Fork trailhead at the end of County Rd. 6, your dog can join you on the southern half of the trail, which goes through a portion of the Arapaho National Recreation Area and the Indian Peaks Wilderness Area. Though dogs do not have to be leashed on the sections of trail in the recreation complex, keep a leash handy and a sharp eye out for Wilderness boundary signs, as you will need to leash your dog on the sections of trail in the Indian Peaks Wilderness.

CYCLING FOR CANINES

Winter Park has developed a reputation for the quality and variety of its mountain biking trails. But you won't be easily able to bike with Rover on the ski resort's network of trails, as dogs are required to be leashed on them. For a ride near the Divide, set out on the **High Lonesome Trail** (see "Tail-Rated Trails"). The **Creekside** and **Flume Trails** make an approximately 4-mile loop that begins and ends at the St. Louis Campground off County Rd. 73, outside of Fraser. In the same vicinity, you can access the **Chainsaw** (about 2 miles one way) and **Zoom** (about 1.5 miles) **Trails;** the Chainsaw Trail goes out of County Rd. 72 and intersects the Zoom Trail, which can also be accessed from County Rd. 159. Water is available at places along all of these trails. For a different type of cycling adventure, bike 2.5 miles in to the **High Lonesome Hut,** outside of Tabernash. See "Powderhounds" for more details.

POWDERHOUNDS

Devil's Thumb Cross-Country Center. This popular nordic ski area, at the end of County Rd. 83 out of Tabernash, allows dogs on three of its trails: the 3.5-kilometer **Foxtrot,** the 3.5-kilometer **Left Field,** and the 2-kilometer **Creekside.** A leash regulation is in effect, but there's no restriction on length, so you can outfit Rover with an extra-long leash to make skiing or snowshoeing with him in tow a bit more manageable. You'll have to pay a trail fee to access the dog-friendly routes as well as buy a $10 season pass for your dog. Because the dog policy has been somewhat controversial, double-check with the ski area before you go to make sure that dogs are still allowed. 970-726-8231.

> The Dog Trail, so called because the Native Americans who traveled it used dogs to carry their possessions, went through an area between Estes Park and Grand Lake.

Grand Lake Touring Center. The center, located about 2 miles west of Grand Lake, features a dog loop for skiers and snowshoers as well as their canine companions. The loop begins and ends near the center's main building and goes for about three-quarters of a mile. Dogs can be off leash, and owners don't need to pay a trail fee to access the loop. A few laps should tucker out Rover enough that you can check out the rest of the terrain while he snoozes in the car. Call 970-627-8008 for additional information.

High Lonesome Hut. A backcountry hut that your dog can come along to—wonders never cease! Actually, there are some good reasons why dogs aren't allowed at most huts, water supply being one of them (you don't want to be melting yellow snow!). But the High Lonesome has a well—and indoor plumbing—making the water source a moot point. The hut, which sleeps up to eight people, is a gentle 2.5-mile ski or snowshoe in from County Rd. 84 out of Tabernash, in the Strawberry region. You can either go the traditional route, humping your own pack with food and drink, or pay extra for the "hut master service," which includes gear transport and three meals a day. Either way, your dog will love being able to accompany you on a ski tour and telemark adventure. The hut is also available during the summer to hikers and mountain bikers. For rates and other details, call 970-726-4099.

Snow Mountain Ranch. The nordic ski area at this YMCA center has two dog-friendly trails, and both are even named after dogs. The 2-kilometer groomed Loppet's Trail permits skiers with leashed dogs; it's also a popular route for skijoring (your dog, wearing a harness, pulls you along) and dog-sled training runs. Peter's Trail, a 5-kilometer loop, is not groomed and is open to skiers and snowshoers; dogs can be off leash. You don't need to pay a fee to use either of these trails. 970-887-2152.

CREATURE COMFORTS

Unless otherwise stated, dogs should not be left unattended in the room or cabin.

Fraser

$$ High Mountain Lodge (at Tally Ho Ranch), 425 County Rd. 50, 970-726-5958 (800-772-9987). The homey High Mountain Lodge has twelve rooms, all with king-size beds and most with fireplaces. A few are designated pet rooms. The ranch sits on 180 acres, and you can take your dog hiking off leash if he's a good voice-command listener. He might also want to sniff out the six resident dogs. During the summer, trail rides are offered at the ranch. Winter rates include breakfast and dinner; summer rates, from May to October, include breakfast only.

Granby

$ Broken Arrow Motel, 843 W. Agate (Highway 40), 970-887-3532 (800-730-3532). Dogs are permitted on a case-by-case basis, with a $5 one-time fee. Those who come with a travel kennel can stay in most rooms; uncrated dogs are limited to certain rooms. The motel is surrounded by two acres where you can walk your dog off leash.

$ Homestead Motel, 851 W. Agate (Highway 40), 970-887-3665 (800-669-3605). The motel's flyer advertises the touches of home, including "colored, printed sheets"—you won't find the standard-issue, tissue-thin motel sheets here. (No word on the carpeting, as far your dog is concerned.) Units with kitchenettes are available.

$-$$ Blue Spruce Motel, 170 E. Agate (Highway 40), 970-887-3300 (800-765-0001). Dogs are allowed in smoking rooms only.

$-$$ Little Tree Inn, 62000 Highway 40, 970-887-2551 (800-359-2551). There's a $5 charge per dog, per night.

$-$$ Trail Riders Motel, 215 W. Agate (Highway 40), 970-887-3738. Small, lap-sized dogs only get the nod.

$$ Gala Marina and Motel, 928 County Rd. 64, 970-627-3220. Located on Lake Granby, the motel offers eight one- and two-bedroom units with full kitchens as well as boat and dock rentals at its full-service marina. Small dogs are welcome for $5 extra per dog, per night. Open year-round.

$$ Longbranch, 185 E. Agate (Highway 40), 970-887-2209. Well-trained dogs are permitted at this two-room guesthouse (it's not a B&B).

$$$ Just Arnolds Vacation Home, County Rd. 641, 303-682-2539 or 303-576-8157. This three-bedroom mountain house, ten minutes from Grand Lake, includes a fireplace, patio, washer/dryer, and gas grill. The owners prefer one dog guest at a time and that you not leave your dog unattended inside (though very well-behaved dogs may merit an exception). The house is available for rental year-round, and there's a two-night minimum.

$$$ Shadow Mountain Guest Ranch, 5043 Highway 125 (8 miles from Granby), 970-887-9524 (800-64-SHADOW). The six fully outfitted log cabins at the ranch range from studios to three bedrooms, and some have fireplaces or wood stoves. The rates include a full breakfast in the central lodge. You'll pay a $10 fee per night, per dog to bring four-legged guests, and Fido can stay inside unattended, preferably in a travel kennel. But he'd probably rather be out with you, exploring the ranch's 1,100 acres leash-free. Horseback rides are offered during the summer.

Grand Lake

$ Elk Creek Camper Cabins and Campground, 143 County Rd. 48 (near the park entrance), 970-627-8502 (800-ELK-CREEK). Dogs are allowed in the seven camper cabins here (more are being built) with a credit-card imprint as a deposit. "We're doggie people," says the owner, "but we don't want things getting torn up." You'll need to supply your own bedding and cooking gear. Open year-round.

$ Mack's Shadow Mountain Motel, 12365 Highway 34, 970-627-8546. Dogs are permitted in the motel's knotty-pine-finished rooms for $5 per night extra as well as a $25 cash deposit. Most of the rooms have a small refrigerator and microwave. If your dog has a travel kennel, he can be left unattended in the room as long as he promises to keep quiet. Otherwise, the friendly owner might be willing to watch your dog at his house nearby.

$–$$ Bluebird Motel, 30 River Dr., 970-627-9314. There's a $5 one-time fee for dogs. Note that the Peaks Point Cottages, which are affiliated with the motel, do not allow dogs.

$–$$ Grandview Lodge, 12429 Highway 34, 970-627-3914. Dogs are welcome at this small motel with a $20 deposit. All rooms come equipped with a microwave, refrigerator, and freezer. Though you won't be able to leave your dog unattended in the room, the motel has a large yard where you can tie up Fido if you need to go somewhere without him.

$–$$ Inn at Grand Lake, 1103 Grand Ave., 970-627-9234 (800-722-2585). The inn is located in one of Grand Lake's historic buildings, which dates from 1890, and rooms have antique furnishings. Dogs are accepted on a case-by-case basis—"We like to meet the dog," says the manager—and you'll have a better chance of being able to stay here with Rover in the off-season (i.e., anytime but summer). There's a $10 one-time fee for a dog.

$–$$ Mountain Lakes Lodge, 10480 Highway 34, 970-627-8448. The rustic cabins are situated in a wooded area on a canal that connects Lake Granby and Shadow Mountain Lake, about 4 miles south of the town of Grand Lake. Ten connected, fully equipped cabin units (some with wood-burning stoves) are available as well as two three-bedroom log houses (for a higher rate). There's a $5 fee per night for a dog, and you can leave yours unattended inside. You'll also be able to walk him on the surrounding 2.5 acres of property, which has great views of the Indian Peaks, and on the pathway that runs along the canal for several miles in each direction.

$–$$ Sunset Motel, 505 Grand Ave., 970-627-3318. Poodle-sized dogs (or smaller) can stay in the motel's older units for a $5 fee per night.

$–$$ Waconda Motel, 725 Grand Ave., 970-627-8312. There's a $10 one-time fee for a dog at this downtown motel. Two of the rooms have fireplaces. You can leave your dog unattended inside as long as you're sure he'll remain quiet.

$$ Columbine Creek Ranch, 14814 Highway 34, 970-627-2429. Dogs are permitted in the ranch's fully equipped four cabins, but not in the B&B rooms in the historic main lodge. There's also a trout pond on the premises. Only one cabin stays open year-round.

$$ Lonesome Dove Cottages, 416 Grand Ave., 970-627-8019. Located in downtown Grand Lake, the eight fully equipped cottages sleep from four to seven guests. Your dog is welcome to join you for $10 extra per night, and you can leave him unattended inside.

$$ Nonehshe Cabins, 450 Broadway, 970-627-8012. The seven fully outfitted cabins with knotty-pine interiors are in the town of Grand Lake. You and your dog can choose a one- or two-bedroom unit, some of which have fireplaces or wood-burning stoves.

$$ Osprey Inn, 12685 Highway 34, 970-627-3461 or 303-237-1438. When the land on which this house was built in 1928 was flooded to create Shadow Mountain Lake, the structure was moved uphill to its present location, two miles south of Grand Lake. The inn has two B&B rooms, one with Victorian decor, the other Santa

Artemis basks in a wildflower-studded meadow near Winter Park. (photo by Karen Pauly)

Fe style. Though you can't leave your dog unattended in the room, the owner may be able to watch him for a few hours, along with Ashley, the resident Samoyed. A plan to fence the inn's yard is also in the works, which will provide another place for Fido to hang out for a short time. And you can walk your dog off leash on the surrounding five acres.

$$ Spirit Lake Lodge, 829 Grand Ave., 970-627-3344 (800-544-6593). Dogs are allowed in two of the motel's rooms, for $5 extra per night. The motel is located in downtown Grand Lake.

$$–$$$ Rocky Mountain Cabins, 12206 Highway 34, 970-627-3061. Not your average cabin, the three units here, 2.5 miles south of Grand Lake on the North Fork of the Colorado River, are custom-built log homes. They're all fully equipped, including washer/dryers and fireplaces. Dogs are permitted on a case-by-case basis, though if yours is a charmer, chances are he'll make the grade: "We'd rather rent to pets than to kids," quips the owner. You can leave your dog unattended inside only if he's in a travel kennel, but you can walk him off leash on the six acres that surround the cabins. He may also want to meet the four resident dogs and cats (two of each). There's a two-night minimum stay.

$$–$$$ Winding River Resort Village, 1447 County Rd. 491, 970-627-3215 or 303-623-1121 (800-282-5121). The resort, located near the entrance to Rocky Mountain National Park, has lodge rooms, cabins, and tent and RV sites. Dogs are allowed in the four cabins, with a $20 deposit, and at the campsites. The fully equipped cabins range from one to two bedrooms, and three have wood-burning stoves. There's plenty for your dog to explore on the resort's 160 acres as long as he's on his leash. For your entertainment, the resort offers horseback rides, hayrides, sleigh rides, and Frisbee golf, among other activities. Open year-round except for April and May.

Hot Sulphur Springs

$ K C Cabins, 417 Byers Ave., 970-725-3329. For a $100 one-time fee (about three times what you'll pay per night for the lodging), you can stay with your dog in one of these seven fully equipped cabins.

$–$$ Canyon Motel, 221 Byers Ave., 970-725-3395. Dogs are assessed a $5 one-time fee. Some rooms with kitchenettes are available.

$–$$ The Stagecoach Country Inn, 412 Nevava St., 970-725-3910 (800-725-3919). This B&B is located in a historic building (from 1874) that once served as the area's stagecoach stop. The fourteen rooms, each individually furnished, are simple but comfortable, with grandmotherly-type decor. There's a $10 fee per night

A barrier-free nature trail constructed by the Bonfils-Stanton Foundation and the Winter Park Outdoor Center allows a guide dog and his owner to enjoy a wilderness experience. The trail is located off Highway 40, across from the entrance to the Winter Park Ski Resort.

for a dog, and you can leave Fido unattended in the room. A restaurant is also on the premises.

$–$$ Ute Trail Motel, 120 E. Highway 40, 970-725-0123 (800-506-0099). There's a $5 fee per night for a dog. Dogs can be left unattended in the rooms on a case-by-case basis.

Silver Creek

$$–$$$$ The Inn at Silver Creek, 62927 Highway 40, 970-887-2131 (800-926-4386). This resort hotel, located at the base of family-oriented Silver Creek Ski Area outside of Granby, offers a range of rooms, from standards to studios and lofts with kitchenettes and fireplaces to suites—but dogs can only stay in smoking rooms. There's a $12 one-time fee for a dog ($24 if he's staying in a suite), and a credit-card imprint is required as a deposit.

Tabernash

$$ Candlelight Mountain Inn, 22 County Rd. 85, 970-887-2877 (800-KIM4TIM). The Candlelight, which bills itself as a family B&B, has two rooms, both with private bath and one with a loft and private deck. The owners prefer that visiting dogs have a travel kennel in which to stay, but they'll consider allowing nonkenneled dogs, too. There's a $5 fee per night for dog guests. If Fido is in a kennel, you can leave him unattended in the room; otherwise, you can arrange for dog-sitting with the owners.

$$ Fireside Inn, 72160 Highway 40, 970-726-4668 (800-531-1251). Dogs are allowed in the summer season only, from May to October, with a $100 deposit. The motel has designated pet rooms.

$$$ Devil's Thumb Ranch, 3530 County Rd. 83, 970-726-5632. Dogs are allowed in six out of the ranch's seven cabins (not in the lodge rooms). The one-room cabins include a sleeping area and bathroom. You'll be asked to sign a damage waiver on behalf of your dog. Devil's Thumb

Cross-Country Center is on the property, and you can take your dog on three of the trails (see "Powderhounds" for more details). The cabins are open year-round.

Winter Park

$–$$ Sitzmark Lodge, 78253 Highway 40, 970-726-5453. The lodge offers six fully equipped chalet-cabins. Dogs are charged $5–$10 per night extra.

$–$$$ Alpenglo Motor Lodge, 78665 Highway 40, 970-726-5294 (800-541-6130). Under the same management as the Winter Park Super 8 (which doesn't allow dogs), the Alpenglo has mostly been converted to meeting space, but there are still three units available for lodging: a motel room with queen-size bed, a two-bedroom apartment-style unit, and a four-bedroom house. There's a $5 fee per night for a dog; you can leave Rover unattended in the room, but housekeeping won't enter during that time.

$–$$$ Valley Hi Motel, 79025 Highway 40, 970-726-4171 (800-426-2094). Dogs are permitted on a case-by-case basis in the motel's older rooms, with a $10 deposit. If your dog is in a travel kennel, he can stay unattended in the room. Otherwise, you can tie up Fido outside as long as he's not a constant barker.

$$–$$$ Beaver Village Lodge, 79303 Highway 40, 970-726-5741 (800-666-0281). Dogs are allowed in any of the lodge's hotel rooms, but not in the condos. Rates from mid-November to April include breakfast and dinner. You can leave your dog unattended in the room.

$$–$$$ The Foxwood Inn, County Rd. 83, 970-726-0456 (888-726-0456). This luxury B&B—each room has a private balcony, jetted tub, and antique and designer decor—allows dogs who are on their best behavior to stay with their owners. You can leave your well-behaved dog unattended in the room as long as he stays in a travel kennel. The inn, a picturesque log home, is surrounded by eight wooded acres.

$$–$$$$ Raintree Inn, 81699 Highway 40, 970-726-4211 (800-726-3340). There's a $10 charge per dog, per night. The hotel's rates include breakfast and dinner.

$$–$$$$ The Vintage Hotel, 100 Winter Park Dr., 970-726-8801 (800-472-7017). Winter Park's resident upscale hotel, the Vintage offers a variety of lodging options, ranging from regular rooms to studios with kitchenettes and fireplaces, that you can share with your dog. And you can leave Fido unattended inside, although housekeeping won't service the room during that time.

$$$ Snow Mountain Ranch YMCA, Highway 40 north of Fraser, 970-726-4628 or 303-443-4743. Located on almost 5,000 acres, the ranch has forty-five fully furnished cabins, ranging from two to five bedrooms, in which you and your dog can stay (dogs are not permitted in the lodge rooms). All the cabins have fireplaces, and you can leave your dog unattended inside. When exploring the ranch property, you'll need to keep Rover on his leash. The complex also offers a restaurant, indoor pool, indoor climbing wall, tennis courts, miniature golf, and a nordic trail system (see "Powderhounds"). Camping and RV sites are also available.

Campgrounds

Rocky Mountain National Park. The park has one campground, Timber Creek, on its western side.

National Forest campgrounds: **Arapaho National Recreation Area,** which includes Lake Granby, Shadow Mountain Lake, Monarch Lake, Willow Creek Reservoir, and Meadow Creek Reservoir, has several campgrounds, among them **Stillwater Campground,** off Highway 34 (148 sites); **Green Ridge Campground,** off County Rd. 66 (78 sites); **Arapaho Bay Campground,** at the end of County Rd. 6 (84 sites); and **Willow Creek Campground,** off County Rd. 40 at Willow Creek Reservoir (35 sites). Also available are **St. Louis Campground,** 4 miles from Fraser off County Rd. 73 (18 sites); **Byers Peak Campground,** 7 miles from Fraser off County Rd. 73 (6 sites); **Idlewild Campground,** 1 mile south of Winter Park off Highway 40 (26 sites); and **Robbers Roost Campground,** 5 miles south of Winter Park on Highway 40 (11 sites).

Private campgrounds: **Elk Creek Camper Cabins and Campground** and **Winding River Resort Village** in Grand Lake; **Snow Mountain Ranch YMCA** outside of Winter Park (see "Creature Comforts" for details on all).

WORTH A PAWS

High Altitude Sled Dog Championships. During the first weekend in March, the heartiest of the huskies gather outside of Grand Lake to compete in these championships, in which winners' points count toward the national championships. More than 100 teams typically compete. The races start at the Winding River Resort and follow 4-mile, 6-mile, and 8-mile routes. A series of cross-country ski and walking trails are set up along the courses for human spectators only. If you'd like to bring your dog to cheer on his fellow tail-waggers, you'll have to stay at the start/finish line— and keep Fido firmly under control. Call the Grand Lake Chamber of Commerce (see "Resources") for more info.

DOGGIE DAYCARE

Fraser
Byers Peak Veterinary Clinic, 360 Railroad Ave., 970-726-8384. $9–$11/day, depending on the size of dog. Open 9 A.M.–12:30 P.M. and 2–5 P.M., Monday to Friday; 10–10:15 A.M. for dropoffs and 6–6:15 P.M. for pickups, Saturday and Sunday.

Granby
Granby Veterinary Clinic, 458 E. Agate (Highway 40), 970-887-3848. $8–$9/ day, depending on the size of dog. Open 9 A.M.–

5 P.M., Monday to Friday; 9 A.M.–noon, Saturday.

PET PROVISIONS

Granby
Granby Mart, 62 E. Agate, 970-887-3843

Grand Lake
Rocky Mountain Sports, 711 Grand Ave., 970-627-8124

CANINE ER

Fraser
Byers Peak Veterinary Clinic, 360 Railroad Ave., 970-726-8384. Open 9 A.M.–12:30 P.M. and 2–5 P.M., Monday to Friday.

Granby
Brooks Veterinary Service, 12 E. Agate (Highway 40), 970-887-2417. Open 8 A.M.–5 P.M., Monday to Friday; 9–11 A.M., most Saturdays.

Granby Veterinary Clinic, 458 E. Agate (Highway 40), 970-887-3848. Open 9 A.M.–5 P.M., Monday to Friday; 9 A.M.–noon, Saturday.

RESOURCES

Fraser Visitor Center, 120 Xerex St., Fraser, 970-726-8312

Granby Chamber of Commerce, 81 W. Jasper, Granby, 970-887-2311

Grand Lake Chamber of Commerce, intersection of Highway 34 and Grand Ave., Grand Lake, 970-627-3402 (800-531-1019)

Sulfur Ranger District, Arapaho and Roosevelt National Forests, 62429 Highway 40, Granby, 970-887-4100

Winter Park/Fraser Valley Chamber of Commerce, 78841 Highway 40, Winter Park, 970-726-4118 (800-722-4118)

8
Steamboat Springs and North Park

THE BIG SCOOP

Steamboat Springs, with its ski-town sensibility (which means lots of dogs) and miles of trails in Routt National Forest close at hand, is a dandy place to take a dog. If you're looking for a truly get-away-from-it trip, head to the North Park area northeast of Steamboat. The region combines ample BLM and National Forest land with a location remote enough that your dog can explore leash-free to his heart's content without disturbing other hikers (keep an eye out for wildlife, though).

Leash laws are enforced within the city limits of Steamboat Springs. In Routt County, you can have your dog under voice command only on agricultural land, which basically rules out any areas you're apt to be visiting. In Jackson County (North Park), dogs can be under voice command on county land; individual towns have their own leash laws.

TAIL-RATED TRAILS

For more hiking ideas, pick up a "Trails Map" brochure at the Steamboat Springs Chamber Resort Association (see "Resources") or a copy of *Hiking the 'Boat,* by Diane White-Crane (the author's dog accompanied her on all of the hikes). The three state parks in the Steamboat area—Stagecoach, Pearl Lake, and Steamboat Lake—primarily focus on water recreation, though all offer some lakeside hiking opportunities, with the longest trail following the eastern shoreline of Stagecoach Reservoir. Colorado State Forest, outside

Walden, is described in more detail later in this section.

Steamboat Springs

Mad Creek. 7.8 miles round-trip to the Mount Zirkel Wilderness boundary. Head west from Steamboat Springs on Highway 40 to County Rd. 129 (you'll see a sign for Steamboat Lake). Turn right and drive 5.5 miles to the parking area and trailhead on the right. *Dogs can be off leash up until the Wilderness boundary.*

Be aware that this trail can get heavy horse use on summer weekends. You'll start out climbing up a rocky hill for the first few tenths of a mile. The trail then meanders along a shelf high above Mad Creek before dropping closer to creek level. After going through a livestock fence, you'll spot a footpath leading down to the creek, a side-trip your dog will no doubt want to take. Shortly after, you'll reach a junction; stay right on Trail 1100 (the sign says "Swamp Park"). A Forest Service building known as the Mad House sits to the south. The trail becomes a narrow singletrack rolling through a pasture. When you come to a fork where a split-rail fence curves to the right, stay to the left. You'll hike through a beautiful stretch of open meadow on an old wagon road. The next section of trail meanders through stands of aspen and again parallels the creek, this time at dog's-eye level. At about 4 miles, you'll reach the clearly marked Wilderness boundary, the turnaround point for this hike.

Remember that if you decide to venture further, Fido will need to leash up.

 Soda Creek. About 3.5 miles round-trip. From downtown Steamboat, take 3rd St. northwest from Lincoln Ave., then make a right at the next block onto Fish Creek Falls Rd. Shortly after, look for a sign for Buffalo Pass and make a left onto Amethyst. Follow Amethyst until it ends in a fork at Strawberry Park Rd.; bear right. You'll see a sign on the right that points toward Buffalo Pass. Drive up Buffalo Pass Rd. to Dry Lake Campground on the left. Park in the large lot across the road. *Dogs can be off leash.*

Begin by walking on a service road just past the campground sign. When the road forks, stay right; you'll come to a gate barring vehicle traffic as well as a small wooden "Soda Creek" sign. After this point, the road turns into a smooth, gentle trail, descending gradually through aspen and ferns toward Soda Creek. When you reach a three-way junction, stay right to follow the trail (though you should consider detouring down the middle path to allow your dog a dip in the creek). You'll eventually reach a large meadow, prime dog frolicking ground and, during the summer, a first-rate place to view wildflowers. The trail, which begins to become less distinct, goes along the meadow's edge. The end of the meadow, where the trail pretty much peters out, makes a good turnaround point.

 Steamboat Ski Area. You and your dog can speed on up the Silver Bullet Gondola, which goes about halfway up the mountain, and hike back down. Most of the summer trail network is open to mountain bikers, so if you're out on foot, your best options are the hikers-only **Vista Nature Trail**, which makes a 1.25-mile loop around near the gondola, and the **Thunderhead Hiking Trail**, an approximately 3-mile trip down to the gondola base area. *Though this is actually National Forest land, the resort requests that you keep your dog leashed.*

The gondola operates daily from 10 A.M. to 4 P.M. during June, July, and August. After Labor Day, it runs on weekends only until mid-September. There is a fee.

 Spring Creek. 8 miles round-trip. From downtown Steamboat Springs, drive northwest on 3rd St. for one block to Fish Creek Falls Rd. on the right. Turn left onto Amethyst shortly after, then right onto E. Spring St. (which is E. Maple on the left). Park along the road. *Dogs must be leashed.*

"All the dogs come here," says one local dog owner about Spring Creek. Unfortunately, this has also resulted in a bit of controversy over leash laws—there are a lot of noncomplying dogs, and property owners near the trail have been getting upset. So make sure you do your bit not to make things worse. The trail is also a popular mountain-biking route, so ask Rover to keep a nose out for riders flying downhill. The first part of the hike follows a single-lane dirt road for about a half mile to the Spring Creek Reservoirs. The reservoirs make a pleasant destination in themselves, and a separate footpath encircles them. After passing the reservoirs, the road narrows and bends to the left; follow the signs to the right to access a newer, rerouted section of the trail. As you ascend the Spring Creek drainage via a consistent, but moderate, climb, you'll crisscross the creek several times over a series of bridges, giving your dog ample opportunity to hydrate. The Steamboat Ski Area becomes visible to the right as you gain elevation. The trail ends partway up Buffalo Pass, in a parking area across from the Dry Lake Campground.

 Yampa Core Trail. Runs for 4 miles along the Yampa River, from West Lincoln Park (next to the

Dream Island mobile home park) to Walton Creek Rd., east of town. *Dogs must be leashed.*

This paved recreation path runs along the river, passing by the southeastern edge of downtown Steamboat Springs, the Howlsen Hill Ski Area, and the rodeo grounds before reaching a more undeveloped area in riparian habitat. It's a great spot for a close-to-town stroll with your dog—just keep an eye out for bicyclists and in-line skaters.

Ski-town watchdogs. (photo by Tim Hancock)

Fish Creek Falls. A little under a mile round-trip to view the falls. From Lincoln Ave. in downtown Steamboat Springs, head northwest on 3rd St. (you'll see a sign for Fish Creek Falls). Take a right at the next block, which is Fish Creek Falls Rd. The falls are 4 miles ahead. *Dogs must be leashed.*

Park in the free parking lot and walk a quarter mile to the main (pay) parking lot. From there, take the gravel-surface Fish Creek Falls National Recreation Trail (the other two trails are paved) to the Historic Fish Creek Bridge, where your dog can salivate at the 280-foot-high waterfall. Reward him with a dip in the creek. If you're feeling ambitious (and are suitably prepared), follow the trail 2 miles farther to the Upper Falls or 5 miles total to Long Lake, at 9,850 feet. As dogs are allowed off leash on this National Forest trail, this could turn your outing into a three- or four-wag hike.

North Park

Colorado State Forest. There is a park entrance off Highway 14 West, about 20 miles from Walden and just before Gould. Highway 14 also runs through the park before reaching Cameron Pass. *Dogs must be leashed.*

The forest is actually a state park, and with 70,000 mostly undeveloped acres along 28 miles from north to south, it's by far the biggest of Colorado's state parks.

There are only five established hiking trails throughout the park. The 2-mile round-trip **Lake Agnes Trail** is the most heavily used, as it's short and incredibly scenic, nestled near the 12,400-foot Nokhu Crags and 12,940-foot Mt. Richthoven, the highest peak in the Never Summer Range in nearby Rocky Mountain National Park. The 10-mile round-trip **American Lakes Trail** is nearby. The trailheads for these hikes are off Highway 14 toward Cameron Pass. The least-used trails are those to **Clear Lake** (10 miles round-trip) and **Kelly Lake** (6 miles round-trip). Both lakes are at timberline, and you'll hike through pine and spruce forest to reach them. The trailhead is accessed via a road heading north shortly after the park headquarters. The **Ruby Jewel Lake Trail** is a relatively short 3 miles round-trip if you're able to get all the way up the four-wheel-drive access road to the trailhead. As this road is often not passable to the end, you'll likely end up parking somewhere along it and extending the hike's mileage. During any of these hikes, but especially the less-traveled ones, keep an eye out for moose, the park's "specialty."

Cycling for Canines

The **Mad Creek Trail** (see "Tail-Rated Trails") is a scenic ride you can take Fido on. So is the **Coulton Creek Trail**, off Seedhouse Rd. (County Rd. 64) north of Steamboat, though you'll want to ride it as an out-and-back rather than as a loop to avoid 1.5 miles of road riding. A network of jeep roads just west of **Steamboat Lake State Park** and north of **Sand Mountain** is a less-frequented cycling area: Begin on Forest Rd. 42, which runs west out of County Rd. 62, and follow Forest Rd. 480 to the left and around to make a loop. The top of **Rabbit Ears Pass** offers a couple of biking options: You and your dog can take an approximately 6-mile round-trip ride to the distinctive **Rabbit Ears Peak** by following Forest Service Rd. 291, which branches out of Forest Service Rd. 311 past the Dumont Lake Campground (park at the beginning of Rd. 291). Or drive farther on Forest Rd. 311 to the Base Camp trailhead (Trail 1102). From here you can ride to **Fishhook Lake, Lost Lake,** and **Lake Elmo,** up to a 6-mile round-trip.

POWDERHOUNDS

Rabbit Ears Pass is one of the most popular ski and snowshoe areas around Steamboat. Several trails start here, including the **West Summit Loop,** a 3.5-mile tour that doesn't cross any avalanche terrain. There are also trails off **Seedhouse Rd.** (County Rd. 64) north of Steamboat, out of the **Hinman Park and Seedhouse Campgrounds**—watch out for snowmobilers in this area. And the road itself is unplowed after a certain point, providing a wide, gentle grade for skiing or snowshoeing. Also see **High Meadows Ranch** in "Creature Comforts."

CREATURE COMFORTS

Unless otherwise stated, dogs should not be left unattended in the room or cabin.

Clark

$$ Hahn's Peak Guest Ranch, 60880 County Rd. 129 (7 miles north of Clark), 970-879-5878. You and your dog can stay in one of four rustic cabins, all fully equipped, that sleep from two to eight guests. There's a $5 fee per night for a dog. The ranch does not have a strict leash law, though if a lot of other dogs are around,

you might be asked to restrain yours. The ranch offers guided horseback rides in summer and snowmobile tours in the winter, and a general store is on the premises. Open year-round except for a few weeks in November and in April.

$$–$$$ Dutch Creek Guest Ranch, 61565 RCR 62, 970-879-8519 (800-778-8519). The ranch, on 100 acres across from Steamboat Lake and bordered by Routt National Forest, offers a total of nine modern, fully furnished log cabins and A-frames. Dogs are allowed for a $5 fee per dog, per night, with a limit of two dogs per unit. The owners ask that you keep your dog leashed when around the main lodge and cabins and the horse area. Open year-round.

Columbine

$–$$ Columbine Cabins, 64505 County Rd. 129, 970-879-5522. Columbine, located about 30 miles north of Steamboat, was once an active mining town. The only buildings that remain are these historic cabins (the oldest is from about 1890), which have been renovated to accommodate guests, and a general store. The thirteen rustic cabins are furnished and vary in their amenities: Most have wood-burning stoves to cook on as well as hotplates, though a few have more modern kitchen facilities; most rely on the central showerhouse for bathing and toilet facilities; and a few lack running water. There's a $5 fee per night, per dog. It'll be a step back in time for you, and your dog is sure to enjoy the surrounding Routt National Forest and miles of trails nearby. Bring your skis or snowshoes to explore in the winter. Open year-round.

Cowdrey

$ Cowdrey Store, Trout Camp & Cafe, 41489 Highway 125, 970-723-8248. This is the only business in Cowdrey, so it'll be hard to miss. Five rustic cabins are for rent; they all have kitchens but use a central bathhouse. If your dog sleeps on the bed, you'll need to provide a blanket to put under him. Open year-round.

Gould

$ North Park KOA, 53337 Highway 14, 970-723-4310 (800-KOA-3596). Dogs are allowed in the Kamping Kabins (you'll need to supply your own bedding and cooking gear), and they must be kept leashed when outside. Open year-round.

$ Powderhorn Cabins, 35336 County Rd. 21, 970-723-4359. There are fourteen cabins, all fully furnished and with kitchens; the "rustic" ones have use of a central bathhouse, and the "modern" ones have their own bathrooms. A $10 deposit is required for a dog, in addition to a $2 fee per night. You'll need to keep your dog leashed on the property. Open May 15 to November 15.

Kremmling

$ Bob's Western Motel, 110 West Park Ave., 970-724-3266.

Oak Creek

$ Oak Creek Motel, 400 Willow Bend, 970-736-2343. You can walk your dog off leash on the 1.5-acre property.

$$$ High Meadows Ranch, 20505 RCR 16 (southeast of Stagecoach Reservoir), 970-736-8416 (800-457-4453). This ranch, about 20 miles from Steamboat, is a perfect place for a getaway with Fido in tow. It's situated on 140 acres, which your dog can check out leash-free with you. Two attractive, modern log buildings are available for guests, one with two bedrooms, two and a half baths, and kitchen and living areas; the other with three bedrooms, three baths, and kitchen and living areas. Both buildings have wood stoves as well as use of an outdoor hot tub. During the summer, the ranch offers a variety of horseback rides. In winter, you and your dog can explore 12 miles of groomed ski trails. You can leave your dog unattended inside, or he can stay in a small outside kennel with dog house. Meals (for humans) are available for an extra charge. Open year-round.

Steamboat Springs

$–$$ Nite's Rest Motel, 601 Lincoln Ave., 970-879-1212 (800-828-1780). Dogs are allowed year-round. Some units come with fully equipped kitchens.

$–$$ Nordic Lodge Motel, 1036 Lincoln Ave., 970-879-0531 (800-364-0331). There's a $10 one-time fee for a dog, and pets are permitted year-round. You can leave your dog unattended in the room as long as you're certain he'll remain well behaved.

$–$$ Rabbit Ears Motel, 201 Lincoln Ave., 970-879-1150 (800-828-7702). Your dog may not know what to make of the neon pink bunny head on the motel's sign. But he's welcome to sniff it out any time of the year.

$$ Best Western Ptarmigan Inn, 2304 Apres Ski Way, 970-879-1730 (800-538-7519). You can stay at this slopeside hotel with your dog during the summer only (from about the end of May to sometime in October). Because the gondola is open for summer hiking, there is still some advantage to being mountainside. The one-time fee for a dog is $10, and the hotel will try to put you in a ground-floor room for easy dog-walking access.

$$ Super 8 Motel, 3195 S. Lincoln Ave., 970-879-5230 (800-800-8000). The motel has designated pet rooms (nonsmoking as well as smoking) and requires either a $20 cash deposit or a credit-card imprint.

$$–$$$ Alpiner Lodge, 424 Lincoln Ave., 970-879-1430. Dogs are permitted throughout the year, though they're usually put in smoking rooms only. There's a $10 fee per night.

$$–$$$ Harbor Hotel, 703 Lincoln Ave., 970-879-1522 (800-543-8888). Dogs are allowed in the summer only (which is broadly defined as mid-April through mid-November), and only short-haired breeds get the nod. Moreover, only the motel units and one- and two-bedroom condos are dog friendly; the rooms in the historic hotel building are off-limits. You're able to leave your dog unattended in the room—you just won't get housekeeping service during that time. And you'll be conveniently located on Steamboat's main street.

$$–$$$ Holiday Inn, 3190 S. Lincoln Ave., 970-879-2250 (800-654-3944). Dogs are welcome year-round with a $25 deposit.

$$–$$$ Scandinavian Lodge, 2883 Burgess Creek Rd., 970-879-0517 (800-233-8102). The lodge consists of condos, from studios to three bedrooms. Dogs are allowed in eight of the units—those that have not been recently remodeled. If your dog has an affinity for 1970s-style ski digs, this is the place. And you can leave your pooch unattended inside.

$$$ Perry-Mansfield Log Cabins, 40755 County Rd. 36, 970-879-1060 (800-538-7519). These seven rustic cabins are located on the expansive grounds of the Perry-Mansfield Performing Arts Camp. If your dog is a budding thespian, he'll enjoy coming here. Though the cabins are open year-round, dogs are only permitted from the beginning of May through the end of October, for a $10 one-time fee. The fully equipped cabins have from two to five bedrooms and wood-burning stoves. Note that cabin reservations are taken through the Best Western Ptarmigan Inn in Steamboat.

$$$–$$$$ Sheraton Steamboat, 2200 Village Inn Court, 970-879-2220 (800-848-8878). Dogs are allowed year-round, in smoking rooms only, for a $50 one-time fee.

Walden

$ Chedsey Motel, 537 Main St., 970-723-8201. This small motel allows dogs for $5 extra per dog, per night.

$ Hoover Roundup Motel, 361 Main St., 970-723-4680. Dogs are allowed in most rooms; small dogs, under 20 pounds, are preferred. Sometimes the motel will make exceptions to the size policy, but if you have a large dog that sheds a lot, expect to get the thumbs-down.

$ North Park Motel, 625 Main St., 970-723-4271. All rooms have kitchenettes.

$ Village Inn Hotel, 409 Main St., 970-723-4378. No, you're not going to find pies and skillet dishes here. But if you're suffering from altitude sickness, the friendly owner may whip up some homemade chicken-noodle soup for you. The small hotel (eleven rooms) dates from the 1930s, and dogs are welcome for $5 extra per night. You can leave your dog unattended in the room as long as he's quiet and doesn't scratch on the door, and he can also sniff around the large yard leash-free.

$ Westside Motel, 441 LaFever, 970-723-8589. You can leave your dog unattended in the room.

Campgrounds

State Park campgrounds: **Colorado State Forest,** off Highway 14 near Gould (104 sites; note that dogs are not allowed in the primitive cabins available for rental at North Michigan Reservoir or the Lake Agnes trailhead); **Stagecoach State Park,** 17 miles southeast of Steamboat Springs on County Rd. 14 off Highway 131 (100 sites); **Pearl Lake State Park,** 26 miles north of Steamboat Springs, via County Rd. 129 to County Rd. 209 (40 sites); **Steamboat Lake State Park,** 27 miles north of Steamboat Springs, via County Rd. 129 to County Rd. 62 (182 sites).

National Forest campgrounds: **Hinman Park Campground,** 20 miles north of Steamboat Springs (13 sites), and **Seedhouse Campground,** 22 miles (25 sites), are off Seedhouse Rd., via County Rd. 129 north; **Dry Lake Campground,** 6 miles east of Steamboat Springs (8 sites), and **Summit Lake Campground,** 15 miles east of town (16 sites), are both on Buffalo Pass Rd.; **Meadows Campground,** 15 miles southeast of Steamboat Springs (30 sites), **Walton Creek Campground,** 18 miles (16 sites), and **Dumont Lake Campground,** 22 miles (22 sites), are all off Highway 40, on Rabbit Ears Pass; **Big Creek Lakes Campground,** west of Cowdrey via County Rd. 6 and Forest Rd. 600 (54 sites); **Aspen Campground** (7 sites) and **Pines Campground** (11 sites) are both on Forest Rd. 740, just outside of Gould.

Private campgrounds: North Park KOA (see "Creature Comforts")

WORTH A PAWS

The Silver Bullet Gondola. Bring your dog aboard Steamboat Ski Area's gondola for a bird's-eye view of the surrounding valley. You can either hike down or make a return trip on the gondola. See "Tail-Rated Trails" for more details.

Felix and Fido, 635 Lincoln, Steamboat Springs, 970-870-6400. Felix and Fido bills itself as a dog and cat boutique store. Though your dog may just turn up his nose at the abundance of cat-related paraphernalia, he'll love sniffing out the selection of unique collars and leashes, bowls, dog packs, dog booties, treats, and squeaky toys. You'll enjoy browsing among the dog-theme items, including clothing, jewelry, accessories, and knicknacks—more than 125 different breeds of dogs are represented.

DOGGIE DAYCARE
Steamboat Springs

Mt. Werner Veterinary Hospital, 35825 E. Highway 40, 970-879-3486. $13.50/day. Open 9 A.M.–5:30 P.M., Monday to Friday; 9 A.M.–noon, Saturday. Weekend day boarding available by appointment.

Steamboat Veterinary Hospital, 30278 W. Highway 40, 970-879-1049. $11.50/day. Open 7:30 A.M.–6 P.M., Monday to Friday; 8 A.M.–noon, Saturday. Weekend day boarding available by appointment.

PET PROVISIONS
Steamboat Springs

Elk River Farm and Feed, 40805 County Rd. 129, 970-879-5383

Moose's Ark Pet Shop, 211 3rd. St., 970-879-8558

Paws 'n Claws 'n Things, 1250 S. Lincoln Ave. (in Sundance Plaza), 970-879-6092

CANINE ER
Steamboat Springs

Mt. Werner Veterinary Hospital, 35825 E. Highway 40, 970-879-3486. Open 9 A.M.–5:30 P.M., Monday to Friday; 9 A.M.–noon, Saturday.

Pet Kare Clinic, Sundance Plaza, 970-879-5273. Open 8:30 A.M.–5 P.M., Monday to Friday; 9 A.M.–noon, Saturday.

Steamboat Veterinary Hospital, 30278 W. Highway 40, 970-879-1049. Open 7:30 A.M.–6 P.M., Monday to Friday; 8 A.M.–noon, Saturday.

RESOURCES

Bureau of Land Management, 1116 Park Ave., Kremmling, 970-724-3437

Hahn's Peak/Bears Ears Ranger District, Routt National Forest, 925 Weiss Dr., Steamboat Springs, 970-879-1870

North Park Chamber of Commerce, Main St., Walden, 970-723-4600

North Park Ranger District, Routt National Forest, 612 5th St., Walden, 970-723-8204

Parks Ranger District, Routt National Forest, 210 S. 6th, Kremmling, 970-724-9004

The Ski Haus, at 1450 S. Lincoln Ave. in Steamboat Springs (970-879-0385)—good selection of trail guides and maps to the area

Steamboat Springs Chamber Resort Association, 1255 S. Lincoln Ave., Steamboat Springs, 970-879-0880 (www.steamboat-chamber.com)

Yampa Ranger District, Routt National Forest, 300 Roselawn Ave., Yampa, 970-638-4516

9

Summit County

THE BIG SCOOP

Summit County is somewhat of a dog paradise, with plenty of great hiking, mountain biking, and skiing opportunities as well as a variety of accommodations that actively welcome four-legged guests. When Denver or other areas along the Front Range become a bit too warm midsummer for those stuck with a permanent fur coat, mountain relief is but an hour's drive away among the towns of Silverthorne, Dillon, Frisco, and Breckenridge.

All of the principal Summit County towns have leash laws within their city limits. On county land, your dog can be off leash if he stays within ten feet of you and is under voice control.

TAIL-RATED TRAILS

What follows are but a few recommendations out of the many hiking options in the region. For more ideas, consult *The New Summit Hiker and Ski Touring Guide*, by Mary Ellen Gilliland.

 Chihuahua Gulch. 6 miles round-trip. From Dillon, head east on Highway 6, past Keystone Resort. Exit onto Montezuma Rd. About 4.5 miles from the exit, turn into a parking area on the left (across from the Paradox Lodge). Peru Creek Rd. begins just beyond the parking area. Drive 2.1 miles to a parking pullout on the right; the trailhead is on the left. *Dogs can be off leash.*

With a name like Chihuahua, the hike begs exploration by dogs. When I brought

Clover and her hiking companion, Tundra, here, they had a blast on this spectacularly beautiful trail that ascends between the backside of Arapahoe Basin Ski Area and Grays and Torreys Peaks, a pair of 14,000-foot mountains, to Chihuahua Lake. Because the hike involves several stream crossings, it's best to wait until the spring runoff has subsided before tackling it. Begin by climbing steadily up a four-wheel-drive road. Stay left at a fork, which will bring you to the first stream to ford. The ascent levels off as you enter a vast meadow, with two more stream crossings. After the beaver ponds, take the left trail fork and stay left again after another stream crossing. At the end of the meadow, the trail resumes its climb. The final approach to the lake involves scrambling up a steep, but short, talus slope to the left. You'll first reach a small pond; continue downslope to reach the emerald-green lake, which shimmers at the base of a cirque of rocky peaks.

 Wilder Gulch. 6 miles round-trip. Turn off I-70 at the Vail Pass rest area and park by the buildings. It can be a bit tricky to find the trailhead from the rest area. Walk down toward a small hexagonal building (not the rest area concession building, which is also hexagonal; this is a small pumphouse farther downhill, toward Copper Mountain). Stand on the access road uphill from the building and look for a small paved path on the right that ultimately leads to the bikeway. From the top of this path you'll also see the faint outline of a footpath through the grass that goes down a hill, crosses a brook, and climbs a gentle hill on the other side. Follow this small path for half a mile; it will bring you to Wilder Gulch. (Though you can also access the trail from the bikeway, you'd spend the first half mile of your hike uncomfortably close to the interstate.) *Dogs can be off leash.*

Turn right at the junction with the Wilder Gulch Trail, which climbs gradually along Wilder Creek. You'll ascend through wildflower-studded meadows surrounded by lodgepole pine. Stop occasionally to enjoy the views of Ptarmigan Hill at the head of the gulch ("hill" is definitely a misnomer), and Jacque Peak, Copper Mountain, and the Tenmile Range to the east. Eventually you'll come to an expansive meadow. Here the slope intensifies somewhat as it climbs through cool and fragrant stands of spruce. If your dog's a mycophile, let him know to keep an eye out for the big brown caps of boletus mushrooms, which grow in profusion in August and September. In about another mile you'll come to a junction with four-wheel-drive Wearyman Road; if you're game to keep going, turn left and climb for another 2 miles to Ptarmigan Pass, which offers great views of the Gore and Tenmile Ranges.

 Crystal Lake. 4 miles round-trip. Drive south from Breckenridge on Highway 9 for 2.5 miles to Spruce Creek Rd. (you'll see a sign for the Crown subdivision). Turn right and continue on Spruce Creek Rd. for 1.2 miles to the trailhead parking area. *Dogs can be off leash.*

This popular hike follows a jeep track up to Lower Crystal Lake, nestled at the base of a cirque. Begin by walking along Spruce Creek Rd. for about a quarter mile, to where the Crystal Rd. takes off to the right. The wide, rocky trail ascends gradually through forested terrain of lodgepole pine, Douglas fir, blue spruce, and aspen.

Lucy and Clover on a Summit County powder day. (photo by Cindy Hirschfeld)

As you hike, you'll become aware of Crystal Creek in the gully to the left, though it remains out of paw-dipping range. Not too far from the trailhead, you'll pass the Burro Trail coming in from the north. About a mile later, the Wheeler National Recreation Trail crosses your route. At this point, the trail breaks out above treeline and follows a short, steep ascent onto a shelf. You may glimpse lovely Francie's Cabin off to the right, part of the Summit Huts Association and available for winter use by reservation only (but dogs are not allowed). After the ascent, it's pretty much a level, straight shot to the lake, through wildflower-filled meadows bordered by craggy Mount Helen to the south. At the lake, your dog can play in the water and sniff out the remains of an old cabin while you savor the scenery. If you're inspired to make the hike longer, it's possible to climb up on a trail that winds north and then southwest to Upper Crystal Lake, hidden from sight at the base of Crystal Peak, which rises to the west from Lower Crystal Lake.

 North Tenmile Trail. 4 miles round-trip to the Eagles Nest Wilderness boundary. Head west on I-70 past Silverthorne to Exit 201. Stay right at the end of the exit ramp and park in the gravel lot by the trailhead. If coming from Frisco, drive west on Main St. and cross under I-70 to reach the parking area.

Dogs can be off leash up until the Wilderness boundary.

This pleasant hike follows an old mining road, alternating between stands of pine and spruce and grassy clearings. Follow the dirt road from the parking area. Right before a large green water tank on the left, take the road that branches off to the right. At the next junction, either option works; they both rejoin shortly after. Then stay right at a fork shortly afterward, as the road takes a short climb. From here on, it's easy going. The trail parallels North Tenmile Creek, with many good access points for dogs, including a crystal-clear beaver pond. The Wilderness boundary was our turnaround point, though you could continue for another 1.5 miles to an intersection with the Gore Range Trail. If you do keep hiking, remember to leash up Fido once you cross that Wilderness line.

Tundra (center) and pals stick three tongues to the wind on Quandary Peak. (photo by Cindy Hirschfeld)

 Rainbow Lake. Approximately 2 miles round-trip. From Main St. in Frisco, go south on 2nd St. until its end; cross the bike path and, if you're driving, park in the dirt lot. *Dogs can be off leash.*

This short hike is great for a close-to-town canine workout. It's also a good place to spot columbine in July and August. Begin by taking a right on the paved bike path, toward Breckenridge and Keystone, *from* the parking lot (keep your dog leashed when on the path). Walk about an eighth of a mile to an opening in the trees, on the right. Then go straight across a clearing and pick up the wide path that leads to a boardwalk across fragile wetlands. After crossing a stream, the trail ascends gradually through lodgepole pine, aspen, and blue spruce. You'll cross an old road and another trail before reaching the lake. For a loop option, look for the blue diamond marker at the right of the lakeside clearing. Almost immediately, you'll come to another dirt road; take a right. Stay to the right when the trail converges with another road, right at the fork shortly after, and right at the junction that follows. When you pass a small wooden post on the right, marked with arrows, turn left, and you'll be back at the original trail on which you came up.

 Tenderfoot Trail. 2.5 miles round-trip. Head east on Highway 6 from Silverthorne. At the stoplight turnoff toward Dillon, make a left, then an immediate sharp right. Signed parking for the trail is 0.6 mile ahead on the right. *Dogs can be off leash.*

In this trail's favor are its accessibility and views. However, the constant drone of traffic from I-70 reminds you that you haven't escaped civilization. This is a dry area, so bring water. Walk up the hairpin curve in the road and past the water treatment plant to access the trail. Follow a dirt road for a quarter mile to a trail sign pointing left and uphill. Wend your way through an odd gate contraption, and you'll be on the trail. As you hike, you'll enjoy wonderful views of Buffalo Mountain and the Gore Range to the north, as well as Dillon Reservoir and Peaks 1 through 10 beyond. The trail switchbacks gently up Tenderfoot Mountain, first through sagebrush, then aspen, and, finally, lodgepole pine. The second bench along the trail, from which you can see Breckenridge and Keystone Resorts, is a good turnaround point. After this, the trail gets considerably steeper and less maintained as it heads to the summit of Tenderfoot.

CYCLING FOR CANINES

Summit County is filled with great riding spots, and because many routes follow trails or old mining roads on National Forest property, they're also dog friendly, as long as you keep an eye on distance. **Wilder Gulch, Crystal Lake, Rainbow Lake,** and **North Tenmile Trail** up to the Wilderness boundary (see "Tail-Rated Trails" for more info) all make suitable dog rides. Or try an out-and-back on the jeep road along **Tenderfoot Mountain** (see Tenderfoot Trail in "Tail-Rated Trails"; keep following the dirt road you start out on instead of taking the trail uphill). You can also bike with your dog (with a gondola ride uphill if you're averse to climbing) at **Keystone Resort.**

For more ideas, check out *The Mountain Bike Guide to Summit County*, by Laura Rossetter.

POWDERHOUNDS

There are many excellent backcountry ski and snowshoe trails throughout Summit County. Some routes that follow roads, which means more room for both skiers/snowshoers and dogs to maneuver, include **Peru Creek, Webster Pass,** and **Deer Creek,** off the Montezuma Rd.; **Keystone Gulch; French Gulch** and **Sally Barber Mine,** outside of Breckenridge; **North Tenmile Trail** near Frisco; and **Mayflower Gulch,** south of Copper Mountain via Highway 91. Refer to *Skiing Colorado's Backcountry*, by Brian Litz and Kurt Lankford, for detailed route descriptions.

Breckenridge Nordic Center, 1200 Ski Hill Rd., and **Frisco Nordic Center, 18454 Highway 9 (on Dillon Reservoir), 970-453-6855.** Though dogs are not allowed on the regular groomed trails, each center has devoted one ungroomed trail to skiers or snowshoers with dogs in tow. At Breckenridge, it's the 3.5-kilometer **Loop de Poop;** at Frisco, the 1-kilometer **Fire Hydrant Loop** (and the owners hope to eventually expand both). You'll need to buy a trail pass (Fido is free) and keep your dog on his leash (an extendable/retractable leash comes in handy here).

CREATURE COMFORTS

As you get into ski resort territory, it gets more difficult to find lodgings that accommodate dogs. For example, none of the hotels or condos at Copper Mountain or Keystone Resorts accept pets. The grumpy man behind the desk at the Breckenridge visitor center told me assuredly that absolutely no place in town takes pets. However, as you'll see below, there are actually several that will welcome your dog as a guest. A little persistent research pays off! And if accommodations are hard to come by, try the town of Fairplay, about a half hour south of Breckenridge on the other side of Hoosier Pass.

Unless otherwise stated, dogs should not be left unattended in the room or cabin.

Breckenridge

$–$$ Wayside Inn, 165 Tiger Rd., 970-453-5540 (800-927-7669). In addition to motel-style rooms, the inn has a condo that sleeps up to twelve guests. Dogs are permitted in both with either a $20 cash deposit or a credit-card imprint. And they'll be in good company, as four dogs call the inn home. You can leave your dog unattended inside, but housekeeping won't enter the room. And be sure to keep him on a leash when outside on the wooded property.

A visit to the Pika Bagel Shop (401 Main St. in Frisco and 500 S. Main in Breckenridge) will not only net you a tasty treat but one for Fido as well: The shops hand out day-old bagel pieces for dogs to nosh on.

$$$–$$$$ Tannhauser Condominiums, 420 S. Main St., 970-453-2136 (800-433-9217). Serviceable but not luxurious, these condos are conveniently located in downtown Breckenridge and, most important, your dog can stay too. Most of the one- and two-bedroom units in the complex allow pets with a $25 one-time fee. You can leave your dog unattended inside.

$$$$ Lodge and Spa at Breckenridge, 112 Overlook Dr., 970-453-9300 (800-736-1607). The lodge, located off the road to Boreas Pass, accepts "smaller" dogs with a $25 fee per night. You can leave your dog unattended in the well-appointed rooms, furnished in a rustic log theme, as long as he's well behaved and quiet. Two suites with kitchenettes are available.

Dillon

$$ Annabelle's Bed and Breakfast, 276 Snowberry Way, 970-468-2476. Annabelle's is in a residential neighborhood near Keystone Resort. Of the three rooms, one in particular is the likely location for a dog guest. Though you can leave your dog unattended in the room, the owner is happy to pet-sit, for a small fee, and keep him out of trouble.

$$ Best Western Ptarmigan Lodge, 652 Lake Dillon Dr., 970-468-2341 (800-842-5939). The motel, located across from the Dillon Marina and a lakeshore path, accepts dogs in two of its buildings for a $15 one-time fee per pet. You can leave your dog unattended in the room.

$$–$$$ Paradox Lodge, 5040 Montezuma Rd., 970-468-9445. Located just east of Keystone Resort on the road to the tiny town of Montezuma, the Paradox is close to a bevy of National Forest trails for hiking, biking, and nordic skiing. And the lodge itself sits on thirty-seven acres along the Snake River. Dogs may stay in the cabins, though not in the main lodge, with a maximum of two canines per cabin. There's a $10 fee per night, and you can leave your dog unattended in the cabin.

Fairplay

$ South Park Lodge, 801 Main, 719-836-3278. The motel allows dogs for $5 extra per night, though if your dog is clearly a nonshedder the fee is usually waived.

$–$$ Fairplay Hotel, 500 Main, 719-836-2565 (888-924-2200). This recently renovated, Victorian-era hotel is dog friendly, says the management, though dogs are usually relegated to the smoking rooms. The twenty-one rooms are furnished with antiques, and you can leave your dog unattended inside as long as he behaves responsibly.

$–$$ Western Inn Motel & RV Park, 490 W. Highway 285, 719-836-2026

$$ Hand Hotel Bed and Breakfast, 531 Front, 719-836-3595. Built as a hotel in the 1930s, the Hand was recently converted to a B&B. The eleven rooms, all with private bath, are individually decorated with a Western theme that commemorates Fairplay's history. One canine guest per room is preferred, and particularly quiet, well-mannered dogs may be left unattended inside.

Frisco

$–$$ Snowshoe Motel, 521 Main St., 970-668-3444 (800-445-8658). The motel has some designated pet rooms where dogs can stay for $5 extra per night and a $15 deposit. You can leave your dog unattended in the room if he's in a travel kennel and promises not to bark.

$$ The Finn Inn, Highwood Terrace, 970-668-5108. A homey B&B in a residential neighborhood, the Finn Inn tends to keep a low profile these days, but the owners do accept pets. And there's a resident dog, Mustaa, whom Clover took a shine to when we visited. Check with the owners about leaving your dog unattended inside.

$$ New Summit Inn, 1205 N. Summit Blvd., 970-668-3220 (800-745-1211). The motel accepts dogs with a $20 deposit, of which you'll get $15 back if your dog leaves the room damage-free.

$$–$$$$ **Best Western Lake Dillon Lodge,** 1202 N. Summit Blvd., 970-668-5094 (800-528-1234). Dogs are allowed in smoking rooms only, with a $50 deposit.

Heeney (Green Mountain Reservoir)

$ **Green Mountain Cabins,** 0255 County Rd. 1782, 970-724-9748. "Dog heaven" is how one of the managers of these cabins describes the area around Green Mountain Reservoir. These three rustic log cabins (you'll have to supply your own cooking utensils) are near the water and close to National Forest trails. You can leave your dog unattended in the cabins and exercise him off leash on the property. Open year-round.

$$ **Melody Lodge,** 1534 County Rd. 30, 970-468-8497 (888-8-MELODY). The lodge accepts "mature" dogs for $5 per night, per pet. There are three cabins as well as a two-bedroom suite in the main lodge building, and it's about a two-minute walk to the reservoir. You can leave your dog unattended inside, but you must keep him on a leash on the lodge's property. Open May to the end of November.

Silverthorne

$–$$ **First Interstate Inn,** 357 Blue River Parkway, 970-468-5170 (800-462-4667). The motel accepts small to medium-sized dogs for $5 extra per night.

$$ **Days Inn,** 580 Silverthorne Ln., 970-468-8661 (800-DAYS-INN). There's a $10 charge per dog, per night.

$$ **Home and Hearth Bed and Breakfast,** 1518 Rainbow Dr., 970-468-5541 (800-753-4386). Located in a residential neighborhood, this five-room B&B allows dogs on a case-by-case basis. If your dog passes muster, he can also hang out with the resident lab, Charlie.

$$–$$$ **Luxury Inn and Suites,** 540 Silverthorne Ln., 970-468-0800 (800-742-1972). Small dogs are permitted, as long as they stay in a travel kennel at all times, for a $5 fee per night.

Campgrounds

National Forest campgrounds: **Blue River Campground,** 9 miles north of Silverthorne off Highway 9 (24 sites); **Dillon Reservoir** has four campgrounds, for a total of 314 sites, plus one group campground; **Cataract Creek Campground** (4 sites), **Elliot Creek Campground** (64 sites), **McDonald Flats Campground** (13 sites), and **Prairie Point Campground** (44 sites) are all at Green Mountain Reservoir in Heeney.

WORTH A PAWS

Keystone Resort Gondola. Enjoy a scenic trip on the Keystone gondola with your dog. Once at the top, you can hike or bike down the mountain (or download on the gondola). *Dogs can be off leash.* The gondola runs from the end of June to the begining of September from 9:30 A.M.–7:00 P.M., Wednesday to Sunday, and 9:30 A.M.–3:30 P.M., Monday and Tuesday. Call the Keystone Activities Desk (970-496-4386) for info on ticket prices.

Canine 4K Walk/Run. This annual race, held the first Saturday of August, is a

Even dogs can pose for tourist shots. (photo by Cindy Hirschfeld)

fundraiser for LAPS, the League for Animals and People of the Summit. You and your leashed dog will follow a course that begins and ends at the Frisco Town Hall. Registration fee (around $20, slightly more on race day) includes a T-shirt for you and a bandanna for your canine companion. Participants also are encouraged to collect money from sponsors to turn in at the race. Following the race, stick around for the Mountain Mutt contest, in which your dog can vie for prizes in categories such as biggest and smallest dog and closest pet-owner lookalike. You can register in advance of the race at the Summit County Animal Shelter (970-669-3230) or at Frisco Town Hall; race-day registration will also be available. Your dog must show proof of current rabies vaccination to participate.

DOGGIE DAYCARE
Breckenridge
DnR Kennels, 0115 Gateway Dr. (SCR 950), 970-453-6708. $12/day. Open 8 A.M.–6 P.M., Monday to Saturday; 2–6 P.M., Sunday.

PET PROVISIONS
Frisco
The Barnyard, 104 Main, 970-668-0238

Pet Stuff, 310 Main, 970-668-2229

Silverthorne
Summit Feed and Mountain Supplies, 330 Warren Ave., 970-468-1669

CANINE ER
Frisco
Animal Hospital of the High Country (AAHA certified), 700 Granite St., 970-668-5544. Open 7:30 A.M.–6:30 P.M., Monday and Wednesday; 7:30 A.M.–5:30 P.M., Tuesday, Thursday, and Friday; 8 A.M.–noon, Saturday.

RESOURCES
Breckenridge Resort Chamber, 555 S. Columbine St., Breckenridge, 970-453-6018 (800-221-1091; www.gobreck.com)

Dillon Ranger District, White River National Forest, 680 Blue River Parkway, Silverthorne, 970-468-5400

Lake Dillon Resort Association, 121 Dillon Mall, Dillon, 970-468-6222 (800-365-6365)

South Park Ranger District, Pike and San Isabel National Forests, 320 Highway 285, Fairplay, 719-836-2031

Summit County Chamber of Commerce Visitor Centers: in Frisco at the intersection of Highway 9 and Main St. (head toward the lake), 970-668-2051; in Dillon on Labonte St. (turn right on the main road to Dillon off Highway 6 East)

10

Vail, Leadville, and Vicinity

THE BIG SCOOP

Situated smack-dab in the middle of the mountains, Vail and Leadville offer the avid outdoor canine lots of trail mileage to sniff out. The more refined dog might prefer Vail, with its faux-Tyrolian decor and upscale boutiques—and where the arm that reaches out to pet him is likely to be sporting a Rolex. The dog with an interest in Colorado's past will relish a visit to Leadville, whose ties to its mining roots are still strong. About the only place your dog won't enjoy is Beaver Creek Resort—because he can't. Dogs are not allowed anywhere in Beaver Creek unless they belong to property owners at the resort. Rumor has it that even Olympic gold medalist Picabo Street was deterred when she tried to bring her pooch along.

In Vail, dogs must be on a leash in Vail Village, Lionshead, and West Vail (specifically, the neighborhood around the Safeway); on any bike path; and in all public parks. Anywhere else in the city limits, as well as in unincorporated areas of Eagle County, dogs can be under voice control as long as they're within ten feet of their owners. In Leadville, a leash law is in effect within the town and in Lake County. There's also a law against public tethering, meaning you can't tie up your dog in front of a store or restaurant, for example, and leave him unattended, even for a few moments.

TAIL-RATED TRAILS

If you're looking for a place to wander in Vail that's close at hand, bring your dog to the paved walkway/bike path that follows **Gore Creek** (from Vail Village to Lionshead, the route parallels W. Meadow Dr. instead of the creek). Or check out the **Vail Nature Center,** next to Ford Park, where a network of four short interpretive trails goes through a meadow and riparian habitat (your dog can be under voice command here). For more hiking options in the beautiful mountains surrounding Vail, refer to *The Vail Hiker and Ski Touring Guide,* by Mary Ellen Gilliland. In Leadville, stop by the Chamber of Commerce (see "Resources") and pick up a copy of the Chamber-issued hiking guide.

Leadville

 Douglass City and Hagerman Tunnel. 5.5 miles round-trip. From Highway 24 in Leadville, take 6th St. west. In approximately 2 miles, you'll come to a T-intersection (Leadville's recreation center will be on your right). Turn right and continue straight on the paved road to Turquoise Lake. As you reach the lake, continue past the dam. You'll climb two separate hills that afford wonderful overlooks of the lake before coming to Forest Rd. 105, a dirt road bearing to the left. Turn here. You'll drive for approximately 3.5 miles before coming to a sharp turn in the road; proceed another quarter mile to a parking area on the right. Across the road is the trailhead and a sign describing the Colorado Midland Railroad. *Dogs can be off leash.*

This hike will let your dog sniff around one of the ghost towns for which Colorado is renowned. Many of these former towns have some connection to the state's fabled mining past. This one does, too, but in a roundabout way.

Douglass City was a wild and woolly construction camp built high above Turquoise Lake and Leadville to house workers building the Hagerman Tunnel. The tunnel was built in 1888 and used until 1897 as a route for the Colorado Midland Railroad between the silver mines of Aspen and the smelters of Leadville. At 11,528 feet, the tunnel was the highest ever built, featuring an 1,100-foot-long curved trestle (both the trestle and the tunnel were engineering marvels at the time). The path to Douglass City and the Hagerman tunnel follows the former railroad grade.

The trail starts out over rough cobble and rocks, but it soon smooths out to a gradual doubletrack. Throughout the ascent, you'll enjoy spectacular views of the valley you just traveled through as well as the northern flank of Mount Massive. After about a mile the grade comes to an abrupt end; this is where the long trestle once stood. If you look hard, you can see where the railroad grade resumes 1,100 feet across the valley. Don't hike to it! Instead, turn around to see a small trail climbing the hill to the left 50 feet behind you. Continue up this trail, which is a bit steeper and more rocky. At the four-way intersection in the trail shortly after, turn left to take a shortcut to the site of Douglass City. No standing structures re-

Susan Hill pauses with Inkah and Yuki near Turquoise Lake. (photo by Alyssa Pumphrey)

main; in fact, many of the "buildings" of Douglass City were tents. Eight saloons and one dance hall were among the first buildings up and among the busiest as long as the work lasted. You'll see a few of their remains among the rocks and wildflowers.

Continue climbing past the town, toward a steep rock wall. Soon you'll come to remnants of the tunnel-making operation; high above and to the right is the old railroad grade leading to the tunnel. Follow the trail up the hill to the railroad grade and turn left. In less than a hundred yards you'll see the entrance to the tunnel, and, just inside, ice. The tunnel was used only briefly by the Colorado Midland. It cost James J. Hagerman, the tycoon who owned the rail line, millions to construct and almost as much to keep open. The high elevation and fierce winter conditions caused so many problems that the Midland was soon routed through another tunnel, the Busk-Ivanhoe (now called the Carlton), which allowed the trains easier passage. Enjoy the coolness of the tunnel's mouth and the quiet dripping sounds from deep within. Your pooch may be tempted at the sight of emerald-green Opal Lake below, which can provide a welcome splash on the hike down.

 Turquoise Lake Trail. Runs 6.4 miles along the lakeshore. From Highway 24 in Leadville, take 6th St. west. In approximately 2 miles, you'll come to a T-intersection (Leadville's recreation center will be on your right). Turn right and continue straight on the paved road to Turquoise Lake. As you reach the lake, continue straight toward the dam, but don't drive onto it. Park at the pullout on the left immediately before it. Cross the road and start down the singletrack that contours along the shoreline. The other main access point for the trail is at the May Queen Campground, though you can also pick up the trail at various points along it. *Dogs can be off leash* (though you may want to leash your dog when in the vicinity of the campgrounds the trail skirts).

This beautiful trail is a great hike. It never strays farther than 25 yards from the water—most times it's a lot closer than that—and winds around several secluded coves with sparkling water and sandy beaches. During the summer, the trail is fairly popular, especially close to the dam. Expect to see plenty of other hikers and cyclists if you go on a holiday weekend. (Hint: Go off-season if you can. On a beautiful autumn day, we had the trail completely to ourselves.) You'll savor spectacular views of the two highest peaks in the Rocky Mountains, Mounts Elbert (14,433 feet) and Massive (14,421 feet), which dominate the skyline across the water. After approximately 4 miles, you'll encounter the remains of some abandoned mines—remnants of Leadville's rip-roaring mining heyday. A sign alongside the trail enumerates many of the dangers posed by the abandoned mine shafts and suggests you turn around here. Don't, but take the warnings to heart, and make sure your dog (and you) stay on the trail, which passes safely through the dilapidated remains. (While you're in Leadville, you may want to stop by the National Mining Hall of Fame and Museum, 120 W. 9th St., which offers fascinating displays and artifacts on mines and mining. Your dog won't be able to accompany you inside, however.) After 6.4 miles, the trail reaches the May Queen Campground at the northern terminus of the lake. The Charles Boustead tunnel empties water collected from the Fryingpan River into this end of Turquoise Lake. The tunnel is one of many that brings water from the Western Slope underneath the Continental Divide for burgeoning Front Range population centers. Water, it turns out, is ultimately the most precious resource—more valuable than all of the gold and silver ever mined in this area.

Vail

Piney Creek Trail. 5.5 miles round-trip. From the Vail exit (176) off I-70, take the North Frontage Rd. west. After approximately one mile, turn right onto Red Sandstone Rd. You'll climb through a few switchbacks and come to a dirt road bearing left (Red Sandstone No. 700). Turn here and follow the signs to Piney River Ranch (12 miles). Park in the public parking lot outside of the fence. Begin by walking through, or around, the gate and follow the road toward the lake. As you approach the water, turn left onto a well-used trail. This is the Piney Creek Trail. Get ready for an amazing hike! *Dogs must be leashed (this is Wilderness area).*

This is a hike with a view: You'll be entering a broad valley flanked by cliffs of red sandstone. As the trail contours along the lake's left shore, you may marvel at the sheer rock walls of the Gore Range reflected in the water. You'll most likely see waterfowl and maybe spot the beaver that live in the lodge at the east end of the lake. As you near the east shore, where the creek enters the lake, you'll see a sign and trail register indicating you are about to enter the Eagles Nest Wilderness Area. After approximately a quarter mile, bear right at the fork (the left one goes to Soda Lakes). Enjoy the vistas of rock walls ahead of you; aspen on the slopes to your left (incandescent in autumn!); and spruce, fir, and pine across the valley. The rock has weathered into rugged spires, sharp horns, knife-edge ridges, and jagged arêtes, offering a striking and photogenic backdrop.

After about 2 miles you'll come to another fork in the trail. Bear left, which will start to bring you up and around the cirque you've been admiring throughout your journey. You'll enter a forest of aspen and pine, which should send your dog's nose into overdrive; the trail will become a bit more rugged as it climbs through the rocks and trees. As you climb you'll encounter several forks along the trail; stay right on the main-traveled route. It will soon bring you along a ridge, crossing several small streams, and, ultimately, to a wonderfully scenic overlook of the valley and Piney Lake beyond. You may be tempted to stop here, but less than a quarter mile away is Piney Creek Falls. It's a bit of a scramble to the falls, but their ambience and the always spectacular vistas make it well worth your collective efforts. If you've been hiking during midafternoon, turn around periodically on the way back, as the steep rock walls turn lustrous hues of apricot and orange as the afternoon light slowly fades.

 Booth Creek Falls Trail. 4 miles round-trip to the falls; 12 miles round-trip to Booth Lake. Take the East Vail exit (180) off I-70 and head west along the Frontage Rd. In less than one mile you'll see Booth Falls Rd. on your right. Drive to the trailhead at the end of the road (0.25 mile) and park. Please be careful not to block or park in the nearby driveways. *Dogs must be leashed (this is Wilderness area).*

Climb about a quarter mile through open, wildflower-studded meadows to exit the noise and bustle of the Vail Valley, and you'll soon travel through cool stands of aspen, white fir, and blue spruce (Colorado's state tree). Keep an eye out for hummingbirds, which are plentiful in the lower areas during summer. You'll hear the rush of Booth Creek to your left as you climb high above it. After 2 miles the trail opens up to reveal vistas of the classic U-shape of this glacially sculpted valley, with the creek bed etching a deep notch at its base. You'll also see evidence of recent avalanches all around.

Before reaching the falls you'll cross two smaller creeks, providing your dog with the opportunity to cool off. After approximately 2 miles you'll reach Booth Falls, which are quite impressive as they cascade 80 feet through a sheer notch in the schist. You'll definitely want to linger here on one of the many perches that loom directly over the plunge.

You might be tempted to turn around at the falls—don't. The falls are a portal to the incredibly beautiful high-alpine environment beyond. Immediately after the falls the trail winds directly alongside the brook through cool and fragrant spruce groves, then climbs somewhat more steeply for a short stretch. Soon it brings you through the grass and wildflowers of a high mountain meadow, which is surrounded by the steep-sided mountains that make up the Gore Range.

Ultimately you'll come to Booth Lake, which sits at the base of a high cirque, surrounded by towering walls of schist—the predominant rock in the Gore Range. In addition to being breathtakingly beautiful and a great place to kick back, it also offers good fishing (and swimming for those with a fur suit).

 Vail Mountain. Though dogs are not allowed to ride the gondola, you can take Rover hiking on the mountain's summertime trail network. A summer trail map lays out the options, and the hiking trails are separate from the biking trails so that pedestrians and downhill cyclists don't suffer any overly close encounters. Pick up the **Berrypicker Trail** behind the gondola loading station in Lionshead. The trail climbs for 5.5 miles to Eagles Nest, where you can grab a cold libation and enjoy live music on the deck throughout the summer. You can also find water for your dog here (the hike itself is dry). You'll be treated to spectacular views of Mount of the Holy Cross and the surrounding peaks in the wilderness area. *Dogs can be off leash, as the mountain is National Forest land.*

 West Grouse Creek. About 10 miles round-trip. Take the Minturn exit off I-70 and drive south on Route 24 toward Minturn and Leadville. After approximately 1 mile, immediately across from the Meadow Mt. Business Park, you'll see the parking area and trailhead for Grouse Lake, West Grouse Creek, and Meadow

Jake and Jazzo accompany Terry DuBeau on a hike near Redcliff. (photo by Greg Zemis)

Mountain. *Dogs can be off leash until the Wilderness boundary, about 4 miles in.*

This is not a destination hike per se; it offers no holy grail, no pot o' gold, no ultimate goal. It is, however, a great trail on which to completely enjoy the process of hiking with your dog. It's also a trail that sees little traffic, so you and your dog can exult in sharing the many sensations that accompany a hike with little chance of interruption. The first thing to do when you get on the trail is stop, close your eyes, and inhale; you'll pick up the unmistakably savory smell of sagebrush. Don't get used to this smell on your hike, however; you'll soon ascend out of the semi-arid basin and pass through several distinct vegetative zones as you hike. The sagebrush quickly gives way to towering lodgepole pine—each one straining to get at the light high above. After a quarter mile bear right at the fork, continuing on the West Grouse Trail (the trail to the left will lead you to Grouse Lake). Climb a gentle grade that parallels the creek. In a little under a mile, you'll come to an old road; continue straight across it, staying on the hiking trail. Eventually you'll come to another fork; bear right, descending to a small log bridge spanning the creek. Cross the bridge and climb into a beautiful high meadow. You may be lucky enough to spot some ripe wild raspberries along the trail. Behind you, to the east, are fabulous views of the Holy

Cross Wilderness Area. Continue along the trail; you'll come to the Wilderness area boundary (leash laws are in effect). The trail meanders alternately through wet spots close to the creek and talus, continuing to gradually climb. Between 4.5 and 5 miles the trail will diverge from the creek. This is where your dog might want to do some exploring to find Waterdog Lake, a small, remote pool in the trees. You'll find it—hopefully—by bushwacking off to the right of the trail as you ascend. As you bushwack, remember which way you came because you'll be retracing your steps as you hike out.

CYCLING FOR CANINES

The **Douglass City/Hagerman Tunnel** trip and **Turquoise Lake Trail** outside of Leadville are both great bike rides that dogs also will enjoy (see "Tail-Rated Trails"). The 7-mile round-trip **Meadow Mountain Trail** near Minturn follows an old road to a former cowboy cabin at the top (see West Grouse Creek in "Tail-Rated Trails" for trailhead location). And you can bring Fido to investigate the trails on **Vail Mountain** (though with dog in tow, you won't be able to take the gondola up).

POWDERHOUNDS

Piney Creek Nordic Center. Located at the base of Ski Cooper, northwest of Leadville, the nordic center has 25 kilometers of trails for skiing and snowshoeing. And your dog is welcome to accompany you on all of them! You'll have to purchase a trail pass; Fido is free (719-486-1750).

As for backcountry trails, there's National Forest land aplenty where you can ski or snowshoe with a canine companion. A trail system begins on the south side of **Tennessee Pass**; the **Powder Hound Loop** would be especially appropriate. Pick up a Lake County ski map at the Leadville Ranger District (see "Resources"). Note that the trails beginning at the Leadville Fish Hatchery are not really appropriate for dog-skiing, as they enter Wilderness, where leash rules apply. The Vail Pass area keeps getting busier and busier, with skiers and snowmobilers alike. Instead, bring your dog to one of the unplowed Forest Service roads off Highway 24 south of Minturn, such as the **Tigiwon Road** (Forest Rd. 707) or **No Name Road** (Forest Rd. 705).

CREATURE COMFORTS

Unless otherwise stated, dogs should not be left unattended in the room or cabin.

Avon

$$–$$$ Comfort Inn, 161 W. Beaver Creek Blvd., 970-949-5511 (800-228-5150). You'll be asked to sign a pet waiver upon checking in with your dog and pay a $15 one-time fee. Note that dogs are not allowed in the lobby or on the elevator, so your pooch will have to race you up the stairs.

Eagle

$$ Best Western Eagle Lodge, 200 Loren Lane, 970-328-6316 (800-4-SKIVAIL). Dogs can stay in smoking rooms only.

Edwards

$$–$$$ The Lazy Ranch Bed and Breakfast, 0057 Lake Creek Rd., 970-926-3876 (800-655-9343). Your dog (and you) are happily welcomed at this charming B&B, which is still in the same family whose ancestors homesteaded the land in the late 1800s. There are three rooms upstairs in the ranch house as well as a two-room suite, with fireplace, on the first floor. Dog guests must put down a $25 deposit. The owners prefer that you not leave your dog unattended in the room, but you can tie him up on the porch or leave him in the company of resident dogs Molly and Jiggs if owner Linda Calhoun is around. The ranch is on sixty acres, with a bucolic stream behind the house, on which you can hike or snowshoe with your dog; you'll want to keep him on a leash so he doesn't chase any of the chickens, peacocks, or other various resident animals. Clover encountered her first pig, Pork Chop, here.

$$–$$$$ Inn at Riverwalk, 22 Main St., 970-926-0606 (888-926-0606). Though not

nearly as beautiful as the striking lobby, the rooms in this new hotel are spacious and comfortable. Dogs are allowed in smoking rooms only, of which there are ten. You'll be asked to sign a "pet agreement" at check-in, which among other things warns that animal control will be summoned to get any dog left unattended in a room; you'll also need to pay a $25 fee per night, per dog. The pet agreement concludes with a nicely expressed sentiment: "Thank you for sharing your pets with us!"

Granite

$$ Win-Mar Cabins, intersection of Highways 24 and 82, 719-486-0785 (800-6-WINMAR). These fully equipped cabins, situated at the turnoff for Independence Pass, aren't in the most scenic setting, but the location—about halfway between Leadville and Buena Vista—is convenient. Small dogs are permitted. From May to mid-November, all cabins are available; during the winter only three are kept open.

Leadville

$ Alps Motel, 207 Elm St., 719-486-1223 (800-818-ALPS). Dogs are allowed in smoking rooms only, with a $7 nightly fee and a credit-card imprint as a deposit. Note that long-haired dogs are not welcome (so if you're set on staying here with your English sheepdog, you'll probably have to get him shaved!).

$ Avalanche Motel, 231 Elm St., 719-486-0881 (888-462-1910). Management's main request (besides not leaving your dog unattended in the room) is that you don't allow Fido on the bed. If your pampered pooch won't even think of settling for the floor, however, the motel will provide some blankets with which you can cover the regular bedspread.

$ Club Lead, 500 E. 7th St., 719-486-2202. Since you can't get your dog into Club Med, why not bring him to Club Lead? He'll probably like it better anyway, since dogs seem to be frequent visitors to this bed and breakfast. Of the eight rooms, some are private, with their own bathroom, and others are dormitory style, with six double beds and shared bath. The rooms are individually decorated in Western-style themes. You can leave your dog unattended in the room; he's also welcome to hang out in all common areas except the kitchen and dining room, which are "no" zones. Digger the dalmatian is the host dog. This is also a popular place for runners to stay while they engage in high-altitude training, and some bring their dogs. Perhaps yours will be inspired to shed that puppy fat in the company of such athletic canines.

$ Hitchin' Post Motel, 3164 Highway 91 (3 miles north of Leadville), 719-486-2783. Your dog is welcome to hang his hat here with a $10 deposit. The motel is on 7.5 acres, with some frontage on the East Fork of the Arkansas River, and you can exercise your dog off leash on the property.

$ Longhorn Motel, 1515 Poplar, 719-486-3155. The motel accepts smaller dogs (i.e., poodle size); sometimes larger dogs can stay, too, with a $7 deposit.

$ Mountain Peaks Motel, 1 Harrison Ave., 719-486-3178 (888-215-7040). There's a $5 fee per night, per dog.

$ Timberline Motel, 216 Harrison Ave., 719-486-1876 (800-352-1876). The mo-

Jazzo enjoys the Vail area's abundant snowfall. (photo by Terry DuBeau)

tel accepts dogs during its off-season, which runs from the beginning of April to Memorial Day and from the end of August to March 1. There's a $5 to $8 fee per night, depending on the size of dog. And the owner stresses that visiting dogs do not have license to climb on the furniture.

$–$$ Pan Ark Lodge, 5827 Highway 24 (9 miles south of Leadville), 719-486-1063 (800-443-1063). The motel has one- and two-bedroom suites with kitchens and fireplaces in most.

$–$$ Silver King Motor Inn, 2020 N. Poplar, 719-486-2610 (800-871-2610). There are two pet rooms, one smoking and one nonsmoking. You'll be requested to make a $10 deposit if you're paying with cash, or you can leave a credit-card imprint as a deposit.

Minturn

$$$ Pando Cabins, Highway 24 at Camp Hale, 970-949-4232. Your dog can step back in history during a stay at these cabins located near Camp Hale, the one-time ski-training ground for the Tenth Mountain Division troops, who courageously fought in the Alps during World War II. The three two-bedroom log cabins (which are almost brand-spanking new) come fully equipped with kitchens, gas fireplaces, decks overlooking Camp Hale, and Southwestern decor. There's a $20 one-time fee to bring your dog along. And if he's not into the historical aspect, he'll certainly enjoy romping leash-free on the surrounding eighty acres. Open year-round.

Twin Lakes

$–$$ Twin Lakes Nordic Inn, 6435 Highway 82, 719-486-1830 (800-626-7812). Here's another opportunity to take a step back in time, as this historic inn was previously a stagecoach stop and then a brothel. The seventeen rooms, most of which have shared baths, are individually furnished with antiques and European featherbeds. But they're not necessarily plush; you'll probably want to spend time hanging out in the cozy lobby and bar area, where your pooch can join you whenever food is not being served in the adjoining restaurant. You can also leave your dog unattended in the room. Open year-round.

$–$$ Twin Peaks Cabins, 6889 Highway 82 (one-half mile west of Twin Lakes Village), **719-486-2667.** Located on the road to Independence Pass, Twin Peaks offers two fully equipped cabins as well as a four-bedroom mobile home for rent. Well-mannered dogs are allowed, with a $5 charge per night for small ones, $10 per night for large dogs. The owner, who loves dogs but not necessarily the messes they make, emphasizes that they should be kept on a leash at all times outside and that you should walk Fido away from the property to do his business. Open mid-May to mid-October.

$$ Mount Elbert Lodge, Highway 82 (4 miles past Twin Lakes Village), **719-486-0594 (800-381-4433).** The Lodge, a former stagecoach stop with an idyllic setting on the banks of Lake Creek, makes a great dog destination. Though dogs are not allowed in the B&B rooms of the main lodge, they are welcome in any of the six fully furnished cabins, for $8 per night, per pet. If your dog would like to explore Mount Elbert itself—Colorado's highest peak—the Black Cloud trail to the summit starts right outside the door. Open year-round.

Vail

$$–$$$ Roost Lodge, 1783 N. Frontage Rd. West, 970-476-9158 (800-873-3065). The Roost is known as Vail's "budget" accommodation, a relative term, of course. It's a cozy place—just don't expect a lot of amenities. The prime draw is that the motel allows dogs, "from a chihuahua to a St. Bernard," according to the desk clerk. Dogs are put in back-facing rooms, which is actually to your advantage, as you'll be farther from the noise of I-70 traffic. There's a $25 one-time fee. Splurge for a deluxe room, much more spacious for you and Fido than the standard lodge rooms.

$$–$$$$ Antlers at Vail, 680 W. Lionshead Pl., 970-476-2471 (800-843-VAIL). About half of the individually owned condos in this very-near-to-slopeside complex allow dogs. For $10 per night in summer ($15 in winter), you and your dog can stay in comfort in units that range from studios to three bedrooms. According to the general manager, "friendly, quiet—with a capital Q—dogs" can be left unattended in the condos. The Antlers is located alongside Gore Creek; a creekside trail runs right behind the building. And the staff is more than willing to dispense free dog biscuits at the front desk.

> When in Vail, bring your dog to see and be seen at Bart & Yeti's restaurant, named after Bart, a golden retriever, and Yeti, a spaniel mix, who used to frequent the place. Woodrow, a cocker spaniel, carries on their legacy. Bart mixed with the movers and shakers, siring dogs belonging to Henry Kissinger, Nelson Rockefeller, and Clint Eastwood (Liberty, former President Ford's dog, was the lucky gal). Enjoy a meal with your dog on the outside patio (though a local dog or two has also been known to sneak into the bar area).

$$–$$$$ Lift House Condominiums, 555 E. Lionshead Circle, 970-476-2340 (800-654-0635). These studio condos, just steps from the gondola, allow dogs except during the two weeks or so around Christmas and New Year's. Each condo is equipped with a gas fireplace and kitchenette. In summer, there's a $50 one-time pet fee; in winter, it increases to $100. If you leave your dog unattended in the room, management prefers that you contain him in a travel kennel. Bart and Yeti's restaurant (see sidebar) is just downstairs.

$$–$$$$ The Lodge at West Vail, 2211 N. Frontage Rd. West, 970-476-3890 (800-543-2814). The Lodge has a big-city-motel atmosphere. In addition to standard hotel rooms, it offers one- and two-bedroom condos, which, with two levels, fireplaces, and homier decor, are the best option for the money. Dogs can stay in either rooms or condos, with a $100 deposit and a $25 fee per night.

Campgrounds

State Park campgrounds: **Sylvan Lake State Park,** 16 miles south of Eagle on West Brush Creek Rd. (50 sites).

National Forest campgrounds: **Gore Creek Campground,** Highway 6, 2 miles from the East Vail exit off I-70 (24 sites); **Camp Hale Memorial Campground,** Highway 24, south of Minturn at Camp Hale (21 sites); **Turquoise Lake,** outside of Leadville (see "Tail-Rated Trails" for directions), with eight campgrounds, for a total of 368 sites; **Lakeview Campground,** Forest Rd. 125, off Highway 82 near Twin Lakes (59 sites).

> If your dog stays in Vail for more than two weeks, you'll have to get him a local license. Call the animal shelter at 970-949-4328 for details.

WORTH A PAWS

Leadville, Colorado & Southern Railroad Company. Bring Fido on a scenic, open-passenger-car train ride along the old Colorado & Southern high line. Though it's ultimately up to each day's conductor to give the final say on whether a leashed dog is allowed, chances are good yours will make the grade. The two-and-a-half-hour round-trip brings you north of Leadville toward Fremont Pass, up to the Climax molybdenum mine, and back again, with a short stop at the French Gulch water tower. The train runs daily from the end of May to the beginning of October, with two runs a day between mid-June and the beginning of September. Catch it at the historic depot, 326 E. 7th St. in Leadville. For price information, call 719-486-3936.

DOGGIE DAYCARE

Avon

Avon Pet Center, 730 Nottingham Rd., 970-949-6467. $12/day. Open 8 A.M.–6 P.M., Monday to Friday; 9 A.M.–6 P.M., Saturday.

Minturn

Animal Hospital of Vail Valley, 23798 Highway 24, 970-949-7733 or 970-949-HELP. $10/day. Open 8 A.M.–6 P.M., Monday to Friday; 8 A.M.–noon, Saturday.

PET PROVISIONS

Avon

Avon Pet Centre, 730 Nottingham Rd., 970-949-6467

Leadville

Mountain Feed and Coal Company, 329 S. Highway 24, 719-486-3566

CANINE ER

Avon

Avon Pet Centre (AAHA certified), 730 Nottingham Rd., 970-949-6467. Open 8 A.M.–6 P.M., Monday to Friday; 9 A.M.–6 P.M., Saturday.

Minturn

Animal Hospital of Vail Valley, 23798 Highway 24, 970-949-7733 or 970-949-HELP. Open 8 A.M.–6 P.M., Monday to Friday; 8 A.M.–noon, Saturday.

RESOURCES

Greater Leadville Area Chamber of Commerce, 809 Harrison Ave., Leadville, 719-486-3900 (800-933-3901; www.colorado.com/leadville)

Holy Cross Ranger District, White River National Forest, 24747 Highway 24, Minturn, 970-827-5715

Leadville Ranger District, San Isabel National Forest, 20p15 N. Poplar, Leadville, 719-486-0749

Vail Valley Tourism and Convention Bureau, two locations: at the Vail Transportation Center and on top of the Lionshead parking structure, 970-479-1394 (800-525-3875)

11
Aspen

THE BIG SCOOP

Aspen is one of the dog-friendliest towns we've visited. Within minutes of our arrival, we were greeted by a man who mistook Clover for an established Aspenite: "I guess if you move to Aspen, you have to get a dog," he commented. "Everyone seems to have one." And, according to one local, golden retrievers and yellow labs are the breeds of choice.

Dogs are welcome on the downtown pedestrian mall, which includes several fountains. The one at the corner of Hyman and Mill—columns of water of varying heights that spurt unpredictably through a grate—is especially appealing to dogs. And your dog need not worry about missing out on any of the chi-chi shopping opportunities for which Aspen is renowned; almost every store allowed Clover as a customer.

Aspen's powers that be recognize that dogs need to recreate too; thus—surprise!—dogs are allowed off leash in almost all city parks (with the exception of Herron, which is maintained as a family park). Be extra diligent in making sure your leash-free dog remains courteous, however, so that Aspen dogs may continue to enjoy this privilege.

TAIL-RATED TRAILS

This is only a small sampling of the many gorgeous trails in the Aspen area. For more ideas, consult *Aspen Snowmass Trails*, by Warren Ohlrich, or the "Aspen/Crested Butte/Gunnison Recreation Topo Map," put out by Latitude 40°.

 Hunter Creek/Hunter Valley Trail. About 4 miles round-trip. Take Main St. to Mill St. north, bear left onto Red Mountain Rd. after the bridge, then take an immediate right onto Lone Pine Rd. Trail access is via the first left, into the Hunter Creek condos parking lot (you'll need to park on the street, however). The trailhead is close enough to town that you can walk to it. There is an upper access point further up Red Mountain Rd. to Hunter Creek Rd.; however, the lower access offers proximity to the creek. *Dogs can be off leash, with the following caveat from the Pitkin County Animal Control officer:* Technically, this trail runs through Pitkin County land as well as National Forest, and county law states that dogs must be leashed when not on private property. But since the animal control officer doesn't regularly patrol this trail, you likely won't be ticketed for having your dog off leash. If Fido harasses someone or something, however, and animal control responds, you will be cited for not having him on a leash. If you're out at a particularly busy time, it's probably best to keep your dog leashed. So assess the risks, and use common sense.

This trail has it all for dogs: water, trees, and a meadow to frolic in. Begin by following Hunter Creek, crossing it via bridges several times. As you ascend, you'll get increasingly better views of Aspen Mountain. The trail becomes steeper and more rocky before reaching the Benedict Bridge, where it merges with the trail from the upper access. Shortly after the bridge, consider a short detour up the hillside to Verena Malloy Park (look for the spur trail to the right and the park sign), where you'll find an overlook, with bench, that provides great views of Aspen and the Elk Mountains. Then continue on the now-wide main trail as it climbs steeply (stay straight at the three-way intersection; a blue blaze marks the way). At the Forest Service boundary sign, the trail opens up into the spacious meadows of the Hunter valley. Follow the wide trail through and to the left, where you'll come to the Tenth Mountain Bridge, 1.5 miles from the trailhead. The meadow beyond is home to several old cabins. To make a short loop, follow the trail east through this meadow. When you come to another, smaller bridge, cross over and come back down the path along the south side of the creek. Rejoin the main Hunter Valley Trail near the Tenth Mountain Bridge. Head back to the trailhead the way you came up.

Dogs love the Hunter Creek Trail in Aspen. (photo by Cindy Hirschfeld)

 Aspen Mountain. During June, July, and August, the Silver Queen Gondola whisks hikers to the top of 11,212-foot Aspen Mountain. Not only can your dog accompany you (at no charge) but you can purchase a souvenir dog gondola pass with your loved one's picture on it for $5 at the gondola ticket office.

Once at the top, you can choose to stroll along the short Richmond Ridge loop or hike 4.5 miles down to the bottom of the gondola. *Dogs are requested, but not required, to be leashed.*

The gondola operates from 10:00 A.M. to 4:00 P.M., and there is a fee.

 Difficult Creek. 4.8 miles round-trip. Head east on Highway 82 from downtown; from the spot where you must turn left to follow the highway (at Original St.), it's 3.5 miles to the Diffi-

cult Campground parking area on the right. When the campground is open (generally from the end of May to the end of September), drive down to the picnic area day-parking lot on the right; the trailhead is at the southeast corner of the lot. When the campground is closed, you'll have to walk 0.6 mile down a paved road to the trailhead. *Dogs must be leashed (this is Wilderness area).*

Don't let the name of this trail mislead you—it's actually a moderate hike. And because the route is mostly in pine and fir forest, this is a good hike for dogs on a hot day. After leaving the parking lot, stay left at the first fork, then follow the brown and white "designated route" markers to a wooden bridge that spans the Roaring Fork River. The trail leads to Difficult Creek, then climbs away from the creek for a bit before rejoining it (you'll cross another small stream en route). You'll eventually pass through a clearing, where your dog may be able to spot the remains of some log cabins, and arrive at a sign indicating that the trail is not maintained beyond this point. This is the "official" turn-around spot.

Rio Grande Trail. Runs about 7 miles from Neal St. in Aspen to Jaffe Park in the neighboring town of Woody Creek. To reach the main access point, which is an easy walk from downtown, take Main St. to Mill St. north, then left on Puppy Smith St. The trail begins across the street from the post office. *Dogs can be off leash as long as they are under voice control.*

The first 2 miles of this popular path along the Roaring Fork River are paved, and because the trail follows the old Denver & Rio Grande railroad bed, it remains fairly level throughout. If your dog is into jogging, this trail would be a perfect venue. At Cemetery Lane, the trail surface switches to gravel. (To reach the unpaved portion by car, drive on Highway 82 west out of Aspen. Just after the road jogs right, then left, you'll cross Castle Creek; turn right at the traffic light, onto Cemetery Lane. After crossing the Roaring Fork River at about 1 mile, look for the parking area on the left.) As you travel westward, you'll go through the river canyon before coming onto a plateau, where the brilliant red tones of the valley are coupled with scenic vistas of the Elk Mountains to the south.

 Sunnyside Trail. About 4 miles round-trip. Take Highway 82 west out of Aspen. Just after the road jogs right, then left, you'll cross Castle Creek; turn right at the traffic light, onto Cemetery Lane. After 1.5 miles you'll see a small parking area on the left; the trail begins on the right. *Dogs can be off leash,* but read the explanation in the Hunter Creek/Hunter Valley Trail description.

This trail features easy access from town as well as scenic views. Because it climbs up a dry, south-facing slope, dogs would enjoy it most in the early morning or evening on warm days (or anytime on cooler days). The narrow trail ascends steeply up the hillside. Ignore the first "trail" sign you come to (which points left) and continue climbing up to the right; however, your dog may want to pause here for a drink from the nearby irrigation ditch. After crossing a second irrigation ditch, the trail levels out briefly before continuing to climb. As you hike, you'll gain great views of Aspen Mountain, Aspen Highlands Ski Area, and Buttermilk Ski Area; the Maroon Bells will eventually reveal themselves behind Buttermilk. At one point the trail goes across a private driveway, and you and your dog will catch glimpses of some of Aspen's multimillion-dollar homes. A good turnaround spot is at the aspen grove and radio tower, when the trail levels out again. Or, if you're up for a longer hike, continue hiking along the ridge. In a couple of miles, the trail meets up with the Hunter Creek Trail, above Hunter valley.

 Ute Trail. About 2 miles round-trip. This trail is also within walking distance of downtown. Head east on Ute Ave. for about 0.4 mile. Shortly after you come to a house with a multitude of windows, look for the small wooden trail sign on the right (across from a parking pullout for Ute Park). *Dogs can be off leash,* but read the explanation in the Hunter Creek/Hunter Valley Trail description.

Because of its proximity to town and its low mileage, the Ute Trail is an efficient way to exercise your dog (as well as yourself). This short trail switchbacks steeply up the lower third of Aspen Mountain. The reward is a bird's-eye view of town from the rock outcroppings at the end. Don't forget water for your dog, as there's no source on the trail—actually, you'll both need it after tackling the 1,700-foot elevation gain.

 Maroon Bells. Take your dog to view two of Colorado's best-known peaks, the 14,000-foot-plus Maroon Bells. From mid-June to Labor Day (and on weekends in September), cars are not permitted to drive up to the Bells between 8:30 A.M. and 5 P.M. Instead, a Roaring Fork Transit Authority bus delivers hikers and sightseers to the spot from the Rubey Park Bus Station in downtown Aspen. Dogs are allowed to ride the bus for free (though they're not allowed on any other local buses). You, however, must pay a $5 fee; children 6 to 16 and riders 65 and older pay $3. Call 970-925-8484 for more information,

Once you're at Maroon Lake, note that dogs must be leashed due to the heavy use of the area. The 1.5-mile **Maroon Lake Scenic Trail** lives up to its name, providing stunning views of the nearby Bells. (Note that dogs are not allowed within 100 feet of Crater Lake, which is 1.75 miles up the Maroon-Snowmass Trail.) To give your dog a chance to enjoy the beauty of this area while encountering fewer people, hike the **Maroon Creek Trail,** which runs 4.5 miles from the upper Maroon Lake parking lot down the valley to the East Maroon Portal. The bus can then pick you up along Maroon Creek Rd. for the trip back to town.

 Conundrum Creek Trail. 17 miles round-trip. The only reason this extremely popular backpack route is

Backpacking up the Conundrum Creek Trail in the Maroon-Bells Snowmass Wilderness. (photo by Marieke Dechesne)

included here is so you'll be aware of its restrictions. The trail leads up a scenic valley to a pair of wonderfully situated hot springs pools (and eventually to Gothic, near Crested Butte), but the trip is not a lot of fun for dogs. *For starters, dogs must be leashed because of the Wilderness designation,* and neither Clover nor I (with both of us wearing packs) enjoyed being linked to each other for 8.5 miles. Because the hot springs see heavy use, camping is limited to designated sites, which become even more limited if you're with a dog. And dogs cannot be brought over to the east side of Conundrum Creek, where the hot springs are. So if the thought of tying your dog to a tree, out of sight, while you luxuriate in the springs evokes a pang of guilt, leave Fido at home for this one.

CYCLING FOR CANINES

Some of the more popular Aspen biking routes—Smuggler Mountain Rd. and the Government Trail—are not suitable to do with dogs due to leash requirements (Smuggler because it's a county road; the Government Trail for wildlife protection). Instead try the unpaved portion of the **Rio Grande Trail** (which is less crowded than the paved part that runs through town); the **Hunter Creek/Hunter Valley Trail** (begin from the upper access—Red Mountain Rd. to Hunter Creek Rd.); or **Aspen Mountain.** (See "Tail-Rated Trails" for descriptions of these three.) Another option is the 10-mile round-trip ride on **Lincoln Creek Rd.** from Grizzly Reservoir to the ghost town of Ruby. For more detailed information about these rides, look at the single-sheet ride descriptions issued at the Aspen Ranger District office (see "Resources"), or pick up a copy of the brochure "Bike Maps of Aspen" at one of the bike shops in town.

POWDERHOUNDS

In addition to the suggestions below, the **Hunter Creek/Hunter Valley Trail** and the **Rio Grande Trail** (see "Tail-Rated Trails") make great ski or snowshoe outings.

Though dogs are not allowed on the trails at the Ashcroft Ski Touring Center, they can accompany their skiing or snowshoeing owners on the unplowed section of **Ashcroft Rd.** beyond, which extends for about 2 miles. Dogs can be off leash as long as they refrain from trotting over to any of the nearby nordic trails. And you can have lunch at the Pinecreek Cookhouse as long as you access it via the Ashcroft Rd. and tie up your dog at least 100 yards from the restaurant.

During the winter and much of the spring, **Independence Pass Rd.** is closed to vehicles just past the Difficult Creek Campground, 3.5 miles east of Aspen, allowing you and your dog to ski or snowshoe. Be aware that there is avalanche danger in areas.

> Retrievers and German shepherds are the most common breed for search-and-rescue dogs, but a rescue poodle? Sure enough, Aspen is home to Cassidy, a standard poodle who has been trained to find avalanche victims. She works with the Aspen Ski Patrol.

CREATURE COMFORTS

Unless otherwise stated, dogs should not be left unattended in the room or cabin.

Aspen

$$ T Lazy 7 Guest and Horse Ranch, 3129 Maroon Creek Rd., 970-925-7254 (888-T7LODGE). This lodge offers dog heaven in the form of a 500-acre ranch near the Maroon Bells–Snowmass Wilderness. Dogs are welcome in one of the main lodge's rooms as well as in five of the outlying cabinlike apartments (which range from studios to five bedrooms). There's a $50 one-time fee. Well-behaved dogs can be left unattended indoors and can romp off leash on the ranch as long as they are supervised. The ranch is open from Memorial Day to the beginning of October and from Thanksgiving to mid-April.

$$–$$$ Alpine Lodge, 1240 East Cooper Ave., 970-925-7351. Dogs are welcome to stay in the cabins (equipped with kitchenettes and teddy bears) at this European-style lodge. There is a $10 fee per night.

$$–$$$ Limelite Lodge, 228 East Cooper Ave., 970-925-3025. It's smoking rooms only for dogs at the basic but comfortable Limelite. The location, across from Wagner Park, is a plus.

$$$–$$$$ Hotel Aspen, 110 W. Main St., 970-925-3441 (800-527-7369). The hotel has eight ground-floor rooms, each with a small, semi-enclosed patio area, in which dogs may stay. A credit card is required as a deposit. Paepcke Park, across the street, offers your dog a chance to stretch his legs.

$$$$ Beaumont Inn, 1301 East Cooper Ave., 970-925-7081. Two of this nicely appointed hotel's deluxe rooms are available for dog stays (one nonsmoking and one smoking). The inn prefers pets under 25 pounds and charges a $20 fee per night. Dogs can be left unattended in the rooms, though the management suggests you inform the housekeeping staff.

$$$$ The Brand, 205 S. Galena, 970-920-1800. One of the more unusual places you can stay with your dog, the Brand has six apartment-style suites, each one individually decorated with exquisite furnishings and art. (The hotel has been featured in *Architectural Digest*.) You can even leave your dog unattended in them—but better tell him that he should not knock down that pre-Columbian vase with his tail! The staff can sometimes be called on for dog walking as well. Why in the world do they allow dogs here? Simple—the manager likes them. There is a three- to four-night minimum visit.

$$$$ Hotel Jerome, 330 E. Main St., 970-920-1000 (800-331-7213). A friend of Clover's was treated like a king when he and his owners stayed at this Aspen landmark. A credit-card imprint is taken as a deposit. You can leave your dog unattended in your large, Victorian-style room so long as you hang the "pet in room" sign to alert housekeeping.

$$$$ The Little Nell, 675 E. Durant, 970-920-4600 (800-THE-NELL). If you have the money, there's no better place than the Little Nell to take a dog. Clover slept in style at this luxury hotel, where dogs are presented with welcome biscuits upon check-in. All the rooms have gas fireplaces, and some have balconies. Dogs can be left unattended in the rooms; put up the "privacy" sign to let the housekeepers know. The staff is also willing to watch your dog down in the lobby, if things aren't too hectic, or periodically take your dog for a short walk. And Glory Hole Park, a pleasant oasis with two small ponds, is down the street, at the corner of Original St. and Ute Ave.

$$$$ The Residence, 305 S. Galena, 970-920-6532. With the benefit of a $1,500 deposit, your pampered pooch can luxuriate in one of this new boutique hotel's seven apartment-style suites. The apartments are lavishly furnished with antiques, museum-quality artwork, and Ralph Lauren linens, each with a different theme. Just don't leave a dog unattended in them; you don't really want to have to use that deposit, do you?

$$$$ The St. Regis Aspen, 315 East Dean St., 970-920-3300 (800-454-9005). It's no longer the Ritz-Carlton, but the hotel, and the pet policy, are very much the same. First-class Fidos are welcome in any of the rooms for a $25 deposit. Dogs cannot be left unattended in the rooms, but you can arrange for pet-sitting through the concierge. For $15 an hour, a staff member will either sit with your dog in the room or take him for a walk. Wagner Park, where your dog can spectate at a rugby game, is a block away.

Basalt
$-$$ Aspenwood Lodge, 220 Midland Ave., 970-927-4747. The motel charges $8 per night for dogs.

Meredith (Ruedi Reservoir)
$$-$$$ Double Diamond Ranch Bed & Breakfast, 23000 Frying Pan Rd., 970-927-3404. If your dog can play well with others, he can stay with you at this eighty-five-acre ranch surrounded by the White River National Forest. He'll have his pick of two rooms in the main ranch house, each with private bath; a cabin with full kitchen (as well as a Jacuzzi); or the "wilderness" cabin, which is equipped with both gas and wood stoves but no electricity or plumbing. And he can even run leash-free on the ranch as long as he doesn't bother the resident horses or mules.

Snowmass
$$-$$$$ Wildwood Lodge, 40 Elbert Lane, 970-923-3550. The Wildwood is affiliated with the Silvertree and has the same pet regulations (see below). The lodge has about ten pet rooms, all with easy access to the outdoors.

$$$-$$$$ Silvertree Hotel, 100 Elbert Lane, 970-923-3520. This deluxe hotel maintains about a dozen rooms suitable for dogs, primarily because they have easy outside access. Dogs can be left unattended in the rooms, but you must sign a pet waiver when you check in, assuming liability for any damage your little charmer may inflict.

Campgrounds
Forest Service campgrounds: **Difficult Campground,** 3.5 miles east of Aspen on Highway 82 (47 sites). **Weller** (11 sites), **Lincoln Gulch** (7 sites), and **Lost Man** (10 sites) campgrounds are farther east on 82, as the road ascends Independence Pass.

WORTH A PAWS
Borrow-a-Dog. If your dog wants a friend to play with, or even if you're in Aspen without your dog and could use some surrogate canine companionship, check out this popular program at the Aspen Animal Shelter. For nothing more than your signature on a release form, you can borrow a

shelter dog, for a few hours or a whole day. Seth Sachson, shelter director, will match you with an appropriate dog. The program operates year-round, and the shelter hours are 8 A.M.–12 P.M. and 2–6 P.M., Monday to Friday, and 8–10 A.M. and 4–6 P.M., Saturday and Sunday. 212 Aspen Airport Business Center, 970-544-0206.

Silver Queen Gondola. Take your dog on the ski gondola up Aspen Mountain. See details in the "Tail-Rated Trails" section.

Golden Retriever Parades. Aspen salutes its furriest finest twice a year, during the annual Winterskol Carnival in January and on the Fourth of July. Dogs and owners parade down Main St., and local lore has it that the canine marching formation has disintegrated into chaos when spectators have thrown tennis balls from the roof of the Hotel Jerome.

Canine Fashion Show. If your dog has a penchant for dressing up, and you're in town during January Winterskol festivities, enter him in the annual fashion show at Paepcke Park. Judges award prizes for categories such as most humorous and most original outfits. There's no fee; just show up with your decked-out pooch.

K-9 Uphill. Aspen local Erik Skarvan organizes this annual snowshoe climb for dogs (on leash) and people up Buttermilk Mountain. It takes place the weekend after Buttermilk Ski Area closes for the season, usually in mid-April. Your dog can choose between the competitive and the recreational divisions and look forward to treats at the top of the 2,000-vertical-foot

Bring your dog to sniff and be sniffed at the Flying Dog Brew Pub (424 E. Cooper Ave.). If you're a "well-behaved owner," he can join you at one of the outdoor tables, and you can quaff an aptly named Road Dog Ale in his honor.

At the start of the K-9 Uphill, a snow-shoe race up Buttermilk Mountain. *(photo courtesy of Mary Sue Bonelli)*

course. Registration fee is about $20 in advance, $25 on event day, and proceeds benefit the Valley Dog Rescue in Basalt.

Doggie Daycare

Aspen
The Aspen Boarding Kennel, 212 Aspen Airport Business Center, 970-544-0206. $12/day, with a walk at lunch and feeding, if requested. $10/half day. Hours are 8 A.M.–12 P.M. and 2–6 P.M., Monday to Friday, and 8–10 A.M. and 4–6 P.M., Saturday and Sunday.

Basalt
Bode's Alpine Meadows Ranch and Kennel, 0329 Holland Hills Rd., 970-927-2688. $11/day for a stay in the heated kennels, with feeding and ball-playing sessions or a short hike as well. Pickup and delivery of your dog are also available. Open 9 A.M.–6 P.M. daily.

Old Snowmass
Aspen Valley Kennels, 30875 Highway 82, 970-923-2022. $11/day. Open 8:30 A.M.–5:30 P.M., Monday to Friday, 11 A.M.–1 P.M., Saturday (and 4–6 P.M. during the winter). Closed Sunday.

PET PROVISIONS

Aspen

C. B. Paws, 420 E. Hyman Ave., 970-925-5848. Though this store doesn't sell pet food, it has just about everything else a dog could desire. It's the sister store to the original C. B. Paws, in Crested Butte.

Rocky Mountain Pet Shop, 107 S. Monarch, 970-925-2010

Tailwaggers, 212 Aspen Airport Business Center (next to the Aspen Boarding Kennel), 970-925-6076

El Jebel

RJ Paddywacks, 19400 Highway 82 (next to City Market), 970-963-1700. The store's ad, which promises the largest selection of rawhide chews in the valley, caught Clover's eye.

CANINE ER

Aspen

Aspen Animal Hospital, 301 Aspen Airport Business Center, 970-925-2611. Open 7:45 A.M.–5:30 P.M., Monday to Friday; 9 A.M.–12 P.M., Saturday. A vet will meet you at the clinic or make a house call in an after-hours emergency.

Old Snowmass

Aspen Valley Veterinary Hospital, 30875 Highway 82, 970-923-2022. Open 8:30 A.M.–5:30 P.M., Monday to Friday, 11 A.M.–1 P.M., Saturday (and 4–6 P.M. during the winter). Closed Sunday.

RESOURCES

Aspen Chamber Resort Association, 425 Rio Grande Pl., 970-925-1940 (800-262-7736)

Aspen Ranger District, White River National Forest, 806 W. Hallam, 970-925-3445

The Ute Mountaineer, at 308 S. Mill St. (970-925-2849)—with a helpful, friendly staff, a good resource for trail maps and hiking/biking guides

12

Glenwood Springs and Vicinity

THE BIG SCOOP

Three hours west of Denver and just about an hour down the road from Aspen, Glenwood Springs makes a pleasant destination in and of itself or a more affordable base camp for exploring the mountains around its tonier sister city. (Your dog, however, will have to sit out the natural hot springs for which Glenwood is famed.) About forty minutes south of Glenwood Springs, the one-street town of Redstone, lined with galleries and antiques stores, and the funky hamlet of Marble also invite a visit. While in Glenwood, be sure to stop by the canine-loving Chamber Resort Association, where Clover scored lots of complimentary dog biscuits.

Leashes are the law within Glenwood city limits, but they are optional in unincorporated Garfield County. Be sure to note that the leash law includes an ordinance against "public tethering" (i.e., you can't leave your dog tied up and unattended outside a store or other business), which can make getting food when it's too warm to leave Fido in the car—on most summer days—problematic.

TAIL-RATED TRAILS

Because Glenwood Springs is in a canyon, most of the nearby trails offer vertical climbs. For strolling on the flats, try one of the paved riverfront trails (see specifics below). A helpful resource is the "Trails Guide to Glenwood Springs, CO," a map that you can pick up at the Forest Supervisor's Office or the Glenwood Springs Chamber Resort Association.

Red Mountain Trail. The "Trails Guide" map gives the one-way mileage for Red Mountain as 2 miles; the sign at the trailhead indicates 3.5 miles. A Parks Department representative says 3 miles is likely, so count on approximately 6 miles for the round-trip. Take 7th St. west from Grand Ave. to the T-stop at Midland. Make a left, and then a right on 10th St. (at the stop sign). Go up 2 blocks to Red Mountain Dr., take a right, cross the one-lane bridge, then take a left on W. 9th St. (not Pl.). There's a parking pullout at the end of the road, adjacent to the trailhead. *Dogs can be off leash.*

This hike follows a dirt road through what was once the Glenwood Springs ski area. Though the area closed in the early 1950s, some of the lift structures remain. Begin by following the road; then cut through an open area to the left of the first water tank you'll come to. (This advised shortcut allows you to avoid walking through the city's water plant.) Hike up the narrow footpath at the far end—a real lungbuster. You'll soon meet up again with the road. The road keeps to a gradual grade; as you ascend, Glenwood Springs unfolds below. About two-thirds of the way up, a bench provides a rest spot with a panoramic view of almost-13,000-foot Mt. Sopris and the Elk Mountains. The road ends at the summit, where the old ski lift used to unload. Though you'll encounter some shady areas along the way, this hike is primarily hot and dry (a stream does flow by the trailhead). Your dog might enjoy it most in the early morning or evening.

Glenwood Canyon Recreation Path. Runs 15 miles from the Vapor Caves, at the east end of 6th St., to about 2 miles west of the Dotsero exit off I-70. *It's suggested, but not required, that dogs be leashed.*

This paved multi-use trail runs the length of spectacular Glenwood Canyon, bordering the Colorado River. Though your dog probably won't appreciate the much-touted engineering marvels of the highway above, he may well enjoy a walk by the water (though he won't be able to actually take a dip). Just keep an eye out for bicyclists and in-line skaters whizzing by.

 Rifle Falls State Park. Since you can't take your dog to Hanging Lake (see below), bring him here to see a triple waterfall. From the Rifle exit off I-70, west of Glenwood Springs, travel north on Highway 13. After about 5 miles, take a right on Highway 325; the park is 9.8 miles ahead on the right. *Dogs must be leashed.*

Once inside the park, go left to access the falls; there is a day-use parking area where the road ends. From there, it's a short walk to the falls. Your dog will appreciate their spray on a hot day. After viewing the plunging water, hike on the **Coyote Trail,** a short, twenty- to thirty-minute walk that meanders past limestone grottos and a small stream before taking you to the top of the falls (you'll be glad to have your dog on a leash here!). Descend via the trail marked "difficult" (it's not, really), and you'll come out by the drive-in campsites. If your dog is into botany, he'll appreciate the trailside markers that identify native plants and trees. The **Squirrel Trail** (did Rover's ears just prick up?), which follows streams for most of its length, is another option for a short walk; it's part dirt road, part path. If you decide to overnight in the park, stay at one of the walk-in campsites, which you'll pass along the Squirrel Trail.

 Scout Trail. About 3.5 miles round-trip. From Grand Ave., take 8th St. four blocks east to the end. There's no trailhead parking lot—just a couple of spaces on the street—so if you're staying downtown, consider walking to the trail. *Dogs can be off leash, keeping in mind the following:* Though the first 1.5 miles are within city limits, the trail is not regularly patrolled by Animal Control. If your dog harasses or injures another hiker or biker, however, you may be cited, among other things, for having a dog off leash. If you're sharing the trail with a lot of other users, it's probably best to keep your dog leashed.

Yuki and Inkah admire the scenery and cool off. (photo by Alyssa Pumphrey)

Because this hike is dry and largely unshaded, it's best for dogs as an evening outing, during the summer. Begin by walking down the driveway on the left of 8th St. to the actual trail. You'll face a short, steep climb before the trail levels off to a more gradual ascent as it snakes around the hillside. Enjoy the bird's-eye view into Glenwood Canyon below. After about half a mile, your dog will find brief respite in the shade of piñon pines. The trail continues to ascend, making a large switchback through sage and oakbrush. At the T-intersection, go left; the trail continues switchbacking up to the right about 200 feet ahead. In about a third of a mile, you'll end up near the top of Lookout Mountain, by the radio towers and an old campground. Savor the views before returning the way you came.

Glenwood Springs River-trails System. At present, just two short sections have been built of this planned paved trail system along the Colorado and Roaring Fork Rivers. The longer section runs from Two Rivers Park to Kiwanis (Veltus) Park, with a shorter section behind O'Leary Park. If you're looking for a short after-dinner stroll to do with Fido, begin at Veltus Park, off of Midland Ave. between 8th and 10th Sts. *Dogs must be leashed.*

 Hanging Lake. This is a great hike up to a gorgeous tropical-style waterfall with ... well, never mind, because your dog can't see it anyway. Because of the immense popularity of this trail, dogs are not allowed, period.

 Harvey Gap State Park. With the exception of hunting dogs, during hunting season, dogs are not allowed in this park, which contains Harvey Gap Reservoir. There are no hiking trails here anyway, so your dog probably won't regret the lack of access.

CYCLING FOR CANINES

The **Red Mountain Trail** is easily bikeable, as it follows a dirt road in fairly good shape. Just remember to allow your dog time to catch up with you on the ride down. You can conceivably bike with your dog on the **Glenwood Canyon Recreation Path,** since leashes are not a requirement; early morning or late evening, when the trail is less crowded, would be the best time to do this. Another option is the 7-mile round-trip **Burnt Tree Ridge Trail** (#18 on the "Trails Guide to Glenwood Springs, CO" map), which follows an old four-wheel-drive road about 15 miles east of Glenwood Springs. Or investigate the **Roan Cliffs** area outside of Rifle. A biking map is available at the Bureau of Land Management office in Glenwood Springs (see "Resources");

the northwest section, accessible from Piceance Creek Rd. outside of Rio Blanco, is generally less used by motorized vehicles than the eastern section.

POWDERHOUNDS

It's strictly backcountry as far as finding a good location near Glenwood Springs to ski with your dog. The Ski Sunlight Nordic Center discourages dogs on its trails, and the Four Mile Park area, which is on National Forest land, is popular for snowmobiling, making it less than ideal for the four-legged set.

CREATURE COMFORTS

Unless otherwise stated, dogs should not be left unattended in the room or cabin.

Carbondale

$ Landmark Bed and Breakfast, 689 Main St., 970-963-1850. Dogs must be brought in and out through the back door because the front entrance opens into a restaurant.

$–$$ Thunder River Lodge, 0179 Highway 133, 970-963-2543. With a $20 deposit and a $5 fee per night, dogs can stay in smoking rooms at this motel.

Glenwood Springs

$ Terra Vista Motel, 52089 Highway 6 & 24, 970-945-6475. The motel offers a choice of knotty-pine paneled rooms or cabins. Expect to pay a $7 fee per night for your dog. Dogs can be left unattended in the rooms, and there is also a yard area where they can run off leash.

$–$$ Red Mountain Inn, 51637 Highway 6 & 24, 970-945-6353 (800-748-2565). The inn offers cabins or motel rooms, and dogs are allowed in either. The rooms are modern, clean, and comfortable. There's a small pet-walking area on the premises, where well-behaved dogs can be unleashed. A $100 deposit is required. You can leave your dog unattended in the room, but housekeeping will not clean it during that time.

$–$$ Sunlight Bavarian Inn, 10252 Road 117 (at base of Ski Sunlight), 970-945-5225 (800-733-4757). The inn, built in 1946, has a 1960s ski-dorm ambiance—and the rooms obviously weren't designed for someone who plans on spending a lot of time in them. The inn's pet policy, however, is great: There are no fees or restrictions, and dogs are allowed to be left unattended in the rooms.

$$ Affordable Inns, 51823 Highway 6 & 24, 970-945-8888 (800-292-5050). A $25 deposit for dogs is required, and they can be left unattended in the rooms.

$$ Best Western Caravan Inn, 1826 Grand Ave., 970-945-7451 (800-945-5495). A $5 fee per pet, per night is charged as well as a $50 deposit. You can leave your dog unattended in the room, but housekeeping won't come in during that time. Note that the Best Western Antlers Hotel, also in Glenwood Springs, does *not* take dogs.

$$ Budget Host, 51429 Highway 6 & 24, 970-945-5682 (800-283-4678). Management says all rooms are "dog-proof," so you can leave yours unattended for a couple of hours.

$$ Buffalo Valley Inn, 3637 Highway 82, 970-945-5297. Rooms with kitchenettes are available. There's a $10 one-time fee per dog.

$$ Frontier Lodge, 2834 Glen Ave., 970-945-5496 (800-366-2285). The lodge has only a couple of rooms set aside for pets. A $25 deposit is required, and a $10 cleaning fee will be taken out of this if your dog decides to leave a lot of his fur in the room.

$$ Ponderosa Motel, 51793 Highway 6 & 24, 970-945-5058 (800-843-5449). All of the units are cabins, most with kitchenettes. Clover found the cabins a bit musty but liked the nice grassy areas outside them. The motel requires a $10 deposit per dog, per night, all of which will be refunded if no damage is done.

$$ Ramada Inn, 124 W. 6th St., 970-945-2500 (800-332-1472). You must put down a $50 deposit per dog, and dogs should not be left unattended for long periods of time.

$$ Riverside Cottages, 1287 Road 154, 970-945-5509 (800-945-5509). New owners, who have a yellow lab named Mars, recently changed the former no-pet policy here. The cottages are a throwback to the 1960s as far as furnishings go, but the setting along the Roaring Fork River can't be beat. A one-time $10 fee per dog is charged. Your dog can romp unleashed to his heart's content, with supervision of course, outside the cottages.

$$ Silver Spruce Motel, 162 W. 6th St., 970-945-5458 (800-523-4742). The motel has eight pet rooms set aside, and they are modern and spacious. A $5 fee per pet is charged per night, and dogs can be left unattended, but housekeeping won't clean the room during that time.

$$ "The" Bed and Breakfast on Mitchell Creek, 1686 Mitchell Creek Rd., 970-945-4002. Though this B&B is technically outside the parameters of this book in that dogs are not allowed in the room, I've included it because the owners of this bucolic haven are nonetheless accommodating to pets. Your dog is welcome to sleep on the patio or in the garage (either leashed or in a travel crate), and a private hiking trail that begins behind the house is open to you and your dog to venture on leash-free. Because the accommodations are for only one set of guests per night, your dog won't run the risk of bothering anyone else. So if you have a dog used to spending time outside, this is an option to consider.

$$–$$$ Hotel Denver, 402 7th St., 970-945-6565 (800-826-8820). We give this hotel high marks for dog friendliness as well as value. The rooms are modern and comfortably furnished, though the building dates from the early 1900s, and you can leave your dog unattended in them. The Glenwood Canyon Brewing Company, which serves its own microbrews and a full menu, is conveniently located off the lobby. In fact, the aroma of hops pervaded the hotel when we arrived.

$$–$$$$ Hotel Colorado, 526 Pine St., 970-945-6511 (800-544-3998; Denver direct line is 303-623-3400). Let your dog be part of history with a stay at this elegant hotel, listed on the National Register of Historic Places, which boasts many past luminaries among its guests, including President Theodore Roosevelt. Clover turned up her nose at the lowest-priced standard rooms but decided that the parlor rooms and suites, recently refurbished and individually decorated with Victorian-style furniture, would more than suffice. Guest dogs receive biscuits on check-in and are even able to order from the room-service menu (dry or moist dog food, delivered in a dog dish). Owners must put down a $25 deposit and can actually leave a dog unattended in the room, though housekeeping won't service the room unless the dog is safely contained in a crate.

Marble

$ Beaver Lake Lodge, 201 E. Silver St., 970-963-2504. There are five rooms in the main lodge building and five rustic cabins, with kitchens. Your dog is welcome to stay with you in either, and he can be left unattended. The lodge is open from mid-May through the end of October.

$$ Chair Mountain Ranch, 0178 County Rd. 3, 970-963-9522. The ranch is situated on eight acres by the Crystal River, and dogs are allowed in any of the five cabins for a $5 fee per night. You can even leave your dog unattended for a few hours or tie him up outside. The owners do ask that you keep your dog leashed on the ranch property because of the abun-

dance of chickens and ducks. If your dog does accidentally have an encounter, you'll be assessed a $25 charge per feathered victim, so keep him close at hand. The ranch is usually closed from December to June.

New Castle

$ New Castle/Glenwood Springs KOA & Kamping Kabins, 0581 County Rd. 241, 970-984-2240 (800-KOA-3240). Dogs are allowed in the camping cabins as well as at the campground as long as they're leashed (you'll need to provide your own sleeping and cooking gear). And "if you leave the campground, your pet goes with you," the owner emphasizes. An enclosed dog area is available, and your dog can run off leash here, but you must supervise him.

Parachute

$ Super 8, 252 Green St., 970-285-7936 (800-800-8000). With a $20 deposit, dogs are welcome and can be left unattended in the room.

Redstone

$$ Redstone Cliffs Motel, 433 Redstone Blvd., 970-963-2691. The motel offers studio or one-bedroom apartments with kitchenettes in a log-cabin-style setup. For $5 a night, your dog can join you.

$$ Redstone Inn, 82 Redstone Blvd., 970-963-2526 or 800-748-2524. Dogs under sixty pounds are welcome to stay in lower-level and first-floor rooms at this turn-of-the-century hotel. And they can romp, leashed, on the inn's twenty-two acres. There's a $25 fee per stay.

$$–$$$ Avalanche Ranch, 12863 Highway 133, 970-963-2846. You've got to love a place that advertises "pets welcome" on the front of its brochure. Owner Sharon Boucher says it's her "mission" to provide lodging that you can enjoy with your dog. Twelve cabins are situated on forty-five acres where dogs can romp unleashed. There is a $10 fee per pet, per night, with a maximum of two dogs per cabin. Along with full kitchens for human convenience, doggie towels are provided in each cabin, and dogs receive biscuits on check-in.

Rifle

$ Red River Inn, 718 Taughenbaugh Blvd., 970-625-3050 (800-733-3152). Dogs are allowed at this motel with a $25 deposit per pet.

$ Rusty Cannon Motel, 701 Taughenbaugh Blvd., 970-625-4004. Four smoking rooms are set aside for pets. There's a $20 deposit, and management says it will call the police if you leave your dog unattended in the room. You've been warned.

$–$$ La Donna Motel, 101 Ray Ave., 970-625-1741. For a $20 deposit, you can stay here with your dog.

Silt

$ Red River Inn, 1200 Main St., 970-876-2346 (800-377-7779). The motel allows small dogs only, and only in smoking rooms. A $10 deposit is required.

Campgrounds

State Park Campgrounds: **Rifle Falls State Park**—see "Tail-Rated Trails" for directions (18 sites); **Rifle Gap State Park,** on Highway 325 outside of Rifle, just a few miles before Rifle Falls State Park (46 sites).

National Forest campgrounds: There are a number of campgrounds along Coffee Pot Rd. (Forest Rd. 600), 2 miles north of Dotsero off I-70, including **Coffee Pot Spring**

> A nice place to eat in the company of your dog is Kiwanis (or Veltus) Park, off of Midland Ave. between 8th and 10th sts., on the banks of the Roaring Fork River.

Campground (15 sites) and **Deep Lake Campground** (45 sites); **Bogan Flats Campground,** on the Marble road off Highway 133 (37 sites); and **Redstone Campground,** about a mile north of Redstone (37 sites).

Private campgrounds: **New Castle/Glenwood Springs KOA** in New Castle (see "Creature Comforts").

DOGGIE DAYCARE
Carbondale

Mid-Valley Kennel, 16478 Highway 82 (west of Carbondale), 970-963-2744. $10–$12, depending on the size of dog. A stay here includes the use of indoor and outdoor runs, exercise and play time, and a choice of four kinds of Iams dog food. Open 8 A.M.–5 P.M., Monday to Saturday; 2–5 P.M., Sunday.

Skyline Ranch and Kennels, 0356 County Rd. 101, 970-963-2915. $7/day. Open 7:30 A.M.–5:30 P.M., Monday to Saturday.

CANINE ER
Carbondale

Alpine Animal Hospital, 17776 Highway 82, 970-963-2371. Open 9 A.M.–noon and 1–5 P.M., Monday to Friday; 9 A.M.–noon, Saturday.

Carbondale Animal Hospital, 234 Main St., 970-963-2826. Open 8 A.M.–5 P.M., Monday to Friday; 9 A.M.–noon, Saturday.

Glenwood Springs

Allpets Animal Hospital, 1605 Grand Ave., 970-945-6762. Open 8 A.M.–5:30 P.M., Monday to Friday; 9 A.M.–1 P.M., Saturday.

Birch Tree Animal Hospital, 1602 Grand Ave., 970-945-0125. Open 8 A.M.–5:30 P.M., Monday to Friday; 8 A.M.–noon, two Saturdays each month.

Glenwood Veterinary Clinic, 2514 Grand Ave., 970-945-5401. Open 8 A.M.–5 P.M., Monday to Friday; 8 A.M.–noon, Saturday.

RESOURCES

Bureau of Land Management, 50629 Highway 6 & 24, Glenwood Springs, 970-947-2800

Eagle Ranger District, White River National Forest, 125 W. 5th St., Eagle, 970-328-6388

Forest Supervisor's Office, White River National Forest, 900 Grand Ave., Glenwood Springs, 970-945-2521

Glenwood Springs Chamber Resort Association, 1102 Grand Ave., Glenwood Springs, 970-945-6589 (www.glenscape.com)

Lodging Reservations, 1-888-4-GLENWOOD

Rifle Ranger District, White River National Forest, 0094 County Road 244, Rifle, 970-625-2371

Sopris Ranger District, White River National Forest, 620 Main St., Carbondale, 970-963-2266

Summit Canyon Mountaineering, 8th and Grand Ave., Glenwood Springs, 945-6994 (800-360-6994), has an extensive collection of guidebooks and maps.

13
Northwestern Colorado

THE BIG SCOOP

The area of Colorado that's west of Craig and north of I-70 embodies the wide open spaces of the West. This is desert and canyon country, though even in the summer temperatures are cooler than in the Grand Junction area, for example, usually topping out in the 80s. But the very characteristic that can make it an appealing place for you and your dog to visit can also be its downfall—there's not a lot here. The principal towns are Craig, Meeker, and Rangely, all small, with just a few even smaller ones dotting the landscape. There's lots of BLM land where you can hike with your dog off leash, but the developed trails are few (and you can't bring your dog on the trails in Dinosaur National Monument). For forested, mountainous terrain, head east of Meeker into the White River National Forest and the Flat Tops Wilderness Area. Several guest ranches in this region welcome canine visitors. Just remember that you'll have to keep your dog on leash in designated Wilderness areas.

TAIL-RATED TRAILS

BLM land. Almost all BLM land in this part of the state is undeveloped, meaning there aren't established trailheads or regularly maintained trails. *But you can bring your dog anywhere, and he can be off leash.* Just be sure to bring a topo map along, as well as lots of water.

The land on either side of Harpers Corner Rd., which leads from the Dinosaur National Monument visitor center outside of Dinosaur to the park itself, is BLM managed. On the west side of the road is the **Bull Canyon Wilderness Study Area,** and on the east side is the **Willow Creek Wilderness Study Area.** From the Plug Hat Butte picnic area, 3.5 miles up Harpers Corner Rd. from the visitor center, you can take a 4- or 5-mile round-trip hike into **Lower Buckwater Draw;** you'll find a waterfall in the draw in spring. For more hiking suggestions, stop by the BLM office in Meeker (see "Resources"), which has some printed route descriptions. *Exploring Colorado's Wild Areas,* by Scott S. Warren, also has information about hiking routes on BLM land in northwestern Colorado as well as for other areas throughout the state.

Dinosaur National Monument. The monument straddles Utah and Colorado and includes Echo Park, at the confluence of the Green and Yampa Rivers, the site of a proposed dam that was scuttled in a celebrated showdown between the Federal government and the Sierra Club in the 1960s. Though the monument's name comes from dinosaur bones discovered in the area, you can only actually see the fossils at the Dinosaur Quarry, 7 miles north of Jensen, Utah. The park's Headquarters Visitor Center is 2 miles east of Dinosaur, Colorado. Dogs are not allowed on trails, anywhere else in the backcountry, or on river trips through the park. You can bring your dog to the quarry, though you'll have to leave him tied up outside while you view the fossil exhibits. And he can come to the campgrounds and picnic areas as long as he's always on a leash.

CYCLING FOR CANINES

The BLM office in Craig (see "Resources") has a handy pamphlet called "Mountain Bike Routes of Moffat County." Note that there's a leash law throughout Moffat County, so unless a bike route is actually on BLM or National Forest land (and not all of the ones listed in the pamphlet are), it won't be practical for Fido to come along. The **Yampa Valley Trail** runs for 100 miles from the town of Maybell to within Dinosaur National Monument. You can access a singletrack section of it from Deerlodge Rd., about 20 miles west of Maybell, near the Cross Mountain turnout.

Sometimes charm can get you in anywhere. (photo by Tim Hancock)

CREATURE COMFORTS

Unless otherwise stated, dogs should not be left unattended in the room or cabin.

Craig

$ **Colorado Inn**, 205 E. Victory Way, 970-824-3274. You can leave your dog unattended in the room.

$ **Craig Motel**, 894 Yampa Ave., 970-824-4481

$ **El Rancho Motel**, 627 W. Victory Way, 970-824-3233 (800-530-2003). There's a $4 one-time fee for a dog.

$ **Trav-O-Tel**, 224 E. Victory Way, 970-824-8171 (888-824-8171). Dogs less than 50 pounds are permitted.

$ **Westward Ho Motel**, 517 E. Victory Way, 970-824-3413. There's a $3 fee per night for dogs.

$–$$ **A Bar Z Motel**, 2690 W. Highway 40, 970-824-7066 (800-458-7228). Dogs are welcome for $5 extra per night, though they're not allowed in the front desk area. The motel is on two acres where you can walk your dog off leash.

$$ **Best Western Inn of Craig**, 755 E. Victory Way, 970-824-8101 (800-528-1234)

$$ **Holiday Inn**, 300 S. Highway 13, 970-824-4000 (800-HOLIDAY). You can leave your dog unattended in the room.

$$ **Ramada Unlimited**, 262 Commerce St., 970-824-9282. If you're paying with cash, you'll need to put down a $50 deposit or leave a credit-card imprint. Management prefers that you not leave your dog unattended in the room, but if you must for a short time, let them know about it.

$$ **Super 8 Motel**, 200 Highway 13, 970-824-3274 (800-800-8000). Dogs are allowed with a $25 deposit.

Dinosaur

$ **Hi-Vu Motel**, 122 E. Brontosaurus Blvd., 970-374-2267. This is the only place in Colorado where your dog can stay at an address that sounds like it's out of *The Flintstones*. The motel allows dogs in six of its eight rooms, for a $4 fee per night. Open April 1 to December.

Meeker

$ **Ducey's White River Resort**, 12830 County Rd. 8 (14 miles east of Meeker), 970-878-4378. This small resort has four one-bedroom cabins, equipped with kitchenettes but not with bathrooms (those are in separate buildings). You must keep your dog leashed at all times on the property and be sure to clean up after him. The White River runs through a part of the property. Open April 1 to November 15.

$ Rustic Lodge, 173 First St., 970-878-3136. The cabins here are actually not quite as rustic inside as they look on the outside. The owner emphasizes that "mean, aggressive" dogs will not be welcome. There's a resident three-legged dog with whom yours might like to socialize.

$ Valley Motel, 723 Market St., 970-878-3656. The motel has four rooms, all smoking, where dogs can stay.

$-$$ Buford Store and Lodge, 20474 County Rd. 8 (22 miles east of Meeker), 970-878-4745. This historic lodge is located on 235 acres along the North Fork of the White River, bordering the National Forest. Ten rustic log cabins are fully furnished but have no bathrooms or running water; there's a central bathhouse for guests. And you'll prepare your meals on a wood-burning cookstove. The oldest of the cabins is more than 100 years old; the "youngest" is about seventy-five years old. You can also rent two modern cabins, which do have full baths. In addition to the cabins, the lodge has a grocery store, gas station, and small museum on the premises. There's a $5 one-time fee for a dog, and you can leave yours unattended inside the cabin. But with hiking trails nearby, as well as off-leash privileges on the lodge's property, you won't have any reason to leave Rover behind. Open May 1 to November 15.

$-$$ Meeker Hotel and Cafe, 560 Main St., 970-878-5255 (800-847-6470). No doubt your dog will be intrigued by the numerous elk and deer heads adorning the lobby walls. The hotel, built in 1896, is on the National Register of Historic Places, and the rooms, though not incredibly luxu-rious, are cozy and furnished with antiques. Several of the twenty-four rooms are dog friendly; a $50 deposit is required. You can leave your dog unattended in the room for an hour or two at a time.

$-$$ Pollard's Ute Lodge, 393 County Rd. 75 (30 miles east of Meeker), 970-878-4669. Eleven cabins, from one to three bedrooms, are at the lodge, which is on 324 acres near the Flat Tops Wilderness Area. The rustic yet cozy log cabins are fully outfitted, and you can leave your dog unattended inside. He can also explore the property, which includes a lake and a creek, off-leash under your supervision. Horseback riding is also available from the lodge. Open from about mid-May to mid-November.

$-$$ Sleepy Cat Guest Ranch, 16064 County Rd. 8 (17 miles east of Meeker), 970-878-4413. Okay, before your dog gets all excited about some unsuspecting cat he can chase around, tell him that Sleepy Cat is actually the name of a mountain in the area. The ranch has twenty-one cabins in a variety of styles, all fully equipped, and dogs can stay for $6 extra per night. There's also a full-service restaurant on premises that gets great reviews. Your dog can sniff out 110 acres, some bordering the White River, off leash. Open year-round.

$-$$ Trappers Lake Lodge, 7700 Trappers Lake Rd. (50 miles east of Meeker), 970-878-3336. Located waaayy out there, the lodge is surrounded by the Flat Tops Wilderness. You and your dog can stay in one of twelve primitive cabins; some have propane heat, some wood-burning stoves, and all share a central bathhouse. There's a $10 one-time fee for a dog, and you can leave yours unattended inside. Dogs are not allowed in the lodge lobby, however, and they need to be kept leashed on the lodge's eleven acres so as not to interfere with the resident working dogs. And make sure your dog stays off the bed! Activities at the lodge include horseback riding, fishing, and boating. There's a restaurant, too. Open year-round, except from November 1 to mid-December. During the winter, one of the lodge's two snow coaches will transport you over the last 17 miles of road.

$$ Adams Lodge, 2400 County Rd. 12 (30 miles east of Meeker), **970-878-4312.** The lodge offers ten fully furnished cabins, and the owners emphasize that visiting dogs cannot lie on the beds. You can walk your dog off leash around the cabins, but be aware that there is a lot of wildlife, as well as llamas and cats, around. Two of the cabins stay open year-round; the others are open from Memorial Day to November 1.

Rangely
$ 4 Queens Motel, 206 E. Main St., 970-675-5035. Dogs can stay for $4 extra per night. You can leave your dog unattended in the room; just let the front desk know so that housekeeping won't go in during that time.

> Canine spectators are discouraged from attending one of Meeker's most famous events—the Meeker Classic Sheepdog Championship Trials, in early September. Leave Fido at home and promise him you'll share some good tips.

Campgrounds
Dinosaur National Monument. The park has six established camping areas, three in Colorado: Gates of Lodore, Deerlodge Park, and Echo Park (38 primitive sites total).

Bureau of Land Management campgrounds: Camping is allowed anywhere on BLM land.

Doggie Daycare
Craig
McCandless Animal Hospital, 2430 E. Victory, 970-824-5964. $8/day. Open 8 A.M.–noon and 1:30–5 P.M., Monday to Thursday; 9 A.M.–noon and 1:30–5 P.M., Friday. Day boarding not available on weekends.

Canine ER
Craig
High Country Veterinary Clinic, 356 N. Ranney, 970-824-2243. Open 10 A.M.–6 P.M., Monday to Friday.

McCandless Animal Hospital, 2430 E. Victory, 970-824-5964. Open 8 A.M.–noon and 1:30–5 P.M., Monday to Thursday; 9 A.M.–noon and 1:30–5 P.M., Friday; 8 A.M.–noon, Saturday.

Resources
Blanco Ranger District, White River National Forest, 317 E. Marker St., Meeker, 970-878-4039

Bureau of Land Management, 1280 Industrial Ave., Craig, 970-824-4441

Bureau of Land Management, 73544 Highway 64, Meeker, 970-878-3601

Colorado Welcome Center, Route 64, Dinosaur, 970-374-2205

Meeker Chamber of Commerce, 710 Market St., Meeker, 970-878-5510

Moffat County Visitor Center, 360 E. Victory Way, Craig, 970-824-5689 (800-864-4405)

Rangely Area Chamber of Commerce, 209 E. Main St., Rangely, 970-675-5290

14
Grand Junction and Vicinity

THE BIG SCOOP

The Grand Valley is dinosaur country. The legacy of these giant reptiles that roamed the area millions of years ago lives on in museums and fossil sites. But if your dog is already panting at the thought of humongous bones, you'll have to break the news to him that most of the dinosaur-related attractions don't allow dogs. Still, there's plenty to do. Spring and fall are the best times to visit Grand Junction and points west if you're a dog; the summer can be just too darn hot, and there aren't very many trees under which to seek respite or creeks to jump into in the desert. If you are in the area during the "nondog"-day months of June, July, or August, consider escaping to the forested lakes of Grand Mesa for the sake of your fur-coated companion.

In addition to the expected leash law throughout Grand Junction, there's an enforced "pooper scooper" law in all city parks. (Of course, you should be cleaning up after your dog on the sidewalks as well.) Neighboring Fruita allows dogs to be under voice command but requires that they be leashed in all city parks. You don't have to go far, however, to find miles of unrestricted dog territory. One of the least regulatory land overseers—the Bureau of Land Management—manages much of the area surrounding Grand Junction, making it a particularly good bet for leash-free dog hikes.

TAIL-RATED TRAILS

There are hundreds of miles of trails on Grand Mesa, which contains the Grand

Mesa National Forest. Unfortunately, many of them are open to all-terrain vehicle (ATV) use as well as to hikers, bikers, and horseback riders. For good dog-hike options, consider the **Coal Creek Trail** (described here) or the **Kannah Creek Trail** (12 miles one way), neither of which permit motorized use. Both can be accessed from Carson Lake off of Lands End Rd. The **Lake of the Woods Trail** (about 11.5 miles round-trip to Cottonwood Lake #1) is another good possibility. *Note that on the immensely popular Crag Crest Trail, dogs must be leashed.*

Coal Creek Trail. 9 miles one way. The trail, which heads up (or down) the Grand Mesa, can be accessed from a lower or an upper trailhead. Hiking from the upper access is not usually available until June, when the snow has melted enough to open the top section of Lands End Rd. To reach the lower trailhead, drive south on Highway 50 from Grand Junction for about 12 miles, to the Lands End Rd. turnoff to the left. Go about 14 miles (the road turns to dirt after 9 miles) to the Wild Rose Picnic Area on the right. The trail begins at the far side of the parking lot. To reach the upper trailhead, head down Lands End Rd. from the top of Grand Mesa for 3.1 miles; turn left on the Carson Lake Rd. Take the road until its end at Carson Lake. The trail begins just below the lower parking area. *Dogs can be off leash.*

From the lower trailhead, the well-maintained trail climbs at a fairly gradual pace toward the rim of the mesa. You'll cross several streams in the first half mile or so. Get your dog to stop long enough so you can admire the wonderful vista of the Kannah Creek Basin below and the Uncompahgre Plateau to the southwest. As the trail ascends the mesa, it winds by large stands of aspen—making this a good candidate for a fall hike—as well as small, scrubby oakbrush. Unless you've arranged a car shuttle at Carson Lake, you'll probably want to turn around before reaching the mesa top.

Whitewater Creek Trail. 7.5 miles one way to rim of Grand Mesa; 3.5 miles farther to West Bench Trail. Take Highway 50 south from Grand Junction. When you reach the town of Whitewater (about 12 miles out of Grand Junction), turn left onto Reeder Mesa Rd. (past the Whitewater General Store). After 2.2 miles, make a left onto White–water Creek Rd. From there, it's 2.5 miles to the trailhead on the right side of the road (if you reach Lumbardy Ranch, you've gone a little too far). There's no parking area, but you'll be able to pull over at the side of the road. The trail sign was knocked over when we visited, but look for a brown carsonite stake that marks the start of the trail. *Dogs can be off leash, but watch for cows.*

If you traveled the entire length of this trail, you'd hike from desert to subalpine zone, as it eventually climbs steeply up a basin to the top of Grand Mesa, connecting to the West Bench Trail. Chances are, however, that you and your dog will stick to the sand and sage of the first several miles. And you may well be able to enjoy some quality solitary hiking time together, as the trail is not heavily used. Moreover, it's free from the dirt-bike and ATV traffic of nearby areas, as it's designated for hiker use only. The trail is well marked at regular intervals with wooden stakes indicating "WWC." Pay attention to your route, however, so you can return the same way—

Artemis soaks up the sun in canyon country. (photo by Karen Pauly)

there's a network of cow trails that could get confusing. Whitewater Creek is, despite its name, slow moving and green. But Clover didn't seem to mind; it gave her a respite from the arid surroundings.

McDonald Creek. About 4 miles roundtrip. The McDonald Creek Cultural Resource Area is part of the BLM's Rabbit Valley Recreation Management Area. One of the beauties of this trail is that no motorized vehicles—or even bikes—are permitted. As you'll quickly surmise from driving to the trailhead, the rest of the Rabbit Valley area is a vast playground for ATVs, jeeps, and motorcycles. From Grand Junction, head west on I-70 for 30 miles to the Rabbit Valley exit (Exit 2). Cross over the highway and pass a parking area for Rabbit Valley Recreation Area. Take the next right. Though the dirt road is narrow and bumpy, my low-clearance Toyota Celica did just fine. Follow the small Kokopelli's Trail decals on brown posts along the road for about 2.3 miles. Just after a small parking pullout on the right, watch for a sign to McDonald Creek and a road to the left. After taking this left, follow the road all the way to a small parking area at the trailhead. *Dogs can be off leash.*

First of all, don't be fooled by the name—there's no actual creek here, just a sandy wash, so bring along plenty of water on this desert hike. The trail allows for some exploring, as several paths wind through the wash, though you'll always be heading south. You'll soon be immersed in a landscape of sculpted sandstone, red sand, and pungent sage. Keep an eye out for rock art as you hike; four panels supposedly grace the canyon (we only spotted three). The trail ends at a set of railroad tracks (stay alert) along the Colorado River. Though it would be difficult to access the river from here, a small tributary comes in near the trail's end, and your dog can take a well-deserved dip.

For another hikers-only venue in the area, try the 5-mile round-trip **Rabbit's Ear Trail,** which leads to the Ruby Canyon overlook of the Colorado River. You can reach it by staying on the road from the I-70 overpass instead of turning right as for McDonald Creek. Drive 4.4 miles to the signed trailhead on the right, where there's also a small parking area.

Old Spanish Trail. Runs about 4 miles along the Gunnison River bluffs. Situated in the Orchard Mesa section of Grand Junction, this area has some historical significance: The North Branch of the Old Spanish Trail, which was used first by traders and trappers and then by wagon trains in the 1800s, passed through. To reach the present-day trail, head south on Highway 50 from downtown Grand Junction. About 2.5 miles from the bridge over the Colorado River, look for a sign that reads "Fairgrounds Livestock entrance" and make a right (you'll also see Lions Park). Go up a block and turn left on 28¹/₂ Rd. Look for the brown-and-white "Old Spanish Trail" sign immediately on the right. Pull into the gravel parking area. This trail can also be accessed from a southern trailhead near the

town of Whitewater. Drive about 2 miles farther on Highway 50. Make a right onto the landfill access road, and follow Old Whitewater Rd. about 1.5 miles to the trailhead. *Dogs can be off leash.*

Don't pack up your dog's leash just yet; you'll have to walk through a few neighborhood streets to actually reach the trail. Once there, the route follows a wide dirt track that stretches off into the distance. This is not the most scenic hike—there are no trees, and you won't actually see much of the river—but it's a great place that's close to town for exercising your dog. And although there's no shade, your dog may enjoy a stiff breeze off the river rippling through his fur. The **Gunnison Bluffs Trail** is also directly accessible from the southernmost trailhead described above as well as by taking various small unmarked paths from the Old Spanish Trail, heading toward the river. The trail seems promising, as it runs directly above the river, but will have to wait for a return visit to get our tail-wag evaluation.

Colorado River Trails. Varying lengths. An extensive trail system has been developed in the past decade at various points along the Colorado River. The system is divided into six main portions: the Palisade Trail; the Corn Lake section of Colorado River State Park; Watson Island; and the Audubon Trail, Blue Heron Trail, and Connected Lakes sections of Colorado River State Park, collectively known as the Redlands Loop. For more detailed information on specific trails, including access points and mileages, pick up the "Colorado River Trails" brochure, produced by the Colorado Riverfront Foundation, at the Grand Junction Visitor Center or Chamber of Commerce (see "Resources").

One recommended hike begins at the Audubon trailhead and continues to Connected Lakes, a series of reclaimed gravel pits that have been turned into lakes. It's about 4 miles round-trip. To access the

Audubon Trail, take Grand Ave. west from downtown. Cross the Colorado River; at the intersection with Dike Rd., turn right into the Brach's Corner shopping plaza. Signed parking for the trail is at the far end of the lot. *Dogs must be leashed.*

Clover and I enjoyed a pleasant amble along this paved trail, which is partially shaded by cottonwoods and borders riparian habitat as it runs along the Redlands Canal. Once at Connected Lakes, your dog will have his choice of gravel trails that wind around and between the lakes. There's lots of water here, obviously, as well as cooling breezes off the river. Note that if you drive into the park rather than hike in via the Audubon Trail, you'll have to pay the standard entrance fee.

 Highline State Park. A 3-mile loop. To reach the park, which is northwest of Grand Junction in Loma, take I-70 west to the Loma exit (Exit 15). Head north on Route 139 for about 5 miles to Q Rd., then make a left and drive 1.2 miles to 11.8 Rd. Turn right; the park entrance is about 1 mile ahead. *Dogs must be leashed.*

The park is a welcome oasis of grass, trees, and water in the midst of arid surroundings. The **Highline Lake Trail** is an easy, level stroll along a combination of dirt road and wide gravel path that circles the lake. While you gaze at the Book Cliffs to the northeast, your dog can amuse himself by splashing in the water and watching the water-skiers go by. Clover particularly enjoyed our evening walk here. There are several bird-watching blinds at the far side of the lake, so take care that your pooch doesn't disturb any birders who may be present (as well as the birds they're watching). Note that dogs are not allowed on the park's swim beach.

 Rabbit Valley Trail Through Time. A 1.5-mile loop. From Grand Junction, head west on I-70 for 30 miles to the Rabbit Valley exit (Exit 2). Turn right and drive to the trailhead parking area straight ahead. *Dogs must be leashed.*

This is the only dinosaur-related activity in the Grand Junction area in which your dog is welcome to participate. In addition to a working dinosaur quarry on the premises, an interpretive trail highlights dinosaur fossil imprints as well as the geology of the area. Do keep your dog on his leash so he's not tempted to start his own quarry excavation—and remind him that fossil collecting is prohibited by law on all BLM lands.

 Colorado National Monument. Your dog can view the wondrous cliffs and canyons of the monument out the car window or from within the confines of the campground, but he's not allowed to set paw on any of the trails.

Cycling for Canines

The area around Grand Junction offers lots of riding opportunities, and nearby Fruita is becoming something of a mountain-biking mecca. The good news is that many of the rides are on BLM land, so your dog is free (literally) to accompany you. The bad news is that you'll definitely want to keep your rides on the shorter side so that your dog doesn't die of heatstroke in the desert. For descriptions and maps of some of the classic routes, pick up a copy of *River City Rides,* by Toby Gold and Alix Craig, at a local bike shop. **Over the Edge Sports,** 202 E. Aspen Ave. in downtown Fruita, is a helpful source of maps and information.

Approximately 7.8-mile-long **Lions Loop** is a popular ride west of Grand Junction that begins near the Mack exit (Exit 11) off I-70. It follows Kokopelli's Trail (which goes all the way to Moab, Utah) for part of its length. Look for a flyer with detailed route information on this ride (along with Mary's Loop and tips for Kokopelli's Trail) at a cycle shop.

Grand Mesa is another good biking choice, and it offers the advantage of fir, spruce, and aspen to make your ride (and your dog's run) a little cooler. Try the **West Bench Trail**, which runs about 5.5 miles from the Mesa Lakes Ranger Station to Powderhorn Ski Area, or the 11.5-mile (round-trip) **Lake of the Woods Trail,** which ends at Cottonwood Lake, allowing your dog to go for a welcome swim.

POWDERHOUNDS

The Grand Mesa is the place to head for wintertime recreation with your dog. The Mesa Lakes Resort (near milepost 36 on Highway 65) maintains 6 to 8 miles of groomed trails that can be accessed from the lodge or at the Jumbo National Forest Service Campground. There's no trail fee, and the lodge's owners graciously allow anyone, including those who aren't guests at the lodge, to use the trails. The lodge also operates a ski rental shop.

Some recommended backcountry trail areas on the mesa (none of which cross through avalanche terrain) include **Water Dog Reservoir, Griffith Lakes,** and **Deep Creek.** The 11-mile round-trip West Bench Trail, which starts from the Mesa Lakes Ranger Station, is also a popular winter ski or snowshoe tour. Stop in at the Forest Service office in Grand Junction (see "Resources") or at the Mesa Lakes Lodge for maps and more trail info.

The Grand Mesa Nordic Council maintains trails at three different sites on the mesa—Ward Creek, County Line, and Skyway; however, they ask that you leave your dog at home.

> Heatstroke is a real risk to your dog when exercising in desert country. If you notice him having difficulty breathing, panting to excess, or refusing to go any farther, get him water immediately; even better, immerse him in water, if possible.

CREATURE COMFORTS

If you can trust your dog on his own, it's a good idea to find lodging where you can leave him unattended while you go out to eat, for example. The high temperatures in the Grand Junction area make it especially inadvisable to leave your dog in the car.

Unless otherwise stated, dogs should not be left unattended in the room or cabin.

Dogs can find respite from the heat in the Grand Mesa National Forest. (photo by Cindy Hirschfeld)

Cedaredge

$–$$ Super 8 Motel, 530 S. Grand Mesa Dr., 970-856-7824 (800-800-8000). Several designated pet rooms are available. There's a $10 fee per night, and if you're paying with cash, a $20 deposit is required. You'll also be asked to sign a "pet rules" form.

Clifton

$$ Best Western Clifton Inn, 3228 I-70 Business Loop, 970-434-3400 (800-528-1234). Dogs 25 pounds and under can stay, and management emphasizes that only adult dogs are welcome.

Collbran

$ Alpine Motel, 102 Spring St., 970-487-3220. "Dogs have to be very friendly" to stay at the motel, says the owner, with his tongue somewhat in his cheek. "We all have dogs here." You can leave your friendly pooch unattended in the room for a few hours at a time.

$ Vega Motel, 6724 64 6/10 Rd., 970-487-3733. There's a $5 fee per night for dogs, and they can be left unattended in the room.

$$ Spruce Inn Bed and Breakfast, 112 Main St., 970-487-0225. "We love dogs," says the friendly operator of this B&B in an 1889 Victorian house, which has a resident heeler. You and your dog have your pick of three individually decorated rooms or a bunk room. And if your dog needs a short break from romping on nearby Grand Mesa, you can leave him in the room unattended. "Our house is your house" is the motto here.

Fruita

$ Balanced Rock Motel, 126 S. Coulson, 970-858-7333

$ H Motel, 333 Highway 6 & 50, 970-858-7198. You'll be in a smoking room here as long as your dog's with you. There's a $5 fee per night as well as a $20 deposit. You can leave your dog unattended in the room.

$ Park Hotel, 150 S. Park Sq., 970-858-3917 (800-878-3917). A funky combination of rooming house and overnight lodging, this small, 100-year-old hotel has cozy rooms nicely furnished with antiques. (All rooms have shared baths.) If you don't mind the comings and goings of the people who actually live here, it's a nice change for you and your dog from the chain-motel lodging that dominates the area. And the rates can't be beat.

$–$$ Super 8 Motel, 399 Jurassic, 970-858-0808 (800-800-8000). Dogs can stay in smoking rooms only, with a $25 deposit. They can be left unattended in the room.

$$ West Gate Inn, 2210 Highways 6 & 50, 970-241-3020 (800-453-9253). It's smoking rooms only for dogs at this motel, but they can be left unattended.

$$–$$$ Grapeland Bed and Breakfast, 1763 K 6/10 Rd., 970-858-0741. This new B&B has gotten rave reviews from dog owners and mountain bikers alike. The three rooms, one of them a suite with sitting area, are decorated country style. Small dogs (lap-size) can stay with their owners

in the rooms (and be left unattended), and a half-acre or so fenced-in area in the back accommodates large dogs. At night, the big dogs get their own sleeping quarters in the Grapeland's barn. Your dog will have plenty of company here, as the animal-loving owners have three yorkies, a border collie/blue heeler mix, and four cats. The B&B has also started hosting "murder mystery weekends" in which your dog can play a part in sniffing out who done it.

Grand Junction

$ Columbine Motel, 2824 North Ave., 970-241-2908. The motel allows one dog per room.

$ El Rio Rancho Motel, 730 Highway 50 South, 970-242-0256. There's a $5 fee per night.

$ Motel 6, 776 Horizon Dr., 970-243-2628. The policy is one small dog per room.

$ Peachtree Inn, 1600 North Ave., 970-245-5770 (800-525-0030)

$ Prospector Motel, 547 Highway 50 South, 970-242-4891. Dogs are allowed in smoking rooms only, with a $5 fee per night. They can be left unattended in the room.

$ Super 8 Motel, 728 Horizon Dr., 970-248-8080 (800-800-8000). With a $25 deposit, dogs are allowed to stay, but only in smoking rooms. They can be left unattended.

$ Value Lodge, 104 White Ave., 970-242-0651. Certain rooms are set aside as pet rooms at the motel, which charges $5 per night for dogs.

$–$$ Country Inn of Grand Junction, 718 Horizon Dr., 970-243-5080 (800-990-1143). The motel has about six designated pet rooms. There's a $5 fee per night for dogs as well as a $50 deposit if you're paying with cash.

$–$$ Two Rivers Inn, 141 North First St., 970-245-8585. The motel allows dogs in its upstairs (i.e., older) rooms, for a $5 fee per night.

$$ Best Western Horizon Inn, 754 Horizon Dr., 970-245-1410 (800-544-3782). Note that the Best Western Sandman, down the street, does *not* accept pets.

$$ Days Inn of Grand Junction, 733 Horizon Dr., 970-245-7200 (800-790-2661). The motel has six pet rooms and requires a $50 deposit.

$$ Holiday Inn Grand Junction, 755 Horizon Dr., 970-243-6790 (800-HOLIDAY). You'll have your choice of a smoking room or a nonsmoking room to stay here with your dog. You can leave him unattended in the room.

$$ Howard Johnson Lodge, 752 Horizon Dr., 970-243-5150 (800-446-4656). Dogs are allowed in smoking rooms only, and there's a $10 one-time fee. You can leave your dog unattended in the room.

$$ Ramada Inn, 2790 Crossroads Blvd., 970-241-8411 (800-2-RAMADA). Dogs 25 pounds and under are welcome at the Ramada, where they can stay in ground-floor rooms. There's a $10 one-time fee. You can leave your dog unattended inside.

$$$ Grand Junction Hilton, 743 Horizon Dr., 970-241-8888 (800-360-4066). Dogs usually stay in second- or third-floor rooms here. You must put a credit card down on the room as well as fill out a pet application. And there will be a room inspection before you and your dog check out. But it's also one of the nicest places to stay in town that accepts pets.

Grand Mesa
$–$$ Grand Mesa Lodge, Highway 65 (near milepost 28), 970-856-3250 (800-551-MESA). Your dog will be greeted here by canine residents Timber and Buffy. The lodge offers motel rooms as well as one- and two-bedroom cabins. Dogs are allowed in both, but the owners prefer that

they stay in the cabins. You can leave your dog unattended in either. Plans are also in the works for kennels outside some of the cabins. Your dog may want to explore Island Lake, the largest lake on the mesa, right behind the lodge buildings; be sure to keep him leashed at all times. Open year-round.

$–$$ Mesa Lakes Resort, Highway 65 (near milepost 36), 970-268-5467. The resort offers motel rooms, rustic cabins (no running water), and modern cabins, and dogs can stay in any of them for a $5 one-time fee. You can also leave your dog unattended in your room or cabin. Open year-round.

Mesa
$ The Wagon Wheel Motel, 1090 Highway 65, 970-268-5224

Palisade
$$–$$$ Orchard House, 3573 E ½ Rd., 970-464-0529. Pets are negotiable at this B&B in Colorado wine country, "but their behavior would have to meet certain standards," emphasizes the owner. The owner is considering adding a kennel for future visiting dogs, so if you have an outdoor dog, keep this possible option in mind.

Campgrounds
Colorado National Monument. Just west of Grand Junction, access off Highway 340, or off I-70 at the Fruita exit. The Saddlehorn Campground, near the visitor center, has 80 sites.

State Park campgrounds: **Highline Lake State Park**—see "Tail-Rated Trails" for directions (26 sites); **Colorado River State Parks/Island Acres**, Exit 47 off I-70, 5 miles east of Palisade (60 sites); **Vega State Park**, Highway 330, 12 miles past Collbran (110 sites).

BLM campgrounds: **Rabbit Valley**—see McDonald Creek in "Tail-Rated Trails" for directions.

National Forest campgrounds: **Grand Mesa** has fourteen campgrounds, with a range of 5 to 42 sites each.

Worth a Paws

Dog Jog. Sponsored by the Grand Valley Veterinary Medical Society, this annual run, usually held the second weekend of October, raises money for Project Pups, a low-cost spay and neuter program. You and your four-legged running partner have your pick of a 1-mile or 3-mile course, both in Grand Junction's Sherwood Park. Your entry fee also includes a T-shirt for you and a bandanna for your dog.

 Riggs Hill and Dinosaur Hill. Dogs are not allowed at either of these outdoor dinosaur fossil-viewing sites.

> Looking for a shady respite in Grand Junction? Bring your dog to Hawthorne Park, just a few blocks north of downtown west of 5th St., or Whitman Park, a few blocks in the other direction of downtown, also west of 5th St. Sherwood Park, bounded by Orchard Ave., 5th St., North Ave., and 1st St., is a popular dog spot, with its grassy expanse and paved path on its perimeter.

Doggie Daycare

Clifton
Upper Valley Kennels, 3460 G Rd., 970-464-5713. $7/day lets your dog choose between inside and outside runs and includes feeding. "We can be accommodating and flexible, because we live here," says owner Donna Bondurant. She'll even do pickup and delivery of your dog if necessary. Open 7 A.M.–6 P.M., Monday to Saturday; 4 P.M.–6 P.M., Sunday.

Fruita
Pet-a-Cure Pet Grooming, Boarding, and Supplies, 242 S. Mulberry, 970-858-0818.

$6/day. Open 8:30 A.M.–5:30 P.M., Monday to Friday. You can also board your dog on weekends with prior arrangement.

Grand Junction
All Pets Center, 424 S. 5th, 970-241-1976, $6.50/day. Open 7 A.M.–6 P.M., Monday to Friday; 8 A.M.–5 P.M., Saturday.

Animal Medical Clinic, 504 Fruitvale Ct., 970-434-4094. $6.50/day. Open 7 A.M.–7 P.M., Monday to Friday; 8 A.M.–5 P.M., Saturday.

Appleton Boarding Kennels, 621 24 Rd. (next to Mesa Mall), 970-242-1285. $5/day. Open 8:30 A.M.–5:30 P.M., Monday to Friday; 8:30 A.M.–noon, Saturday.

The Pet Spa, 2509 Industrial Ct., 970-241-8499. $3/day. Open 8 A.M.–6 P.M., Monday to Saturday; 9–9:30 A.M. (for dropoff) and 5–5:30 P.M. (for pickup) Sunday.

Your Best Friends Boarding Kennel and Grooming House, 2708 Highway 50, 970-244-8865. $5/day. Open 7 A.M.–6 P.M., Monday to Friday; 7 A.M.–1 P.M., Saturday; by appointment, Sunday.

Pet Provisions

Fruita
Nicole's Pampered Pets, 145 N. Mesa, 970-858-7387

Pet-a-Cure Pet Grooming, Boarding, and Supplies, 242 S. Mulberry, 970-858-0818

Grand Junction
Green Fields Seed and Feed, 520 S. 9th St., 970-241-0979

J + M Aquatics and Pet Center, Mesa Mall, 970-241-1456, and 28½ Rd. and North Ave., 970-245-2526

Mesa Feed and Farm Supply, 715 S. 7th St., 970-242-7762

Pet Company, 2830 North Ave. 970-241-3250

The Pet Spa, 2509 Industrial Ct., 970-241-8499

CANINE ER

Grand Junction

All Pets Center (AAHA certified), 424 S. 5th, 970-241-1976. Open 7 A.M.–6 P.M., Monday to Friday; 8 A.M.–5 P.M., Saturday.

Animal Medical Clinic (AAHA certified), 504 Fruitvale Ct., 970-434-4094. Open 7 A.M.–7 P.M., Monday to Friday; 8 A.M.–5 P.M., Saturday.

RESOURCES

Bureau of Land Management, 2815 H Rd., Grand Junction, 970-244-3000

Collbran Ranger District, Grand Mesa National Forest, 218 High St., Collbran, 970-487-3534

Colorado Welcome Center, 340 Highway 340, Fruita, 970-858-9335

Fruita Chamber of Commerce, 325 E. Aspen, Fruita, 970-858-3894

Grand Junction Chamber of Commerce, 360 Grand Ave., Grand Junction, 970-242-3214

Grand Junction Ranger District, Grand Mesa National Forest, 764 Horizon Dr., Rm. 115, Grand Junction, 970-242-8211

Grand Junction Visitor and Convention Bureau, 740 Horizon Dr. (at I-70), Grand Junction, 970-244-1480 (800-962-2547; www.grand-junction.net)

SOUTHWEST
COLORADO

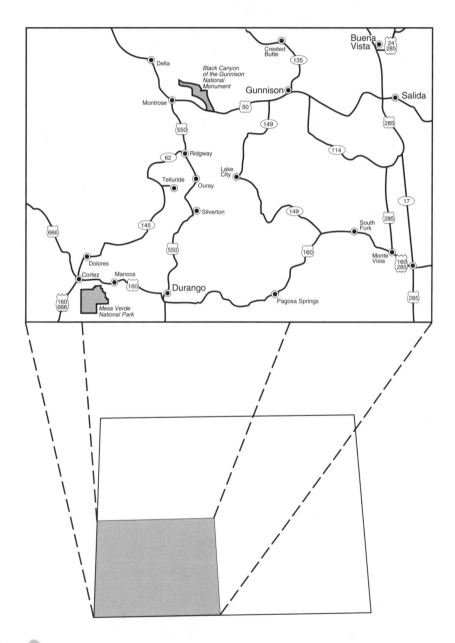

15
Black Canyon Area

The Big Scoop

Not quite desert, not quite mountains, the area surrounding the Black Canyon of the Gunnison River will give your dog a taste of high plateau country. And the eponymous national monument is one of the few where dogs can actually do something besides sit in the car.

The hub towns are Montrose and Delta, about half an hour's drive apart. Montrose has a leash law in both the city and county. Delta's leash law is imposed within city limits but not on county land. And "things are a little different out here," cautions Delta's Animal Control officer. If you tie your pooch outside a store while you run in, keep a close eye on him; apparently dogs are in high demand in the area. If you're out running your dog in the Adobe Hills that encircle the town, tell him to keep a nose out for people taking target practice. And, finally, note that if your dog is in Delta for more than seven days without a current license and rabies tag, you'll be required to purchase those items for him in town.

Tail-Rated Trails

FYI, the three state parks within this region—Paonia, Crawford, and Sweitzer Lake—focus on water recreation. Hiking opportunities are limited to a half-mile nature trail at Crawford and a short canal road at Sweitzer. For some trail ideas in the West Elk Wilderness Area east of Crawford and the western part of the

Curecanti National Recreation Area (dogs must be leashed in both locations), pick up the "North Fork Trails Network" brochure at the Delta Visitor Center or the Forest Supervisor's Office in Delta. Or ask for trail descriptions for the Uncompahgre Basin Resource Area at the BLM/Forest Service office in Montrose (see "Resources").

Delta

Confluence Park. There are about 5 miles of trails in this 265-acre park, formerly an abandoned industrial site, situated at the junction of the Gunnison and Uncompahgre Rivers. Head south on Gunnison River Dr. from Main St. to reach the park entrance. *Dogs must be leashed.*

If you're driving through Delta on a longer trip, a visit to this recently constructed park (1993) is a great way for your dog to stretch his legs. It's also a good destination for a late afternoon or evening stroll. The nicest section of the wide gravel trails that loop around and through the park is by the waterfowl habitat area. For the most direct access, begin walking from the boat ramp on the Gunnison River (at the end of Gunnison River Dr., within the park, turn right and follow the road into a parking area). Another section of trail encircles Confluence Lake. Make sure to keep your dog on the trail with you throughout the park; he may encounter some hazards if he frolics in the water.

Montrose

Duncan Trail. 3 miles round-trip. Drive north out of Montrose for 9 miles on Highway 50 and turn right onto Falcon Rd., on the right just before Olathe. Travel 3.6 miles to the end of the paved portion of the road, then follow it left as it turns into Peach Valley Rd. Staying left at the next fork you come to, drive 4.8 miles to the BLM sign for access to the Duncan Trail on the right. It's about 1.7 miles to the trailhead, where there's a parking area; stay left at the one fork you'll come to. It's inadvisable to drive on the dirt roads when they're muddy; apparently they turn into a sort of quicksand that will trap your car. And though four-wheel drive is recommended for the access road off Peach Valley Rd., my low-clearance Toyota Celica made it all the way to the trailhead. *Dogs can be off leash.*

Quinn enjoys a plunge in the Gunnison River. (photo by Amy Ditsler)

Less heavily used than the neighboring Chukar Trail, this is a rewarding hike for the intrepid dog. And it provides the access to the Gunnison River Gorge that your dog is unable to enjoy in the national monument. The trail begins by traversing a hillside for a half mile or so before beginning the descent to the river. At this point, it gets rather steep—a pair of hiking boots or good shoes are a must. Navigation also gets a little tricky before the final descent to the river. Look for the path of least resistance, as there seem to be several options. To avoid getting minicliffed-out right before the river, stay to the left and somewhat high in the last gully (you'll be able to see the river from here.) Once at the river, your dog can cool off in the current while you relax to the water's soothing rush and muster the energy for the climb back up. Try the nearby Ute Trail if you want a more gradual, but longer (9 miles round-trip), hike; the access road is about 2.4 miles past the Duncan Trail turnoff.

Black Canyon of the Gunnison National Monument. This spectacular canyon reaches depths of up to 2,689 feet. It's 15 miles east of Montrose via Highways 50 and 347. *Dogs must be leashed.*

Unlike at many other sites managed by the National Park Service, dogs actually have a few hiking options at the monument. I'll start with the no-no's. Pets are not permitted on the North Vista and Deadhorse Trails (both on the canyon's north rim) or on the Oak Flat Trail (near the visitor center on the south rim). They are also not allowed in the inner canyon or designated Wilderness areas. You can bring your pooch along on the 2-mile loop hike of the **Rim Rock** and **Uplands Trails** (dogs are allowed on the brief section of the Oak Flat Trail that connects these two trails together) and on either of the short nature trails: **Chasm View,** by the North Rim Campground; and **Warner Point,** at the end of the South Rim Rd. (Note that your dog will have to stop at the end of the Warner Point Nature Trail; the continuation of the trail leads down into the inner canyon.) And your dog is welcome to gaze down to his heart's content from any of the overlooks—just be sure to keep a tight rein on him if he suffers from vertigo! Bring plenty of water to share for hiking.

In the winter, the South Rim Rd. is unplowed past the visitor center and is open for cross-country skiing, but not for dogs.

CYCLING FOR CANINES

The Uncompahgre Plateau west of Montrose offers lots of varied biking opportunities, including the originations of the **Tabeguache Trail,** which travels 142 miles to Grand Junction, and the **Paradox Trail,** which links up with Kokopelli's Trail 100 miles later in Utah. (Of course, I recommend just biking a few miles of these multiday trails if Fido is in tow.) Because the BLM and Forest Service oversee the land on which the trails pass, your dog will be able to run leash-free beside your bike. For route descriptions, look for pamphlets on the Tabeguache and Paradox Trails at the BLM/Forest Service office in Montrose (see "Resources") or check out *Bicycling the Uncompahgre Plateau,* by Bill Harris.

CREATURE COMFORTS

Unless otherwise stated, dogs should not be left unattended in the room or cabin.

Cimarron

$ Cimarron Inn and Motel, 82401 E. Highway 50, 970-249-6222. This motel accepts dogs for a $5 fee per night, but prepare yourself for abrupt service.

Crawford

$$ Last Frontier Lodge, 4020C Highway 92, 970-921-6363. For a quiet retreat with your dog, try the Last Frontier, located on ten acres next to the Crawford Reservoir. Of the eight rooms, two have private baths; the rest share a bath. You can leave your dog unattended inside. And he can be off leash while on the property, free to hobnob—under your supervision—with horses, pigs, and two resident dogs. A stay at the lodge includes three meals a day (for you, not your dog).

$$ Steward Homestead Cabin, Onion Valley (8.5 miles southeast of Crawford), **970-921-6751.** The Homestead Cabin is a vacation house to rent; the owners live nearby but off-site. In addition to a full kitchen and living space, the cabin has one bedroom and a loft. You can leave your dog unattended inside as well as walk him leash-free on the surrounding 160 acres. There's a $20 pet deposit.

Delta

$ El-D-Rado Motel, 702 Main, 970-874-4493. There's a $5 fee per night for dogs.

$ Flying A Motel and Campground, 676 Highway 50, 970-874-9659. The fee for dogs is $2 per night ($1 if you're staying in the campground). A $25 deposit is requested if you pay with cash.

$ Southgate Inn, 2124 S. Main, 970-874-9726 (800-621-2271). This friendly motel allows one adult dog per room (it has ten pet rooms) for a $5 fee per night.

$ Westways Court, 1030 Main, 970-874-4415. The motel allows you to leave your dog unattended in the room.

$–$$ Best Western Sundance, 903 Main, 970-874-9781 (800-626-1994)

$$ Escalante Ranch Bed and Breakfast, 701 650 Rd., 970-874-4121. Your dog can have a field day at this working cattle ranch; you and he won't run out of room to roam together on the ranch's 100,000 acres along the Gunnison River. And, as long as he doesn't chase cows, your dog can be off leash. The B&B has four rooms, and the owners prefer small to medium-sized dogs.

Hotchkiss

$$ Hotchkiss Inn, 406 Highway 133, 970-872-2200. The motel offers four pet rooms, two nonsmoking and two smoking. There's a $5 one-time fee, and you can leave your dog unattended in the room as long as you're sure he won't attack the housekeepers.

Montrose

$ Log Cabin Motel, 1034 E. Main, 970-249-7610. Three or four rooms are set aside for dog guests. There's no deposit for small (i.e., lap-size) dogs; larger dogs require a deposit of $20.

$ Vee Broken Bracket Bed and Breakfast, 67255 Trout Rd., 970-249-5609. Clover had her first encounter with a ferret who was a temporary resident at this B&B during our stay. (The two of them actually got along quite well.) The 1894 Victorian farmhouse has a lot of history—it's been in the same family since the early part of the century—and host Ruby Woods is happy to share its stories with visitors. But Clover was too preoccupied with the ferret to join me in listening.

$–$$ Black Canyon Motel, 1605 E. Main, 970-249-3495 (800-348-3495). The motel has thirty pet rooms, and there's a $4 fee per night. Dogs can usually be left unattended in the rooms for a short time. The motel also has a grassy dog-walking area where four-legged guests can do their thing off leash.

$–$$ Blue Fox Motel, 1150 N. Townsend, 970-249-4595

$–$$ Montrose Super 8 Motel, 1705 E. Main, 970-249-9294 (800-800-8000). Dogs can stay in smoking rooms only. If you're paying with cash, a $20 deposit is required.

$–$$ Red Barn Motel, 1417 E. Main, 970-249-4507. The motel has eleven pet rooms, both smoking and nonsmoking.

$$ Holiday Inn Express, 1391 S. Townsend, 970-240-1800. At this easygoing Holiday Inn no-frills version, dogs can be left unattended in the rooms as long as housekeeping is notified.

$$ San Juan Inn, 1480 Highway 550, 970-249-6644. There's a $6 fee per night for dogs, and they can be left unattended in the rooms.

Paonia

$ Colorado Guest Ranch, 1938 Highway 133, 970-929-6260 (800-521-4055). Dogs won't be able to stay in the main lodge rooms at the ranch, but they are welcome in the bunkhouse, which contains two guest suites. The owner emphasizes that visiting dogs must be well behaved, and because the ranch is in a wilderness setting with lots of deer and elk around, they can't be wildlife chasers. Once a dog has passed muster, however, rules at the ranch are laid-back; for example, he can be left unattended in the room.

Somerset

$–$$ Crystal Meadows Ranch, 30682 County Rd. 12, 970-929-5656. This non-working ranch offers two cabins, four rooms in the main building, and two log houses, one with two bedrooms and one with three bedrooms. Dogs can stay in any of them. You can leave your dog unattended inside, but you must keep him leashed when outside. RV sites are also available. Open from the end of May to mid-November.

Campgrounds

Black Canyon of the Gunnison National Monument, 15 miles east of Montrose via Highways 50 and 347. The monument has two campgrounds, one on the north rim, one on the south rim. There's also a small campground on East Portal Rd., in what is actually part of the Curecanti National Recreation Area.

State Park campgrounds: **Crawford State Park,** 1 mile south of Crawford on Highway 92 (53 sites); **Paonia State Park,** 16 miles east of Paonia on Highway 133 (15 sites).

National Forest campgrounds: **McClure Campground,** 12 miles north of Paonia Reservoir on Highway 133, at the top of McClure Pass (19 sites); **Erickson Springs Campground,** 6 miles down County Rd. 12 (turn off Highway 133, right before Paonia Reservoir; 18 sites).

Private campgrounds: **Flying A Motel and Campground** in Delta (see "Creature Comforts").

DOGGIE DAYCARE
Delta
Deleff Kennels, 1951 B 50 Rd., 970-874-4058. $6/day for small dogs; $7/day for large dogs. Open 7 A.M.–6 P.M., Monday to Saturday, or by appointment.

Montrose
Double Diamond Kennels, 23661 Horsefly Rd., 970-249-3067. $10/day. Open 8 A.M.–5 P.M., Monday to Friday; 8–11:30 A.M., Saturday; closed Sunday.

Redclyffe Kennels, 16793 Chipeta Dr., 970-249-6395. $6–$10/day. Open 8 A.M.–6 P.M., Monday to Saturday; closed Sunday.

PET PROVISIONS
Delta
H & R Aquatics and Supplies, 333 Main, 970-874-1135

Sisson's Feed and Seed, 405 W. 5, 970-874-8376

Montrose
Little Friends Pets, 38 S. Selig Ave., 970-249-1797

CANINE ER
Montrose
Morningstar Veterinary Clinic (AAHA certified), 717 N. Cascade Ave., 970-249-

8022. Open 8 A.M.–5 P.M., Monday and Friday; 8 A.M.–5:30 P.M., Tuesday and Wednesday; 8 A.M.–7 P.M., Thursday; 8:30 A.M.–noon, Saturday.

RESOURCES
Bureau of Land Management, 2505 South Townsend, Montrose, 970-240-5300

Delta Area Chamber of Commerce and Visitor Center, 301 Main St., Delta, 970-874-8616

Forest Supervisor's Office, Grand Mesa–Uncompahgre and Gunnison National Forests, 2250 Highway 50, Delta, 970-874-6600

Montrose Chamber of Commerce, 1519 E. Main, Montrose, 970-249-5000 (800-923-5515)

Montrose Visitor Information Center, 17253 Chipeta, Montrose, 970-249-1726

Ouray Ranger District, Uncompahgre National Forest, 2505 South Townsend, Montrose, 970-240-5300

Paonia Ranger District, Gunnison National Forest, North Rio Grande Ave., Paonia, 970-527-4131

16

Gunnison, Crested Butte, and Lake City

THE BIG SCOOP

Dogs on the go will find attractions aplenty in the Gunnison area: forested hikes, rugged mountains to climb, and lots of water. Just be sure to keep an eye on your dog when you're both out enjoying the natural environment—wildlife and livestock harassment by otherwise well-meaning dogs is a perennial problem in the region.

Gunnison has the expected leash law within city limits. In Gunnison County, dogs can legally be under voice control.

For a generally dog-friendly, laid-back mountain town, Crested Butte has fairly strict dog regulations: There's a leash law within city limits, public tethering (i.e., tying up your dog outside a shop while you run in) is verboten, and dogs are not allowed in any of the five town parks. Nevertheless, dogs here seem to enjoy themselves as much as in any of the ski towns, and your dog won't be at a loss for encountering other butts to sniff. Mt. Crested Butte, which is the separate town at the ski area, allows dogs to be under voice control instead of on leash, and the no-public-tethering rule is confined to the ski resort's immediate base area.

Lake City, tucked in the mountains 55 miles south of Gunnison, requires dogs to be on leash in its downtown area, from 4th through 1st Sts.; they can be under voice control elsewhere in the town as well as on all Hinsdale County land. Unfortunately, dogs must refrain from setting paw in the town park.

TAIL-RATED TRAILS

There is limitless hiking in the Gunnison and Uncompahgre National Forests and BLM lands of which this region is largely composed. I've highlighted just a few of the most accessible trails. For more ideas, consult the "Aspen/Crested Butte/Gunnison Recreation Topo Map" put out by Latitude 40°. Keep in mind that many of the well-known hiking trails around Crested Butte are in Wilderness areas, so your dog will have to stay on a leash. And because the town is a legendary mountain biking hub, choose non-Wilderness trails carefully if you want to avoid dodging avid cyclists.

Crested Butte

Green Lake. 7 miles round-trip. This hike to a gorgeous mountain lake begins right in Crested Butte, at the Nordic Center at 2nd and Whiterock. *Dogs can be off leash.*

Begin hiking up the dirt road that ascends from the left of the Nordic Center parking lot. At the top of the bench, go right on the dirt road (Wildcat Rd.). Walk past the houses to the end of the road, go around some large boulders on the left, and follow a rocky jeep road up what's known as Baby Head Hill. (There are plans for the access up the hill to change slightly; check in at one of the outdoor shops in town for an update.) Eventually you'll come to the proverbial fork in the road; in this case, it doesn't matter which one you take, as both lead to a well-maintained dirt road (Trapper's Crossing Rd.) within less than a hundred yards. Go right at this road. The actual Green Lake Trail can be a little tricky to find, as there's no sign (though plans call for one eventually). About a half mile down Trapper's Crossing Rd., look for a large gravel mound on the left, just before the road curves obviously to the right. This is the access point. (Unfortunately, you can't just drive to this point from town because the road leading to it is private.) From here, the trail is distinct all the way to the lake, as it winds through wildflower meadows and forest. Just before reaching the lake, pass by a trail that climbs steeply up to the right. The lake itself lives up to its name and is picturesquely situated at the base of an alpine cirque. Midsummer, the water temperature may even be warm enough for both you and your dog to enjoy a dip.

Crested Butte Mountain. The ski area is open for hiking in the summer, though you won't be able to ride up the Silver Queen chairlift with your dog. Instead, follow the Yellow Brick Rd. (the summer service road) from the base area to the top of the Silver Queen. From there, trail signs will point you in the direction of the hike to the peak, where you'll top out at 12,162 feet, rewarded by a stunning panoramic view of the Elk Mountains and the backside of the Maroon Bells. *Dogs can be off leash.*

Woods Walk to Peanut Lake. About 5 miles round-trip. Either walk or drive up Kebler Pass Rd. from Crested Butte. Just past Treasury Hill Rd. on the right, there's a place for one or two cars to park (before the dirt road designated private). There's also a pair of small parking pullouts a little farther up Kebler Pass Rd., on both sides of the road. *Dogs can be off leash.*

Head into the woods from the parking area after Treasury Hill Rd. You'll first pass a trail branch coming from the right. Then at the fork, stay right. The trail goes through a stand of aspen, then opens into a flower-filled meadow. Continue hiking west until you draw near a stylish house; turn left here. The trail then parallels Peanut Lake from above, with Crested Butte Mountain and Gothic Mountain dominating the view. Though your dog won't be within paw-dipping access of the lake, you will cross a stream he can get wet in. The trail eventually ends at a fence and some abandoned-looking property and descends about fifty feet to Peanut Lake Rd. If you want to make a loop, walk back on the road along the lake; just before you reach pavement, take the small footpath up to the right. Stay on the straight, narrow path past a branch-off to the left, until you meet up with your original route by the house.

You can also access Peanut Lake Rd. from town by walking to the end of Butte Ave., four blocks north of Elk Ave. This will make for a shorter hike, but you'll forsake the lovely woods part of the hike described above.

> Crested Butte dogs who are feeling a little hot under the collar like to go to easily accessible Long Lake to cool off—it's directly off Washington Gulch Rd.

Gunnison

Curecanti National Recreation Area. Curecanti, administered by the National Park Service, encompasses an area from about 5 miles west of Gunnison to the border of the Black Canyon of the Gunnison National Monument. Its centerpiece is 20-mile-long Blue Mesa Reservoir, created by three dams constructed along the Gunnison River. There are also seven established hiking trails in the recreation area. The Elk Creek Visitor Center, off Highway 50 West, has a brochure that describes them.

The 1.5-mile round-trip **Neversink Trail**, which provides good bird-watching opportunities, is the closest one to Gunnison, just off Highway 50, 5 miles from town. For a less frequented hike that's also near water, try the 4-mile round-trip **Curecanti Creek Trail**, accessed from Highway 92 north, 5.7 miles from the junction with Highway 50. Your dog will have to pass on the boat tours of Morrow Point Lake. *Dogs must be leashed throughout the recreation area, including all trails.*

Backpacking near Crested Butte. (photo by Cindy Hirschfeld)

 Hartman Rocks. From Gunnison, head west on Highway 50 for approximately 1.5 miles to County Rd. 38 (Gold Basin Rd.). Turn left and drive for 2.4 miles to a parking area on the right, indicated by a small blue-and-white "Hartman Rocks" sign. *Dogs can be off leash.*

This 160-acre recreation area, which abuts BLM land, has a network of trails looping over and around hilly terrain, with sage, piñon, and juniper as the primary vegetation. There's no set destination—let your dog lead the way to wherever his nose takes him. Because the area is dry and hot, you'll want to avoid bringing Fido here midday during the summer. Actually, the best times to come are when motocross riding is not allowed on the front side of the trail: before 11 A.M. or after 6 P.M., Monday through Saturday, and all day Sunday. Bring plenty of water for the both of you, though your dog might be lucky enough to come across one of the water-filled stock tanks on the back side of the hill.

 Signal Peak. Up to approximately 8 miles round-trip. From Main St. (Highway 135) in Gunnison, head east on Georgia Ave. Follow the road as it bends to the left, becoming Escalante Drive, and partially circumnavigate the Western State College campus. Turn into a parking lot on the right, just after the water storage tanks

on the right and just before the athletic field. *Dogs can be off leash.*

The route to Signal Peak is actually a spur of the Colorado Trail. Though the hike is not necessarily rewarding enough to merit covering the entire distance (unless you're on a bike), it's nice to have an option so close to town where your dog can hike with you leash-free. Just be sure to access it as described above, even though you may spot another access point along a four-wheel-drive road before the water towers; apparently this latter route crosses private property, and a "no dogs" sign has been posted by the owner to avoid canine-livestock conflict. (I've made an educated guess as to the origins of the sign; neither Gunnison Animal Control nor the BLM was aware of it.) And bring lots of water.

The trail you want begins through the fence at the edge of the parking area. Either take the straight shot up to the first radio tower or, for a more gradual ascent, hike left along the dirt road and follow the "Parcours" markers. Once on top of the hill, hike along the ridge toward the second radio tower. The trail follows a dirt road through the sagebrush and affords a nice panorama of the Gunnison Valley and the surrounding mountain ranges. Signal Peak is the cone-shaped feature to the northeast. Your dog might also just be interested in exploring the network of dirt roads and singletrack that winds around the radio tower hills.

CYCLING FOR CANINES

Any mountain-biking dog worth his snuff will want to say he's been to the Butte to bike, and several trails fit the bill for canine cycling companionship. The **Woods Walk** (see "Tail-Rated Trails") is a nice, gentle ride, as is biking on **Peanut Lake Rd.** For something more technical, try **Snodgrass Mountain** as an out-and-back ride of a few miles, driving to the trailhead past Mt. Crested Butte—the loop that bikers usually do involves riding on trafficked roads. Or drive up Brush Creek Rd. south of town and tackle the 5.5-mile **Farris Creek Loop.**

In Gunnison, **Signal Peak** and **Hartman Rocks** (see "Tail-Rated Trails") are both suitable for taking your dog along on a ride. Dogs visiting Lake City may especially enjoy the 7.6-mile round-trip ride to **Waterdog Lake,** which begins just outside of town a quarter mile up the road from the sewage treatment plant.

POWDERHOUNDS

Two great places to ski or snowshoe with your dog in Crested Butte are **Slate River** and **Washington Gulch Rds.** Both are unplowed after a certain point and provide wide-open touring in breathtakingly scenic surroundings. In the Lake City area, the Lake City Nordic Association discourages dogs from the groomed Williams Creek and Slumgullion Pass trail systems; however, a couple of ungroomed areas make for suitable dog destinations. The **East Lakeshore** area, by Lake San Cristobal, includes an unplowed public road. The **Danny Carl** area, between Slumgullion and Spring Creek Passes on Highway 149 south, features a meadow as well as forested terrain. Note that dogs are not allowed at any of the yurts along the Hindsdale Haute Route system outside of Lake City.

CREATURE COMFORTS

Unless otherwise stated, dogs should not be left unattended in the room or cabin.

Almont

About ten miles north of Gunnison, on the way to Crested Butte, this small town is home to several cabin resorts. A few of the resorts listed here are closer to Taylor Reservoir, about a half-hour drive from Almont.

$–$$ Holt's Guest Ranch, 1711 County Rd. 55 (2 miles from Taylor Reservoir), 970-641-2733. The ranch has sixteen fully equipped cabins, and dogs may stay for a $5 fee per night. You must keep your dog leashed when he's outside. Open mid-May to the end of October.

$–$$ Taylor Park Trading Post, located at Taylor Reservoir, 970-641-2555. Thirty-three cabins, fully furnished, can be shared with your dog. Open February 15 to December 31.

$–$$ Three Rivers Resort and Outfitting, 130 County Rd. 742, 970-641-1303. Situated at the confluence of the Taylor, East, and Gunnison Rivers (hence the name), the resort has thirty fully outfitted cabins, some along the Taylor River. You can leave your dog unattended inside; he must be leashed when outside on the resort's property. The resort also offers guided rafting, kayaking, and fly-fishing trips (for humans only). Open beginning of May to November.

$$ Almont Resort, 10209 Highway 135, 970-641-4009. The resort advertises its accommodations as "rustic cabins with modern conveniences." However, most of the cabins don't have kitchens, something to keep in mind if you're planning a cooking vacation. Dogs can be left unattended inside the cabins; the resort advises that you keep your dog leashed when outside because of the proximity to busy Highway 135. Open year-round.

$$ Char-B Resort, 1730 County Rd. 744 (9 miles northeast of Almont), 970-641-0751. Dogs are allowed in all but two of the resort's nineteen cabins. There's no charge for one or two dogs; more than that, and you'll have to pay a $5 fee per night. Dogs can be left unattended inside. The cabins sit on seven acres bordering the Gunnison National Forest, and Spring Creek runs through the property, giving your leashed dog a great place in which to stretch his legs. Open from mid-May to mid-November as well as Thanksgiving, Christmas, and the last two weeks of March.

$$ Silent Spring Resort, 905 County Rd. 744, 970-641-0583. You and your dog can relax here in one of the two secluded, extremely well-equipped cabins. One cabin has a fireplace, the other a wood-burning stove. There's a two-night minimum stay; many guests rent the cabins for a week at a time. You can leave your dog unattended inside; keep him on a leash outside the cabins. Open May 15 to September 15.

$$ Spring Creek Resort, 880 County Rd. 744 (8 miles from Almont), 970-641-0217. Dogs are permitted in any of the resort's fully furnished twenty-one cabins, ranging from one room to three bedrooms. A deposit is required; call for details. You can leave your dog unattended in the cabin if you're sure he won't pester the neighbors, but you must keep him leashed when outside. From the beginning of July to mid-August, rentals are on a weekly only basis, Saturday to Saturday. Open Memorial Day to Labor Day.

$$–$$$ Harmel's Guest Ranch, 6748 County Rd. 742, 970-641-1740 (800-235-3402). Dogs are allowed in the single cabins here, though not in the lodge rooms or suites. The ranch is on 150 acres surrounded by the Gunnison National Forest, and your dog can hike off leash on the property with you.

Crested Butte

$$ Nordic Inn, 14 Treasury Rd., 970-349-5542 (800-542-7669). Dogs are allowed at this cozy upscale motel only in the summer. There are three designated pet rooms, and a $10 fee per night is required. Though your dog might be tempted to lounge in front of the fireplace in the Scandinavian-themed common rooms, you'll have to break it to him that he's not allowed in the lobby area. Continental breakfast is included (for people).

$$–$$$ The Claim Jumper, 704 Whiterock, 970-349-6471. To call this B&B unique, as it advertises, may be an understatement. Each of the six rooms is packed with memorabilia relating to a specific theme; the sports fan room, for example, is filled to the gills with athletic equipment, baseball hats, autographed pictures, pennants, souvenirs, and so on. And in the midst of all this, your dog (as well as you) is extremely welcome. "Dogs make great guests," emphasizes owner Jerry Bigelow. "I've never had a dog smoke in a room or take a towel." You can even leave your dog unattended in the room, where he certainly won't run out of things to look at until you return. And Otis, the resident Newfoundland, can give your pooch the insider's view of Crested Butte.

$$–$$$ Sheraton Crested Butte Resort, 6 Emmons Rd., 970-349-8000. This new hotel near the ski area base allows dogs from June 1 until the end of October. Dogs can stay in first-floor rooms only, all of which are smoking, and there's a $20 fee per night.

$$–$$$$ San Moritz Condominiums, 18 Hunter Hill Rd., 970-349-5150 (800-443-7459). Dog-friendly condos are a rare find at a ski area. "We love pets," says the manager of these ski-in/ski-out condos. You can even leave your dog unattended inside as long as he doesn't bark the day away (though the housekeepers will leave clean linens and towels outside your door when Fido guards the condo). A credit-card imprint is requested as a deposit, and there's a four-night minimum stay throughout the year.

Gunnison

$ Ferro's Blue Mesa Trading Post, 3200 Soap Creek Rd., 970-641-4671. The trading post is actually located west of Gunnison, on the northwest side of Blue Mesa Lake and within spitting distance of the Curecanti National Recreation Area. You and your dog will have your choice of two fully outfitted cabins, one mobile home, or one cabin with everything but running water. Dogs can be off leash on the post's forty acres. The friendly owner put in a plug for his cats, saying that they're entertained by visiting dogs and vice versa. Open beginning of May to mid-November.

$ Gunnison KOA Kampground, 105 County Rd. 50, 970-641-1358. Canines are allowed in the camping cabins (you'll have to bring your own bedding and cooking gear). Open May 1 to mid-November.

$ Island Acres Motel, 38339 W. Highway 50, 970-641-1442. The motel takes "chihuahuas and toy poodles" (or similar-sized pooches) in smoking rooms only. Closed during January and February.

$ Long's Holiday Motel, 1198 W. Highway 50, 970-641-0536. Large dogs are assessed a $5 one-time fee.

$–$$ Bennett's Western Motel, 403 E. Tomichi Ave., 970-641-1722. There's a $3 fee per night, per dog. Legion Park, across the street, provides ample dog-walking opportunities.

$–$$ Days Inn, 701 W. Highway 50, 970-641-0608 (800-DAYSINN). There's a $4 fee per night, per dog.

$–$$ Hylander Inn, 412 E. Tomichi, 970-641-0700. Dogs are charged $5 per night extra. The motel is across the street from Legion Park, where your dog can stretch his legs.

$–$$ Shady Island Resort, 2776 N. Highway 135, 970-641-0416. The resort has ten cabins, including a three-bedroom house, and dogs can stay in any for a $3 fee per night, per dog. The cabins are located on ten acres along the Gunnison River, and your dog needs to be leashed when outside. Open May 1 to November 15.

$–$$ Swiss Inn Motel, 312 E. Tomichi, 970-641-9962. Small dogs (poodle-sized) get the nod, and well-behaved ones can be left unattended in the rooms.

$–$$ Tomahawk Guest Ranch, 2943 County Rd. 27 (halfway between Gunnison and Lake City), **970-641-2104.** The ranch offers nine fully outfitted cabins, from one to three bedrooms. You can leave your dog unattended inside, though he'd probably rather be out exploring the forty acres of property leash-free with you. The ranch abuts BLM land. Open from the beginning of June to mid-November.

$$ Lost Canyon Resort, 8264 Highway 135, 970-641-0181. The resort's seventeen log cabins are scenically situated on ten acres along the Gunnison River. Many of the fully equipped cabins also have fireplaces or wood stoves. Your dog can explore the property off leash as long as you're there to supervise him. Open year-round.

$$ Rockey River Resort, 4359 County Rd. 10, 970-641-0174. For $3 per night, per dog, your pooch(es) can join you in one of the fourteen fully furnished cabins on seven acres along the Gunnison River. Dogs must be leashed when outside. Open year-round.

Lake City

$ Castle Lakes Cabins and Campground Resort, Cinnamon Pass Rd. (County Rd. 30), **970-944-2622.** Dogs are accepted on a case-by-case basis and can then have their pick of furnished one- or two-bedroom cabins, mobile homes, or RV trailers to stay in. The setting is gorgeous, on forty-five acres above Lake San Cristobal and near 14,000-foot-plus Redcloud and Sunshine

Peaks. It's also along the Alpine Loop Scenic Byway. Open May 15 to November 15.

$ Matterhorn Lodge, 409 N. Bluff, 970-944-2210 (800-779-8028). The Matterhorn has motel rooms, some with kitchenettes, as well as two cabins. Dogs are welcome for $5 extra per night, and they can be left unattended inside. Open year-round.

$ Spruce Lodge, 321 Silver St., 970-944-2279. The lodge has one- and two-bedroom motel units in which dogs are welcome. You can leave your dog unattended in the room. Open May 1 to November 15.

$ Town Square Cabins, 231 Gunnison Ave., 970-944-2236. Four of the eight fully equipped cabins are dog friendly, with a $5 one-time fee per dog. You can leave your dog unattended in the cabin, which you'll have to do if you take a stroll in the town park, across the street, where no dogs are allowed. Open year-round.

$–$$ G & M Cabins, 331 Gunnison Ave., 970-944-2282. For $5 extra per night, you can bring your dog along to these in-town, fully furnished cabins, which range in size from studios to three bedrooms.

$–$$ Lake City Resort, 307 S. Gunnison Ave., 970-944-2866. The eight cabins range from studios to two bedrooms and come with all the necessities. There's a $5 fee per night, per dog. Though the cabins are in town, there's a grassy area around them where you can exercise your dog on leash. Open May 15 to October 1.

$–$$ Lakeview Resort, Lake San Cristobal, 970-944-2401 (800-456-0170). Enjoy a stay with your dog at Colorado's second-largest natural lake, just outside Lake City. The resort offers lodge rooms, one-bedroom lodge suites, and one- to three-bedroom cabins with wood-burning stoves or fireplaces. There's a $2 fee per night, per dog, with a two-dog limit (so no three-dog nights here!). The resort also has guided horseback rides and fishing trips. You must

keep your dog leashed when outside. Open mid-May to October 1.

$$ Alpine Village, 631 N. Silver, 970-944-2266. The Village's one- and two-bedroom, fully equipped log cabins are located in town. Dogs can be left inside unattended. Open June 1 to September 30.

$$ Crystal Lodge, Highway 149 (2 miles from Lake City), **970-944-2201 (800-984-1234).** Dogs are allowed in the lodge suites, which sleep from four to eight, or in the four two-bedroom cabins, but not in the upstairs lodge rooms. There's a $25 deposit per pet, and dogs can be left unattended inside. They should be kept leashed on the lodge's property. There's also a restaurant with a reputation for great homemade meals on the premises. Open year-round except during April and November.

$$ Quiet Moose Lodge (formerly Western Belle), **1221 Highway 149, 970-944-2415.** Dogs are welcome in any of the motel's rooms for $5 extra per night. They can be left unattended inside. Open year-round.

$$ Ryan's Roost, 9501 Highway 149, 970-944-2339. Your dog will likely clamor to stay here when you tell him there are 200 acres that he can explore with you leash-free. Though the Ryans no longer rent out B&B rooms, they offer three fully equipped cabins, which sleep from five to eight people. You can leave your dog unattended in them. If you have a horse, you can bring it along, too, for a true family outing. Open June to October.

$$ Vickers Ranch, Highway 149 (1 mile south of Lake City), 970-944-2249. Located on 3,000 acres just south of Lake City, the ranch has twenty log cabins, ranging in size from two to four bedrooms, all with kitchens and fireplaces. Your dog will want to do some sniffing around on this vast expanse of land—the Lake Fork of the Gunnison River runs on the property—but you'll have to keep him leashed because of the cattle and horses. The ranch has guided horseback trips and rents jeeps. Open May 1 to mid-November (a winter stay can be arranged in advance, but there's a five-day minimum).

$$ Wagon Wheel Resort, 249 Highway 149, 970-944-2264. The resort has cabins ranging from efficiencies to two bedrooms, all fully equipped. Dogs are welcome and can be left unattended in the cabins "as long as they don't raise heck." Open mid-May through mid-November.

$$ Westwood Resort, 413 Gunnison Ave., 970-944-2205. "We love animals," says the owner, who has a dog and cat. One dog per cabin (all are fully equipped) is the policy here. There's a three-night minimum stay during July and August. Open from the beginning of May to mid-October.

$$–$$$ Old Carson Inn Bed and Breakfast, 8401 County Rd. 30, 970-944-2511 (800-294-0608). The well-behaved dog who wants more upscale accommodations in Lake City may be able to stay at this B&B, which on occasion allows dogs in one of its rooms. The inn is in a modern log and frame house, and the potential dog-stay room has a queen-size bed, antique furnishings, and a private entrance for discreet dog walking. Possibly closed in winter.

Ohio City

$ Sportsmans Resort, County Rd. 771, 970-641-0172. The resort, in a town of about fifty people, has nine fully furnished cabins, and you can leave your dog unattended inside. Open from the end of May to mid-November.

Parlin

$ 7-11 Ranch, County Rd. 76 (5 miles north of Parlin), 970-641-0666. This working cattle ranch on 600 acres will let your dog be a guest as long as he doesn't chase the cattle. There are six fully furnished cabins that share a central bathhouse. (There's also a lodge with ten beds available for rental, but dogs are not allowed.) When outside on the property, your dog doesn't have to be on a leash as long as you can keep him under your voice control. Open April 1 to just before Christmas.

Pitkin

$ Pitkin Hotel, 329 Main St., 970-641-2757. To get away from it all, your dog might enjoy a stay at this historic, quaint hotel, which dates back to 1904. There are six private rooms, all with shared baths, as well as three bunkrooms (sleeping eighteen, six, and three, respectively). The teeny town of Pitkin, about 30 miles northeast of Gunnison, has one restaurant, which is open from Memorial Day to mid-November. After that, you'll have to fend for yourself, though you're welcome to bring your own food and use the hotel kitchen to whip up a meal. Rather than leave your dog unattended in the room, the owner prefers that you attach him to one of the dog chains (on the front porch or in back of the hotel), and she'll keep an eye on him.

Campgrounds

Curecanti National Recreation Area, west of Gunnison along Highway 50, has major developed campgrounds at Stevens Creek, Elk Creek, Lake Fork, and Cimarron; smaller campgrounds around Blue Mesa Reservoir are at Dry Gulch, Red Creek, Ponderosa, and Gateview.

National Forest campgrounds: **Cement Creek Campground,** 4 miles up Cement Creek Rd. outside of Crested Butte (13 sites); **Lake Irwin Campground,** at Irwin Lake, west of Crested Butte on Kebler Pass Rd. (32 sites); **Cold Spring, Lodgepole, Lottis Creek, North Bank, One Mile,** and **Rosy Lane Campgrounds** are all along the Taylor Canyon Rd. between Almont and Taylor Reservoir; **Lakeview Campground,** overlooking Taylor Reservoir (46 sites); **Williams Creek Campground,** on County Rd. 30 past Lake San Cristobal, outside Lake City (23 sites); **Slumgullion Campground,** off Highway 149 south of Lake City (21 sites).

Private campgrounds: **Gunnison KOA** (see "Creature Comforts").

WORTH A PAWS

Ashley Whippet Canine Frisbee Invitational. Held in Gunnison's Jorgensen Park (along Highway 50) on the last Sunday in July, this annual event is open to any dog willing to strut his Frisbee-catching skills. Competing dogs are given sixty seconds to catch as many throws as possible; each throw and catch is also rated on a six-point scale. Registration is free. In years past, the Dog Derby has taken place after the Frisbee event, featuring judged categories such as biggest/smallest dog. For more information, contact Trish Winslow at the City of Gunnison offices, 970-641-8000.

C. B. Paws, 303 Elk Ave., 970-349-5606. This pet store deserves special mention as a great place to visit. Within its small confines is packed an enticing array of items for dogs (and cats, too), including specialty collars and leashes, backpacks, booties, toys galore, and gourmet treats. You'll also find pet-themed items such as picture frames, mugs, cards, and jewelry. It's hard to say who will have more fun shopping—you or Fido.

DOGGIE DAYCARE

Gunnison

Critter Sitters and Outfitters (part of Gunnison Veterinary Clinic), 98 County Rd. 17, 970-641-0460. $5.75/day. Open 8:30 A.M.–5 P.M., Monday to Friday; 8:30 A.M.–noon and 5–7 P.M., Saturday; 8:30–9:30 A.M. and 5–7 P.M., Sunday.

Tomichi Animal Hospital, 106 S. 11th St., 970-641-2460. $10/day. Open 8 A.M.–5:30 P.M., Monday to Friday; 9 A.M.–noon, Saturday.

Town & Country Animal Hospital, 1525 Highway 135, 970-641-2215. $4.50/day.

Open 8 A.M.–5:30 P.M., Monday, Wednesday, Friday; 8 A.M.–7 P.M., Tuesday, Thursday; 8 A.M.–1 P.M., Saturday.

PET PROVISIONS

Crested Butte

C. B. Paws. See description in "Worth a Paws."

Gunnison

Critter Sitters and Outfitters, 98 County Rd. 17, 970-641-0460

CANINE ER

Gunnison

Town & Country Animal Hospital (AAHA certified), 1525 Highway 135, 970-641-2215. Open 8 A.M.–5:30 P.M., Monday, Wednesday, Friday; 8 A.M.–7 P.M., Tuesday, Thursday; 8 A.M.–1 P.M., Saturday.

RESOURCES

The Alpineer, 419 Sixth St., in Crested Butte (970-349-5210/www.alpineer. com)—maps, guidebooks, and friendly, knowledgeable advice about area trails

Bureau of Land Management, Gunnison Resource Area, 216 North Colorado, Gunnison, 970-641-0471

Crested Butte/Mt. Crested Butte Chamber of Commerce, 601 Elk Ave., Crested Butte, 970-349-6438 (800-545-4505); www.cbinteractive.com

Gunnison County Chamber of Commerce, 500 E. Tomichi Ave. (Highway 50), Gunnison, 970-641-1501 (800-274-7580)

Lake City Chamber of Commerce, 970-944-2527 (800-569-1874)

Taylor River/Cebolla Ranger District, Gunnison National Forest, 216 North Colorado, Gunnison, 970-641-0471

17
Telluride, Ouray, and Silverton

THE BIG SCOOP

All three of these mountain towns are dog-friendly havens, with Telluride earning top honors. "Telluride has more dogs than people," claimed the guy behind the counter at the local pet supply store. While this may or may not be true, any town that sets aside designated "puppy parking" areas in its business district is definitely in step with the canine set. And pet pickup bags are amply provided throughout town. Telluride's leash laws match its laid-back atmosphere: Dogs can be under voice control almost anywhere. The exceptions—where dogs must be leashed—are Colorado Ave. and any place within a block of it, and Town Park. You can bring your dog to the Mountain Village—on a leash or under voice control—though a common misconception exists that dogs are out-and-out banned (and the actual ordinance regarding dogs has some contradictions within it). The only place in Telluride that truly bans dogs is the Lawson Hill subdivision (by Society Turn). Regulations have been revised to allow dogs to ride the gondola connecting Telluride proper and the Mountain Village: Now one leashed dog at a time can ride in a designated pet cabin. There are only a few such cabins, so be prepared for a potential wait.

Ouray, ringed by mountains on three sides, provides a spectacular setting. Your dog, however, will probably prefer to spend most of his time exploring the nearby trails rather than dodging kids and RVs on the town's busy main street. There is a leash law within city limits.

Silverton, with only one paved road, would seem to be the kind of town where dogs roam the streets; in fact, we did see a couple of dogs on the loose during our visit. Nevertheless, there's a leash law within city limits (though not in surrounding San Juan County).

TAIL-RATED TRAILS

The area around Telluride, Ouray, and Silverton is filled with spectacular mountain hikes, many of them steeped in mining history. Some of the most accessible are described here. For more options, check out *Telluride Hiking Guide,* by Susan Kees; *Ouray Hiking Guide,* by Kelvin B. Kent; and, for Silverton, *Hiking Trails of Southwest Colorado,* by Paul Pixler. A brochure and map put out by an association called The Trail Group, Inc., "Hiking Trails of Ouray County," is another helpful resource.

Ouray

 Bear Creek National Recreation Trail. About 6 miles round-trip to the first creek crossing. Drive south out of Ouray on Highway 550. At about 2 miles from the signed turnoff for Box Canyon Falls, you'll pass through a tunnel; a parking area is immediately after it on the left. The trailhead is across the road, on the south side of the tunnel (which you'll actually hike on top of). *Dogs can be off leash.*

The most taxing part of this trail is the beginning section, which switchbacks dramatically up and up the side of the canyon. You'll encounter loose slate and quartzite along the first half of the trail; Clover didn't have a problem with it, and neither did Bruno, a ten-year-old shepherd mix we met on the trail (who had a bandaged paw, no less). But if your dog's a tenderfoot, keep an eye on him. At the top of the switchbacks, you'll be rewarded with a picture-perfect view of Red Mountain as well as a peek down the precipitous drop into Bear Creek Gorge. The narrow trail, built by miners in the late 1800s, has been carved out of the canyon's sides—if your dog has a fear of exposure you might want to keep him leashed. At 2.5 miles, pass the ramshackle remains of the Grizzly Bear Mine. About half a mile beyond, the trail descends to the creek, traveling through grasses and fir, with some good resting spots for you and your dog. Eventually the trail crosses a side creek. This was our turnaround spot, but you can continue another mile or so farther to the ruins of the Yellow Jacket Mine, and even beyond.

 Weehawken Trail. 6.2 miles round-trip. Take Highway 550 south from Ouray. At the first switchback, turn right at the National Forest access sign for Camp Bird Mine and Box Canyon Falls; then stay left at the fork. Follow the Camp Bird road for 2.6 miles to a small parking area at the trailhead, on the right. *Dogs can be off leash.*

This would be a particularly nice hike in the fall, when the aspen change. Begin by switchbacking up a wooded hillside on a narrow trail. Ascend first through an open meadow, then through aspen, all to the symphonic rumbling of Canyon Creek. Past the junction where a trail to the Alpine Mine heads off to the right (another good hike, which ends at a breathtaking overlook of Ouray), the trail snakes around a hillside, heading up the Weehawken Valley. Imposing volcanic cliffs rise across the ravine. After crossing an avalanche basin, hike along a narrow shelf in the forest to the trail's eventual end at Weehawken

Creek, where your dog can take a dip before the return hike out.

Ridgway

 Ridgway State Park. The park is right off Highway 550, just north of Ridgway, and is divided into three distinct sites: Pa-Co-Chu-Puk (try saying that one ten times in a row!), Dutch Charlie, and Dallas Creek. *Dogs must be leashed.*

Seventeen miles of trail, both paved and gravel, meander through the park. For a complete listing, pick up the trails guide at the visitor center. A few your dog may particularly enjoy: The **Dallas Creek Trail**, a 1-mile loop, begins at the Confluence Nature Area in the Dallas Creek site, following the creek and then ascending a small hill to provide a nice vista of the nearby San Juan Mountains. The **Piñon Park Trail**, in the Dutch Charlie site, runs about a mile from the visitor center to the marina. And the 3.5-mile (one way) **Enchanted Mesa Trail** skirts the edge of the mesa from Dutch Charlie to Pa-Co-Chu-Puk, with views of both the reservoir and the mountains. Be sure to bring water on this hike, as the terrain is dry. And, as in all Colorado state parks, dogs are not allowed on the swim beach at Ridgway.

The spectacular Dallas Divide, north of Telluride. (photo by Cindy Hirschfeld)

Telluride

Jud Wiebe Trail. A 2.7-mile loop. From Colorado Ave., walk three blocks north on Aspen St. to where the road dead-ends. The trailhead is here. (You can also access the Sneffels Highline trail from here, an 8.5-mile loop; because the trail enters a designated Wilderness area, however, remind your dog to leash up.) *Dogs can be off leash.*

Immediately past the trailhead, go left on the bridge over Cornet Creek. Then stay straight as the trail contours across a hillside. You'll ascend steadily, while gaining a bird's-eye view of Telluride along with a face-to-face view of the ski area. Your hiking companion in the fur coat will appreciate reaching the shady respite of aspens and, eventually, fir. The trail then opens up into a hillside meadow, from which you'll be looking directly at Bridal Veil and Ingram Falls. Descend through a lovely aspen stand before crossing another creek and hiking through more fir. When you reach an old road, go right. The trail descends back into town via a series of switchbacks; hiking boots with good tread will help you keep your footing on the loose rocks. The trail ends at a gate opening onto the Tomboy Rd. Turn right to head back to town. After passing a couple of houses balanced on the hillside, you'll wind up at the top of Oak St.

Bear Creek Trail. About 5 miles round-trip. From Colorado Ave., head south on Pine St. for 3 blocks to the end of the road and the trailhead. *Dogs can be off leash.*

This has to be the most popular trail in Telluride, judging from the many people we encountered, and it's no surprise why: It's a relatively short hike, starting from town, with a worthwhile payoff—the thundering Bear Creek Falls at trail's end. The trail follows an old mining road above Bear Creek up a fairly gradual ascent, passing

in and out of forest and meadows. The road ends at a very large rock. From there, it's a short hike up one of the footpaths to the bottom of the falls, where your dog can enjoy the cool spray.

River Corridor Trail. Runs approximately 4 miles from Town Park to Highway 145. You can access it from the southwest corner of the parking lot in the park or by heading south on any of the side streets in town. *Dogs can be off leash.*

This extremely pleasant gravel trail runs right along the banks of the San Miguel River, crisscrossing it several times. Your dog will be able to enjoy water-splashing as well as social sniffing opportunities. The trail remains pancake-flat for its whole length. Maintenance ends past the Telluride town limits, so the condition of the trail slowly deteriorates as you head farther west.

CYCLING FOR CANINES

You can find several good biking options close to Telluride, including the **Bear Creek** and **River Corridor Trails** (see "Tail-Rated Trails"). Regarding Bear Creek, unless your dog enjoys dodging lots of unaware hikers, early morning or early evening would be the best times to ride. The popular **Mill Creek Trail,** a 7-mile loop that begins past the Texaco station west of town and winds up at the beginning of the Jud Wiebe Trail, is another recommended possibility; you can ride out of town on the paved bike path that begins near the high school so you and your dog won't have to bike on the road. The **Galloping Goose Trail** (part of it's known as the **Ilium Trail**) follows an old railroad bed for 18 miles, from Society Drive in Telluride to Lizard Head Pass. Given the fairly gentle grade, riding a portion of the trail would make a good canine cycling outing. Because parking is limited at the Society Drive trailhead, pick up the trail off of South Fork, or Ilium Valley, Rd. Head west from Telluride on Highway 145; after about 6 miles, look for a sign indicating National Forest Access/South Fork Rd. After turning left, it's about 3.5 miles or so to the trailhead, on the left; parking is across the street.

Ouray and Silverton are not as conducive to canine mountain biking, as most of the areas where you can reasonably ride are on county or four-wheel-drive roads that have their share of vehicle traffic.

POWDERHOUNDS

Dogs are not allowed on any of the groomed nordic trail systems in Telluride, which include ones in Town Park and down the valley as well as by the ski area. You can, however, ski or snowshoe with your dog along the **River Corridor Trail** (see "Tail-Rated Trails"). The Ouray Nordic Council oversees a trail system south of town; although dogs are not permitted on the groomed trails, they can accompany you on the unmaintained ones. A map at the trailhead will show you which is which. The **Ironton trailhead** is 8 miles south of Ouray on Highway 550, on the left side, and the **Silver Bell trailhead** is 10 miles south of town, also on the left. In addition, see the write-ups on the **St. Paul Lodge** (outside of Silverton) and the **San Juan Guest Ranch** (in Ridgway) under "Creature Comforts."

If you're running into a store (for thirty minutes or less) in downtown Telluride, put your pooch in designated "puppy parking." The biggest spot is on the 100 block of S. Fir, conveniently across from Baked in Telluride, and there's another one on N. Pine, across from the post office. You're encouraged—not required—to tie up your dog here. Whatever you do, don't tie your dog to the bumper of your car—there's a town ordinance against doing so.

CREATURE COMFORTS

Unless otherwise stated, dogs should not be left unattended in the room or cabin.

Naturita

$ Bunkhouse Motel, 1118 Highway 97, 970-865-2893. The motel will sometimes allow small dogs to stay if owners "promise not to let the dog on the bed." Consider this an option only if you're really stuck, however; in general, the motel operators would prefer not to have dog guests.

$ Ray Motel, 123 Main St., 970-865-2235. There is one pet room available, and you can leave your dog unattended in it.

Norwood

$ Annie's Country Bed and Breakfast, 551 County Rd. 44ZN, 970-327-4331. Small dogs (e.g., poodle size) are welcome to stay in one of the three rooms at this B&B on a 160-acre working ranch. There's a $10 fee per night. You can leave your dog unattended in the room; however, he must remain on his leash when outside because the ranch abounds with sheep, cattle, and chickens.

$ Lone Cone Elk Ranch Bed and Breakfast, 900 Z42 Rd., 970-327-4300. This elk and cattle ranch on 150 acres allows dogs to visit. But before your dog starts quivering his nostrils at the possibility of chasing elk, let him know that he'll have to be on a leash when he's outside. You may be able to leave your dog unattended in your room, at the discretion of the owners.

$ Mug and Muffin Bed and Breakfast, 1245 W. Grand Ave., 970-327-4707. This friendly B&B welcomes dogs on a case-by-case basis; due to some unhappy dog experiences in the past, the owner prefers to "interview" your dog beforehand, so be sure to call ahead. If your dog passes muster, the two (or more) of you can stay in a huge upstairs room with a king-size bed, two twins, and private bath. Though you can't leave your dog unattended inside, there's a fenced yard where a nonbarker could hang out while you grab a bite to eat. The B&B is usually closed from about mid-December to mid-January.

$ **Westward Ho Motel and Trailer Court,** 1160 W. Grand Ave., 970-327-4232. Dogs can stay for $10 extra per night.

$–$$ **Back Narrows Inn,** 1550 Grand Ave., 970-327-4417. The inn has two sections: "the Lodge," with modern-style rooms, and a 100-year-old building, with rooms furnished with antiques. Dogs are allowed in about half of the rooms.

$$ **Norwood Inn,** 1415 Grand Ave., 970-327-4982. The inn welcomes dogs in any of its twelve antique-furnished rooms with a $10 nightly fee. You'll also be asked to leave a credit-card imprint as a deposit.

Ouray

$ **Ouray KOA,** 225 County Rd. 23, 970-325-4736. Dogs are allowed in the camper cabins (you'll have to supply your own bedding and cooking gear). Open May through September.

$–$$ **Ouray Cottage Motel,** 4th and Main Sts., 970-325-4370. There's a $5 one-time fee for a dog. Suites with kitchens are available. Open mid-May to mid-October.

$–$$ **Polly's Riverside Inn,** 1805 N. Main St., 970-325-4061 (800-432-4170). The inn is located aside the Uncompahgre River, as the name implies, though it also fronts busy Highway 550. But the important thing is, your dog is welcome.

$–$$ **Red Mountain Lodge,** 1510 N. Main St., 970-325-4087. For the less discriminating dog.

$–$$ **River's Edge Motel,** 110 7th Ave., 970-325-4621. "We treat a dog just like an extra person," says the owner of this motel that's pleasantly situated on a side street and along the Uncompahgre River. There's a $5 fee per night. Rooms with kitchens are available.

$$ **Ouray Victorian Inn,** 50 3rd Ave., 970-325-7222 (800-84-OURAY). This upscale motel has eight pet rooms and requests a $50 deposit. If you're confident that your dog is not a barker or whiner when left alone, you can leave him in the room unattended. Note that dogs are *not* allowed in the Victorian Inn Townhomes.

$$ **Singer Cabin,** 210 Portland Rd., 970-325-4016. For $5 extra per night, your dog can feel at home in this two-story, two-bedroom cabin on sixteen acres between Ouray and Ridgway. The cabin's decor is "moderately rustic," and a deck provides views of the San Juans. You can leave your dog unattended inside. There's a three-night minimum stay.

$$ **Timber Ridge Motel,** 1515 North Main St., 970-325-4856 (888-325-4856). This pet-friendly motel has designated thirteen ground-floor rooms for four-legged guests. "We have more problems with children than we ever have with pets," says the astute owner.

Ridgway

$ **The Adobe Inn,** 221 Liddell St., 970-626-5939. This Mexican restaurant rents out three rooms (which share a bath). Because the focus is on food, however, the owners' interest in providing lodging takes a backseat. You can leave your dog unattended in the room.

$$ **Super 8 Lodge of Ridgway/Telluride,** intersection of Highways 550 & 62, 970-626-5444 (800-368-5444). Dogs are allowed in first-floor smoking rooms only, with a $25 deposit.

$$–$$$$ **San Juan Guest Ranch,** 2882 County Rd. 23, 970-626-5360 (800-331-3015). If your dog passes muster during an over-the-phone screening (you can do the speaking for him), he can accompany you for a stay at this scenically located ranch. There are nine lodge units, each with two bedrooms, and your dog can be unattended in them. The ranch itself is on twenty-five acres, with another 2,500 acres adjacent for horseback riding and other activities. Your dog can explore either on leash or under voice control. During the summer, the ranch offers six-day stays, which include lodging,

meals, and activities for one price. In the winter, the ranch operates as a B&B, with nightly rates. The owners also maintain a set of cross-country ski trails that you and Fido can sniff out together.

Silverton

$ Molas Lake Camper Cabins and Campground, Highway 550 (5 miles south of Silverton), **970-387-5848.** Dogs can stay in the camper cabins at this scenic site on Molas Lake (you'll have to bring your own sleeping and cooking gear). And hiking is literally at the doorstep—the Colorado Trail runs right through the property.

$–$$ The Miner's Mansion, 325 W. 13th St., 888-699-3086. You and your dog can relive Silverton's past in this fourth-generation family cabin that dates from the turn of the century, now completely remodeled. It rents out weekly from May through October. You'll need to consult with the owners about whether you'll be able to leave your dog unattended inside.

$–$$ Prospector Motel, 1015 Greene St., 970-387-5466. The motel does not accept pets during the summer, but dogs are allowed from March 1 until Memorial Day and from after Labor Day to the end of November (the motel is closed during the winter).

$$ Alma House Bed and Breakfast, 220 E. 10th St., 970-387-5336 (800-267-5336). It's a lucky dog who gets to stay in the beautifully decorated rooms at this luxurious, Victorian-themed B&B. The house dates from 1898. You'll be asked to sign a damage waiver for your dog, but no deposit is required. Open mid-May through mid-October.

$$ Grand Imperial Victorian Hotel, 1219 Greene St., 970-387-5527 (800-341-3340). Built in 1882, the hotel has spacious rooms furnished with Victorian antiques, which are getting a little bit worse for the wear. But your dog won't notice.

$$ Red Mountain Motel and Campground, 664 Greene St., 970-387-5512 (888-970-5512). Open May to the end of September.

$$ Smedley's Bed and Breakfast, 1314 Greene St., 970-387-5713. The B&B, which has three rooms, will accept dogs on a case-by-case basis. Your dog might be interested to know it's located above an ice-cream parlor.

$$ St. Paul Lodge, P.O. Box 463, Silverton, 81433, 970-387-5367 or 970-387-5494 (winter). This rustic ski lodge, in a building dating from the 1880s, hosts backcountry skiers from mid-December to mid-April. Depending upon the circumstances of your stay (i.e., whether other skiers will be there, if they mind dogs), you may be able to bring along your dog. Because the only way to access the lodge is by skiing in, Rover should be comfortable with snow travel. You can purchase lodging and three meals a day, or opt for the same with guide service. The owners also rent out a cabin in summer that's 1 mile east of Red Mountain Pass and is reachable by four-wheel drive or a half-mile hike. Dogs are welcome in the cabin, which is available nightly or by the week and sleeps up to six.

$$ Villa Dallavalle Inn, 1257 Blair St., 970-387-5555. This comfortable bed and breakfast allows small and medium-sized short-haired dogs in three of its seven rooms, furnished with antiques and family memorabilia. There's a $10 deposit.

$$–$$$ Wyman Hotel and Inn, 1371 Greene St., 970-387-5372 (800-609-7845). Dogs are allowed in ground-floor rooms (there are seven, including two suites with whirlpool tubs) at this plush, elegant hotel. There's a $10 fee per night. Open approximately mid-April to November and December to mid-February.

Telluride

$$ Z Lodge, 308 San Juan Vista Dr. (near the Dallas Divide, off Lost Dollar Rd.), **970-728-5767.** "Dogs really enjoy being here," says Barbara Zabel, the owner of this secluded mountain retreat. And with thirty-seven acres at the base of the Sneffels Range, where your dog can hike with you leash-free, it's no wonder. (If your pooch is prone to taking off after deer, elk, or the like, you'll want to keep his leash close at hand, however.) The lodge's two rooms, which share a bath, feature handmade log beds and other niceties. Though you can't leave your dog unattended in them, Barbara will sometimes keep your dog company (if he's comfortable with that) while you go out for a couple of hours. Though the lodge is open year-round, the last mile of access in the winter is by snowmobile ride, courtesy of the owner—Fido can either ride along or run behind.

$$$–$$$$ Hotel Columbia, 300 W. San Juan Ave., 970-728-0660 (800-201-9505). Dogs love it at the Hotel Columbia, where they are truly welcomed. And you'll love the individually decorated, luxuriously appointed rooms. Upon check-in, your pooch will receive a biscuit, and you'll get pet pick-up bags as a gentle reminder to clean up after him on your walks through town. The hotel prefers one dog per room, and there's a $10 nightly fee. Certain rooms are the first to be given to canine visitors, and you can leave your dog unattended in the room.

$$$–$$$$ Telluride Resort Accommodations, 800-538-7754, rents out condos and private homes, some of which allow dogs with a deposit. You can leave your dog unattended in your rental accommodation.

$$$$ The Peaks at Telluride, Mountain Village, 970-728-6800 (800-789-2220). For $15 extra per night, your dog can join you at this ultra-luxury hotel and spa. Management prefers that canine guests be under 30 pounds. If your dog is tipping the scales a bit, perhaps you can promise that he'll shed those extra pounds during your stay; this is a spa, after all! Though you can't leave your dog unattended in the room, dog-sitting can be arranged through the concierge for a fee.

Campgrounds

Ridgway State Park. Highway 550, just north of Ridgway. The park has 281 sites total among its three recreation sites.

Another successful peak climb: Sean McCullough and Frostbite. (photo by Cindy Hirschfeld)

Town Park, Telluride. Located at the east end of town (42 sites).

National Forest campgrounds: **Ilium Campground,** 6 miles west of Telluride on Ilium Valley Rd. (8 sites); **Matterhorn Campground,** off Highway 145, west of Telluride (26 sites); **Amphitheatre Campground,** 1 mile south of Ouray off Highway 550 (30 sites); **South Mineral Campground,** 5 miles west on Forest Rd. 585 (turn off of Highway 550 2 miles north of Silverton; 26 sites).

Private campgrounds: **Ouray KOA, Red Mountain Motel and Campground,** and **Molas Lake Camper Cabins and Campground** in Silverton (see "Creature Comforts").

Worth a Paws

Jeep touring. The San Juan Mountains are probably the most popular area in Colorado for four-wheeling, and several companies will allow your dog either in a rental jeep or on a guided tour. **Triangle Jeep Rental, 864 Greene St. in Silverton (970-387-9990)** will let you bring one dog along for the ride as long as you can provide a protective covering (e.g., a blanket or tarp) to prevent his claws from puncturing the vinyl seat. Rentals are available May through September. And **Switzerland of America Jeep Tours, 226 7th Ave., Ouray (800-432-5337)**, will let your dog come along if you arrange for a private tour and actually purchase a seat for Fido. The tours go out from April 15 to October 15.

Bridal Veil Falls, Telluride. Bring your dog (he can be off leash) to see Colorado's tallest free-falling waterfall (325 feet), at the east end of Telluride's box canyon. Drive east on Colorado Ave. past the Liberty Bell Mill to the beginning of a jeep road. Park either in the lot at the bottom or in one of the switchback turnouts off the jeep road. From here, it's about a 1-mile hike to the bottom of the falls and about another mile to the top, by the Bridal Veil Hydroelectric Plant (now restored as a private residence as well as a functional plant).

 Box Canyon Falls and Park, Ouray. Your dog will have to forgo viewing this popular Ouray attraction. (But did you really want to pay to see a waterfall, anyway?) Instead, take him to see Lower Cascade Falls, a short walk (leash required) from the east end of 8th St.

 During the annual **Telluride Bluegrass Festival** (the third weekend in June), do yourself, and your dog, a favor and leave him behind. Dogs are not allowed in Town Park (where the performances take place) during the fest, and most of the campgrounds erected for the long weekend don't allow dogs either. To top it off, the only way you can get into town by vehicle is via special shuttle buses, which—you guessed it—don't take dogs. Put a tape of Charles Sawtelle and the Whippets on the kennel sound system and let Fido do his paw-tapping at home.

DOGGIE DAYCARE
Norwood
San Miguel Veterinary Clinic, 40775 Highway 145, 970-327-4279. $7–$9, depending on the size of dog. Open 8:30 A.M.–5:30 P.M., Monday to Friday.

PET PROVISIONS
Telluride
Telluride Pet Supply, 138 E. Colorado Ave., 970-728-0484

CANINE ER
Norwood
San Miguel Veterinary Clinic, 40775 Highway 145, 970-327-4279. Open 8:30 A.M.–5:30 P.M., Monday to Friday.

Telluride
Telluride Veterinary Clinic, 547$^{1}/_{2}$ W. Pacific Ave., 970-728-4461. Open 9 A.M.–5 P.M., Monday through Friday; until 8 P.M. on Thursday.

RESOURCES
Between the Cover Books, at 224 W. Colorado, Telluride (970-728-4504), and Ouray Mountain Sports, 772 Main, Ouray (970-325-4284), carry good selections of guidebooks and maps.

Lodging Reservations, 1-88-TELLURIDE

Norwood Ranger District, Uncompahgre National Forest, 1760 E. Grand Ave., Norwood, 970-327-4261

Ouray Chamber Resort Association, 1222 Main (in front of the Hot Springs pool), 970-325-4746 (800-228-1876; www.ouraycolorado.com)

Silverton Visitor Center, 414 Greene St., 970-387-5654 (800-752-4494; www.silverton.org)

Telluride Visitor Center, 666 W. Colorado Ave., 970-728-3041 (800-525-3455; www.telluridemm.com)

18

Mesa Verde and Vicinity

The Big Scoop

Your four-legged companion won't be able to join you in viewing this area's main attraction—Mesa Verde National Park—but you'll still be able to explore much of the fascinating history and natural beauty of the area surrounding the "Green Table." And if your dog really wants to have something to tell his stay-at-home friends about, drive him 38 miles southwest from Cortez to the Four Corners National Monument, where he can put one paw in each state.

Activity in the area surrounding Mesa Verde is centered in the small towns of Cortez, Dolores, and Mancos, which form a triangle. In Dolores, dogs can be off leash as long as they are under voice control. Cortez and Mancos both have leash laws. Cortez Centennial Park, located behind the Colorado Welcome Center in Cortez, provides a nice expanse of green for the dog who's feeling carbound.

Tail-Rated Trails

Trails in the region range from hot, sandy desert hikes to routes through the heart of the forest. The Visitor Information Bureau in Cortez puts out a great brochure with detailed descriptions, called "Guide to Scenic Hiking Trails in Mesa Verde Country." All the trails are on National Forest (non-Wilderness) or BLM land, meaning lots of leash-free jaunts on which to take your dog. A few other options are described here.

 Mancos State Park/Chicken Creek Trail. Up to 16 miles round-trip. From

Mancos, head north on Highway 184 for a quarter mile, then east (right) on County Rd. 42. Go 4 miles to County Rd. N, and turn left, which leads to the park entrance. To reach the trailhead, drive over the dam and around to the north side of the lake, where you'll see a parking area and trailhead sign on the left. *Dogs must be leashed on the portion of trail that begins in the state park; they can be off leash on National Forest land.*

This trail would be a good one for a dog during the day in summer—there's access to water as well as the pleasant shade of spruce and ponderosa pine once you reach the creek. Begin by hiking through a meadow. After about a quarter of a mile, when the trail bends to the right, it forks in the grass; stay to the left. Continue walking through tall grasses and, in summer, colorful wildflowers. Hike across and down a small clearing, after which you'll pass through a fence; this is the park boundary. The trail heads down a wide, gradual pitch to Chicken Creek. From here, it runs alongside the creek, crisscrossing the water several times and allowing your dog to cool his paws. Because this is an out-and-back hike, follow the creekbed for as long as you like. One note of caution: Because the trail receives a lot of horse use, the first mile may be heavily "cratered" when the dirt dries after a rainstorm.

 Sand Canyon Trail. 12 miles round-trip. From Cortez, drive south on Highway 160/666. Make a right onto McElmo Rd. (across from the

M&M Cafe). Go 12.5 miles to a trailhead parking area on the right. Alternate access is from the north, at Sand Canyon Pueblo: Drive north from Cortez on U.S. Highway 666 for 5.3 miles; make a left on Road P. Go 4.5 miles, then left on Road 18, at the T-intersection. After half a mile, follow the road as it makes a sharp curve to the right, turning into Road T. Turn left on Road 17 (1.4 miles); drive for a little over 3 more miles (follow the road as it bears right, becoming Road N). Look for a small parking area and BLM signage for Sand Canyon Pueblo on the left. *Dogs can be off leash.*

This is true desert hiking, best to do in the spring or fall. Be sure to bring a lot of water. As the "Sleeping Ute" mountain formation snoozes to the south, head north from the parking area at the southern trailhead, traveling across slickrock before picking up the red dirt trail. Your dog will have the chance to sniff out piñon, juniper, yucca, and prickly pear cactus. The level trail, which is easy to follow, is also marked with the occasional rock cairn. Along the way, the dog with an archaeological bent will enjoy viewing several Anasazi cliff dwellings, the first of which is in a large dome about half a mile from the trailhead. Other trail highlights include intriguing rock formations and sculpted canyons.

If you begin hiking from the north, the trail starts out somewhat rootier and rockier as it descends into the canyon. You may want to walk around the Sand Canyon Pueblo, which is in the process of being excavated, near the trailhead. The lack of interpretive material, however, may have you and your dog guessing at what you're supposed to be looking at.

Dolores Walking Trail. Runs for about half a mile along the Dolores River in the town of Dolores. Access is at either the 4th St. Bridge (take 4th St. south from Highway 145 through Dolores) or behind Joe Rowell Park, off Highway 145 North just before entering downtown Dolores. *Dogs can be off leash.*

This wide gravel trail is great for a short stop or, if you're staying in Dolores, a morning or evening walk with Fido. Hot and thirsty canine travelers will appreciate the easy river access.

Dominguez and Escalante Ruins Hike. 1 mile round-trip. The hike starts at the Anasazi Heritage Center, 27501 Highway 184, in Dolores. *Dogs must be leashed.*

A paved trail winds up a gradual ascent to the Escalante Ruins, which were first documented by Spanish Franciscan friars in the eighteenth century and then excavated in 1976. Several shaded picnic tables are available along the trail for dining al fresco with your dog. At the top, take in the panoramic view of the surrounding area, including McPhee Reservoir and Mesa Verde. The Dominguez ruins are located right next to the museum building.

Mesa Verde National Park. As with all national parks, dogs are not allowed on any of the trails here. Their presence in the park is limited to parking lots and campgrounds (always on leash) and the Far View Lodge.

CYCLING FOR CANINES

Sand Canyon (see "Tail-Rated Trails") is a scenic cycling option, best to do with your

Checking out the Anasazi ruins in Sand Canyon. (photo by Cindy Hirschfeld)

dog when temperatures are moderate. Biking from south to north gives you better riding terrain, and turning around before the trail gets too rocky will keep the round-trip distance under 10 miles. Or try the 10-mile round-trip **Cannonball Mesa** ride, which begins off McElmo Canyon Rd. about 8 miles past the Sand Canyon trailhead. For a detailed route description, pick up the brochure "Mountain and Road Bike Routes" that's put out by the Visitor Information Bureau in Cortez.

> Yes, there was a canine component to Anasazi culture; the "ancient ones" kept dogs for work and companionship.

POWDERHOUNDS

Note that though the groomed trails in the Chicken Creek area near Mancos are on National Forest land, the volunteers who maintain the ski trails ask that you leave Fido at home in winter. To access trails where you can ski or snowshoe with your dog, head northeast of Dolores up Highway 145 to the **Lizard Head Pass** area. Pick up maps at the Mancos-Dolores Ranger District (see "Resources").

CREATURE COMFORTS

Unless otherwise stated, dogs should not be left unattended in the room or cabin.

Cortez

$ Sand Canyon Inn, 301 W. Main, 970-565-8562 (800-257-3699)

$ Ute Mountain Motel, 531 S. Broadway, 970-565-8507. The motel tends to put dogs in smoking rooms but will accommodate a request for a nonsmoking room.

$–$$ Aneth Lodge/Budget Six, 645 E. Main, 970-565-3453. Small dogs can be left unattended in the room if you let housekeeping know. The motel will direct you and your dog toward a particular side of the building for bathroom excursions.

$–$$ Arrow Motor Inn, 440 S. Broadway, 970-565-3755 (800-727-7692). The Arrow doesn't allow dogs in its newest rooms, but they are welcome in all others. If you're paying with cash, you'll need to put down a $20 deposit.

$–$$ Tomahawk Lodge, 728 S. Broadway, 970-565-8521 (800-643-7705). There's a $3 one-time fee for dogs, and they can be left unattended as long as they promise to be quiet.

$$ Anasazi Motor Inn, 640 S. Broadway, 970-565-3773 (800-972-6232). The motel tries to put all dog guests in downstairs rooms for easy access outside. A credit-card imprint or a $50 cash deposit is requested, and you can leave your dog unattended in the room as long as you notify housekeeping. There's a walking path behind the motel, with grass and trees, where you can exercise your leashed dog.

$$ Bel-Rau Lodge, 2040 E. Main, 970-565-3738. One of the motel's buildings—about ten rooms—is designated for pets.

$$ Comfort Inn, 2308 E. Main, 970-565-3400. You can leave your dog unattended in the room.

$$ Days Inn, Highway 145/160, 970-565-8577 (800-628-2183). Small dogs only get the nod here. They can be left unattended in the room "as long as they don't bark or cause any trouble."

$$ Far View Lodge, Mesa Verde National Park, 970-529-4421 (800-449-2288). The lodge is one of the few places in the park where you can take your dog with you. However, there are only three dog-friendly rooms (out of 150), and they're also for smokers. A $50 deposit is required. The lodge is open from April to October.

$$ Holiday Inn Express, 2121 E. Main, 970-565-6000 (800-626-5652). Dogs are allowed in downstairs smoking rooms only.

$$ Ramada Ltd., 2020 E. Main, 970-565-3474 (800-272-6232). Dogs 45 pounds and under are welcome as guests. You can leave your dog unattended as long as you let the front desk know so they can alert housekeeping.

$$–$$$ Best Western Turquoise Inn & Suites, 535 E. Main, 970-565-3778 (800-547-3376). Dogs are allowed in smoking rooms and suites only. The hotel operators prefer that you not leave your dog alone in the room. (Note that the other Best Western in town, the Sands Motel, does *not* accept pets.)

Dolores

$ Groundhog Fishing Resort and Outfitter, Groundhog Lake, 970-565-8974, then dial 20184 after the beep. "Dogs can have as much fun here as they want," promises owner Jim Wagoner. "Just turn 'em loose and let 'em run." While the isolated mountain setting (the lake is 32 miles north of Dolores) and two rustic cabins may not be for everyone, dogs are bound to have a great time in a place that has no restrictive rules. Open June to October.

$–$$ Dolores Mountain Inn, 701 Highway 145, 970-882-7203 (800-842-8113). For a $5 one-time fee, your dog can be a guest at this motel, and he can also be left unattended in the room. In addition to standard motel rooms, one- and two-bedroom units with kitchens are available.

$–$$ Dolores River Cabins and RV Park, 18680 Highway 145, 970-882-7761. The cabins include four fully furnished housekeeping units and six camper ones (bring your own bedding to the latter). Dogs are allowed in all, and they can be left unattended in them, too. You'll find a pet-walking area near the road as well as one by a pond; the owners ask that you keep your dog leashed. There's also a walk along the Dolores River behind the cabins. Open May 15 to November 1.

$–$$ Historic Rio Grande Southern Hotel Bed and Breakfast, 101 S. 5th, 970-882-7527 (800-258-0434). How would your dog like to stay in the same hotel as Teddy Roosevelt once did and where noted Western writer Zane Grey wrote *Riders of the Purple Sage?* If he's particularly well behaved, he's welcome to join his distinguished predecessors as a visitor to this former railroad hotel, which dates from 1893 and is on the National Register of Historic Places. The eight cozy rooms (four with private bath) are furnished with turn-of-the-century antiques. You can leave your dog unattended for up to a few hours. A credit-card imprint is required as a deposit.

$–$$ Outpost Cabins, Motel, and RV Park, 1800 Highway 145, 970-882-7271 (800-382-4892). The Outpost allows dogs in all its lodging options. You can leave your furry companion unattended in the cabins or motel rooms, but housekeeping will not come in to clean during that time. There's also a large deck overlooking the Dolores River for hanging out and watching the current go by.

$$ Green Snow Oasis and Cabins, 28434 Highway 145, 970-562-3829. Located north of Dolores, near Rico, the five fully outfitted cabins here are along the Dolores River. For a $20 one-time fee, your dog can stay with you, be left unattended in the cabin, if necessary, and walk with you unleashed on the small property—just be sure to clean up after him. Open May 15 to September 30.

$$ Priest Gulch Lodge, Cabins, and Campground, 27646 Highway 145, 970-562-3810. Dogs may stay in any of the four full-service cabins or at the RV sites but not in the lodge rooms. The complex is on thirty acres bordering the Dolores River, which your dog is welcome to explore on a leash. Open May to October.

$$ The Red Elk Lodge, 27060 Highway 145, 970-562-3849. The lodge has two fully outfitted cabins; one sleeps up to five people, the other sleeps up to eight. Dogs are $10 a day extra.

$$–$$$ Lebanon Schoolhouse Bed and Breakfast, 24925 Road T, 970-882-4461

(800-349-9829). This is probably the only chance your dog could have to stay overnight in a schoolhouse, and, to be expected, he should be on his best behavior. Dating from 1907, the converted building features an intriguing mix of architecture, with two separate living room/kitchen areas and five antique-furnished bedrooms, including a master suite and the bell-tower room. Though you won't be able to leave your dog unattended here, there's a nice fenced-in area outside where he can relax while you go out to dinner. And the "schoolyard" features colorful gardens and a picnic area.

Dove Creek

$ **Country Inn Motel, 442 W. Highway 666, 970-677-2234.** The motel allows one dog per room.

Mancos

$ **A&A Mesa Verde Camper Cabins and RV Resort, 34979 Highway 160** (directly across from the entrance to Mesa Verde), **970-565-3517 (800-972-6620).** In addition to tent and RV sites, the A&A has three camping cabins where you can stay with your dog (you'll have to bring your own bedding, and there are no cooking facilities). You can leave your dog unattended in the cabin; keep him leashed at all times when outside. As an added bonus, pet-sitting is available for $5 per day, a handy option if you want to tour the national park.

$ **Mesa Verde Motel, 191 Railroad Ave., 970-533-7741 (800-825-MESA).** You may have to pay a $5 one-time fee to stay here with your pooch.

$ **The Old Mancos Inn, 200 Grand, 970-533-9019.** The inn, located in a 103-year-old building, is a work in progress. Currently, there are three downstairs rooms with private baths and antique furnishings, with #2 designated as the pet room. The upstairs rooms are hostel style, with shared bath, though plans are in the works to convert some to rooms with private baths. But

no matter what, "we'll always be pet friendly," promises the owner. Quiet dogs can be left unattended in the rooms. Or guest dogs might like to socialize with the five resident dogs at the inn. An antique shop and the Dusty Rose Cafe round out the premises.

$$ **Country West Motel, 40700 Highway 160, 970-533-7073**

$$ **Echo Basin Dude Ranch, 43747 County Rd. M, 970-533-7000 (800-426-1890).** Dogs are welcome to stay in the A-frame cabins or tent and RV sites on this 600-acre former working ranch. A $100 deposit is requested for a canine cabin stay. You can leave your four-legged dude unattended in the cabin; be sure to keep him leashed when exploring the ranch's vast property.

$$ **Ponderosa Cabins, 14068 Road 37, 970-882-7396.** The two cabins here are "pet friendly," says the owner. One sleeps up to four people, and the other sleeps up to seven. You can leave your dog unattended in them as well as let him romp leash-free on the surrounding eight acres, which are next to Summit Reservoir. Open April to November.

Rico

$$ **Rico Motel, 24 S. Silver St., 970-967-2444.** A $75 deposit is requested for dogs. They can be left unattended in the rooms.

Campgrounds

Mesa Verde National Park. Off Highway 160, about 10 miles east of Cortez. The park's Morefield Campground has 490 sites.

Mancos State Park. See "Tail-Rated Trails" for directions (33 sites).

Forest Service campgrounds: **McPhee Campground,** at McPhee Reservoir near Dolores (73 sites); **House Creek Campground,** also on the reservoir, reached via Forest Rds. 526 and 528 from Dolores (55 sites); **Transfer Campground,** north of

Mancos on Forest Rd. 561 (12 sites); **Mavreeso Campground** (14 sites), **West Dolores Campground** (13 sites), and **Burro Bridge Campground** (15 sites) are located on Forest Rd. 535, 12.5 miles from Dolores on Highway 145 East.

Private campgrounds: **Dolores River Cabins & RV Park** in Dolores; **A&A Mesa Verde Camper Cabins & RV Resort** and **Echo Basin Dude Ranch** in Mancos; **Groundhog Fishing Resort & Outfitter** at Groundhog Lake (see "Creature Comforts").

Worth a Paws

Anasazi Heritage Center, 27501 Highway 184, Dolores, 970-882-4811. Though your dog can't accompany you inside the museum to view the exhibits on Anasazi culture and artifacts on display, you're welcome to secure him to one of the benches outside while you wander through. The dog-friendly management can sometimes supply water dishes, and you can always fill up your dog's own dish from the "icy-cold water fountain," in the words of one museum staffer. Your dog can join you on the short hike up to the Dominguez and Escalante ruins; see "Tail-Rated Trails" for more information. The Heritage Center is open year-round except on Thanksgiving, Christmas, and New Year's Day. Hours are 9 A.M.–5 P.M. during the summer; 9 A.M.–4 P.M. in winter. There's a $3 admission fee to the museum.

Lowry Pueblo. Excavated in 1928, the pueblo dates from A.D. 1090. It reflects styles of both the Chaco Anasazi (from the south) and the Northern Anasazi. You and your dog can take a self-guided tour of the pueblo and the adjoining Great Kiva, as long as your dog remains on his leash. To reach the ruins, head north from Cortez on Highway 666 to Pleasant View (about 28 miles). Turn left on County Rd. CC and drive 9 miles to reach the pueblo.

Hovenweep National Monument. The monument, established in 1923, lies about 43 miles west of Cortez, straddling the Colorado/Utah border. The Square Tower Ruins, in Utah, are accessible by car; the other five ancestral Puebloan sites require short hikes. Your leashed dog is welcome to accompany you on this walk back through time (around A.D. 1200). Bring lots of water. Expect to pay $3 per person, or $6 per vehicle, at the entrance. For more information, call Mesa Verde at 970-529-4461.

 Ute Mountain Tribal Park, Towaoc (970-565-3751, ext. 282, or 800-847-5485). The park, which contains about 125,000 acres, is a primitive area containing hundreds of Anasazi ruins, and admission is only with a Ute guide, by prior reservation. Dogs are discouraged as visitors, mainly because of the archaeological work in progress. The staff member I spoke with relayed an incident in which a dog had run off, only to come back carrying a vertebra in its mouth. To prevent similar scenarios, consider dayboarding Fido in Cortez if you want to visit the park.

> If your dog tends to wander off trails, it's a good idea to keep him leashed in the desert, so he doesn't damage the fragile cryptogamic soil, which can take up to 100 years to form.

Doggie Daycare
Cortez

Cedarwood Animal Clinic, 1819 E. Main, 970-565-6531. $7–$9/day, depending on the size of dog. Open 8 A.M.–5 P.M., Monday to Friday; 9 A.M.–noon, Saturday.

Cortez Animal B&B, 6815 Highway 160, 970-564-1385. $7.50–$9.50/day, depending on the size of dog. Your dog will have plush accommodations in the indoor/outdoor heated kennels as well as a large yard to play in with his fellow boarders. Hours are 8 A.M.–5 P.M., Monday to Friday; 8–10 A.M., Saturday. Late Saturday pickups and Sunday day-boarding can also be arranged in advance.

Cortez Animal Clinic, 11314 Highway 145, 970-565-4458. $10.50/day. Open 8 A.M.–5 P.M., Monday to Friday; 9 A.M.–noon, Saturday.

High Country Kennels, 27516 Highway 160, 970-565-4910. $10/day. Open 8 A.M.–1 P.M. and 2–6 P.M., Monday to Friday; 8 A.M.–noon, Saturday.

PET PROVISIONS
Cortez
Cortez Animal B&B, 6815 Highway 160, 970-564-1385

Dolores
Dolores Feed & Supply, 28101 County Rd. T½, 970-882-2359

CANINE ER
Cortez
Cedarwood Animal Clinic, 1819 E. Main, 970-565-6531. Open 8 A.M.–5 P.M., Monday to Friday; 9 A.M.–noon, Saturday.

Cortez Animal Clinic, 11314 Highway 145, 970-565-4458. Open 8 A.M.–5 P.M., Monday to Friday; 9 A.M.–noon, Saturday.

Montezuma Veterinary Clinic, 10411 Highway 666, 970-565-7567. Open 8 A.M.–5 P.M., Monday to Friday; 8 A.M.–noon, Saturday.

RESOURCES
Colorado Welcome Center, 928 E. Main St., Cortez, 800-253-1616 (www.swcolo.org)

Dolores Visitor Center, 600 Railroad Ave., Dolores, 970-882-4018 (800-807-4712)

Mancos-Dolores Ranger District, San Juan/Rio Grande National Forest, 100 N. 6th St., Dolores, 970-882-7296

Mancos Visitor Center, 200 Main Ave., Mancos, 970-533-7434

151

19

Durango and Vicinity

THE BIG SCOOP

Dogs will find plenty to do in Durango, from sniffing out good hikes near town to wagging their tails at the world-class mountain bikers who frequent many of the trails. This is definitely a town geared toward outdoor activities. In addition, the resort area of Vallecito Lake, some 20 miles northeast of Durango, contains numerous dog-friendly accommodations (most along the order of cabins and campgrounds) and is surrounded by National Forest land and hiking trails. And Pagosa Springs, an hour east of Durango, boasts the "world's largest hot springs" (for people only) in addition to nearby National Forest trails (for dogs and people).

Note that in addition to the expected leash and dog-waste cleanup laws, Durango City Code prohibits tied-up dogs left unattended on any public property. In other words, if you want to leave your dog outside while you dash in for a bagel and coffee, don't. (For your dog's safety, find a friendly passerby who's willing to dog-sit for a few minutes rather than leave your pet in the car on a warm day.) Within surrounding La Plata County, dogs can legally be off leash as long as they are under voice control. In Pagosa Springs, dogs must be restrained, whether by leash or voice control. The Animal Control officer emphasizes, however, that you should be extra vigilant if you choose to have your dog under voice control to ensure against any wildlife-chasing escapades.

TAIL-RATED TRAILS

With the nearby San Juan National Forest as well as several trails in town, Durango is somewhat of a hiking mecca for dogs. The pamphlet "Hiking in and around Durango," available at the Durango Area Chamber Resort Association, and Paul Pixler's *Hiking Trails of Southwest Colorado* describe many fine options in addition to those given here.

Durango

Colorado Trail/Junction Creek. 8 miles round-trip. From Main Ave. in town, turn west on 25th St. After 3.4 miles, turn left into the gravel parking area, just after the cattle guard. *Dogs can be off leash.*

This hike begins at the southwest terminus of the 469-mile Colorado Trail, completed in 1988. This portion of the trail offers excellent hiking, biking, and horseback riding, so be prepared to meet lots of other outdoor enthusiasts. Climb a fairly gentle grade for the first 2.5 miles. As it ascends, the trail clings to the side of a steep, walled ravine, providing breathtaking views (and challenging cycling if you're on a bike—you'd take a heckuva long tumble if your pooch got tangled up in your spokes). At 2.5 miles, cross a bridge and begin climbing a series of switchbacks for the next 1.5 miles to Gudy's Rest. The spectacular overlook is named for Gudy Gaskill, the driving force behind the construction of the Colorado Trail. Stay for awhile and let your dog savor the view before heading back the way you came.

 Red Creek. 6 miles round-trip. From Main Ave. in town, turn east on 32nd St. (by the City Market). Make a right on County Rd. 250 (toward Lemon Lake and Vallecito Lake), then go left at the next stop sign (Rd. 240). After a little over 7 miles, turn left on County Rd. 246 (at the sign marked "Colvic Silver"). Stay on this road for 1.2 miles, where you'll come to a gate; you may have to open (and close) it. After driving another 0.3 miles, you'll see a small clearing on the right and another road leading up from it; you may want to park here, as the road gets a little rough after this point. If your car has four-wheel drive, continue straight through to the trailhead at road's end. *Dogs can be off leash.*

The trail follows Red Creek for most of the way, crisscrossing it several times, until about the last half mile, when it veers away to switchback steeply to the top of Missionary Ridge. A good hike for the active dog; you and he can enjoy a peaceful route through aspen, pine, and spruce, accompanied by the symphony of the rushing creek. If you're feeling more ambitious, it's possible to make a slightly longer loop hike: Take a right on Missionary Ridge where the Red Creek Trail intersects the Missionary Ridge Trail (it's not signed). Look for the next distinct trail to the right after a short, steep climb. Descend down the ridge between Red Creek and the west fork of Shearer Creek; you'll end up back at the road to the Red Creek trailhead.

 Animas Mountain. 6 miles round-trip. From Main Ave. in town, turn west on 32nd St. At the T-intersection with West Fourth Ave., make a right. The road ends in a small parking lot at the trailhead. *Dogs must be leashed.*

Check out the sign at the trailhead to see the various loops available on this hike.

In order to minimize hiker/biker conflict, a suggested hiking-only route is delineated by white arrows, and a suggested biking-only route is shown with blue arrows. Signs with white or blue arrows mark the routes along the way. The trail is dry, so bring water for you and your pooch.

Begin by climbing a series of gradual switchbacks; as you climb, the scenic Animas River Valley unfolds below. And you may hear the distinctive whistle of the Durango-Silverton narrow-gauge train as it leaves town. Follow the route marked with the white arrows; it ascends through piñon, juniper, and stands of ponderosa pine. You'll eventually come to a series of vista points where you and your dog can enjoy views of the La Plata Mountains to the west and the Animas River as it snakes its way from the north through verdant flatlands. You can then either turn around once you've had your fill of views or continue up the trail, which loops back to the trailhead by way of the bike route. When you come to an unmarked juncture near the bottom of the mountain, stay left and head down the switchbacks to return to the parking area.

Savoring the view from up high. (photo by Cindy Hirschfeld)

 Animas River Trail. Enjoy an easy stroll along this 5-mile paved trail that follows the Animas River through Durango. Currently the trail exists in segments: About 1.5 miles from 32nd St. to Rotary Park, and 4 miles from the Holiday Inn parking lot to K-mart at the Durango Mall. The newest section to be completed connects Albertson's to the 9th St. bridge, near Snyder Park. An easy place to access the trail is behind the Durango visitor center in Gateway Park, where parking is available. The trail runs close enough to the river that your dog can dip his toes in. And several parks along the way offer opportunities for a "green break." *Dogs must be leashed.*

Durango Mountain Park. From Main Ave. in town, turn west on 22nd St., which turns into Montview Parkway. Drive until the road ends; several parking spots are available along the street. *Dogs must be leashed.*

This area, popular with mountain bikers (it's also known as the Test Tracks), consists of a network of crisscrossing trails. There are actually several access points, in addition to the one described above, from any of the streets that back up to the park. Don't expect to find any named or signed trails; this is a place to explore. You'll encounter two starting options from the Montview access: Go left on the trail at the road's end. A couple of hundred feet later, another trail comes in from the north, which ascends up along a ridge. Or, stay on the lower trail and hike in the shade. You may have to do some puddle jumping in the spring. During the summer, the area is pretty dry. Let your dog decide the route since there's no particular destination for these hikes.

Pagosa Springs

In addition to the trail described below, **Town Park** and the adjoining short, paved **River Trail** along the San Juan are pleasant respites for a dog. During our visit to town, we enjoyed watching an agile black lab jumping in and out of the river to retrieve a stick while kayakers played in the current nearby.

Reservoir Hill. 6 miles of trail on 117 acres. From Hot Springs Blvd. off

Highway 160, make a left on San Juan St. (across from the visitor center). Take the first right, which leads directly to the parking area. *Dogs can be off leash.*

You can make an infinite number of short loop hikes within the network of trails here. All the routes are clearly marked with blazes on the trees. You can ascend to various overlooks, including ones of the town, the hot springs, Wolf Creek Pass, and Pagosa Peak. A hike up to the San Juan overlook is a relatively quick way to view a nice panorama; your dog will discover lots of ponderosa pine and gambel oak to sniff through at the top as well as what could only be Paul Bunyan's picnic table.

There's no water along the trails, but you can fill up a water bottle at pumps at the main trailhead and at the water tower overlook.

> One attraction that dogs will have to skip is the Durango & Silverton Narrow Gauge Railroad. If you opt to take the full-day trip on this historic coal-fired steam train, your dog can wait in comfort at one of several boarding kennels in Durango (see "Doggie Daycare").

CYCLING FOR CANINES

Because Durango offers such a bonanza of biking opportunities, picking up tips on suggested rides from locals is easy to do. Some areas to consider for short rides with Rover include the **Colorado Trail/Junction Creek** (see "Tail-Rated Trails"); the **Log Chute,** a short loop in the vicinity of the Colorado Trail that's not as heavily used; **Horse Gulch,** accessible from E. 8th Ave. and 3rd St. in Durango (your dog might enjoy the 4-mile **Meadow Loop**—go right at the first intersection you'll come to); **Lime Creek Rd.** (Forest Rd. 591), off Highway 550, a couple miles north of Purgatory (ride this old stagecoach route out and back for as long as you want); or the **Tuckerville Trail,** which starts at mile marker 11 off Middle

Mountain Rd. near Vallecito Lake and follows an old jeep road to a former mining site. Stop by **Hassle Free Sports**, 2615 Main, 970-259-3874 (800-835-3800), for maps and more specifics. In Pagosa Springs, the **Reservoir Hill** trail network (see "Tail-Rated Trails") is a great place to take along your dog for a short spin.

POWDERHOUNDS

Chimney Rock Archaeological Area. Though dogs are not allowed here during the summer, the Forest Service says that you're welcome to bring yours along as a ski or snowshoe partner in the winter. The 3-mile road up to the archaeological area is unplowed from about November to March, providing for an easy winter workout. To reach the area, drive 17 miles west from Pagosa Springs on Highway 160. At the Route 151 turnoff (by Lake Capote), turn south and continue for about three miles to the Chimney Rock entrance.

Pine River Valley Nordic Ski Club Trail System. A local nordic club maintains a network of groomed trails located on the east side of Vallecito Lake that wind along an unplowed road as well as through campgrounds and surrounding area. Your dog can accompany you, and because this is Forest Service land, he can be off leash. The Vallecito Lake Chamber of Commerce (970-884-9782) can provide more info.

CREATURE COMFORTS

Unless otherwise stated, dogs should not be left unattended in the room or cabin.

Bayfield

$$ Horseman's Lodge, 7100 County Rd. 501, 970-884-9733. Located halfway between Bayfield and Vallecito Lake, the motel allows dogs in any of its nine units. There is a small dog run in the back where well-behaved dogs can be tied up, and some dog kennels may be available in the future.

$$ Mountain Trails Inn and Cafe, 399 N. Mountain View Dr., 970-884-2780. Dogs are allowed to stay in some of the motel's rooms for a $5 fee per night. They can be left unattended in the rooms, and there is a dog-walking area behind the motel (dogs should be kept leashed).

Durango

$ Brookside Motel, 2331 Main Ave., 970-259-0150. There's a $20 deposit for dogs. Kitchen units are available.

$ Country View Lodge, 28295 Highway 160 East, 970-247-5701. Dogs are allowed in smoking rooms only. Rooms with kitchens are available.

$ Durango East KOA & Kamping Kabins, 30090 Highway 160, 970-247-0783 (800-KOA-0793). Dogs are allowed in the cabins (you'll need to supply your own sleeping and cooking gear). There's a dog walk along a creek where you can bring your leashed companion. Open April to October.

$ Hermosa Court Hot Springs Lodge, 7397 County Rd. 203, 970-247-2413. The motel, which is open between Memorial Day and Labor Day, accepts small dogs. Most units have kitchenettes.

$ Lightner Creek Camper Cabins & Campground, 1567 County Rd. 207, 970-247-5406. Dogs are allowed in the cabins as well as in the campground. The cabins are bare bones—you must bring sleeping bags and cooking equipment, and they have lighting but no electricity. Be sure to keep your dog leashed when outside. Open from the beginning of May to the end of September.

$ Valley View Lodge, 5802 County Rd. 203, 970-247-3772

$–$$ Budget Inn, 3077 Main Ave., 970-247-5222 (800-257-5222). The motel has a few pet rooms available for $5–$10 extra per night.

$–$$ Caboose Motel, 3363 Main Ave., 970-247-1191. Dogs can stay in smoking rooms for a $3–$5 fee per night.

$–$$ Highland Motel, 474 College Dr., 970-247-0452. Dogs can stay for a $10 fee per night, and they can even be left unattended in the room.

$–$$ Rodeway Inn, 2701 Main Ave., 970-259-2540 (800-752-6072). For a $5 one-time fee, dogs can stay here (though the management reserves the right to turn away very large or aggressive dogs). If you pay with cash, the motel also requests a $20 deposit.

DeChelly takes a rock-chewing break in Durango. (photo by Cindy Hirschfeld)

$$ Adobe Inn, 2178 Main Ave., 970-247-2743. This motel accepts dogs for a $5 fee per night. Units with kitchens are available.

$$ Alpine Motel, 3515 N. Main Ave., 970-247-4042 (800-818-4042)

$$ Comfort Inn, 2930 N. Main Ave., 970-259-5373. Selected pet rooms are available, with a $10 fee per night.

$$ Days End, 2202 Main Ave., 970-259-3311 (800-242-3297). For a $5 fee per night, per pet, you can stay here with your dog; however, dogs are not permitted in the motel's newest building. Kitchen units are available.

$$ Days Inn Durango, 1700 Animas View Dr., 970-259-1430 (800-329-7466)

$$ Dollar Inn, 2391 Main Ave., 970-247-0593 (800-727-DRGO). Though very large dogs are "questionable," according to management, smaller canines are welcome to stay in the motel's smoking rooms for a $3 fee per night.

$$ Siesta Motel, 3475 Main Ave., 970-247-0741. The motel allows one dog per room for a $5 fee per night. Management tries to limit dogs to smoking rooms but will put them in nonsmoking rooms if the former are not available.

$$ Thrifty Inn Sunset, 2855 Main Ave., 970-247-2653 (800-414-5984). The motel will sometimes accept small dogs, in smoking rooms, if it's not full. You'd pay $5 extra per night for the privilege.

$$ Travel Lodge, 2970 Main Ave., 970-247-1741. Selected pet rooms are available, with a one-time fee of $4 for small dogs or $8 for large dogs. A $25 deposit is required.

$$ Vagabond Inn, 2180 Main Ave., 970-259-5901. For $5 per night, your dog can stay with you at this motel and can hang out in the room unattended.

$$ Wapiti Lodge, 21625 Highway 160 West, 970-247-3961. Some rooms at this motel are available for dogs to stay in. You'll need to give a credit-card imprint for a deposit if you're paying in cash.

$$–$$$ Holiday Inn, 800 Camino del Rio, 970-247-5393 (800-HOLIDAY). Dogs are welcome for a $5 fee per night, per pet. The hotel has kennels out back where Fido can stay, at no extra charge, while you're out on the town.

$$–$$$ Iron Horse Inn, 5800 N. Main Ave., 970-259-1010. All of the motel's rooms are bilevel, with a queen-size bed, sitting area, and fireplace downstairs and another queen-size bed upstairs. You can leave your dog unattended in the room as long as you notify housekeeping.

$$$ Doubletree Hotel, 501 Camino del Rio, 970-259-6580 (800-222-TREE). One of the more upscale accommodations in town that accepts pets, the hotel prefers to put dogs in the lower-level river-facing rooms. You'll pay a $10 fee per night. Quiet dogs may be left unattended in the room.

$$$ Quality Inn and Suites, 455 S. Camino del Rio, 970-259-7900 (888-259-7903). Dogs under 20 pounds who put down a $50 deposit are welcome as guests.

$$$ Rochester Hotel, 726 E. 2nd Ave., 970-385-1920 (800-664-1920). The most interesting place for dogs to stay in Durango is this tastefully updated historic hotel, especially if yours is a fan of Western movies. Two of the hotel's fifteen Western-themed rooms are available for dog stays, and both open onto a lovely courtyard garden. There's a $10 fee per night. Note that the affiliated Leland House Bed & Breakfast, across the street, does *not* accept dogs.

$$$$ Residence Inn by Marriott, 21691 Highway 160 West, 970-259-6200. You'd have to really have an affinity for Residence Inns to want to stay here with your dog, as you'll be required to fork over a $200 fee per visit.

In what may be a disappointment to the erudite canine, dogs are not allowed anywhere on the Fort Lewis College Campus, located on the eastern end of town.

Hesperus
$ Canyon Motel, 4 County Rd. 124, 970-259-6277 (800-273-5673)

Pagosa Springs
$ Bruce Spruce Ranch, 231 West Fork Rd. (16 miles northeast of Pagosa Spgs.), **970-264-5374.** Dogs are welcome in all of the ranch's cabins as well as in the RV and tent sites, on forty acres bordered by National Forest land. The large group facility known as the Faris House Lodge, however, does not allow pets. There's a $2.50 fee per night, per pet for the cabins. Dogs must be kept leashed when outside. Open May to October.

$ Elk Meadows Camper Cabins & Campground, 5360 E. Highway 160, 970-264-5482. The campground has three cabins (bring your own bedding and cooking gear) in which dogs are allowed to stay for a $10 deposit. There's a trail on the property, and the San Juan River flows through part of the grounds; keep your dog leashed and be sure to pick up after him. Open May to mid-October.

$ Indian Head Lodge, 631 Williams Creek Rd. (FS 640; 24 miles north of Pagosa Spgs.), **970-731-2282.** Small to midsize dogs are allowed in the four cabins here, two of which come with kitchen facilities. Open early May to late November.

$ Pagosa Riverside Cabins & Campground, 2270 E. Highway 160, 970-264-5874. As the name implies, the campground has 1,100 feet of frontage on the San Juan River. Dogs are allowed in the cabins (bring your own bedding). Keep your dog on his leash when outside and be diligent about picking up after him. Open April to November.

$ Piedra River Resort, Highway 160 and Piedra River (20 miles west of Pagosa Spgs.), **970-731-4630 (800-898-2006).** Dogs are allowed to stay in any of the cabins here. The owners request a credit-card imprint as a deposit against any damages. Keep your dog leashed (and picked up after) on the resort's seven acres. Open May to mid-November.

$ Sportsman's Supply & Campground, 2095 Taylor Lane (18 miles north of Pagosa Spgs.), **970-731-2300.** The campground has five cabins that dogs can stay in. The owners prefer that you not leave your dog unattended in a cabin—"We don't appreciate barking dogs"—and require that you keep your dog leashed and clean up after him when exploring the campground's ten acres.

$–$$ Be Our Guest Bed & Breakfast/Guest House, 19 Swiss Village Dr., 970-264-6814. The invitation extends to dogs, too, at this super-friendly B&B, which is also home to two dogs and a cat. You can pick from a variety of accommodations: five private rooms, a lower-level area that sleeps sixteen, and an open sleeping loft. Expect a $10 fee the first night for a dog, $5 per night thereafter. Dogs can be left unattended inside, and there's a lot next door where they can play while on a leash.

$–$$ Pinewood Inn, 157 Pagosa St. (Highway 160), 970-264-5715 (888-655-7463). There's a $5 fee per night for dogs. One cabin is available, as are rooms with or without kitchenettes.

$–$$ Skyview Motel, 1300 Highway 160 West, 970-264-5803. Dogs are welcome for a $5 fee per night. If you're paying with cash, a deposit might be required.

$$ Best Western Oak Ridge Lodge, 158 Hot Springs Blvd., 970-264-4173. Dogs 25 pounds and under are allowed in smoking rooms only.

$$ Fireside Inn, 1600 E. Highway 160, 970-264-9204 (888-264-9204). As far as dogs go, "just bring them and make sure they behave," say the operators of these one- and two-bedroom cabins. Just a quarter mile outside of Pagosa Springs, the cabins are situated on seven acres bordering the San Juan River.

$$ First Inn Motel, 260 E. Highway 160, 970-264-4161 (800-903-4162). Very small pets only are allowed in a few of the motel's rooms; there's a $5 one-time fee.

$$ Pagosa Springs Inn, 3565 W. Highway 160, 970-731-4141 (888-221-8088). The hotel has designated pet rooms where dogs can be left unattended as long as you notify housekeeping. If you pay with cash, a $75 deposit is requested.

$$ Spa Motel, 317 Hot Springs Blvd., 970-264-5910 (800-832-5523). There's a $15 fee per night, per pet. Some rooms have kitchenettes or full kitchens.

$$ Super 8 Motel, corner of Piedra Rd. and Highway 160, 970-731-4005 (800-800-8000). Dogs can stay here for $5 per night and can be left unattended in the rooms.

$$–$$$ Spring Inn, 165 Hot Springs Blvd., 970-264-4168 (800-225-0934). Dogs are only allowed in smoking rooms. There is also an adjoining cabin, which sleeps four to six people, where dogs are permitted.

$$$ Pagosa Realty Rentals, 970-731-5515 (800-367-2140), has some dog-friendly homes available for short-term stays, with a $50 deposit.

$$$ Sunetha Management, 970-731-4344 (800-365-3149), has some short-term condo and home rentals available that will allow dogs with a $150 deposit.

Purgatory

$$–$$$ Best Western Lodge at Purgatory, 49617 Highway 550 North, 970-247-9669 (800-637-7727). For $6 per pet, per night, your dog can stay with you at the base of Purgatory Ski Area. All units are condo style, with full kitchens, ranging from studios to two bedrooms. You can leave your dog unattended inside as long as he refrains from barking a lot.

$$–$$$ The Nugget Cabin, 48721 Highway 550 (one half mile south of Purgatory), 970-749-4742 or 970-385-4742. Owner Dale Butt, who rents out this two-bedroom, 900-square-foot log cabin with outdoor hot tub, says dogs are "absolutely no problem" to have as guests. As he puts no restrictions on four-legged occupants, you can leave yours unattended in the cabin (and go skiing, perhaps). You can view the cabin on the Web at www.big-mountain.com/Purgatory/Nugget.

Vallecito Lake

$ Lake Haven Resort, 14452 County Rd. 501, 970-884-2517. The resort allows dogs in about two-thirds of its cabins, which overlook the lake. There's a $5 fee per night, per pet, and you must sign a damage release upon check-in. Open from April to mid-October.

$ Scottie's Resort, 17454 County Rd. 501, 970-884-2506. Depending on a variety of factors (call to find out), dogs can stay in either the motel rooms or cabins here. Open from May to mid-November.

$ Vallecito Resort, 13030 County Rd. 501, 970-884-9458 (800-258-9458). The resort allows small dogs (around 30 pounds and under) in its cabins and travel trailers as well as in the campground sites. They should be leashed everywhere on the property. If your dog feels like picking up a new hobby, let him know that this is the place to come for square dancing and line dancing. The resort, which is just south of the lake, is open from May to October.

$$ Bear Paw Lodge, 18011 County Rd. 501, 970-884-2508. Dogs are welcome to stay in any of the lodge's one- to three-bedroom cabins for a $10 fee per night. They must be kept leashed when exploring the wooded property. The lodge, which is open year-round, is one mile from the lake.

$$ Circle S Lodge, 18022 County Rd. 501, 970-884-2473. You can bring along your dog to stay in the one- to four-bedroom cabins for a $10 one-time fee. The lodge is open year-round.

$$ Croll Cabins, 4557 County Rd. 501A, 970-884-2083. There's a $5 fee per night for dogs to stay at these lakeside two- to four-bedroom cabins. They must be kept leashed on the cabin property. Open from May to November.

$$ DLR Lakefront Units, 14518 County Rd. 501, 970-884-4161. Dogs are welcome in any of the two- or three-bedroom cabins, which overlook the lake, and can be left unattended inside. Open May to September.

$$ Forest Lakes Chalets, 260 Alpine Forest Dr., 970-884-2411 (800-525-5424). "We love pets," says the manager of these A-frame cabins 7 miles south of Vallecito Lake. A deposit is required (call for specifics). There's lots of area nearby for dog walking, preferably done with a leash. Open May to September.

$$ Lone Wolf Lodge, 18001 County Rd. 501, 970-884-0414. For an extra $10 per night, dogs can stay in any of the cabins here, which are a bit north of the lake. Keep your dog leashed when outside. The lodge is open year-round.

$$ Sawmill Point Lodge, 14737 County Rd. 501, 970-884-2669. The lodge itself houses motel rooms with kitchenettes and apartments, but it also books one- to three-bedroom cabin rentals around the lake. Dogs are allowed in all but one of the units, for $5 per night, per dog. Cabin rentals are available from Memorial Day to Labor Day; the motel rooms are open year-round.

$$ Silver Spruce Lodge, 18849 County Rd. 501, 970-884-2866. With prior approval only, the lodge permits small dogs (poodle size and under) in any of its cabins, which all have three bedrooms. The lodge, a mile from the lake's north end, is open April to October.

$$ Valley of Spruce Chalet, 19007 County Rd. 501, 970-884-2623. The friendly folks here welcome dogs in any of their eight cabins, situated on nine acres along the Vallecito River. You can leave your dog unattended in the cabin, and he can even run leash-free on the property as long as he "behaves and doesn't bite anyone." Open May to October.

$$$ Granite Peaks Ranch, 25080 County Rd. 501, 970-884-2626. Three cabins are available for rent on this working horse and cattle ranch bordering National Forest land. Your dog is welcome and can be left unattended in the cabin, too. The owner asks that you keep your dog leashed while near the ranching operations, but you can let him run free elsewhere on the 135 acres. The Forest Service's Pine River Trail is also nearby. The ranch is open to guests from June to the beginning of November.

Campgrounds

National Forest campgrounds: Three campgrounds (**Florida, Miller Creek,** and **Transfer Park**) are at Lemon Reservoir, 17 miles northeast of Durango, via County Rds. 240 and 243; **Vallecito Lake** has seven campgrounds, including the 80-site **Vallecito Campground; Junction Creek Campground,** just west of Durango on 25th St. (38 sites); **East Fork Campground** (26 sites), **Wolf Creek Campground** (26 sites), and **West Fork Campground** (28 sites) are all reached via Highway 160 East from Pagosa Springs, heading up Wolf Creek Pass.

Private campgrounds: **Durango East KOA** and **Lightner Creek Campground** in Durango; **Bruce Spruce Ranch, Elk Meadows Campground, Pagosa Riverside Campground,** and **Sportman's Supply and Campground** in Pagosa Springs; **Vallecito Resort** at Vallecito Lake (see "Creature Comforts" for all).

WORTH A PAWS

Pet Fair and Show. In May, the La Plata County Humane Society hosts this fundraising event at the Durango High School. Your dog can compete in judged categories such as "funniest looking," "most resemblance to owner," "best tail wagging," and "worst behaved." Call 970-259-2847 for information.

Pet Pride Day. Held in Pagosa Springs the second or third weekend of July in Pagosa Springs' Town Park, this owner/dog event includes the 1-mile Paws Walk, with dogs

in costume; competitions in categories such as best trick, best costume, and "longest" dog; information and pet products booths; and the K-9 9-K race, which you can run with or without a four-legged partner. The "pet blessing," done by a different denomination each year, opens the festivities. Proceeds from the day benefit the Upper San Juan Humane Society (970-731-4771).

Pack Rack (Humane Society thrift store), 180 S. 6th St., Pagosa Springs, 970-264-6424. As long as your dog is a well-behaved, housebroken shopper, you can bring him along to explore the goods here, where sales fund the Upper San Juan Humane Society.

 Chimney Rock Archaeological Area. Guided tours only are available at the site of this one-time Anasazi community, located between Durango and Pagosa Springs, and dogs are not allowed to participate. But dogs are welcome in wintertime (see "Powderhounds").

DOGGIE DAYCARE
Durango

Durango Animal Hospital, 2461 Main Ave., 970-247-3174. $19/day. Open 7:30 A.M.–5:30 P.M., Monday; 7:30 A.M.–7 P.M., Tuesday to Friday; 8 A.M.–5 P.M., Saturday; and 10 A.M.–noon and 1–4 P.M., Sunday.

Happy Paws Pet Care, 1301 Florida Rd., 970-259-7917. $12/day. Special hours for passengers on the Durango & Silverton Narrow Gauge Railroad are available at no extra charge. (The kennel is five minutes from the train station.) Regular hours are 7:30 A.M.–5:30 P.M., Monday to Friday; 7:30 A.M.–1 P.M., Saturday.

Puppy Love, 130 County Rd. 234, 970-259-3043 (800-521-3843). $8–$10.50/day, depending on the size of dog. For an extra fee, the kennel will allow Durango & Silverton train passengers to drop a dog off early, pick him up late, or bring him in on a Sunday. (The kennel is ten minutes from the train station.) Regular hours are 7 A.M.–5 P.M., Monday to Saturday.

Willow Tree Kennels, 6510 County Rd. 203, 970-259-0018. $20/day. Open 8 A.M.–5 P.M., Monday to Saturday.

PET PROVISIONS
Bayfield
Bayfield Feed & Supply, 24 Mill St., 970-884-2094

Durango
Creature Comforts, 1119 Camino del Rio, 970-247-2748

Pagosa Springs
Pagosa Pet Parlor & Palace, 457 S. Highway 84, 970-264-5923

CANINE ER
Durango
Durango Animal Hospital (AAHA certified), 2461 Main Ave., 970-247-3174. Open 7:30 A.M.–5:30 P.M., Monday; 7:30 A.M.–7 P.M., Tuesday through Friday; 8 A.M.–5 P.M., Saturday; and 10 A.M.–noon and 1–4 P.M., Sunday.

Pagosa Springs
San Juan Veterinary Services, 102 Pike Dr., 970-264-2629. Open 9 A.M.–5 P.M., Monday to Friday.

RESOURCES
Bureau of Land Management, 701 Camino Del Rio, Durango, 970-247-4082

Columbine Ranger District East, San Juan/Rio Grande National Forest, 367 S. Pearl St., Bayfield, 970-884-2512

Durango Area Chamber Resort Association, 111 S. Camino del Rio, Durango, 970-247-0312 (800-525-8855; www.durango.org)

Pagosa Ranger District, San Juan/Rio Grande National Forest, 180 Second St., Pagosa Springs, 970-264-2268

Pagosa Springs Area Chamber of Commerce, 402 San Juan Ave., Pagosa Springs, 970-264-2360 (800-252-2204; www.pagosa-springs.com)

San Juan/Rio Grande National Forest Annex, 701 Camino Del Rio, Rm. 301, Durango, 970-247-4874

Vallecito Lake Chamber of Commerce, 1245 County Rd. 500, Vallecito Lake, 970-884-9782

SOUTHEAST
COLORADO

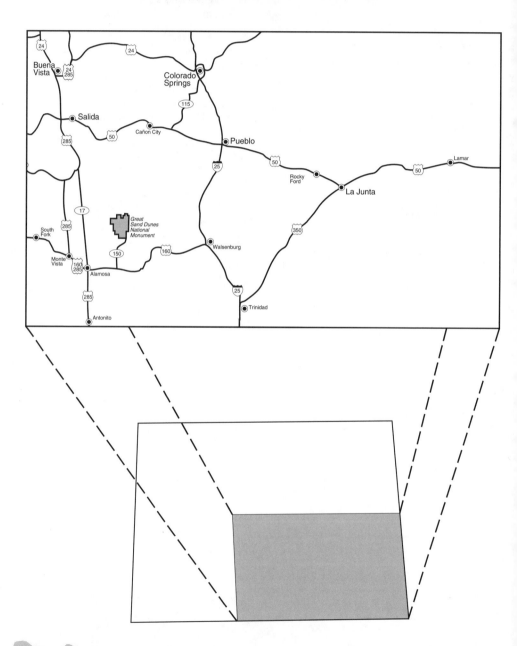

20

San Luis Valley and Vicinity

THE BIG SCOOP

The San Luis Valley encompasses a large portion of south-central Colorado. Though towns are few, small, and far between, your dog will exult in the thousands of acres of Rio Grande National Forest that stretch across the area. You'll be pleased that a wide variety of accommodations welcomes dogs, from remote cabin resorts to luxury inns. There's even a motel in Monte Vista from which you and your dog can watch movies at the drive-in theater next door. Note that dogs will have to pass up a ride on the Cumbres and Toltec Scenic Railroad, one of the area's few "organized" attractions, which runs between Antonito and Chama, New Mexico.

TAIL-RATED TRAILS

 Great Sand Dunes National Monument. Located 38 miles northeast of Alamosa via Highways 160 east and 150 north. *Dogs must be leashed.*

The sand dunes are the closest thing to the beach that your dog can experience in Colorado—minus all the water. At heights of nearly 700 feet (higher than many midwestern ski areas), the dunes are the tallest in North America. Though your dog might not quite appreciate the stunning contrast between snowcapped peaks in the background and 39 square miles of sculpted sand, he'll certainly enjoy burrowing his nose in something new and different. There are no set trails across the dunes,

so you're free to explore, as long as Fido stays leashed. In June, July, and August, the temperature of the sand can get as high as 140°—which will burn paw pads—so stick to hiking during the early morning or evening if you visit during those months. The only water you'll find is that of Medano Creek, which borders the dunes on the east, so bring plenty along. For a change of pace from the sand, head east on the **Mosca Pass Trail**, which borders Mosca Creek and is on Forest Service land; your dog can hike here off leash.

CREATURE COMFORTS

Unless otherwise stated, dogs should not be left unattended in the room or cabin.

Alamosa

$ Alamosa KOA and Kamping Kabins, 6900 Juniper Ln., 719-589-9757 (800-KOA-9157). Dogs are allowed in the three camper cabins here (you'll need to provide your own sleeping and cooking gear). Open May 1 to October 1.

$ Narrow Gauge Motel, A811 Highway 285, 719-589-6651

$–$$ Rio Grande Motel, 2051 Main, 719-589-9095. Dogs are usually placed in smoking rooms here, though they can stay in nonsmoking rooms on request. There's an $8 fee per night.

$–$$ Sky-Vue Motel, 250 Broadway, 719-589-4945 (800-805-9164). The motel has eight pet rooms, one of which is nonsmoking. There's a $3 one-time fee per pet, and you can leave your dog un-attended in the room.

$$ Best Western Alamosa Inn, 1919 Main, 719-589-2567 (800-528-1234). Dogs 30 pounds and under can stay for $6 extra per night.

$$ Cottonwood Inn Bed and Breakfast, 123 San Juan Ave., 719-589-3882 (800-955-2623). "Well-behaved dog owners"—and their dogs—are welcome in the inn's suites, adjacent to the main building, with a $50 deposit. Two suites, one with modern, "Pottery Barn–style" decor, the other furnished with 1920s-era antiques, are open to all dogs. The other two suites are also available to dogs who are traveling in a crate. All suites have a living room area, bedroom, bath, and kitchen. Quiet, non-destructive dogs may be left unattended in the rooms, as can all crated canines. There are two resident dogs at the inn.

$$ Holiday Inn of Alamosa, 333 Santa Fe Ave., 719-589-5833 (800-HOLIDAY). You need to put down a $25 deposit for your dog, and you can leave him unattended in the room. You'll also be asked to notify the front desk half an hour before you check out so that they can inspect your room and, hopefully, refund your deposit.

Antonito

$ Josey's Mogote Meadow, 34127 High-way 17 (5 miles west of Antonito), 719-376-5774. Two cabins and two mobile homes on seven grassy acres are available to you and your dog. Open May 1 to mid-October.

$ Menkhaven Lodge, 20900 Highway 17 (20 miles southwest of Antonito), 719-376-5767. "All pets are welcome" in the nine-teen fully furnished cabins, ranging from one to four bedrooms. There's a $5 one-time fee, and you can leave your dog unat-tended inside. RV sites are also available. Open year-round.

$ Park Motel, 115 Main, 719-376-5582 (888-892-5701). You can leave your dog unattended in the room. The motel opera-tors will also dog-sit, for no extra charge, if you want to spend a day riding the Cumbres and Toltec Scenic Railroad.

$ Ponderosa Campground, 19600 High-way 17 (16 miles west of Antonito), 719-376-5857. The campground has five cabins available, furnished and equipped with a refrigerator and a hot plate for cooking. Dogs are welcome as long as they're kept leashed when outside. Open Memorial Day to October 1.

$–$$ Narrow Gauge Railroad Inn, 5200 Highway 285, 719-376-5441. Dogs are accepted with a $5 one-time fee.

$–$$ Rocky Mountain Lodge, Forest Rd. 250 (about 32 miles from Antonito), 719-376-5597. The fourteen rustic log cabins are on an old ranch that borders the Na-tional Forest. Dogs can be left inside unat-tended. Open May 15 to November 1.

$–$$ Skyline Lodge, Forest Rd. 250 (about 45 miles from Antonito), 719-376-2226. The lodge, near Platoro Reservoir, wins the prize for remoteness of all the accommo-dations listed for Antonito. Luckily, there's

Bart catches air, with Pam Simich, at Great Sand Dunes National Monument. (photo by Elizabeth Oppen)

a restaurant on site. You could have an idyllic stay here with your dog, in either a lodge room or one of sixteen fully outfitted cabins. You'll be asked to put down a $25 deposit per pet. Dogs can be left unattended inside, and they can also romp off leash with their owners on the property, which is next to the Conejos River. Open from Memorial Day to the end of October.

$–$$ Twin Rivers Guest Ranch and RV Park, 34044 Highway 17 (5 miles west of Antonito), **719-376-5710.** There's a two-dog limit in the eight fully equipped cabins, which are on fifteen acres by the Conejos River. Keep your dog on a leash on the property. If you happen to be traveling with your horse, he's welcome here, too. Open May 1 to November 15.

$$ Conejos Cabins, Forest Rd. 250 (about 43 miles west of Antonito), **719-376-2547** (417-842-3279 in winter, which is a good time to book in advance, according to the proprietor). Near the Continental Divide and well into the Rio Grande National Forest west of Antonito, these cabins on the banks of the Conejos River afford you and your dog relative solitude. The eleven cabins are fully equipped, and some have fireplaces. There's a limit of one dog per cabin and a $5 fee per night. Open Memorial Day to mid-October.

$$ Conejos River Guest Ranch, 25390 Highway 17 (14 miles west of Antonito), **719-376-2464.** Choose from among the eight lodge rooms or six fully equipped, one- to three-bedroom cabins. Part of the ranch's main building is 104 years old. There's a $10 one-time pet fee, and you can leave your dog unattended inside. But he'll probably be more eager to explore the ranch's twelve acres within the Rio Grande National Forest, which he can do leash-free with you, or play along the mile of Conejos River frontage. If you do need to leave Fido behind for any length of time (say, to ride the Cumbres and Toltec Scenic Railroad), Shorty, the woman in charge, is willing to dog-sit; there are two resident dogs who may keep him company. There's also a restaurant on the premises. Open March through November.

Blanca

$$ Mt. Blanca Game Bird and Trout, County Rd. CC, 719-379-3825. You and your dog can stay together at this eight-room B&B if you have a travel kennel in which he can stay. As long as he remains in the kennel, you can leave your dog unattended in the room. His reward will be the surrounding 6,000 acres on which he can run and sniff leash-free. And there are three lakes within steps of the house that are perfect for a quick doggie paddle.

Creede

$ Broken Arrow Ranch, 32738 Highway 149 (12 miles southwest of Creede), **719-658-2484.** For a $10 one-time fee, well-mannered dogs are allowed in the ten one- or two-bedroom rustic cabins, which are fully furnished and have wood cook stoves (as well as propane). Your dog can walk the sixty acres of property (bounded by National Forest) off leash with you. Open Memorial Day to September 15.

$ Snowshoe Motel, Highway 149 and 8th St., 719-658-2315. Small to medium-sized dogs are considered on a case-by-case basis.

$$ Antlers Rio Grande Lodge, 26222 Highway 149 (5 miles southwest of Creede), **719-658-2423.** Dogs are allowed in both the fully furnished cabins and the motel rooms, with a $5 fee per night, per pet. You must keep your dog leashed on the ranch's seventy acres. Open May 1 to September 30.

$$ Wetherill Ranch, Highway 149 (17 miles southwest of Creede), **719-658-2253.** The ranch accepts dogs that aren't "vicious," and if your dog is a particularly heavy shedder, you might be asked to put down a $25 deposit. Dogs can be left unattended in the cabins but should be kept leashed when outside. Open May 1 to mid-November.

Crestone

$$ Alder Terrace Inn, Alder St., 719-256-4975. You can stay with your dog here—just don't expect the red-carpet treatment. The inn offers one- and two-bedroom suites with kitchens. One small to medium-sized dog is allowed per unit, for an undisclosed fee. And if you leave your dog unattended inside, the owner threatens that she'll turn him out.

$$ White Eagle Village, 67485 County Rd. T (4 miles west of Crestone), **719-256-4865 (800-613-2270).** The hotel offers some designated pet rooms for $5 extra per night.

Del Norte

$ Del Norte Motel, 1050 Grand Ave., 719-657-3581 (800-372-2331). Dogs are allowed in smoking rooms only.

$ El Rancho Motel, 1160 Grand Ave., 719-657-3332 (800-266-6573). Again, it's smoking rooms only for dogs.

Fort Garland

$ The Lodge, Highway 160 West at Gilpin, 719-379-3434. The owner of the motel says she's used to having dog guests, especially when field trials are being held in nearby Blanca. There are several designated pet rooms, and a $5 one-time fee per pet is charged. You can leave your dog unattended in the room.

La Jara

$ Travelers Motel, 305 Spruce St., 719-274-5872

Monte Vista

$ El Campo Motel, 401 Ulysses Blvd., 719-852-5952. Dogs are permitted in most rooms.

$–$$ Best Western Movie Manor, 2830 W. Highway 160, 719-852-5921 (800-771-9468). Unique in its own right, your stay here can be enhanced by the company of your dog. True to its name, the Movie Manor provides big-screen entertainment (from May to September) via the drive-in theater next door. Your room is equipped with speakers, so you can just lie on the bed and watch away. Dogs are restricted to smoking rooms only, but you can leave yours unattended inside if he wants to get in more movie viewing than you're up for. There's a $5 one-time pet fee.

$–$$ Rio Grande Motel, 25 N. Broadway, 719-852-3516. There's a $4 fee per pet, per night.

$$ Comfort Inn, 1519 Grand Ave., 719-852-3584 (800-221-2222)

Mosca

$–$$ Great Sand Dunes Oasis and Camper Cabins, 5400 Highway 150 North (at the entrance to the national monument), **719-378-2222.** "We love pets," say the owners of the Oasis. Dogs are allowed in the four camping cabins and at the teepee sites as well as in the two motel rooms, though the owners prefer that dogs be kept in travel kennels in the latter. Open May 1 to October 31.

$$ Great Sand Dunes Lodge, 7900 Highway 50 North (at the entrance to the national monument), **719-378-2900.** The motel allows dogs with a $10 deposit.

$$$$ Inn at Zapata Ranch, 5303 Highway 150, 719-378-2356 (800-284-9213). For the luxury Sand Dunes experience, bring your dog to this 100,000-acre working bison ranch, which just happens to have an eighteen-hole golf course on the premises. Of the fifteen rooms, dogs are allowed to stay in the nine that have outside access, for a $25 one-time fee. Both you and he will rest in comfort in the upscale, rustic-style rooms featuring Western decor and handmade furniture. But Fido will have to be content with just a doggie bag from the resort's highly touted restaurant. Open March 1 to October 30.

Saguache

$ Hillside Motel, 440 Gunnison Ave. (Highway 285), 719-655-2524

$$ Saguache Creek Lodge, 21495 Highway 285, 719-655-2264. There's a $5 fee per dog, per night.

San Acacio

$–$$ The Depot Bed and Breakfast, 1 Rio Grande Ave. (Highway 142), 719-672-3943 (800-949-3943). Housed in a former train depot built in 1910, the B&B takes dog guests on a case-by-case basis. The four rooms include two suites with private baths and wood-burning stoves. Dogs are $5 extra per night, and you can leave Fido unattended in the room.

$$ Casa de Salazar, 603 Main, 719-672-3608. Two B&Bs in the tiny town of San Acacio may very well qualify the town for most B&Bs per capita out of any in Colorado! The Casa allows dogs in any of its three rooms, all furnished with Victorian-style antiques, for a $5 one-time fee. You may be able to leave your dog unattended inside after discussing it with the owner.

South Fork

Because Wolf Creek Ski Area is so close to South Fork, all cabin resorts, in addition to the motels, stay open year-round.

$ Budget Host Ute Bluff Lodge, 27680 Highway 160 West, 719-873-5595 (800-473-0595). The lodge offers furnished cabins and motel rooms, and dogs are welcome in either for a $5 one-time fee. Extra bedspreads are also available for your dog's sleeping comfort.

$ Grandview Cabins and RV Park, 613 Highway 149 West, 719-873-5541. Nine out of the ten fully furnished cabins (all have fireplaces) are dog compatible. There's a $5 per night pet fee, up to $25.

$ The Inn Motel, 30362 Highway 160 West, 719-873-5514 (800-233-9723). Dogs are allowed in smoking rooms only for $2.50 per night, per dog. You can leave

your dog unattended in the room if he's in a travel kennel.

Every backpacker deserves a rest. (photo by Cindy Hirschfeld)

$ South Fork Lodge and RV Park, 0364 Highway 149, 719-873-5303 (800-457-9156). Dogs can stay in any of the twelve fully furnished cabins for a $5 one-time fee per dog. You can leave your dog unattended in the cabin and must keep him on a leash when outside.

$ Spruce Lodge, 29431 Highway 160 West, 719-873-5605 (800-228-5605). The lodge, a log structure built in 1924, offers motel rooms and B&B rooms as well as two cabins with two bedrooms and a kitchen (the only difference between the motel and B&B rooms is that the motel rooms have private baths). The best news: If you're skiing at nearby Wolf Creek, not only can you leave your dog unattended inside but the owners will gladly walk him every few hours, at no extra charge.

$–$$ Aspen Ridge Cabins, 0710 Highway 149 West, 719-873-5921. These seven fully equipped one- and two-bedroom cabins allow dogs for $5 extra per night.

$–$$ Riverbend Resort, 33846 Highway 160 West, 719-873-5344 (800-621-6512). For a $10 one-time fee, your dog can stay with you in one of the eleven fully equipped cabins with fireplace at this resort that once did double service as a movie set for *National Lampoon's Vacation.* Though you should keep your dog leashed when walking around the property, he can play down by the river (the South Fork of the Rio Grande) under your voice control.

$–$$ Wolf Creek Ranch Ski Lodge, Highway 160 (9 miles west of South Fork), **719-873-5371 (800-522-9653).** For $5 extra per night, your dog can join you in either the fully equipped riverside cabins or motel rooms with kitchenettes.

$–$$ Wolf Creek Ski Lodge and Motel, 31042 Highway 160, 719-873-5547 (800-874-0416). Some of the motel rooms are also available with kitchenettes.

$$ Cottonwood Cove Lodge and Cabins, HC 33 Highway 149 West (13 miles from South Fork), **719-658-2242.** Dogs are welcome in the resort's cabins, though not in the lodge, for a $10 one-time fee. The thirty fully outfitted cabins range from studio-size to three bedrooms, and you can leave your dog unattended inside. There's also a restaurant on the premises. Though the resort is open year-round, only six of the cabins are winterized.

$$ Rocky Mountain Associates, 719-873-5688. This rental operation has units ranging from one bedroom, one bath to a six-bedroom, three-bath house. The units include two single-family homes, with three bedrooms and two baths, known as the Moore Cabins. Dogs are permitted on a case-by-case basis, with a deposit possible; you can leave your dog unattended inside.

Villa Grove

$ Escuela Lodging, 34040 Highway 285, 719-655-2343. Well-behaved dogs are allowed to visit at this 6,000-square-foot former school built in 1937, which now houses four lodging rooms as well as an art gallery and studios; "a big, wild building" is how one of the owners describes it.

The guest rooms, with Southwestern decor, share a bath. There's a large dog run in the yard where Fido can hang out if you need to leave him temporarily behind. Definitely a place to sniff out.

$ Inn at Villa Grove, 34094 Highway 285, 719-655-2203. The motel has three rooms and accepts dogs with a $25 deposit. You can leave your dog unattended in the room.

$ Valley View Hot Springs, County Rd. GG, 719-655-4315. Your dog will fit right in at this clothing-optional hot springs resort. There are five cabins where dogs are allowed (three of them have kitchens); the motel rooms and communal bunkhouse do not accept canine guests. You can leave your dog unattended inside the cabin, which you'll have to do if you want to soak, as dogs are understandably not allowed near the hot springs (and must be kept leashed at all times on the property). During part of each weekend, the resort is open only to members; from 3 P.M. Sunday to 11 P.M. Friday, nonmember guests are welcome. Note that entrance to the hot springs requires a fee in addition to the lodging price.

Campgrounds

Great Sand Dunes National Monument, 38 miles northeast of Alamosa via Highways 160 and 150. The Pinyon Flats campground is open year-round.

San Luis Lakes State Park, about 25 miles northeast of Alamosa via Highway 17 and Six Mile Lane (51 sites).

National Forest campgrounds: **Highway Springs Campground,** west of South Fork on Highway 160 (11 sites); **Big Meadows Campground,** at Big Meadows Reservoir, Forest Rd. 410 off Highway 160, west of South Fork (53 sites); **River Hill Campground** (20 sites), **Thirty Mile Campground** (35 sites), and **Lost Trail Campground** (7 sites) are all on Forest Rd. 520 by Rio Grande Reservoir, off Highway 149, 21 miles southwest of Creede; **Mogote Camp-**

ground (41 sites) and **Aspen Glade Campground** (34 sites), both on Highway 17 west of Antonito; **Trujillo Meadows Campground,** by Trujillo Meadows Reservoir at Cumbres Pass, west of Antonito on Highway 17 (50 sites).

Private campgrounds: **Alamosa KOA** in Alamosa; **Ponderosa Campground** and **Twin Rivers Guest Ranch and RV Park** in Antonito; **Great Sand Dunes Oasis** at the entrance to Great Sand Dunes National Monument (see "Creature Comforts" for all).

Doggie Daycare
Alamosa
Alamosa Valley Veterinary Clinic, 7038 Highway 160, 719-589-2615. $7–9/day. Open 8 a.m.–5:30 p.m., Monday to Friday; 8 a.m.–noon, Saturday.

Monte Vista
Alpine Veterinary Hospital, 2835 Sherman, 719-852-2561. $12–18/day. Open 8 a.m.–noon and 1–5:30 p.m., Monday to Friday; 9 a.m.–noon, Saturday.

Pet Provisions
South Fork
Mountain Meadow Country Feed Store, 30362 Highway 160, 791-873-1060

Canine ER
Alamosa
Alamosa Valley Veterinary Clinic, 7038 Highway 160, 719-589-2615. Open 8 a.m.–5:30 p.m., Monday to Friday; 8 a.m.–noon, Saturday.

Del Norte
Del Norte Animal Hospital, 630 Grand, 719-657-3440. Open 8 a.m.–5:30 p.m.,

Monday, Tuesday, Thursday, Friday; 8 a.m.–noon, Wednesday and Saturday.

Monte Vista
Alpine Veterinary Hospital, 2835 Sherman, 719-852-2561. Open 8 a.m.–noon and 1–5:30 p.m., Monday to Friday; 9 a.m.–noon, Saturday.

Monte Vista Animal Clinic, 1851 Highway 160, 719-852-5504. Open 8 a.m.–5:30 p.m., Monday to Friday; 8 a.m.–noon, Saturday.

Resources
Alamosa County Chamber of Commerce, Cole Park, Alamosa, 719-589-3681 (800-BLU-SKYS)

Bureau of Land Management, 1921 State St., Alamosa, 719-589-4975

Conejos Peak Ranger District, Rio Grande National Forest, 15571 County Rd. T-5, La Jara, 719-274-8971

Creede/Mineral County Chamber of Commerce, Creede Ave., Creede, 719-658-2374

Divide Ranger District/Creede Office, Rio Grande National Forest, 3rd and Creede Ave., Creede, 719-658-2556 (closed from the end of October to May 1)

Divide Ranger District/Del Norte Office, 13308 W. Highway 160, Del Norte, 719-657-3321

Saguache Ranger District, Rio Grande National Forest, 46525 Highway 114, Saguache, 719-655-2547

San Luis Valley Visitor Center, 947 1st Ave., Monte Vista, 719-852-0660

Supervisor's Office, San Juan/Rio Grande National Forest, 1803 W. Highway 160, Monte Vista, 719-852-5941

21
Arkansas River Valley and Vicinity

THE BIG SCOOP

The San Isabel National Forest figures prominently in the area described in this chapter, which includes the Arkansas River towns of Buena Vista, Salida, and Cañon City as well as Monarch Pass to the west and the Wet Mountains to the south. This translates into a wide range of dog-friendly hikes, many with no leash requirements. The buff dog might want to hike up one of the eleven 14,000-foot-plus peaks that dot the Sawatch Range in the area west of U.S. Highway 285. You can also bring Fido to several more traditional tourist attractions. However, he will have to sit out the raft trips that draw crowds to the area during the summer.

All the major towns in this vicinity have leash laws in effect. In Fremont County (home to Cañon City), dogs can be under voice control as long as they remain within ten feet of their owner. And unfortunately, all town parks in Salida are closed to canines.

TAIL-RATED TRAILS

The Forest Service offices in Salida and Cañon City and the BLM office in Cañon City can provide details on the hundreds of trails in the area. One easily accessible option is given below if you want to escape the Royal Gorge–focused bustle of Cañon City. In addition, the Cañon City visitor center has a brochure with nine local trail descriptions. And the visitor center in Salida sells *Back Country Trails in the Heart of the Rockies,* by Jim Stotler.

(See "Resources" for the locations of the visitor centers.)

 Waterdog Lakes. Although we haven't actually hiked this trail, the name itself may cause your dog's ears to prick up with interest. The trail is a 3.4-mile round-trip to a pair of lakes scenically situated at the base of the Continental Divide near the top of Monarch Pass. Take Highway 50 west to the Monarch Park turn-off past Garfield. Parking is at the side of the highway. *Dogs can be off leash.*

 Arkansas Riverwalk. About 2.5 miles of trail along the Arkansas River plus 1.2 miles around John Griffin Regional Park. Though there are a few different access points, this one is the most central: From Highway 50 in Cañon City, head south on Raynolds Ave. (the second traffic light in town if coming from the east). After crossing the Arkansas (in less than a mile), look for a trailhead sign and a large parking area on the left. *Dogs must be leashed.*

Though just a short distance from busy Highway 50, the wide gravel riverfront trail seems miles away. It's just you and your dog, the rushing of the water, and the rustle of cottonwood leaves in this verdant setting. Benches are strategically placed in shady spots along the route. If you're looking for a good jogging path for you and the pooch, this is the place. Head west (under the bridge) from the parking area, and you'll get a nice view of the jagged Sangre de Cristo Mountains rising to the west. This direction will bring you to the loop around John Griffin Regional Park, an eighty-acre nature park that also has some unmaintained paths leading through it.

CYCLING FOR CANINES

Mountain-biking options abound in this area, but keep in mind that many of the ones you'll see mentioned in guides involve riding on dirt roads with vehicle traffic. When you want to take your dog along, try a section of the **Rainbow Trail,** which runs for 100 miles from southwest of Salida to Music Pass south of Westcliffe. One of the best parts to try is the one known as **Silver Creek,** which runs for 13 miles from the west end of the Rainbow Trail to U.S. Highway 285. Motorized vehicles (e.g., trail bikes) are prohibited from a portion of the route. Reach the trail by driving 5 miles south of Poncha Springs on 285. You can access a 5.5-mile (one-way) section of singletrack on the **Old Midland Railroad Grade** by going 5 miles east of Johnson Village on Highway 285/24, then heading north on Forest Rd. 315. The **South Fooses Creek Trail,** which includes 3 miles of jeep road and 3 miles of singletrack, is another good ride. Take Highway 50 about 4 miles west of Maysville to County Rd. 225 south.

POWDERHOUNDS

Dogs in search of snow have lots of great trails to sniff out in the area. One to check out is the **South Fooses Creek Trail** (see "Cycling for Canines").

The **Browns Creek Trail** is an 11-mile round-trip ski or snowshoe to picturesque Browns Lake. Take U.S. Highway 285 about 11 miles north of Salida to County Rd. 270. Drive 1.5 miles to County Rd. 272; take 272 for 2 miles to an intersection, where you'll turn left. The trailhead is 1.5 miles farther.

North Cottonwood Creek Rd. runs into the heart of the Collegiate Range, near the base of the Continental Divide. From

Judy Nishimoto and Bohdi on the trail up Mount Princeton. (photo by Cindy Hirschfeld)

the stoplight in Buena Vista, drive north to County Rd. 350. Take a left, then a right at the intersection with County Rd. 361. A sharp left will bring you onto County Rd. 365 and to a plowed parking area, from where you'll commence skiing.

CREATURE COMFORTS

Unless otherwise stated, dogs should not be left unattended in the room or cabin.

Buena Vista

$ Aspen Families, 225 Brookdale Ave., 719-395-3750. If you're looking for a solitary retreat with your dog, this is the place. Formerly a ranger station, this one-room rustic cabin is nestled among aspen in the San Isabel National Forest, and the nearest neighbor is seven miles away. The cabin is fully furnished and has a woodstove, but there's no running water or electricity; you'll have to use the nearby outhouse and get water from a handpump. You can leave your dog unattended in the cabin, but chances are you won't be going anywhere out here that he can't join you. The cabin is available for rent year-round, but during the winter, the road leading up to it isn't plowed.

$ Bar VV Cabins, 40671 Highway 24 (14 miles north of Buena Vista), **719-395-2338.** Dogs are allowed in any of the five cabins here with a $10 deposit. All cabins are one room, with two double beds, and three have kitchens. Keep your dog leashed on the property, where there's plenty of room to run with him. Open mid-May to the end of September.

$ Piñon Court Motel, 227 Highway 24 North, 719-395-2433. The motel rents apartment-style cabins that are fully equipped. You can leave your dog unattended inside. There's a park across the street where your dog can stretch his legs.

$-$$ Alpine Lodge Resort, 12845 Highways 24 & 285 (Johnson Village), 719-395-2415 (800-395-8900). The motel permits short-haired, lap-sized dogs in three of its smoking rooms. There's a $35 deposit as well as a $5 fee per night. You can leave your dog unattended in the room as long as he's in a travel kennel.

$-$$ Collegiate Peaks Family Inn and RV Park, 516 Highway 24 North, 719-395-2251(888-PEAK-INN). It's nice to know that "family" includes the dog at this Christian-run motel. There's a $5 fee per night.

$-$$ Lakeside Motel, 112 Lake St., 719-395-2994 (800-248-7684). Extremely well-behaved dogs and their responsible owners are welcome at the motel, with a $10 fee per dog, per night. There are only two rooms in which dogs of all sizes are allowed, though small, lap-sized dogs are also permitted in the other rooms. The motel is near one of the town parks.

$-$$ Strelow Haus, 29994 County Rd. 354, 719-395-8410. The haus is a cozy, two-bedroom cottage located in a residential area, with a fenced yard perfect for a traveling pooch. Small dogs are the preferred canine guests. The nightly rate gets lower the longer you stay.

$-$$ Topaz Lodge, 115 Highway 24 North, 719-395-2427 (800-731-5906). The motel, across from a town park, accepts dogs for $5 extra per night.

$-$$ Vista Court Cabins and Lodge, 1004 W. Main, 719-395-6557. Though dogs are not allowed in the lodge rooms, smaller ones (i.e., no lab- or shepherd-sized dogs) can stay in any of the eight log cabins, which are fully equipped, for $5 extra per night. You'll need to keep your dog leashed on the three acres surrounding the cabins.

$$ Cottonwood Hot Springs Inn and Spa, 18999 County Rd. 306, 719-395-8036 (800-241-4119). Don't be misled by the "spa" in the name and go looking for luxury here. The rustic inn's lodging includes motel-style rooms, creekside cabins, and two tepees. Dogs are allowed in any of them. The pet charge is $5 per night for a small dog, $7.50 for a large dog. Which category does your dog fit into? Well, if he's bigger than the inn's resident lab/shepherd mix, Bubba, he's a large dog; if he's smaller than Bubba, he's a small dog. And if he's just Bubba's size, who knows? Maybe the toss of a coin will settle it!

$$ The Mountain Shack Bed and Breakfast, 15120 County Rd. 306, 719-395-6745. The B&B features one fully furnished "upscale" cabin, which you and your dog can rent with or without breakfast served. You can leave your dog unattended in the cabin, though the owners prefer that he be in a travel kennel if you do so. There are several acres around the cabin where your dog can romp off leash, but keep a watchful eye on him, as a well-trafficked road runs nearby. Open mid-May to mid-October.

$$ Potter's House Bed and Breakfast, 28490 County Rd. 313, 719-395-6458. You and your dog can stay riverside in a log cabin on the Arkansas, with Mexican-style decor, hardwood floors, and a deck from which you can almost cast your fishing line. "Dogs love it here, especially if they like the water," says the owner. Your dog must promise, however, to be a good canine guest and not jump on any of the beds. There are resident dogs as well. Open May 1 to the end of September.

$$ Sagewood Cabins, 38951-B Highway 24 (11.5 miles north of Buena Vista), 719-395-2582. You and your dog can enjoy a quiet, relaxing stay in these fully furnished log cabins, decorated in a country style with some antiques. A few of the cabins have fireplaces. There's a $1.50 fee per dog, per night. You'll need to keep your dog leashed on the property, but the San Isabel National Forest is right next door. Open from April to the end of October (exact dates depend on the weather).

$$ Thunder Lodge, 207 Brookdale Ave., 719-395-2245 (800-330-9194). The lodge, on Cottonwood Creek in downtown Buena Vista, offers seven fully furnished log cabins that sleep from two to six, plus dog.

$$ Vista Inn, 733 Highway 24 North, 719-395-8009 (800-809-3495). Dogs are allowed in four designated pet rooms (two nonsmoking, two smoking) in this newer motel, with a $50 deposit and a $10 one-time fee.

$$ Woodland Brook Cabins, 226 S. San Juan, 719-395-2922. Fourteen fully equipped log cabins, ranging from studios to two bedrooms, are situated on 4.5 acres. Visiting dogs can explore the grounds off leash as long as they are under voice control. Open year-round.

Cañon City

$ Fort Gorge Camper Cabins, Campground, and RV Park, 45044 Highway 50, 719-275-5111. Dogs are allowed in two of the three camper cabins at this complex located close to the Royal Gorge Bridge. Though you'll have to bring your own bedding and cooking gear, the cabins do come equipped with a small fridge. There's about a $10 deposit for a dog. You can't leave your pooch unattended in the cabin, but there's a small fenced area with some hay and a doghouse where he can hang out if you need to leave him temporarily behind. Open May 1 to October 15.

$ Knotty Pine Motel, 2990 E. Main, 719-275-0461. There's a $10 one-time fee for a dog. Though you can't leave your dog unattended in the room, there's about a half acre of property in back of the motel where you can tie him up for a short time.

$ Parkview Motel, Highway 50 and 3rd St., 719-275-0624. Dogs are allowed in most rooms.

$ Royal View Camper Cabins and Campground, 43590 W. Highway 50, 719-275-1900. There are three camper cabins at the Royal View, which is ten miles west of Cañon City, near Royal Gorge. Leashed dogs are allowed, although they can't be brought into the service building (which houses a grocery, game room, etc.). Open March 15 to November 15.

Shanda, the mayor of Guffey. (photo courtesy of Bruce Buffington)

Perhaps the coolest town government in Colorado belongs to the hamlet of Guffey, northwest of Cañon City off Highway 9. The mayor, Shanda, is a golden retriever. She took office in 1993, when her feline predecessor, Whiffy Legone, retired from politics. Shanda presides over the town from her home at the Guffey General Store and Bootlegger Spirits, where you can visit her year-round. And Shanda's mayoral platform? "Her only platform is the front porch of the general store," says owner Bruce Buffington.

$ Sky Valley Motel, Highway 50 and Greydene, 719-275-2783. Dogs are allowed for nightly stays only (the motel also has weekly and monthly rentals) in lower-level rooms.

$ Thunderbird Motel, 28 County Rd. 3A (at intersection of Highway 50 and Royal Gorge Blvd.), **719-275-3168.** Dogs can be left unattended in the rooms for short periods of time.

$–$$ Cathy's Old-Fashioned Boarding House, 507 Greenwood, 719-275-4989. Certainly one of the most unique places to stay in Cañon City would be this more than 120-year-old house that once belonged to relatives of former President Warren Harding. The lodging consists of "quarters," which are kind of like suites. Canine visitors are generally directed to the first-floor quarter, a 300-square-foot room with hardwood floors, sleeping and living area, full bath, and a private entrance. All rooms are furnished Victorian style, with antiques, and guests have use of the house's full kitchen. Now about your dog: The amount of the deposit depends on the size and type of dog, and you will be able to leave Fido unattended in the room. Both nightly and longer-term rentals are available.

$–$$ Holiday Motel, Highway 50 and 15th St., 719-275-3317. With a $25 deposit (if you're paying with cash) and a $5 standard nightly fee, dogs are allowed in any of the motel's rooms. You can leave Fido unattended in the room.

$–$$ The Historic St. Cloud Hotel, 631 Main St., 719-276-2000. The St. Cloud is one of the oldest hotels in Colorado that your dog has the opportunity to stay in. Built in 1879 in the nearby town of Silver Cliff, the hotel was dismantled and rebuilt in Cañon City, reopening in 1886. Today, each of the characteristically high-ceilinged twenty-five rooms is individually decorated, with some period furnishings. One four-legged guest is allowed per room.

$$ Best Western Royal Gorge Motel, 1925 Fremont Dr., 719-275-3377 (800-231-7317). Small to medium-sized dogs are permitted in smoking rooms only for a $10 one-time fee. You can leave your dog unattended in the room.

$$ Cañon Inn, 3075 E. Highway 50, 719-275-8676 (800-525-7727). The motel has three (out of 152) designated pet rooms, all of which have sliding glass doors that open to the outside. A $50 deposit is required.

Coaldale

$ Hidden Valley Camper Cabins and Campground, 340 City Rd. 40, 719-942-4171. Dogs are permitted in the five camper cabins (bring your own sleeping and cooking gear). They must be kept leashed on the property, which includes several ponds. Open year-round.

$ Lazy J Resort and Rafting Company, 16373 Highway 50, 719-942-4274 (800-678-4274). The resort has a combination of motel rooms, "chalets" (one-room units without private baths), and fully equipped log cabins (though you'll have to supply your own cooking utensils due to one too many forks walking out the door). You can leave your dog unattended inside—perhaps if you sign up for one of the rafting trips the resort also offers—as long as you let the housekeeping staff know. Keep him leashed outside. Open year-round.

Cotopaxi

$ Arkansas River KOA and Loma Linda Motel, 21435 Highway 50, 719-275-9308 (800-562-2686). This KOA offers you and your dog a whole slate of options: camping cabins (bring your own sleeping bag), furnished cabins without kitchens, motel rooms, and fully equipped cabins with kitchenettes. And there's access to the river for when your dog wants to cool off. Open mid-April to the end of October.

Florence

$–$$ River Valley Inn, 4540 Highway 67 South, 719-784-4800. Small dogs (about

20 pounds and under) are accepted at the motel, with a credit-card imprint required as a deposit.

Monarch Pass Area

$$ Monarch Mountain Lodge, Highway 50, near the top of Monarch Pass, 719-539-2581 (800-332-3668). In its third decade of operation, the 100-room lodge, across from Monarch Ski Area, allows dogs in smoking rooms only. Because you can't leave your dog in the room unattended, you'll need to find other lodging if you're bringing Fido along on a ski trip. But during the summer, you'll both be in the heart of the outdoor action.

$$ The Old Mine–Mt. Shavano Bed and Breakfast, 16780 W. Highway 50, 719-539-4640. Located at the eastern base of Monarch Pass, this luxurious four-room B&B features such niceties as Persian rugs and handmade quilts. Small, well-mannered dogs can join their owners.

$$ Ski Town Condominiums, Highway 50, next to the Monarch Mountain Lodge, 719-539-7360 (800-539-7380). Enjoy a stay with your dog in these two-bedroom condos near the top of Monarch Pass and the Continental Divide.

$$ Wagon Wheel Guest Ranch, 16760 County Rd. 220, 719-539-2264. The ranch has six cozy one-room cabins, all fully furnished and with extra touches such as handmade quilts and curtains. Well-trained dogs can recreate leash-free with their owners on the 2.5 acres. Open Memorial Day to Labor Day.

Nathrop

$–$$ Love Ranch, 18670 County Rd. 162, 719-395-2366. The guest ranch, on fourteen acres in Chalk Creek Canyon, has nine cabins, all of which dogs can stay in for a $10 one-time fee. Though fully furnished, some cabins are served by a main bathhouse rather than private bathrooms; others have full baths. Keep your dog leashed on the property. Open May to the end of September.

$$ Inn at Chalk Cliffs, 16557 County Rd. 162, 719-395-6068. Dogs are allowed in any of the three rooms at this homey B&B between Mounts Antero and Princeton. There's a $2 fee per night, and it's okay to leave your dog unattended in the room. The house sits on six acres where you can walk your leashed pooch.

Poncha Springs

$ Poncha Lodge, 10520 Highways 50 & 285, 719-539-6085 (800-315-3952). Small, nonshedding dogs get the okay here; three rooms (one nonsmoking) are pet designated.

$ Rocky Mountain Lodge and Cabins, 446 E. Highway 50, 719-539-6008 (888-539-6008). Dogs are permitted in smoking rooms at the motel and in both of the one-room cabins for a $5 fee per night.

Salida

$ Circle R Motel, 304 E. Highway 50, 719-539-6296 (800-755-6296). Dogs 30 pounds and under are accepted, for $5 extra per night in summer, $3 per night in winter.

$ Motel Westerner, 7335 W. Highway 50, 719-539-5432. You can leave your dog unattended in the room at this small motel.

$ Mountain Motel, 1425 E. Highway 50, 719-539-4420. The motel has five newer rooms and three cabins; dogs are permitted in all.

$ Palace Hotel and Gallery, 204 North F, 719-539-4688 (800-205-4680; in-state only). The hotel is in a historic building, erected in 1904, though it doesn't offer the kind of upscale, restored Victorian accommodations that some other historic Colorado hotels do. Dogs are allowed in six of the fourteen rooms (all smoking), some of which share a bath. The gallery part of the hotel is a large crystal shop—no tailwaggers allowed!

$–$$ Aspen Leaf Lodge, 7350 W. Highway 50, 719-539-6733 (800-759-0338). The motel has six designated pet rooms, three of which are nonsmoking. There's also a pond on the property, and dogs can be off leash as long as they're under voice control.

$–$$ Econo Lodge, 1310 E. Highway 50, 719-539-2895 (800-55-ECONO). The lodge offers four pet rooms—two non-smoking—and charges a $5 fee per dog, per night. You can leave your dog unattended in the room. There's also a yard in back of the motel where you can walk your dog off leash if he's well behaved.

$–$$ Rainbow Inn, 105 E. Highway 50, 719-539-4444 (800-539-4447). Lots of open space and picnic areas surround the motel, which your dog can enjoy as long as he is leashed.

$–$$ Western Holiday Motel, 545 W. Highway 50, 719-539-2553. There's a $5 fee per night for a dog.

$–$$ Woodland Motel, 903 W. 1st St., 719-539-4980 (800-488-0456). The motel has efficiency units and two-bedroom suites, and it welcomes dogs. Particularly well-trained canines can be left unattended inside.

$$ Cedar Ridge Ranch/Lost Lake Ranch, 12500 County Rd. 258 (between Salida and Buena Vista), **719-539-6639.** Dogs will love either of these ranches, as they'll have lots and lots of property to explore leash-free. At the 1,300-acre Lost Lake Ranch, you can rent a three-bedroom, two-bathroom cabin situated beside a lake. The 1,400-acre Cedar Ridge Ranch has a two-bedroom guesthouse that sleeps up to twenty people. Open year-round.

$$ Redwood Lodge, 7310 W. Highway 50, 719-539-2730. Dogs are allowed in seven smoking rooms only, for $5 per dog, per night. Each of the lodge's rooms is individually decorated.

$$–$$$ Tudor Rose Bed and Breakfast, 6720 Paradise Rd., 719-539-2002 (800-379-0889). The B&B actually falls outside the parameters of this book because dogs are not allowed to stay in the rooms; however, dogs are accommodated by means of an outside fenced area with two pens and a doghouse. So if your dog is accustomed to staying outdoors, you might want to bring him along. His reward will be the surrounding thirty-seven acres that he can explore leash-free with you. The B&B does charge a $4 fee per night for dogs, and you must show proof of your dog's vaccinations at check-in.

San Isabel

$$ The Lodge at San Isabel, Highway 165 (10 miles north of Rye), **719-489-2280.** This family-style resort in the Wet Mountains includes cabins situated on the shores of Lake Isabel (though some have kitchens, you'll have to bring your own cooking and serving dishes). There's a $15 one-time fee for a dog, and he can be left unattended in the cabin. Open mid-May through October.

Texas Creek

$ Whispering Pines Resort, 24871 Highway 50 West, 719-275-3827. The resort has four motel rooms and six camper cabins in which your dog can stay with you for $5 extra per night. You and your leashed dog can also check out the Arkansas River, which runs for a mile through the grounds. Open April 1 to Labor Day.

Westcliffe

$ Antlers Motel, 102 S. Sixth St., 719-783-2426. If your dog gets a hankering for beer and chips, Antlers Liquor and General Store is conveniently located next door.

$ Westcliffe Inn, Highway 69 and Hermit Rd., 719-783-9275 (800-284-0850). Dogs are allowed to stay in the motel's older rooms.

Campgrounds

Arkansas Headwaters Recreation Area. Part of the State Parks system, the recreation area consists of 148 miles of the Arkansas River and the area immediately surrounding it. Several campgrounds along the way are accessible by vehicle, including Ruby Mountain (22 sites) and Hecla Junction (21 sites), off Highway 285 South between Buena Vista and Salida, and Rincon (15 sites) and Five Points (21 sites), off Highway 50 east of Salida.

National Forest campgrounds: **Cottonwood Lake Campground,** south on County Rd. 344 from Cottonwood Pass Rd. (28 sites); **Collegiate Peaks Campground,** west of Buena Vista on Cottonwood Pass Rd. (56 sites); **Cascade Campground,** 9 miles west from Nathrop on Chalk Creek Rd. (23 sites); **Monarch Park Campground,** Highway 50, near the top of Monarch Pass (38 sites); **Oak Creek Campground,** south of Cañon City on 4th St. to County Rd. 143 (15 sites); and **Alvarado Campground,** southwest of Westcliffe—take Highway 69 south to Schoolfield Rd. west (47 sites).

Private campgrounds: **Arkansas River KOA** in Cotopaxi, **Hidden Valley Campground** in Coaldale, **Royal View** and **Fort Gorge campgrounds** in Cañon City (see "Creature Comforts" for all).

WORTH A PAWS

Royal Gorge Bridge. Your dog won't want to miss out on one of Colorado's most popular tourist attractions. The gorge boasts the world's highest suspension bridge, which spans the Arkansas River at 1,053 feet. You won't be able to treat your dog to a ride on the incline railway or the aerial tram, but you can take him (and his leash) on a walk across the bridge. And Royal Gorge Park encompasses 5,000 acres with lots of scenic overlooks that you and your dog can enjoy together. The whole complex is 8 miles west of Cañon City, via Highway 50, and it's open year-round. There is an entrance fee. For more information, call 719-275-7507.

Buckskin Joe Park and Railway. Let your dog experience the Wild West during a visit to Buckskin Joe's (and he won't have to run behind a covered wagon to get there). A re-created Western town, the park allows leashed dogs to join you in touring the "historic" buildings, watching staged gunfights, and, of course, stocking up on souvenirs. Or maybe your dog would like to try his paw at panning for gold. The park also operates the Royal Gorge Scenic Railway, which will take you and Fido on a thirty-minute round-trip ride to the rim of the gorge. The park is open May 1 to October 1. From Memorial Day to Labor Day, hours are 9 A.M.–6 P.M.; hours are shorter during the rest of May and September. The railway stays open from March to November 15; hours are 8 A.M.–8 P.M., Memorial Day to Labor Day, with shorter hours before and after those dates. Located 8 miles west of Cañon City, at Royal Gorge. For more information and ticket prices, call the park at 719-275-5149 or the railway at 719-275-5485.

Monarch Scenic Tram. The gondola whisks you and your leashed dog from the top of Monarch Pass to 12,000 feet in a matter of minutes, giving you a bird's-eye view of the neighboring peaks. There's a glass-enclosed observatory at the top for your viewing comfort, though you're free to wander around outside as well. This is a good option for the dog who doesn't want to work too hard for a panoramic vista. The gondola runs continuously throughout the day from May through September. Call 719-539-4789 or 800-332-3668 for current ticket prices or more information.

Bishop Castle. Your dog is welcome to tour this massive stone and iron work-in-progress with you as long as you keep him under control. Since 1969, Jim Bishop has worked on creating the castlelike structure, which is intended for public use, completely on his own. There's no admission charge, and the castle is open year-round. To reach it, drive 6 miles north from Lake San Isabel on Highway 165. You'll see a sign on the right side of the road; park alongside the roadway and cross it to get to the castle.

Pet Parade. Held annually in late September or early October, this mile-long walk for pets and their people benefits the Ark Valley Humane Society. Past walkers have included ponies, horses, goats, and even cats, as well as dogs. The walk has traditionally taken place in Salida, but might be moving up the road to the Humane Society's home in Buena Vista. The Phi Alpha Chi sorority handles the organizational details, and proceeds come from the sale of "Pet Parade" T-shirts. For more information, contact the Humane Society at 719-395-2737.

DOGGIE DAYCARE
Cañon City
Country Kennels, 301 Fourmile Ln., 719-275-5681. $7–$9/day, depending on the size of dog. Open 8:30 A.M.–5 P.M., Monday, Tuesday, Thursday, and Friday; 9–10 A.M. and 4–5 P.M., Wednesday and Saturday.

Nathrop
Double J Cross Kennel, 17605 Highway 285, 719-539-4080. $10/day. Open 7 A.M.–6 P.M., Monday to Friday; weekends by appointment.

Salida
Mountain Shadows Animal Hospital, 9171 W. Highway 50, 719-539-2533. $6/day. Open 8 A.M.–noon and 1:30–5:30 P.M., Monday to Friday; 8 A.M.–noon, Saturday; 6–7 P.M., Sunday (for pickups).

PET PROVISIONS
Buena Vista
Martin Feed, 15415 County Rd. 306, 719-395-4044

Cañon City
Lamala-Kim Pet Shop, 430 Main, 719-269-3732

Westcliffe
Feed Barn, 61199 Highway 69, 719-783-9398

CANINE ER
Buena Vista
Buena Vista Veterinary Clinic, 30400 Highway 24 North, 719-395-8239; after hours: 719-395-6408. Open 8:30 A.M.–noon and 1:30–5 P.M., Monday to Friday; 9 A.M.–noon, Saturday.

Cañon City
Kenline Veterinary Clinic (AAHA certified), 1426 S. 9th St., 719-275-2081. Open 8 A.M.–6 P.M., Monday to Friday; 8 A.M.–5:30 P.M., Saturday.

Salida
Mountain Shadows Animal Hospital, 9171 W. Highway 50, 719-539-2533. Open 8 A.M.–noon and 1:30–5:30 P.M., Monday to Friday; 8 A.M.–noon, Saturday.

RESOURCES
Bureau of Land Management, 3170 E. Main St., Cañon City, 719-269-8500

Cañon City Chamber of Commerce, 403 Royal Gorge Blvd., 719-275-2331 (800-876-7922)

Chaffee County Visitors Bureau Online: www.colorado.com/chaffee

Custer County Chamber of Commerce, 2 Bassick Pl., Westcliffe, 719-783-9163

Greater Buena Vista Area Chamber of Commerce, 343 Highway 24 South, Buena Vista, 719-395-6612

Heart of the Rockies Chamber of Commerce, 406 W. Highway 50, Salida, 719-539-2068

Salida Ranger District, Pike/San Isabel National Forests, 325 W. Rainbow Blvd. (Highway 50), Salida, 719-539-3591

San Carlos Ranger District, Pike/San Isabel National Forests, 3170 E. Main St., Cañon City, 719-269-8500

22
Pueblo and Points Southeast

THE BIG SCOOP

This chapter covers an area from the southeast plains of Colorado to Trinidad, about 20 miles north of the New Mexico border, up through the Cuchara Valley, and north to Pueblo, the metropolis of the region. It's a lot of territory for your dog to sniff, but the attractions he'll most want to explore tend to be spread out. Pueblo and the eastern plains, especially, can be ovenlike during the summer, so for your dog's sake, plan excursions to areas near water (see "Tail-Rated Trails," below, for some ideas). The dry Comanche National Grasslands area is best suited for a spring or fall visit.

In Pueblo, dogs must be leashed within city limits; on county land, they can be under voice control. Because the extensive River Trail system is overseen by the city, dogs must be kept leashed on all of the trails.

TAIL-RATED TRAILS

Lathrop State Park. From Walsenburg, head west on Highway 160 for a little more than 3 miles to the park entrance on the right. *Dogs must be leashed except in the animal exercise area.*

The **Hogback Trail,** an easy 2-mile loop, winds through large stands of piñon and juniper as it ascends, via a series of moderate switchbacks, the Hogback Ridge. From the top, you'll have a nice view of the twin Spanish Peaks to the south and the Wet Mountains to the north—and, on a clear day, Pikes Peak. Pamphlets for a self-guided nature tour are available at the trailhead, which is on the north side of Martin Lake. Bring enough water for you and your dog, as the trail is dry.

Perhaps the best part of the park, if you've got a water-loving hound, is the animal exercise area, where your dog can frolic off leash under your supervision. Though marked on the park map, it's not signed in any way. About 0.3 mile north of the visitor center, keep an eye out for a very small dirt "pullout" on the right; if you reach Martin Beach, you've gone too far. You can park at this pullout and let your dog run in the undeveloped area between the road and the lake. To reach water's edge most directly, stay to the left. Prevent your dog from running as far as the Martin Beach area, however, as dogs are not allowed there.

For picnicking with your dog in a less-frequented area of the park, try the North Martin Inlet.

Vogel Canyon (Comanche National Grasslands). 2.25 miles round-trip. The route to Vogel Canyon feels something like driving down an airport runway, so flat and open is the landscape. From La Junta, take Highway 109 south for 13 miles. Look for a sign to Vogel Canyon on the right. After 1 mile, turn left (at the sign) and proceed 2 miles to the parking lot. *Dogs are supposed to be on leash, though we couldn't find a sign to that effect.*

Hiking Vogel Canyon is a bit like a step back in time to the frontier days of the prairie. You and your dog will likely be the only ones there. Four trails begin at the trailhead; a pleasant loop combines portions of three of them. Start on the **Canyon Trail,** making your way through a cattle guard just past the parking area. The trail is marked by large stone cairns as it makes a gradual descent among large stands of juniper. It soon heads through the namesake grasslands, which also feature flowers and cacti. Eventually you'll reach some standing pools of water—actually a spring—where your dog may want to cool off, as the canyon is otherwise hot and dry. There's a three-way fork here, as well as a cairn; turn right to take the **Mesa Trail.** After crossing a dry streambed, go left, then through the fence opening, and follow the diagonal tracks in the grass. The trail is fairly clear, with some cairns along it. Keep hiking below a series of rock outcroppings, ignoring any cairns that you may spot above, until you come to a rectangular foundation. These are the remains of a stagecoach stop that operated in the 1870s. Just beyond them are three cairns in front of a rocky area. Scramble east up through the rocks, keeping to the left. At the top, look to the northeast for another cairn. Once you reach this cairn, you should be able to spot another to the east. The rest of the Mesa Trail follows a series of cairns. Shortly after climbing over a stile, your route intersects with the **Overlook Trail,** a wide gravel path. A left brings you back to the trailhead.

 Lake Pueblo State Park. From Pueblo, take Highway 50 west to Pueblo Boulevard. Go left (south) for about 4 miles to Thatcher Ave. and turn left (west); the park entrance is 6 miles ahead. You can also access the park from the north, farther west on Highway 50, via McCulloch Boulevard. *Dogs must be leashed.*

The park boasts 16.5 miles of paved trail, known as the **Dam Trail,** which runs along the north side of the lake and connects with the Pueblo River Trail system. The most scenic portion of the trail runs east from the Juniper Breaks Campground to the Rock Canyon area. There's also a short (1.5 miles round-trip) interpretive trail on the south side of the park, which begins at the Arkansas Point Campground and leads up a bluff.

Note that dogs are not allowed at the Rock Canyon swim beach area.

 Pueblo River Trails. A paved trail system runs for about 21 miles through Pueblo, east-west along the Arkansas River and north-south along Fountain Creek. The Arkansas River Trail connects with the paved trails in Lake Pueblo State Park. *Dogs must be leashed.*

Though there are numerous trail access points in Pueblo, by far the nicest place to pick up the trail is at the Greenway and Nature Center just west of downtown. The most straightforward way to get there is to take Highway 50 west from town to Pueblo Boulevard. Turn left (south) and travel about 2.5 miles to Nature Center Rd. on the right (it's W. 11th St. on the other side of Pueblo Blvd.). Take the road to its end, where there's lots of parking at the Nature Center complex.

From here, either head east toward town (after about 2 miles, the trail gets a little sketchy and is not as scenic, however) or head west, where 3.5 miles of trail bring you to the state park. Hiking near the Nature Center is especially serene. The mighty Arkansas just purrs along at this point, and abundant cottonwood drape over the river. A small network of gravel paths begins behind the Nature Center and goes by the river, allowing your dog to dip his paws in. The Nature Center includes a large picnic area as well as a full-service restaurant, the Cafe del Rio, with outdoor seating—perfect for enjoying a beverage by the river with your dog.

If you're looking for a short walk closer to the center of town, the **Runyon**

Lake Trail travels 1.2 miles around its namesake lake. Parking is available at the end of Juniper, by Runyon Field.

Trinidad Lake State Park. From Exit 14A off I-25 at Trinidad, follow the signs for Route 12; the park is about 3 miles west on Route 12, on the left. *Dogs must be leashed.*

The park has several hiking trails, the busiest of which is the 1-mile **Levsa Canyon self-guided nature trail.** For more secluded hiking with your dog—though you'll need to keep an eye out for mountain bikers—try the 4-mile (one way) **Reilly Canyon Trail,** starting from its west end. To reach the trailhead, drive about 3 miles past the main park entrance and take a left at the Cokedale turnoff to access the Reilly Canyon entrance. Cross over two cattle guards; the trailhead is about 200 yards past the second one, on the left. The trail is hot and dry, so early morning—as well as spring and fall—are the best times to hike here with your dog. Bring lots of water. The trail meanders, with moderate ups and downs, through piñon and juniper woodlands along a mesa above the lake. You and your dog can enjoy photo-worthy views of the lake as well as of square-topped Fisher's Peak, which looms above Trinidad. You can also reach this trail from the east via the first quarter mile of the Levsa Canyon Trail, which begins at the Carpios Ridge Campground at the main park entrance. The Reilly Canyon Trail, clearly marked, branches off to the west. Hiking from east to west, you'll encounter a fairly steep descent into Levsa Canyon.

To allow your panting pooch access to the lake, continue on the road to Reilly Canyon (see above), past the trailhead. Once the road turns east, it dead-ends shortly afterward close to the lake. Also at this junction, **Old Highway 12,** now unmaintained, heads west. Park your car along the shoulder and take your dog for a solitary walk near the Purgatoire River.

The road ends about 2 miles later, at the park's western boundary.

The 2.5-mile **South Shore Trail,** while providing scenic views of the lake, follows a rather overgrown road bed next to railroad tracks. Skip it.

CREATURE COMFORTS

Unless otherwise stated, dogs should not be left unattended in the room or cabin.

Don't leave us behind! (photo by Cindy Hirschfeld)

Beulah

$$$–$$$$ Beulah House, 8733 Pine Dr., 719-485-3201. "Good" dogs are welcome to stay with their owners in any of this B&B's four rooms, including a Spanish hacienda–style suite. You can leave your dog behind, while you go out to eat, say, as long as you let the owners know. Keep Fido leashed on the B&B's six acres because of abundant wildlife (the two resident German shepherds are under the same restriction). The owners also have a two-bedroom house in San Isabel, in the Wet Mountains, where you can stay with your dog.

Colorado City

$ Pueblo South/Colorado City KOA & Kamping Kabins, 9040 I-25 South, 719-676-3376 (800-KOA-8646). Small dogs (poodle size) are allowed in the cabins here. You'll have to supply your own bedding and cooking gear. Open year-round.

$$ Greenhorn Inn, I-25 at Exit 74, 719-676-3315. The motel has designated rooms at the back of the motel for dogs—closest to where you should take Fido to do his thing.

> The Cuerno Verde Rest Area at the Colorado City exit off I-25 (Exit 74) has a large dog-walking area for pups on a leash.

Cuchara

$$ Cuchara Inn, 73 E. Ave., 719-742-3685 (800-851-0687). Dogs are very welcome at this hotel, and you can leave yours in the room unattended as long as he won't bother the neighbors. In fact, the whole town of Cuchara is a popular dog spot; "Dogs are everywhere," says the inn's manager. The Boardwalk Saloon, across the street from the hotel, has become unofficially known as the Dog Bar because so many dogs hang out in front of it. Is your dog already pulling at his leash to go here? The inn offers a 10 percent discount if you mention that you read about it in this book.

Fowler

$ Blue Spruce Inn, 2nd and Highway 50, 719-263-4271. No more than two dogs per room, please.

Holly

$ Gateway Motel, 1016 W. Colorado, 719-537-6805. You can leave your dog unattended in the room, but if he does any damage, "you're buying it," warns the motel operator. A recent guest ended up paying for a bathroom door and some carpeting in addition to his room fee.

La Junta

$ La Junta Travel Inn, 110 E. First St., 719-384-2504. There's no fee for dogs 25 pounds and under; dogs weighing more require you to pay $3 extra per night, and larger dogs are generally put in smoking rooms. You can leave your dog unattended in the room if he's in a travel kennel.

$ Mid-Town Motel, 215 E. Third St., 719-384-7741. Pascal the poodle enjoys greeting dog visitors at this friendly place. You can leave your dog unattended in the room if he's in a travel kennel.

$ Stagecoach Motor Inn, 905 W. Third St., 719-384-5476. The motel takes small dogs only.

$ Westerner Motel, 1502 E. Third St., 719-384-2591. Small dogs are allowed in smoking rooms only.

$$ Holiday Inn Express, 27994 Highway 50, 719-384-2900. Small to medium-sized dogs are welcome.

$$ Quality Inn, 1325 E. Third St., 719-384-2571 (800-LA-JUNTA). Dogs are only allowed in smoking rooms in the motel's older wing. They can be left unattended.

Lamar

$ Blue Spruce Motel, 1801 S. Main, 719-336-7454. There's a $2 fee per night, per dog.

$ El Donna Motel, 404 North Main, 719-336-2286

$ Golden Arrow Motel, 611 E. Olive St., 719-336-8725. Small dogs are allowed in smoking rooms only, with a $3 fee per night.

$ Lamar Super 8, 1202 North Main, 719-336-3427

$ Motel 7, 113 North Main, 719-336-7746 (888-596-3100). There's a $5 fee per night, per dog.

$ New Stagecoach Inn, 1201 North Main, 719-336-7471. Dogs require payment of a $5 nightly fee.

$$ Best Western Cow Palace Inn, 1301 N. Main, 719-336-7753 (800-678-0344). You can leave your dog unattended in the room, though if he barks excessively (till the cows come home?), the motel management will call Animal Control.

Las Animas

$ Colonial Inn, 638 Bent Ave., 719-456-0303. The motel accepts smaller dogs, with a $20 deposit.

$$ Best Western Bent's Fort Inn, 10950 E. Highway 50, 719-456-0011 (800-528-

1234). You can leave your dog unattended in the room "as long as he's not a barker."

La Veta

$ Circle the Wagons Motel, 124 N. Main, 719-742-3233. Dogs are welcome with a $5 deposit.

$$–$$$ La Veta Inn, 103 West Ryus, 719-742-3700. The inn will consider small dogs on a case-by-case basis and with a $20 deposit. The fifteen rooms, some of which are suites, are individually decorated with antiques and handsewn quilts.

Ordway

$ Hotel Ordway, 132 Colorado Blvd., 719-267-3541. The hotel is located in a historic three-story brick building, and small dogs (e.g., lap size) can check out the premises.

Pueblo

$ Country Bunk Inn, 3369 I-25 South (Exit 91), 719-564-1840. The motel has had "the whole gamut of critters" as guests, according to the owner, including horses, mules, goats, cats, ferrets, and, of course, dogs. You can leave your dog unattended in the room as long as you let the front desk know.

$ Motel 6, 4103 N. Elizabeth, 719-543-6221. You can leave your dog unattended in the room as long as he's in a traveling kennel.

$ Motel 6 West, 960 Highway 50 West, 719-543-8900. You can leave your dog unattended in the room as long as he's in a traveling kennel.

$ Pueblo KOA & Kamping Kabins, 4131 I-25 North, 719-542-2273 (800-KOA-7453). Dogs are allowed in the cabins and can be left unattended for a short time. You'll need to bring your own bedding and cooking supplies. Open year-round.

$–$$ Bel Mar Motel, 414 W. 29th St., 719-542-3268. Dogs are allowed in the motel's older rooms with a $20 deposit. You can leave your dog unattended in the room.

$–$$ Pinon Inn, 4803 North I-25, 719-545-3900. There's a $10 fee per night, per pet, and you can leave your dog unattended in the room.

$–$$ Pueblo Motor Inn, 800 Highway 50 West, 719-543-6820. Small to medium-sized dogs are accepted, but you must put down a $50 cash deposit (even if you're paying by credit card).

$–$$ Super 8 Motel, 1100 Highway 50 West, 719-545-4104 (800-800-8000). Just a few rooms have been designated for pets.

$$ Best Western Townhouse Motel, 730 N. Sante Fe, 719-543-6530. Small to medium-sized dogs get the nod for one of the several pet rooms.

$$ Hampton Inn, 4703 N. Freeway, 719-544-4700 (800-HAMPTON). There's a $25 one-time fee for a dog. Management usually puts dogs and their owners in smoking rooms; if you prefer a nonsmoking room, the one-time fee is upped to $50. You can leave Fido unattended in the room, but housekeeping won't come in to clean during that time.

$$ Holiday Inn of Pueblo, 4001 N. Elizabeth, 719-543-8050. Dogs can stay in smoking rooms only.

$$ Ramada Inn, 2001 N. Hudson, 719-542-3750. Dogs are accepted with a $75 deposit. You can leave yours unattended in the room if he's in a traveling kennel.

Rocky Ford

$ Melon Valley Inn, 1319 Elm Ave., 719-254-3306 (800-357-5991). Dogs are welcome with a $10 deposit.

Springfield

$ J's Motel, 265 Main, 719-523-6257. Dogs can stay for $2 extra per night.

$ Plum Bear Ranch, 29461 County Rd. 21, 719-523-4344. Though this B&B doesn't allow dogs in the rooms, it does maintain outside kennels (unheated) where your dog might be happy to stay if he's an outdoor type. The five rooms are decorated according to theme, including the Cowboy Room, the Sunrise Room (facing east), and the Garden Room. Your dog can romp leash-free on the ranch's 2,800 acres, and there are two resident dogs for him to share sniffs with.

$ The Stage Stop, 1033 Main, 719-523-4737. This older hotel (the building dates from 1906) has two downstairs rooms, with private baths, where dogs are usually put. However, if you'd prefer an upstairs room with shared bath for you and your dog, it can be arranged.

$ Starlite Motel, 681 Main, 719-523-6236. There's a $5 fee per night for a dog.

Stonewall

$ Picketwire Lodge and Store, 7600 Highway 12, 719-868-2265. The motel has kitchenettes in the rooms, and you can leave your dog unattended inside.

Trinidad

$ Budget Host Trinidad, 10301 Santa Fe Trail Dr., 719-846-3307 (800-BUD-HOST). The motel has some designated pet rooms where dogs can stay for $3 extra per night.

$ Cawthon Motel, 1701 Santa Fe Trail, 719-846-3303

$ Frontier Motel, 815 Goddard Ave., 719-846-2261

$ Royal Motel, 1115 E. Main, 719-846-3361. There's a $5–$10 fee per night, depending on the size of your dog.

$ Trail's End Motel, 616 E. Main, 719-846-4425. You may be asked to pay a $3 one-time fee for a large dog.

$–$$ Days Inn, 702 W. Main, 719-846-2271 (800-DAYS-INN). There are four designated pet rooms, and the fee for your dog is $5 per night.

$–$$ Downtown Motel, 516 E. Main, 719-846-3341. Small dogs only, please.

$–$$ Super 8 Motel, 1924 Freedom Rd. (Exit 15 off I-25), **719-846-8280** (800-800-

8000). You can leave your dog unattended in the room at this new Super 8.

$$ Best Western Country Club Inn, 900 W. Adams, 719-846-2215 (800-955-2215). Dogs 25 pounds and under are allowed in smoking rooms only. They can be left unattended.

$$ Budget Summit Inn, 9800 Santa Fe Trail Dr., 719-846-2251. Dogs are welcome in outside-facing rooms for $10 per night. You can leave Fido in the room unattended.

$$–$$$ Chicosa Canyon Bed and Breakfast, 32391 County Rd. 40 (12 miles from Trinidad), **719-846-6199.** This B&B, on a century-old ranch, has a cozy cabin that sleeps up to four in which your dog is welcome to join you (he can't stay in the main guest rooms). He'll have plenty to explore on the ranch's sixty-four acres, where he can hike off leash with you. Two bird dogs are permanent residents at the inn; they might be able to show your dog a trick or two.

$$–$$$ Holiday Inn, 9995 County Rd. 69.1 (Exit 11 off I-25), **719-846-4491 (800-HOLIDAY)**

Walsenburg

$ Sands Motel, 533 W. 7th, 719-738-2342 (800-373-4126). Dogs can be left unattended in the room.

$ Western Inn Motel, 521 North Walsen Ave., 719-738-3362

$–$$ Alpha Motel, 715 Walsen Ave., 719-738-2890. There's a $20 fee per night, per dog, and the owners have had their share of unfortunate experiences with dogs, so make sure yours doesn't test the limits.

$–$$ Country Budget Host, 553 Highway 85/87, 719-738-3800 (800-BUD-HOST). Dogs are allowed in smoking rooms only.

$$ Best Western Rambler Motel, Highway 85/87, Exit 52 (off I-25), **719-738-1121**

$$ Rio Cucharas Inn, 77 Taylor Rd., 719-738-1282. Your dog will definitely get the welcome mat at this friendly place near the Cuchara Ski Valley. "We love any kind of animals," says the owner, who describes himself as an "animal activist." In addition to motel-style rooms, the inn has three suites, each with fireplace, priced higher than the price category given here.

Weston

$$ Monument Lake Resort, 4789 Highway 12, 719-868-2226 (800-845-8006). You and your dog can stay in either adobe cottages or Southwestern-style lodge rooms at this lakeside resort west of Trinidad, situated at the base of the Sangre de Cristo Mountains. There's a $4 nightly fee for dogs. You must keep your dog leashed at the resort, but you'll be surrounded by the San Isabel National Forest, where he can romp leash-free. Open May to mid-September.

Campgrounds

Lake Pueblo State Park. See "Tail-Rated Trails" for directions (401 sites).

Lathrop State Park. See "Tail-Rated Trails" for directions (96 sites).

Trinidad Lake State Park. See "Tail-Rated Trails" for directions (62 sites).

National Forest campgrounds: Camping is allowed in the parking area at **Vogel Canyon** (see "Tail-Rated Trails" for directions).

Private campgrounds: **Pueblo KOA** and **Pueblo South/Colorado City KOA** (see "Creature Comforts").

Worth a Paws

Bent's Old Fort National Historic Site (719-383-5010). 8 miles east of La Junta and 15 miles west of Las Animas, on Highway 194. An influential frontier trading post on the Arkansas River, the fort was in operation from 1833 to 1849. Today a reconstruction, operated by the National Park Service, allows visitors to reexperience the fort's heyday through tours and interpretive activities. Your dog is welcome to accompany you throughout your visit as long as you keep him on a leash and with you at all times. Open 8 A.M.–5:30 P.M. daily, Memorial Day to Labor Day; 9 A.M.–4 P.M. the rest of the year. There is an entrance fee.

Feet and Fur. If you and Fido are in the Pueblo area during the first part of May, sign yourselves up for this annual run/walk fundraiser. A 10K race (for humans) and a 5K fun walk (for humans and canines) begin and end at Pueblo's Mineral Palace Park, just off I-25 at 17th and Main. The athletic events are followed by contests, including pet/owner lookalike, best dog costume, and best kisser (dogs, that is!). You and your dog can also get pet care information and various freebies at booths set up in the park, view demonstrations by local 4-H groups and police K-9 units, or check out the dog agility course. Money raised through registration fees and pledges benefits the Pueblo City/County Animal Shelter, the Southern Colorado Spay/Neuter Association, the Pueblo Humane Society, and the Animal Welfare Society. You can register in advance at the shelter, 1595 Stockyard Rd. in Pueblo (719-542-3474), or at the park on event day.

A You Do It Dogwash, 3853 Goodnight Ave., Pueblo, 719-561-1382. Is your lovable pooch starting to smell up the back seat after rolling in that suspicious-looking stuff out at the reservoir? Bring him here for a quick spruce-up. For $8 you can clean your dog in one of the special wash bays—shampoo, towels, and blow dryer are provided. You'll need to call for an appointment; walk-ins are not accepted. But appointments are readily available days, evenings, and weekends, including Sundays.

Doggie Daycare

Lamar

Eaton Veterinary Clinic, 1004 E. Maple, 719-336-5068. $5/day. Open 8 A.M.–5 P.M., Monday through Friday; 8 A.M.–noon, Saturday.

Pueblo

Kamp-4-Paws, 1412 32nd Lane, 719-545-PAWS. $4/day. Open 8 A.M.–6 P.M., Monday through Friday, 8 A.M.–2 P.M., Saturday.

Pets & Friends Animal Hospital, 3625 Baltimore Ave., 719-542-2022. $6.50–$7.50/day, depending on the size of your dog. Open 8 A.M.–5:30 P.M., Monday to Friday; 8 A.M.–noon, Saturday.

Pueblo Small Animal Clinic, 1400 Highway 50 East, 719-545-4350. $5.50–$7/day, depending on the size of your dog. Open 8 A.M.–12:30 P.M. and 1–5:30 P.M., Monday through Friday; 8 A.M.–noon, Saturday.

Pueblo West Boarding Kennels, 776 E. Paseo Dorado Dr., 719-547-3815. $12/day (day boarders are required to pay a two-day minimum, at $6 per day). Open 9 A.M.–5:30 P.M., Monday through Saturday.

Rawhide Ranch, 4284 36 Lane, 719-948-0008. $4/day. Your dog can enjoy a fenced-in exercise area outside his kennel. Open 9 A.M.–6 P.M., Monday through Friday; call for weekend hours.

Trinidad

Fisher's Peak Veterinary Clinic, 1617 Santa Fe Trail, 719-846-3211. $5–$7/day, depending on the size of your dog. Open 8 A.M.–5 P.M., Monday to Friday; 8 A.M.–noon, Saturday.

Walsenburg

Rio Cucharas Veterinary Clinic, 22540 Highway 160, 719-738-1427. $8–12/day, depending on the size of your dog. Open 8 A.M.–4 P.M., Monday to Friday; 8–11 A.M., Saturday.

PET PROVISIONS

Lamar

Sportzoo, 117 W. Beech, 719-336-4464. If you need to pick up a stereo for your dog along with some pet food, you can apparently find it here, too.

Pueblo

Aspen Grooming, 2403 Santa Fe Dr., 719-543-9315

Pet Paradise I & II, 339 S. Santa Fe (719-544-4510) and 1501 Moore (719-564-6191)

PetsMart, 4230 N. Freeway, 719-595-9000

Pueblo Feed & Supply, 1811 Santa Fe Dr., 719-542-6787

Sweeny Feed Mill of Southern Colorado, Inc., 403 E. 4th, 719-544-1041

Rocky Ford

Rocky Ford Pet Food, 26242 Highway 71, 719-254-4242

Trinidad

Marty Feeds, 326 N. Commercial, 719-846-3376

Walsenburg

Sporleden Feeds, 215 E. 4th, 719-738-1920

CANINE ER

La Junta

Colorado Veterinary Clinic, 30488 Highway 50, 719-384-8111. Open 8 A.M.–noon and 1–5:30 P.M., Monday through Friday, 8 A.M.–noon, 1–3 P.M., Saturday.

Krugman Small Animal Clinic, 502 E. 1st, 719-384-5050. Open 8 A.M.–noon, 1–5:30 P.M., Monday, Tuesday, Wednesday, Friday; 8 A.M.–noon, Thursday and Saturday.

Lamar

Eaton Veterinary Clinic, 1004 E. Maple, 719-336-5068. Open 8 A.M.–5 P.M., Monday through Friday; 8 A.M.–noon, Saturday.

Lamar Veterinary Clinic, 1209 E. Olive, 719-336-8484. Open 8 A.M.–5 P.M., Monday through Friday; 8 A.M.–noon, Saturday.

Pueblo

Pets & Friends Animal Hospital (AAHA certified), 3625 Baltimore Ave., 719-542-2022. Open 8 A.M.–5:30 P.M., Monday to Friday; 8 A.M.–noon, Saturday.

Pueblo Small Animal Clinic (AAHA certified), 1400 Highway 50 East, 719-545-4350. Open 8 A.M.–12:30 P.M. and 1–5:30 P.M., Monday through Friday; 8 A.M.–noon, Saturday.

Trinidad
Fisher's Peak Veterinary Clinic, 1617 Santa Fe Trail, 719-846-3211. Open 8 A.M.–5 P.M., Monday to Friday; 8 A.M.–noon, Saturday.

Trinidad Animal Clinic, 1701 E. Main, 719-846-3212. Open 8 A.M.–5 P.M., Monday to Friday; 8 A.M.–noon, Saturday

Walsenburg
Rio Cucharas Veterinary Clinic, 22540 Highway 160, 719-738-1427. Open 8 A.M.–4 P.M., Monday to Friday; 8–11 A.M., Saturday.

RESOURCES
Carrizo Unit, Comanche National Grasslands, 27162 Highway 287, Springfield, 719-523-6591

Colorado Welcome Center, Lamar, 109 E. Beech, 719-336-3483

Colorado Welcome Center, 309 Nevada Ave. (Exit 14A off I-25), Trinidad, 719-846-9512

Forest Supervisor's Office, Pike and San Isabel National Forests, 1920 Valley Dr., Pueblo, 719-545-8737

Pueblo Chamber of Commerce, 302 N. Santa Fe Ave., 719-542-1704 (800-233-3446)

Pueblo Visitors Information Center, Highway 50 and Elizabeth (Exit 101 off I-25), 719-543-1742

Timpas Unit, Comanche National Grasslands, 1420 E. Third St., La Junta, 719-384-2181

23

Colorado Springs and Vicinity

THE BIG SCOOP

Despite being Colorado's second-largest urban center, Colorado Springs, picturesquely situated near the base of massive Pikes Peak, is an exceedingly good place to bring your dog for a vacation. National Forest hiking trails are within a twenty-minute drive of downtown, and some forward-looking folks have established several off-leash areas in city and county parks. (There are leash laws within city limits as well as in many areas of El Paso County.) Many area lodging places allow pets. And you can even bring Rover along to some of the many locales to which tourists in the Springs traditionally flock (see "Worth a Paws"). If your dog has a special interest in old mining towns, ghosts, or, perhaps, gambling, pay a visit to nearby Victor and Cripple Creek (though he will have to sit out any casino forays). Whatever activities you choose, your dog is likely to find something to catch his interest in or around Colorado Springs.

TAIL-RATED TRAILS

Of the state parks in the area, two—Eleven Mile and Spinney Mountain—don't have hiking trails, and the one that does—Mueller—doesn't allow dogs on them. But there are plenty of hiking opportunities in city and county parks as well as in the Pike National Forest that you can enjoy with your dog. To research options in addition to the ones described here, stop by the Pikes Peak Ranger District office in Colorado Springs (see "Resources").

Seven Bridges Trail. About 4.5 miles round-trip. From downtown Colorado Springs, take Tejon Ave. south; follow the road as it bends to the right and turns into Cheyenne Blvd. After 2.5 miles you'll come to a fork and some signs pointing left for Seven Falls, right for North Cheyenne Cañon Park; stay right. Follow the road through the park. At Helen Hunt Falls, the road begins to switchback. Shortly after, you'll reach a fork where Gold Camp Rd. goes off to the right, and High Dr. is straight ahead. Park in the dirt lot on the left here. *Dogs can be off leash.*

Begin your hike by walking past the wooden gate at the west side of the parking area. The first half mile, which leads to the actual trail, takes you and your dog along a closed section of Gold Camp Rd. The road, which was a rail line at the turn of the century, stretches all the way to Cripple Creek; because of a tunnel cave-in that's never been repaired, an approximately 8-mile section is closed to vehicle traffic. Just before you would cross North Cheyenne Creek, take an unmarked trail that heads uphill on the right side of the road; stay straight rather than continuing uphill at the first switchback, and you'll be on the Seven Bridges Trail. (An alternate access point is off Gold Camp Rd. on the other side of the creek: There's a rusted metal sign indicating the North Cheyenne Creek Trail, the name by which this hike used to be known. However, you'll merely recross the creek on a couple of planks and wind up intersecting the first trail.) You'll hike along the north side of the creek for just a short while before reaching the first bridge. The trail then follows the twists and turns of the creek, ascending up the scenic drainage via a moderate grade. In addition to the plentiful water, your dog will appreciate the shade of ponderosa pine and Douglas fir. Altogether, you'll cross six bridges, despite the trail's name (there's been some bridge reconstruction and relocation due to flooding). After the sixth bridge, the trail climbs more steeply, away from the creek. Tell your dog to take care when crossing the section of exposed, sandy slope.

The Seven Bridges Trail officially ends when it intersects the Pipeline Trail, 1.5 miles from its start off Gold Camp Rd. However, when we hiked this trail, that intersection wasn't clear. We continued along the trail as it paralleled a smaller creek, ultimately reaching a plateau and a large stand of aspen, which made a good turnaround point. On the way back, you'll get a good down-canyon vista of the eastern plains. Shoes with good traction come in handy on the return trip, as some of the downhills are a bit slippery. Your dog, with his grippy paws, should have no problem.

 Bear Creek Regional Park. This 1,235-acre park has 10 miles of trails, with several access points. The section your dog will be most interested in is the *voice command area, where dogs can be off leash.* The trailhead is in the parking area west of 21st St., just past the intersection with W. Rio Grande Ave. *Dogs must be leashed in the rest of the park, and they are not allowed on the Nature Center trails in the western portion of the park.*

The off-leash area includes a wide trail that makes a 0.75-mile loop. It's a great spot for an after-work hike for local dogs or a close-to-town break for travelers. Look for the red "voice command area" sign at the west side of the parking lot. Though

you'll never get far from the noise of traffic on 21st St., your dog will be too excited at having an area set aside for him and his friends to notice. And he can even splash in nearby Bear Creek. You can also reach the trail that leads into the park's western section from the 21st St. parking area; just remember that your dog will have to leash up.

 Garden of the Gods. From downtown Colorado Springs, drive north to Fillmore St. and make a left to head west (it turns into Fontmore once you cross Mesa Rd.). At 30th St., turn right to reach the park's visitor center. If you're coming from Highway 24, head north on Ridge Rd., near Old Colorado City to arrive at the park. There is no entrance fee from either access. *Dogs can be off leash in the dog run area; they must be leashed elsewhere.*

On its own, the Garden of the Gods would only rate about one-and-a-half tail wags. However, the dog who's done his homework will know to sniff out the off-leash dog run area, which covers about eighteen acres on either side of the Foothills Trail, near Rock Ledge Ranch. To access this area, park at the visitor center and walk through the tunnel from the parking

Dakota (right) and Pony dry off from a swim. (photo by Jennifer Cook)

lot, which comes out at the Foothills Trail. Head south on the trail for about an eighth of a mile; you'll see two signs that demarcate the dog run area, which encompasses a section of open field surrounding the trail. Alternate access is from the Rock Ledge Ranch parking area; look for the signs from 30th St., just south of the Garden of the Gods visitor center. The dog run area begins near the parking lot. (Note that dogs are not allowed at Rock Ledge Ranch, which is a living history site.)

The main attraction of Garden of the Gods itself, a city park, is the vivid red sandstone formations that are clustered in the area. Several short trails, some natural surface, some paved, wind around the rocks. The longest, at 2.25 miles, encircles part of the park. Though you'll likely marvel at the landscape, your dog may find the Garden less than heavenly: There are no water sources for him, and the trails can be crowded. During the summer, try to visit early in the day or late in the afternoon for cooler temperatures and less company.

Palmer Park. From downtown Colorado Springs, head north on N. Nevada Ave.; turn right onto Fillmore St. and left onto Union Blvd. Turn left at the next intersection (Paseo Rd.) and drive into the park. *Dogs can be off leash in the voice-command area; they must be leashed in the rest of the park.*

Palmer Park is primarily an area for you and your dog to explore. Lots of unnamed trails meander throughout; just look for the dirt roads and parking pullouts to access them. However, your dog will first want to head to the **Yucca Area,** where there are 27.5 acres on which he can run off leash (as long as he stays under voice control). To reach the dog run, turn left off Paseo Rd. at the Lazy Land/Ute Crest sign, then follow signs to the Yucca Area/ Ute Crest parking section. The voice-command area encompasses a gravel road, which runs across the mesa top, and the

land on either side of it, providing great views of Pikes Peak to the west. Just keep an eye out for the signs to make sure your dog stays within the parameters of the dog run. If you visit during June, you'll catch the beauty of flowering yucca.

North Cheyenne Cañon Park. From downtown Colorado Springs, take Tejon Ave. south; follow the road as it bends to the right and turns into Cheyenne Blvd. After 2.5 miles you'll come to a fork and some signs pointing left for Seven Falls, right for North Cheyenne Cañon Park; stay right. *Dogs must be leashed.*

This city park, with scenic North Cheyenne Cañon at its center, has several hiking trails for dogs to sniff out. The park's western end borders National Forest land, where even more trails await discovery (see the Seven Bridges Trail description, for one example). You might begin with a stop at the well-stocked visitor center at the Starsmore Discovery Center located at the park's entrance. The **Columbine Springs Trail** runs for three miles through the park; you can access it from the lower trailhead behind Starsmore, from a midpoint trailhead off the park road, and from the upper trailhead across from Helen Hunt Falls. The 2-mile round-trip **Mount Cutler Trail** begins to the left of the park road, 1.4 miles from the park entrance. It makes a gradual ascent up the flanks of Mount Cutler, providing panoramic views of Colorado Springs, including the renowned Broadmoor Hotel and grounds. Near the top, you'll also be able to see the Seven Falls in South Cheyenne Cañon. And you might hear the hourly chiming of the Will Rogers Shrine on nearby Cheyenne Mountain. Though there's no water along the trail itself, North Cheyenne Creek is across from the trailhead. Driving farther west up the canyon brings you to **Helen Hunt Falls,** where your dog can enjoy the cool spray. A short trail leads past these falls up to Silver Cascade Falls.

 Fountain Creek Regional Park. Located south of Colorado Springs between Widefield and Fountain. Take I-25 south to Highway 160 (Exit 132); turn left and drive about half a mile, where you'll come to the exit for South Highway 85/87. Take this exit and make an immediate right onto Willow Springs Rd. Turn left before the parking lot onto the dirt road, then left again to reach the parking area and trail access. *Dogs must be leashed.*

The **Fountain Creek Trail** runs for a level 2.5 miles through the park, allowing your dog ample sniffing opportunities among the creek's riparian habitat. The wide, flat dirt trail also makes a good jogging venue. Though you'll never really get away from the drone of highway noise in the background, the park provides a welcome refuge from the surrounding development. If you head north on the trail, you'll come to the Willow Springs Fishing Ponds and the 0.75-mile **"Fishing Is Fun"** loop trail, where your dog can learn all about fishing from interpretive signs

Snow might be a dog's best friend.
(photo by Cindy Hirschfeld)

(though the ponds themselves have been closed to fishing due to PCE concentration in the water). Past the ponds you can also access the **Fountain Creek Regional Trail,** which extends for 6.5 miles from the northern end of the park to Circle Dr. in Colorado Springs. Heading south on the Fountain Creek Trail brings you to two wildlife observation pavilions, where your dog can gaze out on a ten-acre pond and the resident waterfowl. (Note that dogs are not allowed on the nature center trails in the Cattail Marsh Wildlife Area, which lies east of the Fountain Creek Trail.) The trail continues through two open meadow areas before ending near the Hanson Nature Park in Fountain.

 Monument Valley Park Trail. Runs for 2.2 miles along Monument Creek through Monument Valley Park. From the downtown business district on Tejon St., head east on Bijou St. for two blocks to the park. If you're driving, park on West View Pl. This brings you to the southern terminus of the trail. *Dogs must be leashed.*

Monument Valley Park is where your dog can come to sniff and be sniffed by the dogs who call the Springs home. The trail makes for a nice urban stroll as it follows the creek. In the park's southern end, you may want to detour to get a closer look at the various ponds, fountains, and the Horticultural Art Society demonstration gardens. For the first 1.3 miles, the trail runs along both sides of the creek (with a slight detour at Uintah St.), providing a loop option. Another loop (0.7 mile), in the park's northern end, makes up the **Monument Valley Fitness Trail,** good to know if your dog is really interested in getting a workout.

 Florissant Fossil Beds National Monument. It's best to bypass this national monument when you're with your dog: Not only are dogs not allowed on any trails but they're also discouraged from being in the picnic areas. In case Fido wonders what this place is all about anyway, you can let him know that 35 million years ago, a 15-mile-long lake dominated the landscape of the present-day monument site. Over the next 700,000 years, repeated eruptions from a nearby volcano eventually buried the lake's entire ecosystem, and over the ensuing millions of years, the plant and animal remains became fossilized. Today, the monument's visitor center presents fossil displays, and hiking trails lead visitors to petrified tree stumps. The monument is about 30 miles west of Colorado Springs off Highway 24.

 Mueller State Park. The park, located off Highway 67 on the way to Cripple Creek, offers more than 85 miles of hiking trails, and your dog is not allowed on any of them. Dogs are allowed in the park's camping and picnic sites.

CYCLING FOR CANINES

The 7-mile **Waldo Canyon Trail** is one of the most popular hiking and biking routes near Colorado Springs. It begins right off the north side of Highway 24, about 2 miles west of Manitou Springs. The upper part of the trail is actually a 3-mile loop. The 5.5-mile **Lovell Gulch Trail** starts at County Rd. 22, north of Woodland Park, and features great views of Pikes Peak.

Close to downtown Colorado Springs, the 4-mile **Captain Jack's Frontside Loop** begins at the closed section of Gold Camp Rd.; follow the Seven Bridges Trail (see "Tail-Rated Trails"), but continue to follow the switchbacks up the trail as it leaves Gold Camp Rd. Take a right at the intersection with the Jones Park Trail, then another right on High Dr. to return to the parking area. It's best to do this ride between October 31 and May 1, when High Dr. is closed to vehicle traffic.

You can also bring your bike and your dog to **Rampart Reservoir** outside of Woodland Park (there's a $3 day-use fee for the area). The **Rampart Reservoir Trail** extends around the lake for 11.6 miles. Begin from the Dikeside Boat Ramp and ride counterclockwise; that way your dog will be ready to turn around before you ever reach the campgrounds, where he'd be treading close to leash-required territory.

POWDERHOUNDS

The 3-mile round-trip **Crags Trail** is one of the closest places to Colorado Springs with consistent snow coverage for skiing and snowshoeing. To access the trail, take Highway 24 west to 67 south. Just past the entrance to Mueller State Park, look for Forest Rd. 383 on the left; follow it to the Crags Campground and the trailhead. Some unmarked spur trails lead off the main trail, providing more opportunities for snow travel.

The **Horsethief Park trail system** starts from Highway 67 a few miles south of the Crags Trail turnoff. It's about a 3-mile round-trip to Horsethief Park and back, a little over 2 miles round-trip to Horsethief Falls, and about 5 miles round-trip via the Pancake Rocks Trail.

After a storm or during a good snow, the trail around **Rampart Reservoir** is skiable/snowshoeable. Forest Rd. 306, which goes directly to the reservoir, is closed during the winter, so you'll need to access the Rampart Reservoir Trail via the 1.4-mile Rainbow Gulch Trail, off Forest Rd. 300.

CREATURE COMFORTS

Unless otherwise stated, dogs should not be left unattended in the room or cabin.

Colorado Springs

$ Colorado Springs Motel, 1116 S. Nevada, 719-632-7780. There's a $2 charge per pet, per night during the summer; the rate goes down to $1 per night during the winter.

$ Motel 6 Colorado Springs, 3228 N. Chestnut, 719-520-5400 (800-466-8356)

$–$$ Best Western Palmer House, 3010 Chestnut St., 719-636-5201 (800-223-9127). There's a $25 deposit for a dog plus a $10 fee per night. You can leave your dog unattended in the room.

$–$$ Beverly Hills Motel, 6 El Paso Blvd., 719-632-0386. The motel accepts "mature dogs and mature adults." You can leave your dog in the room unattended.

$–$$ Budget Inn, 1440 Harrison Rd., 719-576-2371. If you're traveling with a teeny-tiny dog, you can stay with him here; dogs 10 pounds and under get the nod. As far as fees or a deposit, that depends on the owner's assessment of you and the dog.

$–$$ Cottonwood Court Motel, 120 Manitou Ave., 719-685-1312. The motel has some designated pet rooms, and dogs are accepted on a nightly basis year-round (on a weekly basis during the summer only). There's a $5 fee per dog, per night, and you can leave your dog unattended in the room for up to an hour.

$–$$ Days Inn, 2850 S. Circle Dr., 719-527-0800 (800-874-4513). Dogs are allowed in smoking rooms only, with a $25 deposit.

$–$$ J's Motel, 820 N. Nevada Ave., 719-633-5513 (800-472-6009). There's a $4 fee per dog, per night.

$–$$ Maple Lodge, 9 El Paso Blvd., 719-685-9230. The motel accepts dogs for nightly stays in some of its rooms from May to the end of September. There's a $5 fee per night, per pet.

$–$$ Red Roof Inn, 8280 Highway 83, 719-598-6700 (800-THE-ROOF). You can leave your dog unattended in the room as long as he's in a travel kennel. The motel is across from the Air Force Academy south gate.

$–$$ Stagecoach Motel, 1647 S. Nevada, 719-633-3894. Small dogs more than two years old are allowed in one of the motel's

four designated pet rooms. You can leave your pooch unattended in the room.

$–$$ Swiss Chalet, 3410-3420 W. Colorado Ave., 719-471-2260 or 719-471-3758. Dogs 15 pounds and under (with a few exceptions) are allowed in the motel's rooms and cabins. You'll be asked to put down a $20 deposit, half of which you'll get back at checkout time, assuming no damage has been done. You can leave your dog unattended inside.

$$ Apollo Park Executive Suites, 805 S. Circle, 719-634-0286 (800-666-1955). This place rents out one- and two-bedroom units with kitchens on a nightly, weekly, or monthly basis. Dogs are allowed in the lower-level units with a $100 deposit. You can leave your dog unattended inside.

$$ Buffalo Lodge, 2 El Paso Blvd., 719-634-2851 (800-235-7416). This historic lodge, which is practically in Manitou Springs, dates from the early 1900s, and the exterior has that classic 1950s vacation-spot look. But the rooms are large, modern, and comfortably furnished. Dogs are permitted in three of the rooms, all of which have wood floors, for a $50 deposit. You must keep your dog leashed on the four-acre property.

$$ Drury Inn, 8155 N. Academy Blvd., 719-598-2500. The motel prefers dogs that weigh less than 50 pounds, but if you have a larger dog that is quiet and well behaved, chances are he won't be turned away. You can leave your dog unattended in the room.

$$ Hampton Inn North, 7245 Commerce Center Dr., 719-593-9700 (800-HAMPTON). There's a $25 deposit per pet. You can leave your dog unattended in the room as long as you put up the "do not disturb" sign to alert the housekeeping staff. Rates include continental breakfast.

$$ Radisson Inn Airport, 1645 N. Newport Rd., 719-597-7000 (800-333-3333). Dogs 25 pounds and under are allowed in first-floor rooms only. If you're staying in one of the newer rooms, you'll also be asked to put down a $50 deposit. You can leave your dog unattended in the room for a short time if you're on the hotel premises, say, at the restaurant. Rates include a breakfast buffet.

$$ Raintree Inn, 2625 Ore Mill Rd., 719-632-4600 (800-929-5478). Dogs are allowed in nine of the motel's ground-floor rooms for $5 extra per pet, per night.

$$ Ramada Inn East, 520 N. Murray, 719-596-7660 (800-272-6232). You'll be asked to put down a $25 deposit if you're paying with cash, and you can leave your dog unattended in the room as long as you notify the front desk.

$$ Ramada Inn North, 3125 Sinton Rd., 719-633-5541 (800-272-6232). This Ramada charges a whopping $100 one-time fee for a dog. You can leave your dog unattended in the room, but housekeeping won't enter during that time.

$$ Rodeway Inn, 2409 E. Pikes Peak Ave., 719-471-0990 (800-228-2000). A $40 deposit is required for a dog. You can leave your dog unattended in the room as long as you put out the "do not disturb" sign to alert the housekeepers.

$$ Sleep Inn, 1075 Kelly Johnson Blvd., 719-260-6969 (888-875-3374). Dogs are put in smoking rooms only, with a $50 deposit. You can leave your dog unattended inside.

$$–$$$ Antlers Doubletree Hotel, 4 S. Cascade, 719-473-5600 (800-222-TREE). This is one of the more upscale hotels in Colorado Springs, and it's conveniently located downtown. The pet policy is a little unusual in that you'll have to put down a $50 deposit per day, which is then refunded each day as long as there's no doggie damage (and then the process starts over again if your stay is several days). You can leave your dog unattended in the room. Rates include continental breakfast.

$$–$$$ Comfort Suites of Colorado Springs, 1055 Kelly Johnson Blvd., 719-536-0731 (888-515-3131). The rooms here are large one-room suites with microwave and refrigerator. You and your dog will generally be put in a smoking room, and a $50 deposit is required.

$$–$$$ Hampton Inn South, 1410 Harrison Rd., 719-579-6900. The hotel has suites and minisuites available in addition to standard rooms. There's a $5 fee per pet, per night, with a limit of two dogs per room. You can leave your dog unattended inside as long as you put the inn's "pet in room" magnet on your door and let the front desk know. You'll also be asked to sign a pet agreement form and refrain from bringing Fido into the lobby. Rates include continental breakfast.

$$–$$$ Holiday Inn Express, 8th and Cimarron Sts., 719-473-5530. Your dog can stay with you for a $25 one-time fee, and you can leave him unattended in the room as long as you put out the "do not disturb" sign.

$$–$$$ Holiday Inn Garden of the Gods, 505 Popes Bluff Tr., 719-598-7656 (800-962-5470). Dogs 20 pounds and under are permitted in the hotel's older rooms. If you're paying with cash, a $50 deposit is required. You can leave your dog unattended in the room as long as you let the front desk know so they can pass that on to the housekeepers.

$$–$$$ La Quinta Inn, 4385 Sinton Rd., 719-528-5060 (800-531-5900). You can leave your dog unattended in the room, but housekeeping won't clean it during that time.

$$–$$$ Quality Inn Garden of the Gods, 555 W. Garden of the Gods Rd., 719-593-9119 (800-828-4347). Dogs are allowed in smoking rooms only, with a $50 deposit.

$$–$$$$ Colorado Springs Marriott, 5580 Tech Center Dr., 719-260-1800 (800-962-6982). Dogs 30 pounds and under are welcome. A credit-card imprint is required as a deposit, and you can leave your dog unattended in the room as long as he's in a travel kennel.

$$–$$$$ Doubletree World Arena, 1775 E. Cheyenne Mountain Blvd., 719-576-8900. Formerly the Red Lion Hotel, this is another of the nicer hotels in the Springs. Dogs are welcome for $10 extra per night.

$$–$$$$ Radisson Inn North, 8110 N. Academy Blvd., 719-598-5770 (800-333-3333). The hotel offers standard rooms, minisuites, and larger suites with Jacuzzi. Your dog is welcome, too, if he's 25 pounds or under, with a $50 deposit, and he can be left unattended in the room.

$$–$$$$ Residence Inn North by Marriott, 3880 N. Academy Blvd., 719-574-0370. Dogs are allowed at this apartment-style hotel for $15 extra per night, with a maximum total of $150 (if your stay extends past ten nights). You can leave your dog unattended inside.

$$–$$$$ Residence Inn South by Marriott, 2765 Geyser Dr., 719-576-0101. This Residence Inn charges a $50 one-time fee for a dog, plus $5 extra per night, with no maximum. You can leave your dog unattended inside as long you're positive he'll remain quiet.

$$–$$$$ Sheraton Colorado Springs, 2886 S. Circle Dr., 719-576-5900 (800-981-4012). Dogs 30 pounds and under can rest in comfort at the Sheraton, though they're only allowed in smoking, ground-floor rooms. There's a $50 deposit. You can leave your dog unattended in the room as long as you contact the front desk so that the housekeeping staff can be alerted.

Cripple Creek

$–$$ Cripple Creek Hotel, 350 E. Carr, 719-689-3709. You can leave your dog unattended in the room.

$$ Cozy Cabins, 232 Thurlow, 719-689-3351. Dogs are accepted on a case-by-case basis. There are two cozy cabins, the actual Cozy Cabin and the Cowboy Cabin. The one-bedroom Cozy was built in 1930 and features a fireplace and some antique furnishings. The modern Cowboy, next door, has two bedrooms and a boatload of cowboy decor; in fact, the cabin is dedicated to Roy Rogers and Dale Evans. The refrigerators in both cabins are stocked with breakfast goodies and snacks for your enjoyment. You might be able to leave your dog unattended inside at the owner's discretion. Open year-round.

$$ Greyhound Ranch Bed and Breakfast, 401 S. Second, 719-689-2599. Living up to its name, this B&B does take dogs, of any variety. There's plenty of open space in the area to walk Fido, and you can leave him unattended in the room for short periods of time, e.g., the length of a dinner.

$$ Sarahouse, 216 W. Masonic, 719-689-3384. One well-behaved dog at a time is welcome to stay with you at this cozy two-bedroom house dating from the early 1900s. A $100 deposit is required, and you can leave your dog unattended inside only if he's in a travel kennel. Note that two other houses in Cripple Creek under the same management—the Ironhouse and the Keeping Room—do not allow pets.

$$–$$$ Double Eagle Hotel and Casino, 442 E. Bennett, 719-689-5000 (800-711-7234). Your dog is welcome to accompany you here on a gambling vacation if you put down a $100 deposit. You can leave Fido in the room unattended while you try your luck in the adjoining casino.

$$–$$$ The Victorian Lady Bed and Breakfast, 127 W. Carr, 719-689-2143 or 303-421-4093. Dogs are allowed on a case-by-case basis, depending on size and temperament. If your dog makes the grade, you'll need to pay $10 extra per night for him. If the owner decides that your dog is too big to stay in the room or if you're heading off to the casinos, your dog can hang out in the yard—just make sure you have a way to restrain him, as the fence is not super secure. Open Memorial Day to Labor Day.

Fountain

$ Colorado Springs South KOA and Kamping Kabins, 8100 S. Bandley Dr., 719-382-7575 (800-KOA-1507). Dogs are allowed in the one- and two-room cabins for a $2 fee per dog, per night (there's no extra charge to have them at the campsites). You'll have to bring bedding and cooking supplies. You can leave your dog unattended inside the cabin, and there are two large fields on site, as well as Fountain Creek, where you can exercise him on a leash. Open year-round.

Green Mountain Falls

$–$$ Falls Motel, 6990 Lake St., 719-684-9745. The motel has about four designated pet rooms—those in which the carpet has not been recently replaced.

Lake George

$–$$ Lake George Cabins and RV Park, 8966 County Rd. 90, 719-748-3822. Dogs are allowed in the log cabins as well as in the RV and tent sites. You'll need to keep your dog leashed on the property, but plenty of hiking trails in Pike National Forest are nearby. Open year-round.

Jasmine finds the perfect cool-down spot. (photo by Helmut Tingstad)

Manitou Springs

$–$$ Green Willow Motel Cottages, 328 Manitou Ave., 719-685-9997. Dogs are allowed in any of the cottages, some of which have kitchens. There's a stream on the property and an adjacent lot where you can walk your dog to do his stuff. Open May 1 to September 30.

$–$$ LaFon Motel, 123 Manitou Ave., 719-685-5488. The motel accepts pets from Memorial Day to Labor Day, and no more than two dogs are allowed in one unit. The rooms have some homey touches that elevate them above standard motel style. You can leave your dog unattended inside.

$–$$ Park Row Lodge, 54 Manitou Ave., 719-685-5216 (800-818-PARK). If you have a teeny dog, you can bring him to the Park Row: The motel accepts dogs 10 pounds and under, with a very occasional exception for a larger dog. There's a $10 one-time fee. Some of the rooms have kitchenettes.

$$–$$$ Red Eagle Mountain Bed and Breakfast, 616 Ruxton Ave., 719-685-4541 (800-686-8801). This five-room B&B is in a house that dates from 1894, and the rooms are furnished in a country Victorian decor. The owner accepts dogs on a case-by-case basis. If your dog does become a guest here, you can leave him unattended in the room for short periods of time.

Tarryall

$$ Ute Trail River Ranch, 21446 County Rd. 77 (21 miles from Lake George), 719-748-3015. This rustic fishing camp on Tarryall Creek features turn-of-the-century log cabins outfitted with wood stoves and Western decor. For $5 extra per night, dogs are allowed to stay in six of the eight cabins, one of which has a private bath (the other five share a central showerhouse). The owners ask that you keep your dog leashed on the property's thirty-five acres, but the ranch is surrounded by Pike National Forest land, where you and Fido can hike leash-free (though you will need to leash him back up if you venture into the nearby Lost Creek Wilderness). The cabin with private bath (as well as two others that don't permit dogs inside) is open year-round; the other cabins are open from mid-May to mid-October.

Victor
$$ Victor Hotel, Fourth St. and Victor Ave., 719-689-3553 (800-748-0870). Originally a bank, this century-old property, which is on the National Register of Historic Places, now houses the Victor Hotel. The cozy, modern rooms have exposed brick walls and nice woodwork. There are three designated dog rooms in which your pooch can stay for a $10 one-time fee. And you can leave him unattended inside. The hotel reputedly has a resident ghost, Ed, so if your dog starts barking at seemingly nothing in the hallway, don't tell him he's just being silly.

Woodland Park
$ Camper Cabins and Campground at Woodland Park, 1125 W. Bowman Ave., 719-687-7575 (800-808-CAMP). Dogs are allowed in the camper cabins; you'll have to supply your own bedding and cooking gear. Open May 1 to September 20.

$–$$ Rainbow Falls Park, Highway 67 (10 miles from Woodland Park), **719-687-9074.** "We're pet friendly, but we don't want the aggressive types," say the owners. If you're traveling with your doberman, rottweiler, German shepherd, or pit bull, they'd prefer you look elsewhere for accommodations. Otherwise, dogs are welcome in both the cabins and RVs for rent; RV hookups and tent sites are also available. Trout Creek and five lakes are located on the property. Open year-round.

Campgrounds
Eleven Mile State Park. About 11 miles from Lake George via County Rd. 92 (350 sites).

Mueller State Park. About 3.5 miles south of Divide on Highway 67 (132 sites).

National Forest campgrounds: **Meadow Ridge Campground** (19 sites) and **Thunder Ridge Campground** (21 sites) are both at Rampart Reservoir, 4.2 miles east of Woodland Park via County Rd. 22 and Forest Rd. 300; **South Meadows Campground** (64 sites), **Colorado Campground** (81 sites), and **Painted Rocks Campground** (18 sites) are north of Woodland Park off Highway 67; The **Crags Campground,** at the end of Forest Rd. 383 off Highway 67, south of Divide (17 sites).

Private campgrounds: **Colorado Springs South KOA and Kamping Kabins** in Fountain; **Lake George Cabins and RV Park** in Lake George; **Camper Cabins and Campground** at Woodland Park; and **Rainbow Falls Park** in Woodland Park (see "Creature Comforts" for all).

WORTH A PAWS
U.S. Air Force Academy. Your leashed dog is welcome to tour the grounds of the Air Force Academy with you, but he won't be able to go in any of the buildings. The **Falcon Trail** makes a 12-mile loop around and through the academy; pick up the "Visitors Map and Guide" at the academy visitor center to see the trail's route and access points. The **New Santa Fe Regional Trail** begins at Ice Lake and skirts the academy's eastern side, running north for about 14 miles to Palmer Lake. Eventually this gravel trail will extend south to connect with other trails in Colorado Springs. If you're doing the driving tour of the Academy and want to let your dog stretch his gams, stop at the Environmental Overlook, off Academy Drive just south of the turnoff for the visitor center. A short trail leaves from the northeast end of the parking lot (look for the signs). For a quick out-and-back, stick to the wide gravel trail that goes to the overlook. There's also a nice loop option through ponderosa pine and gambel oak: Take the path leading to the right from the overlook, then stay right at the small trail intersection to return to the parking lot. You can reach the academy from Exits 156B or 150B off I-25.

Cripple Creek Narrow Gauge Railroad. Small to medium-sized dogs (this includes retriever sized) can accompany their owners on the 4-mile round-trip ride that goes from Cripple Creek halfway to Victor and back. The narrated tour passes by historic mines and ghost towns. Trains leave every 45 minutes from the station at Bennett Avenue in Cripple Creek from mid-May to mid-October. Call 719-689-2640 for more information and rates.

Pikes Peak Highway. Second only to the road up Mount Evans as the quickest way to bring your dog to the top of a fourteener, the Pikes Peak Highway snakes 19 miles to the 14,110-foot summit of legendary Pikes Peak. Once at the top, your dog can feel his fur ripple in the breeze and enjoy a breathtaking view of the eastern plains, up and down the Front Range, and the Sawatch and Mosquito ranges to the west. The road, a combination of pavement and gravel, is open year-round (Wednesday to Sunday from December to March). Access is from Highway 24 just outside of Cascade, and you will have to pay a toll fee. For more information, call 719-684-9383 or 800-DO-VISIT.

Manitou Cliff Dwellings Museum. Leashed dogs are welcome to tour the outdoor areas of this reconstructed example of Anasazi architecture and culture built in 1906. Genuine Anasazi artifacts are also on display. The Cliff Dwellings, located off Highway 24 just west of Colorado Springs, are open year-round (weekends only in January and February). Call 719-685-5242 or 800-354-9971 for more information.

Seven Falls. You're welcome to bring Fido and his leash to this series of seven waterfalls that cascade 181 feet in South Cheyenne Cañon, on the southwestern side of Colorado Springs. An elevator brings you to the Eagle's Nest viewing platform, or you and your dog can tackle the 224 stairs along the falls, which lead to a 2-mile round-trip nature trail that ends at an overlook of Colorado Springs and the plains beyond. Open year-round, the falls are illuminated at night by multicolored lights from mid-May to Labor Day. Admission is charged. Call 719-632-0765 for recorded information.

Gigi's, 728 Manitou Ave., Manitou Springs, 719-685-4772. Billed as the "animal lovers' giftshop," Gigi's is more than your typical pet supply store. You'll find all manner of collars, leashes, and other pet accessories as well as dog-themed items for humans. Your dog, who is welcome to browse along with you, will want to sniff out the array of treats and toys.

Bark in the Park. Has your dog ever attended a minor-league baseball game (or even a major-league game, for that matter)? You can bring Fido along to cheer on the Colorado Springs Sky Sox—one of the Colorado Rockies' farm teams—at this annual event. The stadium has a large, grassy picnic area where dogs and their owners can sit during the game. Before the game, your dog can wear himself out competing in Frisbee competitions put on by the Front Range Flyers Canine Disc Club and other events, like the obstacle course; that way, he won't be as tempted to chase down baseballs during the main event. For more information, call the sponsor, the Humane Society of the Pikes Peak Region, at 719-473-1741.

Dirty Dog Wash. If your pooch is starting to resemble the name of this event, bring him by for a scrub courtesy of Humane Society volunteers and zookeepers from the Cheyenne Mountain Zoo. The wash takes place in July at the Humane Society of the Pikes Peak Region, 633 S. 8th St. in Colorado Springs. A yard sale and bake sale (with goodies for people and dogs) are also held. Proceeds are split between the Humane Society and the American Association of Zookeepers at the Cheyenne Mountain Zoo.

Canine 5K Pet Fest. Held in Colorado Springs on the third or fourth Saturday in September, this annual 5K run/walk is for dogs and their owners. The course goes through Monument Valley Park. After the race, your dog can stroll among the booths of pet products and information, compete in contests such as pet tricks or dog/owner lookalike, or check out Frisbee dog demonstrations. Your $25 registration fee (as well as pledges that you raise for the event) nets a T-shirt, a bandanna for your dog, breakfast snacks, and a goodie bag for you and Fido. All proceeds benefit the Humane Society of the Pikes Peak Region (719-473-1741).

Ashley Whippet Canine Frisbee Invitational. During the last Saturday in May or the first one in June, Frisbee-toting dogs gather in Cottonwood Creek Park in the Springs to show off their leaping and catching prowess. The competition, put on by the Front Range Flyers Canine Disc Club, features two events: the minidistance, in which dogs receive points for catching distance and style in sixty-second rounds; and the free flight, in which they demonstrate their best freestyle tricks. There's no entrance fee, and anyone and their dog is welcome, regardless of your dog's previous competitive experience. You can also just bring your dog to watch; maybe he'll get inspired to compete the next year. For more information, contact Rob Provost at 719-495-9661.

 Cave of the Winds. Dogs are not allowed on the cave tours of this mile-long cavern or at the nighttime laser show.

 Cheyenne Mountain Zoo and Will Rogers Shrine of the Sun. It's probably no surprise that dogs aren't allowed in the zoo, but you should be aware that they're also not allowed at the Will Rogers Shrine (Rover can ride up in the car with you, but he's not supposed to set paw outside). The zoo does have one kennel where a poodle-sized dog can stay, at no charge; it's available on a first-come, first-served basis. For more information, call 719-633-9925.

 Ghost Town Wild West Museum. Dogs are discouraged from visiting this re-

constructed frontier town in Colorado Springs.

 North Pole and Santa's Workshop. Your dog won't be able to visit Santa at his mid-May through Christmas Eve residence west of Colorado Springs.

 Pikes Peak Cog Railway. You won't be able to bring your dog on the Swiss-made cog train that climbs to the summit of Pikes Peak; however, if he's small to medium sized, you may be able to leave him at the train station for dog-sitting free of charge. "We'll provide water and plenty of TLC," says one of the station attendants. The round-trip takes just over three hours, and trains operate from late April to late October, leaving from the depot on Ruxton Ave. in Manitou Springs. Call 719-685-5401 for reservations and fee information.

DOGGIE DAYCARE

Black Forest

Canine Care Center, 7580 Ponca Rd., 719-495-4209. $7.25–$8.50/day, depending on the size of dog. Open 8 A.M.–6 P.M., Monday to Friday; 8 A.M.–3 P.M., Saturday; 5–6 P.M. (summer), 4–5 P.M. (winter), Sunday (pickups only).

Dogs' Best Friend Bed and Breakfast, 7305 Maine Ln., 719-495-2983. $8/day. Open 8–11 A.M. and 2–6 P.M., Monday to Saturday; 5–8 P.M., Sunday (pickups only).

Colorado Springs

Airway Boarding Kennels, 5280 E. Edison, 719-574-1886. About $5/day. The owner stresses that proof of an internasal bordatella vaccination received every six months is required, and all vaccinations must be vet-administered. Open 8 A.M.–5:30 P.M., Monday, Tuesday, Thursday, Friday; 8 A.M.–7 P.M., Wednesday; 8 A.M.–4 P.M., Saturday; 8–11 A.M. and 3–5:30 P.M., Sunday.

Broadmoor Bluffs Kennel, 43 E. Old Broadmoor Rd., 719-636-3344. $8–$11/

day, depending on the size of dog. Open 7 A.M.–5:30 P.M., Monday to Friday; 8 A.M.–5:30 P.M., Saturday; closed for lunch, 12:30–1:30 P.M., all days.

Clearview Animal Lodge, 3928 S. Hancock Expressway, 719-392-1800. $4.25–$7/day, depending on the size of dog. Open 8 A.M.–6 P.M., Monday to Saturday.

Countryside Kennel, 7945 Maverick Rd., 719-495-3678. $7/day includes a 15-minute nature walk. Open 7 A.M.–5:30 P.M., Monday to Saturday; 4–5:30 P.M., Sunday.

Sunrise Kennels, 6580 Vincent Dr., 719-598-8220. $5/day. Open 7 A.M.–5:30 P.M., Monday to Friday; 7:30 A.M.–3:30 P.M., Saturday.

Woodmen Kennels, 6440 Vincent Dr., 719-598-4154. $5/day. Open 7 A.M.–6 P.M., Monday to Friday; 7 A.M.–4 P.M., Saturday.

Falcon
Fox and Hounds, 5335 JD Johnson Rd., 719-683-5544 (888-K9SCHOOL). Call for rates and hours.

Grand Paws Pet Care Center, 13750 Canter Rd., 719-683-3852

Fountain
Land of Ahs Kennels, 12599 Jordan Rd., 719-382-1126. $7.50–$11/day, depending on the size of dog. Open 7 A.M.–5 P.M., Monday to Friday; 7 A.M.–noon, Saturday; Sunday by appointment only.

Pet Provisions
Colorado Springs
Brookhart's Farm and Ranch Store, I-25 and Baptist Rd., 719-488-1300

Circle F Ranch Supply, 115 E. Garden of the Gods Rd., 719-599-5100; 711 N. Union Blvd., 719-578-0666; 1020 Ford St., 719-596-1900

Colorado Agri-Feed, 4625 Park Vista Blvd., 719-599-5961

ENOB Feed and Pet Supply, 6480 N. Academy Blvd., 719-522-9208

Petco, 1820 W. Uintah, 719-578-1123; 5720 N. Academy Blvd., 719-536-0160. Both locations have a self-service dog wash, which includes use of a washing bay, shampoo, towel, and dryer for $8.

PetsMart, 571 N. Academy Blvd., 719-570-1313

Pikes Peak Animal Supply, 5286 E. Edison, 719-591-1448

Fountain
Dawn Meadows Feed Tack and Horsetel, 8250 Highways 85 and 87, 719-382-7069

Canine ER
Colorado Springs
Animal Emergency Care, 5752 N. Academy Blvd., 719-260-7141. Open 6 P.M.–8 A.M., Monday to Saturday morning; noon on Saturday to 8 A.M. Monday; 24 hours on holidays.

Animal Emergency Center of Colorado Springs P.C. (AAHA certified), 2812 E. Pikes Peak Ave., 719-578-9300. Open 5:30 P.M.–8 A.M. Monday to Friday; 24 hours on Saturday, Sunday, and holidays.

Resources
Colorado Springs Convention and Visitors Bureau, 104 S. Cascade, Suite 104, Colorado Springs, 719-635-7506 (800-DO-VISIT; www.coloradosprings-travel.com/cscvb/)

Cripple Creek Chamber of Commerce, 337 E. Bennett Ave., Cripple Creek, 719-689-2169

Manitou Springs Chamber of Commerce, 354 Manitou Ave., Manitou Springs, 719-685-5089 (800-642-2567)

Pikes Peak Ranger District, Pike and San Isabel National Forests, 601 S. Weber St., Colorado Springs, 719-636-1602

Appendices

FOURTEENER DOGS

Climbing "fourteeners," or peaks with elevations 14,000 feet or above, has become an increasingly popular summertime (and occasionally wintertime) activity in Colorado. It's also somewhat controversial, as many believe that the large numbers of hikers tromping up and down the trails is causing irreparable damage to the alpine environment. You can easily deduce that many people are even less thrilled about dogs on fourteeners.

If you and your dog share most hiking outings, however, chances are you're not going to be easily dissuaded from bringing him along for the really spectacular stuff. With this in mind, I've compiled the following listing of fourteeners, grouped according to dog suitability. After turning back about half a mile from the summit of Snowmass Mountain because Clover and another dog couldn't handle the knife-edge ridge, I realized that some advance knowledge would have saved us the frustration of an "incomplete" trek. Athletic dogs can successfully summit many fourteeners. Be sure to bring plenty of water. Dog booties (see the "Gearhound" appendix) are also an excellent accessory to take along, as tender paws can easily get worn ragged on talus or scree slopes, or other rough terrain. And if you're out to tackle peaks that require heavy-duty rock scrambling or knife-edge ridges, do both of yourselves a favor and leave Rover at home.

The categories that follow assume you'll ascend via the easiest routes. Nearly all fourteeners have alternate ascents that may or may not be suitable for dogs. For more specifics on routes, refer to *Colorado's Fourteeners: From Hikes to Climbs*, by Gerry Roach; *A Climbing Guide to Colorado's Fourteeners*, by Walter R. Borneman and Lyndon J. Lampert; and *Dawson's Guide to Colorado's Fourteeners*, volumes 1 and 2, by Louis Dawson.

"I Can Do This!"

Mount Antero
Mount Belford
Mount Bierstadt
Mount Bross
Mount Columbia
Culebra Peak
Mount Democrat
Mount Elbert
Mount Evans
Grays Peak
Handies Peak
Mount Harvard
Humboldt Peak
Huron Peak
La Plata Peak
Mount Lincoln
Mount Massive
Missouri Mountain
Mount Oxford
Pikes Peak
Mount Princeton
Quandary Peak
Redcloud Peak
San Luis Peak
Mount Sherman
Mount Shavano

Sunshine Peak
Tabeguache Peak
Torreys Peak
Uncompahgre Peak
Mount Yale

"Give Me a Boost up That Rock, Will Ya?"

Blanca Peak
Castle Peak
Challenger Point
Ellingwood Point
Mount of the Holy Cross
Mount Lindsey
Windom Peak

"Please Leave Me Behind"

Capitol Peak
Crestone Needle
Crestone Peak
El Diente Peak
Mount Eolus
Kit Carson Peak
Little Bear Peak
Maroon Peak
North Maroon Peak
Pyramid Peak
Mount Sneffels
Snowmass Mountain
Sunlight Peak
Wetterhorn Peak
Mount Wilson
Wilson Peak

"I Couldn't if I Wanted To"

Longs Peak—it's in Rocky Mountain National Park, where dogs are prohibited from all trails.

GEARHOUND

These days, as much thought is going into dog gear as into people gear; you can find an array of canine accessories that will make your dog's travels and hikes easier and more enjoyable. The well-equipped dog will want to have at least some of the following items in his travel bag. Phone numbers and websites are provided for each manufacturer; call to find out which stores near you carry the items that your dog can't wait to get his paws on.

Dog Packs

Backpacks for dogs are a great invention: they allow Rover to schlep his own food, water, treats, or poop bags on long day hikes or multiday outings (assuming you don't overburden him, of course). And at the end of a backpacking trip, you can make your dog carry out the trash! Just as with packs for people, your dog should come in for a fitting before purchase to make sure the pack carries comfortably on his back. With the variety of packs available, your dog should be able to find at least one that suits him. Mountaineering or high-end pet specialty stores are your best bets for pack shopping. A few of the sturdier packs we've found are listed here.

Rocky Mountain K-9 Accessories, in Boulder, has developed a unique modular pack system that can be customized for you and your dog's outings. The basic K-9 Trailblazer pack includes the harness, a Cordura pack that sits on top of the dog's back, a collapsible water bowl, a nylon emergency leash, two insulated water-bottle holders with 28-ounce bottles, and even a small

Dogs want to see the view from the top, too. (photo by Alyssa Pumphrey)

pouch that hooks on the pack's outside for holding poop pick-up bags. Two accessory packs can replace the Trailblazer, which zips off the harness: The Oasis contains two additional water bottles, and the Adventurer includes a twenty-two-piece dog/human first-aid kit. Both accessory packs come with the poop bag and extra leash. 303-448-1942.

Mountainsmith, a Colorado company well known for its human packs, offers three sizes of dog packs, with carrying capacity keyed to the dog's weight. All packs feature Cordura panniers, polypro webbing to prevent chafing, compression straps, and a double-layer construction. 800-426-4075; www.mountainsmith.com.

Wolf Packs, out of southern Oregon, makes three styles of dog packs in six sizes and ten colors. All packs are made out of water-repellent, urethane-coated Cordura nylon; the side-release buckles are padded with Polartec 300 fleece for Fido's comfort. The top-of-the-line Banzai Explorer pack has ballistic nylon side guards, compression straps, and reflective trim. The Trekker Reflector pack features reflective material for safety. The Trekker is the basic pack. The Wolf Packs web site has helpful information on fitting your dog's pack and training him to hike with it. 541-482-7669; www.wolfpacks.com.

Granite Gear, a northern Minnesota company that also produces people packs and canoe gear, manufactures the Ruff Rider dog pack. With a Cordura exterior and a Polartec 200 fleece underside, the packs comes in three sizes and three colors. There's also a D-ring on the pack so you can connect the leash directly to it. 800-222-8032; www.granitegear.com.

Ruffwear, in Bend, Oregon, offers the canine-specific Palisades Pack in three sizes. These packs have lots of bells and whistles, including removable saddle bags (handy for stream crossings), an integrated hydration system (à la Camelbak) so you can empty water directly into your dog's bowl, a webbing handle you can grasp to lift your dog over obstacles on the trail, compression straps, and two leash attachment points. 888-783-3932; www.ruffwear.com.

Caribou, out of Chico, California, produces the Woofer dog pack. Made out of nylon pack cloth and Cordura, the pack comes in two sizes. Quick-release buckles make for easy attachment, and a mesh yoke keeps your dog's back cool. 800-824-4153; www.caribou.com.

Dog Booties

The cutest thing next to infant socks may be dog booties, sturdy little "shoes" that slip on your dog's paws to protect them from snow and ice balls, hot desert rock, or sharp-edged talus. Clover always gets lots of compliments when she's sporting her set. The key is to find booties that will stay on. Allow your dog to get accustomed to his booties by letting him wear them around the house a few times before your first outing. And on snowy days, he'll get the snuggest fit if you put his booties on before he gets out of the car.

Ruffwear makes Bugaboos in five sizes. The booties, made of nylon pack cloth, have a band that wraps around the dog's leg at the top of the bootie and secures with a Velcro closure. 888-783-3932; www.ruffwear.com.

Duke's Dog Fashions, in Beaverton, Oregon, produces fashionable two-tone booties out of 1,000-denier Cordura or fleece, with double-soled construction. The booties stay on by means of a Velcro strap that snugs around the top. Duke, the company's namesake, was a Lab from Crested Butte. 800-880-8969; www.dukesdog.com.

Wolf Packs manufactures Summer Pad Protectors, with a double sole of ballistic nylon and a Cordura upper, and Winter Pad Protectors, made of Polartec 300. Both styles of booties close with a Velcro strap. 541-482-7669; www.wolfpacks.com.

Cool Paw Productions, in Tempe, Arizona, offers three styles of booties available in six sizes: Polar Paws, designed for winter use, are made of heavy fleece and Cordura, with a nonskid Tough-Tek sole and a Velcro strap closure. Tuff Paws, intended for hiking, are constructed of ballistic nylon lined with fleece and have double-layer soles and a double Velcro strap closure. Innovative Cool Paws protect paws from scorching surfaces by means of special insulating granules in the sole that activate to form a cool, gel-like layer when water is added. The booties are made of heavy-duty nylon with Velcro straps. 800-650-PAWS.

Travel Bowls

A collapsible food/water bowl is an invaluable travel aid. It's lightweight and can easily be stashed in a backpack or fanny pack so your dog has something to drink out of on the trail. The sturdiest we've found so far are made by **Ruffwear** and feature the tag line "for dogs on the go." The bowls come in 1- and 2.5-quart sizes and are made of nylon or polyester pack cloth with a waterproof, ripstop nylon liner. One of the two styles features a cinchable top, so you can leave some food in it without worrying about spillage. 888-783-3932; www.ruffwear.com. **Cool Paw Productions** makes similar bowls, with Cordura and pack cloth outers and ripstop nylon interiors, in 1- and 2-quart sizes. 800-650-PAWS.

Other Cool Stuff

People have PowerBars for quick energy pick-me-ups during outings; now active dogs have **PowerBones.** Made by A Guy and His Dog Company in New Mexico, the nutritious treats contain beef, high-fructose corn syrup, durum wheat flour, dried beet molasses, brewer's yeast, apple, carrot, canola and flax-seed oils, and a complement of vitamins and minerals. Yum! 888-364-7693; www.powerbone.com.

For toting your dog's stuff on the road, check out the **W.A.G. (water and gear)** bag by Ruffwear. It holds all of Fido's supplies and even has an internal water storage system. 888-783-3932; www.ruffwear.com.

Unless your dog can read, you'll appreciate *DogGone* more than he will. This bimonthly travel newsletter gives the inside scoop on dog-friendly lodgings, places, and activities around the country. You'll never be at a loss for where to take Rover once you subscribe. Call 888-364-8728 or e-mail doggonenl@aol.com.

Happy tails. (photo by Lowell Hart)

Index

About the Author

Photo by Arlan Flax.

Cindy Hirschfeld is currently a copyeditor for SKIING magazine. She has been a freelance writer and editor, specializing in outdoor activities, for a number of magazines and books. She lives in Boulder, Colorado, with two of her best friends: Clover, a golden retriever, and Blue, a cat.